CONTESTING
SLAVERY

CONTESTING SLAVERY

The Politics of
Bondage and Freedom
in the
New American Nation

EDITED BY JOHN CRAIG HAMMOND
AND MATTHEW MASON

University of Virginia Press   *Charlottesville and London*

University of Virginia Press
© 2011 by the Rector and Visitors of the University of Virginia
All rights reserved
Printed in the United States of America on acid-free paper

First published 2011

First paperback edition published 2012
ISBN 978-0-8139-3305-4 (paper)

1 3 5 7 9 8 6 4 2

The Library of Congress has cataloged the hardcover edition as follows:
LIBRARY OF CONGRESS CATALOGING-IN-PUBLICATION DATA
Contesting slavery : the politics of bondage and freedom in the new American nation /
edited by John Craig Hammond and Matthew Mason.
    p.   cm. — (Jeffersonian America)
Includes bibliographical references and index.
ISBN 978-0-8139-3105-0 (cloth : acid-free paper) — ISBN 978-0-8139-3117-3 (e-book)
    1. Slavery—Political aspects—United States—History—18th century. 2. Slavery—Polit-
ical aspects—United States—History—19th century. 3. Antislavery movements—United
States—History—18th century. 4. Antislavery movements—United States—History—
19th century. 5. United States—Politics and government—1775–1783. 6. United States—
Politics and government—1783–1865. 7. Sectionalism (United States)—History—18th
century. 8. Sectionalism (United States)—History—19th century. I. Hammond, John
Craig, 1974– II. Mason, Matthew.
    E446.C71 2011
    326'.80973—dc22

                                                                        2010037050

For Hallie, Hannah, and Addison

Stacie, Emily, Hannah, and Rachel

and Lance and Ira, too

Contents

Contents

Acknowledgments

It has been a privilege to work with so many fine people and institutions in the preparation of this volume. Jim Oakes's astute and insightful commentary at a 2007 Society for Historians of the Early American Republic (SHEAR) panel provided the rationale for this volume. Peter Onuf and Dick Holway at the University of Virginia Press have enthusiastically supported this project since we first pitched the idea to them. Peter, along with Don Ratcliffe, graciously served as unofficial, unindicted coeditors of the volume: both offered constant good advice about the shape and direction of the volume; both provided needed critical readings of the introduction. François Furstenberg also offered sharp criticism that forced us to rethink the introduction along with the significance of the volume. The outside readers for the University of Virginia Press also provided helpful criticism and support as this volume moved from conception to finished manuscript.

Institutions as well as individuals provided important support. The Rocky Mountain Seminar in Early American History, sponsored by Brigham Young University, the University of Utah, and the Obert C. and Grace A. Tanner Humanities Center in Salt Lake City provided a valuable forum for thinking about the focus of the collection at a critical time. The Sixteenth Annual Meeting of British American Nineteenth Century Historians provided an equally valuable opportunity to rethink our arguments as we readied the volume for publication. The Purdue Research Foundation provided a Summer Faculty Development Grant that helped get this project started. Penn State University and Brigham Young University generously provided the time and support needed to see a project like this through to completion. That included support for Britt Wilkinson's excellent services as a research assistant in the preparation of an early version of the manuscript by BYU's History Department.

Under the auspices of SHEAR, specialists in the early American republic continue to produce some of the best scholarship in American history, as indicated by the excellent essays in this volume. The robust, high quality of scholarship on the early republic is well represented by two of the persons to whom we have dedicated this volume, Lance Banning and Ira Berlin. It is hard to imagine two scholars whose interests are more different, yet it is testimony to their commitment to scholarship that two of their former students have collaborated to produce a volume that treats social and cultural history as critical to understanding the politics of slavery. Finally, thanks and praise are due to the authors who contributed such fine pieces of scholarship to this collection.

Foreword

PETER S. ONUF

Slavery has shaped our national narrative. It has been the dark counterpoint to the progress of democracy, a stark reminder that the American Revolution's promise would long remain unfulfilled for many Americans. The juxtaposition between American slavery and American freedom has led recent generations of historians to subject the founding generation to relentless and penetrating criticism. Echoing antebellum opponents of slavery, modern critics turn the revolutionaries' exalted professions—"All men are created equal"—against their sordid, self-interested practices. Revisionists thus simultaneously reject the Founders and identify with them, positioning themselves at the endpoint of the history the Founders envisioned.

The Revolution enabled white Americans to pursue happiness and enjoy the benefits of self-government, but it also gave rise to a dynamic and expansive "empire of slavery." A few idealistic Americans struggled to keep the Spirit of 1776 alive by redeeming the new nation from its original sin. Overcoming tremendous obstacles, including the great wealth slavery created for white Americans and racist Northerners' indifference to the fate of bondsmen, the antislavery vanguard precipitated a great sectional conflict that destroyed the Union. The Civil War's "new birth of freedom" initiated another century of fitful progress toward racial equality. Only now can the descendants of slaves begin to claim their full share of the freedom the Revolutionary fathers fought for.

The conventional understanding of early American history has a history of its own, dating back to the Civil War. In 1859, as the sectional crisis deepened, Abraham Lincoln looked back to the American Revolution, offering a preliminary sketch of the new narrative. "All honor to Jefferson," Lincoln wrote to correspondents in Springfield, the Illinois state capital. "In the concrete pressure of a struggle for national independence by a single people," the author of the Declaration of Independence "had the coolness, forecast, and capacity to introduce into a merely revolutionary document, an abstract truth, applicable to all men and all times, and so to embalm it there, that to-day, and in all coming days, it shall be a rebuke and a stumbling-block to the very harbingers of re-appearing tyranny and oppression."[1] Jefferson's elo-quent assertion of natural rights principles cast a bright light across the generations, reaffirming the new nation's purpose in world history. The Revolution had been fought to vindicate "abstract truths," not to defend the revolutionaries' contingent, "concrete" interests—including their "property" in slaves. Lincoln's generation would honor the slaveholding fathers by set-ting slavery "in the course of an ultimate extinction."[2]

Lincoln's interpretation of the Revolutionary fathers' intentions was pro-foundly and radically anachronistic, projecting the values of his own gen-eration of Northern nationalists back to the Founding, and equating the Southern "slave power" with a despotic and corrupt imperial government. Southern secessionists returned the favor, of course, equating tyrannical "black Republicans" with their British prototypes. The inevitable result of these divergent interpretations was to read the history of previous decades as an extended prologue to a single great conflict over the meaning of the American Revolution. As they sought to explain and justify their ultimate descent into the violent maelstrom of civil war, Northerners and South-erners alike reaffirmed their fealty to Revolutionary principles. Telescop-ing the distance between the two great nation-making wars that defined the subsequent course of American history, these patriots—and succeeding generations of Americans and their historians—either overlooked the inter-vening decades or failed to interpret them on their own terms. Modern historians thus argue about the impact of Revolutionary values on the de-mocratization of political and social life (for whites), or about the escalating conflicts that led to the coming of the Civil War, with the Age of Jackson providing the battleground for clashing historiographical perspectives.[3] In either case, the Revolution and Civil War have dominated—and continue to dominate—popular and scholarly understandings of early American history.

The essays in this volume suggest that the time has come for rethinking the conventional narrative. Editors Craig Hammond and Matthew Mason take advantage of an extraordinary outpouring of excellent work on the history of slavery and antislavery in the early American republic to challenge the way we think about American history more generally. This new scholar-ship has begun to shift our focus away from the decades immediately pre-ceding the Civil War to the generally neglected period after the Revolution when its idealism seemed to subside, cresting with the gradual end of slavery in the "first emancipation" in the Northern states, with their relatively small enslaved populations. Yet even as its dominion was sectionalized and North-erners began to distance themselves from slavery, and so cultivate a sense of the superiority of their own, "free" institutions, the increasingly "peculiar" institution played an increasingly important role in the political economy of the nation as a whole. It was during these decades that slavery proved to be such a dynamic and prosperous institution.

Conflicts over slavery were pervasive in this period, but they have not attracted much attention because they were not *only* about slavery—nor were they therefore generally cast in the highly polarized, non-negotiable, moral terms that became characteristic during the deepening sectional crisis leading up to the Civil War. Of course, there were conspicuous exceptions: great national crises over the future of slavery in the new state of Missouri and the implications of a protective tariff for South Carolina and the cotton South previewed the arguments and intersectional alienation that ultimately wrecked the Union. But if Americans cherished their Union and stepped back from the precipice, this did not mean that the slavery problem could be banished or suppressed. To the contrary, slavery was omnipresent in the new nation's political life.

These essays illuminate the multiple contexts and the conflicts over eco-nomic interests and value commitments in which slavery figured, some-times conspicuously, often not. The struggle over slavery was not the cen-tral, overarching narrative of American national history before 1840: there were instead many different, interdependent narratives, and slavery was important to all of them. By taking a fresh look at these many narratives, we might in turn be able to recast the national narrative, and so move beyond its exceptionalist premises. American history can only make sense in our in-creasingly interdependent world if we situate the new nation's Founding—and the history of slavery and antislavery—in a global context.[4]

Lincoln seized on the Founders' uneasiness with the peculiar institution, echoing and amplifying their hopes that it would ultimately wither away: the contradiction between slavery and freedom was simply too conspicuous to ignore. Yet Lincoln misinterpreted the Revolution, confusing justifications for intentions and thus losing sight of the Founders' overarching goal: to create "a more perfect union" that would secure the peace and prosperity of the new American republics. Lincoln's determination to preserve the Union in the Civil War was a contradiction in terms, for his "Union" was the antithesis of the Founders' Union—a consensual union bound by common interests and values and a shared dedication to collective security. Making war to save the Union subverted the Founders' original intention: to prevent war.[5] It was hardly surprising, then, that Lincoln should redefine the revolutionaries' goals, and so deflect attention away from the Union's collapse and irrevocable transformation. If the original Union had been designed as a "peace pact," or model world order, Lincoln presented the rump Union of Northern states as a model for the world. His Union had become an embattled "nation," the *only* truly republican regime in the modern world. On the battlefield at Gettysburg, he famously resolved "that these dead shall not have died in vain—that this nation, under God, shall have a new birth of freedom—and that government of the people, by the people, for the people, shall not perish from the earth."[6]

Lincoln justified Civil War carnage as the price his generation had to pay to fulfill the promises he believed Jefferson and his colleagues made to themselves and to the world. His "new birth of freedom" was thus predicated on a creative recasting of the Founders' intentions. If they dreamed of world peace and fashioned a federal union that could at least keep the peace among themselves, they did not imagine that they were launching a worldwide "democratic" revolution that would liberate oppressed peoples everywhere —including their own slaves.[7] In the fullness of time, the American example might indeed inspire nation-makers elsewhere to determine their own political destinies: perhaps the enlightened nations of the Old World might embrace the federal principle and so promote the cause of world peace; and it was even possible, on the *eve* of the Revolution, to imagine a glorious future in which the ultimate extinction of the old regime and its archaic institutions would lead to universal emancipation. But this Revolutionary ideology—this provincial Anglo-American gloss on radical Enlightenment principles—did *not* unleash an irresistible "contagion of liberty."[8] Quite to the contrary, natural rights principles, however sincerely embraced, were invoked and disseminated for instrumental reasons: patriot elites invoked these principles to promote political and military mobilization and they proved remarkably successful in containing their contagious consequences —particularly when it came to the future of the peculiar institution.

American revolutionaries faced daunting challenges. They had to convince provincial populations that they were sovereign "peoples" and, as such, the only legitimate source of authority in their own self-constituted polities; they had to convince these peoples that they were embarked on a "common cause" that in some sense and for some purposes made them a single people; and they had to create constitutional structures that would enable these peoples—or this people—to govern themselves. In the circular logic of this Revolutionary constitutionalism, popular sovereignty was the point of departure. The challenge then was to make the idea of peoplehood meaningful by forging new collective identities. To become "Americans," provincial Anglo-Americans had to define themselves against internal and external enemies, excluding racial "others"—the "merciless savages" and insurrectionary slaves of Jefferson's Declaration—even as they invoked natural rights arguments to justify their assault on monarchical authority. Nation-making was inextricably linked to state-making, as new American governments developed the coercive capacity to make war and secure recognition from the "powers of the earth."[9] Continental union was the indispensable means toward securing "national independence" and guaranteeing American rights. But a more perfect union and the reign of peace and prosperity it would make possible was also the end, the great achievement of a new American science of politics.

The "new order for the ages" that the Founders hopefully initiated was not the same one Lincoln celebrated in retrospect. The Founders recognized slavery as an unjust institution, ultimately incompatible with their republican principles, but emancipation was not their immediate or most pressing goal. To the contrary, their Union would necessarily accommodate the interests of slaveholders, who played such a crucial role in mobilizing resistance to the Crown's despotic power. Far from being seen as a fatal compromise with evil, or what William Lloyd Garrison called a "covenant with death," the ratification of the new federal Constitution was celebrated as a "miracle" that would guarantee peace, prosperity, and moral progress to the American state-republics. The pregnant paradox was that their Union strengthened slavery, even while seeming to promise its ultimate demise. Just as the experience of war gave rise to an increasingly racialized conception of national identity, the Constitution secured slave property and opened a vast hinterland for the institution's expansion and consolidation.

The tension between white freedom and black slavery became increasingly conspicuous in later generations, as Lincoln so eloquently testified. But previous generations did not see the slavery problem in such clear-cut, binary terms. Slavery was everywhere, but it did not dominate the moral imagination of most Americans. In principle they might endorse Jefferson's "abstract truths," but few were acutely or consistently troubled by slavery's pervasive presence. The authors in this volume seek to recover and reconstruct the worlds of these Americans, to look at the many problems slavery presented to them from their own contemporaneous perspectives—and so to eschew Lincoln's radical and reductive reinterpretation of early American history. Looking forward, with their subjects, our authors focus on neglected contests involving slavery that only come into clear focus when we recognize their distinctive contexts. The ways in which Americans engaged with slavery in the early period would shape a subsequent history of deepening sectional polarization that ultimately would lead to the Union's collapse. Until the outbreak of war itself, most patriotic Americans recoiled at the prospect of disunion, the betrayal of the Founders' most precious legacy. Freedom was a paramount value; the preservation of the Union was both freedom's essential precondition and an end in itself.

Americans contested slavery even when they thought they were arguing about other issues—precisely because slavery was so vitally important to regional and national prosperity. These struggles do not point to a necessary, inevitable denouement in freedom's triumph: the end of slavery was not the inevitable, natural consequence or by-product of the progressive enlightenment of a self-governing people. To the contrary, it was Lincoln's reconception of the American nation and its role in world history, not Jefferson's "abstract truth," that led to slavery's demise. And the Union's victory in the Civil War finally depended on the capacity of the federal government to exercise and enforce its will—a capacity, ironically, that had been largely developed in the antebellum decades in service of the "slave power." Emancipation was the unintended consequence of a war to preserve a Union.

Idealistic revolutionaries imagined that slavery would ultimately disappear in their enlightened new nation. They were wrong. In fighting a great war to preserve the Union, Lincoln and his fellow nationalists transformed the Union and so destroyed slavery—a surprising, unanticipated, and anything but inevitable outcome. The essays in *Contesting Slavery* restore a sense of complexity and contingency to the preceding decades, thus situating the sectional crisis and Civil War in a broad new narrative framework. These essays will help us understand the many different ways in which contests over slavery shaped the course of American history, even as they move us beyond the story that Lincoln told us and that we have been telling ourselves ever since.

NOTES

1. Lincoln to Henry L. Pierce and Others, Springfield, April 6, 1859, in *The Collected Works of Abraham Lincoln*, ed. Roy P. Basler (New Brunswick, N.J.: Rutgers University Press, 1953), 3:375.

2. Lincoln's Rejoinder, Fourth Debate with Stephen Douglas, Charleston, Sept. 18, 1858, ibid., 3:180.

3. The state of the field is defined by two recent, magisterial syntheses: Sean Wilentz, *The Rise of American Democracy: Jefferson to Lincoln* (New York: Norton, 2005); and Daniel Walker Howe, *What Hath God Wrought: The Transformation of America, 1815–1848* (New York: Oxford University Press, 2007).

4. For new approaches to the Founding, emphasizing geopolitics and state formation, see David Hendrickson, *Peace Pact: The Lost World of the American Founding* (Lawrence: University Press of Kansas, 2003); and Max Edling, *A Revolution in Favor of Government: Origins of the U.S. Constitution and the Making of the American State* (New York: Oxford University Press, 2003). For a conceptual history of American nation-making in the early republic and antebellum decades, see Nicholas Onuf and Peter Onuf, *Nations, Markets, and War: Modern History and the American Civil War* (Charlottesville: University of Virginia Press, 2006).

5. Hendrickson, *Peace Pact*; David Hendrickson, *Union, Nation, or Empire: The American Debate over International Relations, 1789–1941* (Lawrence: University Press of Kansas, 2009).

6. Lincoln, Gettysburg Address (Final Text), Nov. 19, 1863, in *The Collected Works of Abraham Lincoln*, 7:22. The rich literature on the Gettysburg Address depicts it as a re-founding document, simultaneously renewing and repudiating the Declaration. See, for instance, Garry Wills, *Lincoln at Gettysburg: The Words That Remade America* (New York: Simon and Schuster, 1992).

7. R. R. Palmer, *The Age of the Democratic Revolution*, 2 vols. (Princeton, N.J.: Princeton University Press, 1959–64).

8. The phrase is Bernard Bailyn's, from his *Ideological Origins of the American Revolution* (Cambridge, Mass.: Harvard University Press, 1967). The most influential argument for the importance—and "conditional" limits—of Revolutionary antislavery thought is William F. Freehling's *The Road to Disunion*, vol. 1, *Secessionists at Bay, 1776–1854* (New York: Oxford University Press, 1990).

9. For the text of the Declaration, see *Thomas Jefferson: Writings*, ed. Merrill D. Peterson (New York: Library of America, 1984), 19–24.

CONTESTING
SLAVERY

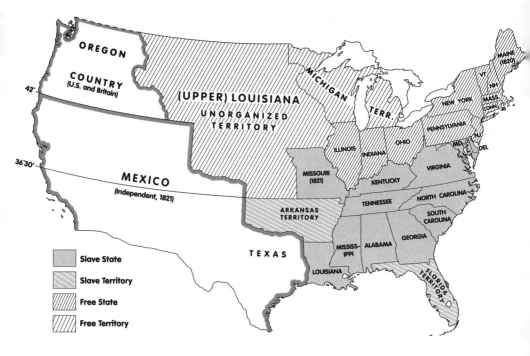

THE UNITED STATES, 1820

Slavery, Sectionalism, and Politics in the Early American Republic

John Craig Hammond and Matthew Mason

The great thirty-year drama that stretched from 1831 to 1861 has dominated historians' accounts of the politics of slavery and sectionalism in the United States. Historians generally agree that the parallel emergence of immediate abolitionism and Deep South extremism, punctuated by Nat Turner's rebellion, initiated the great sectional conflicts that would overtake American politics after David Wilmot introduced his famous Proviso in 1846. From 1846 onward, state and national politics roiled from one sectional crisis to another, eventuating in disunion and civil war. By comparison, the politics of slavery and sectionalism in the early republic—from the American Revolution through 1830—seem tame, sporadic, even insignificant. Reflecting these differences, the historiography on antebellum and Civil War America is vast and rich, characterized by great diversity in subject matter, along with numerous interpretive disputes. Until quite recently—and again, by comparison—the historiography on the politics of slavery and sectionalism for the early republic has been thin, limited in focus to the Founders, and characterized by consensus on fundamental issues.

Consequently, the politics of slavery in Revolutionary America and the early American republic—the long, crucial period stretching from the 1760s through the 1820s—has been largely treated as a prelude to the great conflicts that began with the emergence of immediate abolitionism and Deep South extremism in the 1830s. Because historians know the outcome of the great conflicts over slavery—disunion and civil war, the destruction of slavery and the perpetuation of racism—they have tended to look backward from the antebellum period rather than forward from the Revolution when analyzing the politics of slavery in the early republic. Rather than analyzing the early republic's politics of slavery on its own terms, historians have rummaged through the early republic searching for the roots, origins, and antecedents of antebellum sectional conflict and civil war.[1]

As recently as 2000, historians could agree on something like a standard narrative, situating the early republic's politics of slavery into the larger saga of slavery and sectionalism, disunion, and civil war. That narrative began with Revolutionary challenges to bondage that resulted in the gradual abolition of slavery in the North, a brief surge of manumissions in the Upper South, and the passage of the Northwest Ordinance of 1787. From this high point of Revolutionary antislavery fervor, the politics of slavery devolved into a long history of slaveholder triumphs. The Constitution granted slaveholders extraordinary political power that allowed them to protect their institution from outside interference. In the 1790s, Northern challenges to slavery were repeatedly compromised, then thwarted by self-interested political calculations and endemic white racism. After 1800, antislavery politics was confined to back-bencher New England Federalists, who could pose only token opposition to policies favored by Southern slaveholders and supported by their Northern Republican allies. Consequently, in the thirty years after the implementation of the Constitution, Southerners quietly fashioned the United States government into a slaveholders' republic, expanding the geographical reach of slavery while solidifying their political power and control over the institution. The same three decades saw only brief political battles over the closing of the international slave trade and the expansion of slavery in the Missouri Controversy. Though the Constitution structured later conflicts over slavery, and the Missouri Controversy anticipated the sectional politics of the 1840s and 1850s, historians generally agreed that there was no lasting significant sectional politics through the 1820s. That the furor displayed during the Missouri Crisis subsided as quickly as it appeared confirmed that few white Americans believed that slavery was a pressing political issue. Only in the 1830s did radical abolitionists, Deep South extremists, and rebelling slaves begin to force slavery into the national political agenda.[2]

Recent scholarship on the period between the Revolution and the 1830s has significantly revised this understanding of slavery and American politics. This volume builds on the best of that literature to reexamine the politics of slavery in Revolutionary America and the early republic. Together, this new scholarship and the essays in *Contesting Slavery* establish the enduring importance of slavery and sectionalism in American political life by challenging historians' long-standing assumptions about the origins, extent, and significance of slavery in the politics of the new nation.[3]

To begin, the essays in this volume expand their analysis beyond the Founders and the best-known actors in the early republic's politics. To be sure, such political luminaries as Thomas Jefferson and Timothy Pickering appear frequently in these essays. However, they are joined by a complicated cast of Northern and Southern farmers, Eastern and Western planters, men and women, minor Federalists and Republicans, blacks and whites, the free and the enslaved, the politically marginalized and the politically potent. While much previous scholarship placed the Founders at the center of the politics of slavery, the essays in *Contesting Slavery* instead show that political elites found themselves reacting to events that forced slavery into local, state, regional, and national politics. Richard Newman's essay demonstrates the direct role African Americans took in debates over their place in American life, while Robert Parkinson and Edward Rugemer illustrate how African Americans' willingness to fight and flee for their freedom shaped white concerns about slavery and abolition. Similarly, while Matthew Mason traces how farmers pushed for abolition in New York, John Craig Hammond examines how Western planters shaped the course of slavery expansion. Directly confronting decades of Founders-centered scholarship, Padraig Riley looks past Thomas Jefferson and other prominent party leaders to examine how obscure Northern Jeffersonians reconciled their passion for democracy and equality with the reality of their political alliance with aristocratic slaveholders. As the essays in this collection demonstrate, the politics of slavery could not be confined to a select group of founding fathers—not with so many diverse groups affected by the institution in so many different ways.

The omnipresence of slavery also meant that its politics extended beyond Congress and the presidency, and beyond the Chesapeake and Carolina plantations, which have been the traditional focus of the politics of slavery in the early republic. As the essays here demonstrate, the issue of slavery repeatedly entered into state, regional, sectional, and international conflicts, in turn feeding into and impinging upon politics at the national level. While Rachel Hope Cleves traces the intersecting regional, national, and trans-Atlantic paths that led New England Federalists to condemn slavery on deeply moral grounds, Hammond charts the local and geopolitical conflicts that ultimately determined slavery's expansion. More broadly, this volume demonstrates the continuing influence of the Atlantic world on American history. Edward Rugemer's attention to Caribbean slave revolts; Andrew Shankman's reminder that Latin American independence shaped the thinking of American statesmen on slavery; Brian Schoen's emphasis on the Atlantic dimensions of the Deep South's plantation economy; and Robert Parkinson's and Matthew Mason's illustrations of the ongoing presence of the British in American debates about slavery—all both draw from and add to the fast-growing body of scholarship connecting American history to its Atlantic and international context. Ten years ago, historians could analyze the politics of American slavery with only fleeting references to Haiti and the closing of the trans-Atlantic slave trade. But as these essays reveal, developments in the Atlantic world and on the North American continent continuously shaped and influenced the politics of slavery at home.

Looking beyond the Founders, Congress, and the presidency also demonstrates the need to rethink the old chronological divisions of the politics of slavery. As this volume shows, race, slavery, and sectionalism had an abiding presence in the politics of the early republic, one that extended beyond such well-known incidents as the closing of the international slave trade and the Missouri Controversy. Indeed, political conflicts over slavery did more than submerge and re-emerge in an expanded period of quietude through the 1820s. David Ericson's and George Van Cleve's essays illustrate the long-term effects of slavery on state-formation—and vice versa—in often surprising ways. Mason's and Schoen's narratives feature very different groups driving the politics of slavery over extended periods of time, giving a sense of the intersections of slavery and seemingly unrelated issues. So does Shankman's discussion of the inextricable links between political economy and slavery. As he notes, in the 1820s Mathew Carey and Henry Clay "could barely think a thought, plan a program, or imagine the nation's happy republican future without running into slavery and all the issues with which it intersected." Perhaps none of these essays challenges scholars' common chronological consensus so strongly as Donald Ratcliffe's bracing, revisionist essay tracing the rise of antislavery politics after 1815 and its decline after 1825. The enormous and significant presence of slavery in the early American republic dictated that its politics would be contentious, prolonged, and ultimately unresolved.

But if the essays in *Contesting Slavery* reveal slavery's presence in American political life to be constant rather than ephemeral, they also demonstrate the need for careful attention to the contingent and varied circumstances that made slavery a political issue in the new nation. The early republic was a place of intense and rapid change, which took place in a vortex of postcolonial nation-building. The early republic witnessed an aggressive expansion of democracy for white men, greater assertions of independence from women and African Americans, and a scramble by elites to solidify their economic, social, and political power. An increasingly democratic culture challenged, remade, and at times entirely bypassed established institutions and practices. Economic turmoil produced periods of rapid economic growth and sudden decline. States, regions, and sections jealously protected themselves against a potentially too-powerful federal government, at the same time that they sought to use federal powers to promote their interests. Finally, hasty territorial expansion into the Trans-Appalachian West and the search for new markets and allies in the Atlantic world provoked challenges to the new nation's sovereignty and the constant threat of war. In this milieu stood slavery: an institution whose immense importance spread far beyond the one-fifth of the population who were enslaved and the Southern states where it was most deeply entrenched.

Slavery would have a lasting political presence in the early republic precisely because it became an adjunct to other issues—as political, partisan, social, cultural, sectional, and economic concerns repeatedly forced slavery into politics in unforeseen ways. Thus, the ascension of the Republicans to power after 1800 forced the democratic egalitarians in Jefferson's party to come to terms with their political dependence on aristocratic slaveholders. Similarly, the fall of the New England Federalists from power found them grappling with fears that the degeneracy of democracy was compounded by the deep immorality of slavery. Moving beyond party politics, Eva Sheppard Wolf attends to changes in white Americans' views of slavery's economic efficiency, tracing the emergence of an incipient free-soil ideology, and then examining its transformation into a political, economic, and moral critique of America's not-so-peculiar institution. More generally, Mason shows the precise conditions under which antislavery politics could thrive and prove effective, while Brian Schoen probes the unforeseen paths that drew Lower South politicians into ever more strident defenses of slavery. Finally, Andrew Shankman highlights the effect changing economic and geopolitical realities had on the theorizing of two of the nation's leading politicians and political economists. The deep and abiding presence of slavery and racial consciousness meant that the issue would frequently—and often unexpectedly—enter into debates and conflicts over seemingly tangential issues.

The contingencies and complications of the politics of slavery are especially evident in the collection's treatment of the place of race and slavery in the ideologies and actions of the major political parties. The nuanced chapters from Rachel Cleves and Pedraig Riley contrast well with past scholarly attempts to brand Jeffersonians as pro-slavery (or anti-slavery) and Federalists as anti-slavery (or pro-slavery). Scholars have attempted to assault or vindicate the Democratic-Republicans and the Jacksonians, at the expense not only of a more nuanced reading of these parties but also of their opponents. Scholars have proven especially prone to assume, rather than investigate, the place of slavery in the National Republican and Whig Parties. This collection helps redress this balance. While Donald Ratcliffe charts changes in Northern Democrats', National Republicans', and Whigs' engagement with slavery, Andrew Shankman explores the intersection of slavery with political economy in the writings of two key National Republicans. Although historians will no doubt continue to debate the relationships of these parties with race and slavery, the essays here suggest a way past the polemics that too often dominate such disputes. The political parties of the early republic were broad coalitions cobbled together to address a variety of concerns unrelated to slavery. Yet because of the institution's ubiquity, everything from raw political calculations to increased racial consciousness, from efforts to secure a continental republic to attempts to create a national economy, could and did determine the shifting importance of race and slavery in party politics.

Above all else, by analyzing the Revolutionary era and the early republic on their own terms rather than as mere precursors of the antebellum and Civil War eras, the essays in *Contesting Slavery* offer fresh insights into the politics of slavery. In the end, these essays depict a world in which nothing was automatic, in part because the struggles over slavery could not be confined to a few leading politicians or founding fathers. With so many players participating in response to so many contexts over such a sustained period, the new picture has a certain unpredictability about it. All of this renders composing a grand synthetic narrative about slavery and politics in the new nation that much more daunting. All of us involved with this collection nevertheless hope to have contributed toward the construction of that new narrative.

NOTES

1. For recent works that treat the early republic as a prelude to antebellum sectional conflicts, disunion, and civil war, see James L. Huston, *Calculating the Value of the Union: Slavery, Property Rights, and the Economic Origins of the Civil War* (Chapel Hill: University of North Carolina Press, 2003); and Elizabeth R. Varon, *Disunion! The Coming of the American Civil War, 1789–1859* (Chapel Hill: University of North Carolina Press, 2008), which covers the period between 1789 and 1831 in a single chapter, while devoting eight chapters to the period between 1831 and 1861.

2. For the major works which have advanced this narrative of the politics of slavery from the Revolution through the Mexican War, see Don Fehrenbacher, *The Dred Scott Case: Its Signifi-*

cance in American Law and Politics (New York: Oxford University Press, 1978); idem, *The Slaveholding Republic: An Account of the United States Government's Relations to Slavery* (New York: Oxford University Press, 2001); William W. Freehling, *The Road to Disunion,* vol. 1, *Secessionists at Bay, 1776–1854* (New York: Oxford University Press, 1990); and idem, "The Founding Fathers and Conditional Antislavery," in *The Reintegration of American History: Slavery and the Civil War* (New York: Oxford University Press, 1994). For the major works on slavery and politics in the early republic, see David Brion Davis, *The Problem of Slavery in the Age of Revolution, 1770–1823* (Ithaca, N.Y.: Cornell University Press, 1975); Donald L. Robinson, *Slavery and the Structure of American Politics* (New York: Harcourt Brace Jovanovich, 1971); Edmund S. Morgan, "Slavery and Freedom: The American Paradox," *Journal of American History* 59 (June 1972): 5–29; Duncan J. MacLeod, *Slavery, Race, and the American Revolution* (Cambridge: Cambridge University Press, 1974); William Wiecek, *The Sources of Antislavery Constitutionalism in America, 1760–1848* (Ithaca, N.Y.: Cornell University Press, 1977); Gary Nash, *Race and Revolution* (Madison, Wis.: Madison House, 1990); Leonard L. Richards, *The Slave Power: The Free North and Southern Domination, 1780–1860* (Baton Rouge: Louisiana State University Press, 2000); and Paul Finkelman, *Slavery and the Founders: Race and Liberty in the Age of Jefferson,* 2nd ed. (Armonk, N.Y.: M. E. Sharpe, 2001).

   3. A partial listing of this new scholarship includes David Waldstreicher, *In the Midst of Perpetual Fetes: The Making of American Nationalism, 1776–1820* (Chapel Hill: University of North Carolina Press, 1997); Richard Newman, *The Transformation of American Abolitionism: Fighting Slavery in the Early Republic* (Chapel Hill: University of North Carolina Press, 2002); Adam Rothman, *Slave Country: American Expansion and the Origins of the Deep South* (Cambridge, Mass.: Harvard University Press, 2005); Matthew Mason, *Slavery and Politics in the Early American Republic* (Chapel Hill: University of North Carolina Press, 2006); Eva Sheppard Wolf, *Race and Liberty in the New Nation: Emancipation in Virginia from the Revolution to Nat Turner's Rebellion* (Baton Rouge: Louisiana State University Press, 2006); David N. Gellman, *Emancipating New York: The Politics of Slavery and Freedom, 1777–1827* (Baton Rouge: Louisiana State University Press, 2006); Robert Pierce Forbes, *The Missouri Compromise and Its Aftermath: Slavery and the Meaning of America* (Chapel Hill: University of North Carolina Press, 2007); John Craig Hammond, *Slavery, Freedom, and Expansion in the Early American West* (Charlottesville: University of Virginia Press, 2007); Richard Newman, *Freedom's Prophet: Bishop Richard Allen, the AME Church, and the Black Founding Fathers* (New York: New York University Press, 2008); Edward B. Rugemer, *The Problem of Emancipation: The Caribbean Roots of the American Civil War* (Baton Rouge: Louisiana State University Press, 2008); Rachel Hope Cleves, *The Reign of Terror in America: Visions of Violence from Anti-Jacobinism to Antislavery* (New York: Cambridge University Press, 2009); Brian Schoen, *The Fragile Fabric of Union: Cotton, Federal Politics, and the Global Origins of the United States Civil War* (Baltimore: Johns Hopkins University Press, 2009); Steven Hahn, *The Political Worlds of Slavery and Freedom* (Cambridge, Mass.: Harvard University Press, 2009); David Waldstreicher, *Slavery's Constitution: From Revolution to Ratification* (New York: Hill and Wang, 2010); idem, "The Nationalization and Racialization of American Politics: Before, Beneath, and Between Parties," in *Contesting Democracy: Substance and Structure in American Political History, 1775–2000,* ed. Byron E. Shafer and Anthony J. Badger (Lawrence: University Press of Kansas, 2001), 37–64; François Furstenberg, "Beyond Freedom and Slavery: Autonomy, Virtue, and Resistance in Early American Political Discourse," *Journal of American History* 89 (March

2003): 1295–1330; and Sean Wilentz, "Jeffersonian Democracy and the Origins of Political Antislavery in the United States: The Missouri Controversy Revisited," *Journal of the Historical Society* 4 (Fall 2004): 375–401. Many of these works draw on the new political history examined in Jeffrey L. Pasley, David Waldstreicher, and Andrew Robertson, eds., *Beyond the Founders: New Approaches to the Political History of the Early American Republic* (Chapel Hill: University of North Carolina Press, 2004).

PART I

Slavery and Ideology,
Action and Inaction

Necessary but Not Sufficient

Revolutionary Ideology
and Antislavery Action
in the Early Republic

MATTHEW MASON

For decades, scholars have debated what effect the ideology of the American Revolution had on slavery. For some, the Revolutionary ideals of universal liberty and equality presented a fundamental and straightforward challenge to slavery. Bernard Bailyn, for instance, has posited that the ideology of the Revolution touched off a "contagion of liberty" that struck down entrenched institutions like slavery, as previously oblivious white revolutionaries became aware of the contradictions between their yelps for liberty and the continued bondage of African Americans. Their unease touched off a "movement of thought that was rapid, irreversible, and irresistible."[1] The best evidence of these ideas' effectiveness came when majorities in a succession of Northern states abolished slavery within their limits between 1777 and 1804. Winthrop Jordan summed up the thinking of this group of scholars when he wrote that for American revolutionaries "it was an easy step" from vindicating their rights as Englishmen to "the universalist assertion that all men had a right to be free."[2]

Scholars who ascribe less causal power to ideas have run in the opposite direction. Gary Nash has led this charge. He grants that the Revolution enlightened the minds of some white patriots on the issue of slavery, but in his narrative that enlightenment was woefully short-lived. Indeed, "abolitionist sentiment was already receding" by the time the Founders met in Philadelphia in 1787 to draft the new nation's constitution. That document's protection of slavery constituted a "tragic failure" to realize the Revolutionary moment's opportunity to abolish slavery throughout the land—a gratuitous capitulation on the part of the North to the Southern disunionist bluff. When push came to shove, Northerners rather easily let their "economic interests" trump their shallow antislavery commitment.[3] Nash's writings build on the work of other scholars who likewise insist that when it came to American slavery, the ideology of the Revolution had a superficial impact on both white Northerners and white Southerners.[4]

Given the pounding the Revolution and its Founding Fathers have been taking at the hands of recent scholarship, the Nashian interpretation seems to be winning. Recent studies of Northern abolition have challenged the role of egalitarian ideas in this process by accenting its glacial pace and the hostile racial environment that freed black Northerners faced.[5] The antislavery commitment of the supposedly abolitionist Founders, other historians have argued, has been overrated.[6] Recent books detailing the blows the British army struck for black freedom during the Revolutionary War, and depicting "the vaunted war for liberty" as "a war for the perpetuation of servitude," have reached large audiences.[7] Still other literature has examined the halting response of white Southerners to the Revolutionary challenge to slavery. In one such study, Eva Sheppard Wolf has revised the number of slaves manumitted by Virginia's Revolutionary generation downward.[8] Meanwhile, James McMillin has revised the figures for the volume of the post-Revolutionary foreign slave trade upward.[9] In an influential article, François Furstenburg has drawn out the proslavery implications of the Revolutionary notion that those who would be free must fight for their own freedom.[10] Paul Finkelman's argument that the Constitution constituted a capitulation to slaveholders has deeply influenced both scholarly and popular literature on the Founding.[11] Taking the story beyond 1787, a growing number of scholars have shown just how implicated the new republic's government was in protecting and even expanding human bondage.[12] In the face of this scholarship, one is left to wonder if the ideas of the American Revolution made any significant or lasting contribution to antislavery in the new American nation.

That contribution was at once more and less than the historiography suggests. On the one hand, Revolutionary ideas clearly nourished antislavery activism in the United States. Indeed, only in the age of the American Revolution did scattered and vague discomfort with slavery become organized action against the institution.[13] And it seems extraordinarily cynical to dismiss the constant reference to those ideals within antislavery discourse as mere window dressing. But on the other hand, far more people professed antislavery sentiment than acted on that sentiment. This has misled many scholars into dismissing ideas as incapable of producing the meaningful historical change that they could and often did foster. The distinction between belief and action—between individuals passively lamenting slavery and group initiatives against slavery—offers an alternative to the stark choices in this historiography. It suggests a more nuanced way to understand the significance of Revolutionary ideology by delineating the circumstances under which antislavery ideology became meaningful and effective.[14]

From the Revolution forward, only when slavery became personal in some way did those who harbored an ideological antipathy to slavery act in any organized way against it. Ideas hostile to slavery were thus a precondition for antislavery deeds, but they generally proved insufficient to move people from belief to action. Only when these ideas intersected with political, social, economic, and/or cultural factors did antislavery realize its possibilities. When those factors worked against antislavery action, on the other hand, the limits of antislavery ideas were on full display.

It took the wedding of religious and Revolutionary ideas to create the first serious challenges to slavery in the would-be United States. Antislavery in North America began with objections to slavery as antithetical to such Christian precepts as the Golden Rule. But colonial opponents to slavery only spoke to their own religious communities, and only succeeded in dividing those communities over the issue.[15] The secular philosophies upon which the Revolution was based did not provoke a uniformly hostile response to slavery either. The Enlightenment's emphasis on natural rights brought some minds to the conclusion that slavery was unnatural and immoral. Yet to other Enlightenment thinkers the slave trade and colonial plantation slavery were key elements in a grand, even "divinely contrived system" that was beneficial to all.[16] These religious and secular philosophies, however, proved unfriendly to slavery when they converged in the late eighteenth century.

This mixture was most explosive in the minds of those who felt a powerful personal connection to slavery for the first time. Many people throughout the Atlantic world in this era felt that they were living through a crisis between freedom and tyranny. This apocalyptic appreciation of the stakes involved turned their faith and political precepts into strong rhetoric—and often effort—against human bondage. But some felt more impelled to deeds—such as organizing antislavery societies—than others. For instance, when the Revolution gave evangelical preachers a heightened sensitivity to tyranny, they began to connect the damning sin of "oppression" to slavery. This sense of slavery as a sin, as one historian has aptly written, "gave their antislavery appeals a note of urgency that was absent from the sermons of liberal clergymen who touched upon the subject." During the years in which the very existence of the new nation was in serious doubt, denominating slavery as a crying iniquity for which the whole country would have to answer "before the bar of God" was a powerful call to action.[17]

And act they did. This generation formed the first antislavery organizations in

North American history, struck down slavery north of the Mason-Dixon Line and the Ohio River, and limited and then abolished the foreign slave trade to the United States. Whether part of the "New Divinity" movement within Puritanism or leaders of flourishing new denominations, evangelicals—along with Quakers —founded a flurry of antislavery societies during the Revolutionary era.[18] Besides founding these organizations, which typically pressured state legislators to embrace abolition and sought to shepherd freed blacks into full freedom, many abolitionists of this era proposed several schemes to abolish slavery throughout the land. These plans are easy to dismiss because they countenanced only gradual abolition and varied in their practicality, but they represented the search for pragmatic solutions to a deeply rooted social and political evil.[19]

Religious and Revolutionary qualms about slavery also helped achieve the gradual abolition of slavery in the Northern states, but even that combination was not always enough. Slavery died much more easily in some states than in others, but it always took a combination of motives to push statewide majorities to declare their determination to become free states. Many white residents of Massachusetts, for instance, expressed doubts about the institution of slavery as early as the 1760s, but these scruples alone did not spur them to release their state's slaves. Bay State slaves who committed high-profile crimes, and especially those who appealed to Revolutionary ideology in petitions and freedom suits in the early 1780s, rendered concrete and local what had been abstract and general. They thus helped create the public opinion that supported the judicial abolition of slavery in Massachusetts by the mid-1780s.[20] The more common form of abolition in Northern states, however, was gradual and legislative. Pennsylvania blazed that particular trail in 1780, and it took both Revolutionary ideology and the factional struggle for moral supremacy within the state's tangled denominational politics to achieve it.[21]

New York has become many scholars' best evidence of the weakness of Revolutionary ideals' impact on slavery, as its government did not adopt even gradual abolition until 1799. But to argue, along with historian David Gellman, that "the delayed beginning of gradual abolition in New York precludes ascribing emancipation to Revolutionary fervor or the inevitable realization of Revolutionary ideals," does not help us understand the circumstances under which those ideals helped free the state's slaves. Gellman's study of New York abolition demonstrates that Revolutionary and religious principles actuated both black and white abolitionists, who kept abolition on the state's political agenda for more than two decades. Given the power of slaveholders in the state, however, these reformers could not effect emancipation on the strength of their ideas alone. At the new state's 1777 constitutional convention, delegate Gouverneur Morris proposed inserting a gradual abolition provision into the document, out of regard to "the rights of human nature and the principles of our holy religion." But the New York convention refused to include abolition in its handiwork.[22]

After the Revolutionary War, abolitionists continued to agitate for abolition, but their appeals to the ideals of the Revolution met with continued failure. British troops' recent liberation of thousands of slaves as they left New York and other occupied American ports tainted abolition for some New Yorkers. And influential New Yorkers hungered for social order after the dislocations of the war years, and thus balked at the major social re-engineering program the abolitionists proposed. Still, legislators in Connecticut and Rhode Island adopted gradual abolition in the face of similar concerns, so in the end in New York it continued to come down to the balance of power between opponents and defenders of slavery. The latter actually increased their weight in the legislature in the immediate postwar years, so that almost half of its members owned at least one slave. And the savvy spokesmen for this powerful interest linked abolition to the prospect of black citizenship, which was a bridge too far for most white New Yorkers.[23] Yet the Revolution had infused the zeitgeist with such hostility to slavery in principle that the situation resolved itself into a standoff wherein the slavery interest sought to preserve itself against abolitionist attempts to sway public opinion.

Partisan politics, political economy, and a demographic shift finally broke the impasse in favor of emancipation. By the late 1790s a population boom in the non-slaveholding regions of northern and western New York, and an accompanying reapportionment of the lower house of the legislature, had rendered slaveholders a dwindling minority. But the size of the non-slaveholding majority would have meant little had that majority not roused itself to action against slavery. It took a host of seemingly unrelated concerns to bring slavery home to that majority. Boosters of maple sugar production, for instance, touted its economic benefits to New York cultivators, as well as its moral superiority to slave-produced cane sugar. In the widespread newspaper debate over encouraging maple sugar, antislavery ideas appeared alongside economic self-interest in the preachments of maple sugar devotees. Also in the 1790s, New York Federalists began castigating slaveholders in Republican-dominated Virginia for avowing the rights of man with whips in their hands. For their part, New York's Republicans were not eager to stand with their Virginian co-partisans, with slavery as the basis of brotherhood. "Amid bruising partisan-inflected rhetorical battles for political hegemony," Gellman has summarized, "relatively few Federalists or Republicans in New York found themselves holding a political stake in saving slavery." Abolition followed in 1799, and despite the law's gradualism, slavery died more rapidly in the state than the law required—although it had been growing quickly in some areas of the state right up until the passage of the law.[24]

New York neatly encapsulated both the power and the limits of ideas in effecting abolition. The state had no antislavery society before the Revolution. After 1785, it had the New York Manumission Society; and, in turn, the NYMS had the ideology of the Revolution, combined with a humanitarian version of Christianity, upon which to base its appeals.[25] Contrary to the thrust of recent scholarship, I argue that this rhetoric manifestly diffused discomfort with slavery widely throughout New York's population. Indeed, the ideological legacy of the Revolution was precisely what made West Indian sugar production morally unacceptable and antislavery appeals politically profitable in New York. But given the very real obstacles that stood in the way of a meaningful antislavery movement in New York, it took the welding of humanitarian arguments with the prospects of partisan political gain and profits from the production of maple sugar to effectively mobilize that antislavery sentiment.

Early national debates about the expansion of slavery also reveal that Revolutionary ideals needed to mesh with favorable practical considerations to become active. Congressmen's vague angst over slavery proved no match for the nation's obvious interest in seeing the new western territories become a strength to the Union. For, as late as the first decade of the nineteenth century, emigration to the Southwest far outpaced that flowing north of the Ohio River, where the Northwest Ordinance had decreed that the labor needs of new settlements could not be met by increases in the slave population. Seeking to proscribe slavery in the West might also further alienate a population of dubious loyalty to that Union. Finally, many of those who harbored hostility to slavery in the abstract were disinclined to apply it to the Southwestern territories, because of their generation's popular notion that only enslaved laborers of African descent could work in that climate.[26] Thus, the proponents of a congressional proscription of slavery in places like Mississippi and Louisiana were voices in the congressional wilderness.

Local control, then, was the order of the day in the early national politics of slavery expansion, which imbued local debates over this issue with inherent significance. For those territories with a functioning two-party system, such disputes gave the rival parties many opportunities to mobilize voters around the issue. As Ohio moved toward statehood, for instance, both parties knew that the legality of slavery would be a central question to be decided by the new state constitution. Federalists, who had become a forlorn minority in the territory, sought to boost their political fortunes by linking Republicans' desires for statehood with a conspiracy to fasten slavery on the region. While Republicans elsewhere in the nation publicly expressed contempt for African Americans' claims to rights and liberties, Ohio Republicans understood their constituents' animus toward the prospect of slavery spreading to the Northwest and thus put as much distance as possible between themselves and anything smacking of proslavery. Although they would later enact restrictions on black Ohioans' rights, during the campaign for statehood Ohio Republicans were not to be outdone on questions of either liberty or equality. As they phrased it, to allow slavery would be to allow a Federalist-style aristocracy, the ultimate bugbear for democratic Ohioans.[27]

In the Indiana Territory, which eventually became the states of Indiana and Illinois, the politics of slavery expansion also got so tangled up with factional and party warfare that principle and partisan interest proved inextricable. As John Craig Hammond has written, for Indianans moving toward statehood, "the slavery question became a political question intertwined with larger conflicts over what type of republican society Indianans would create." As in Ohio, if one could tar his enemy as a friend to slavery, then that enemy would also be seen as a friend to aristocracy and tyranny. Only if Indianans resisted the scheme to fasten slavery on the new state, the argument went, would they enjoy a future in keeping with the legacy of the Revolution, "where no proud nabob can cast on" any industrious freeman "a look of contempt." The Republican framers of Indiana's 1816 state constitution thus acted on both egalitarian ideals and on partisan imperatives when they proclaimed that "the holding of any part of human Creation in slavery, or involuntary servitude, can only originate in usurpation and tyranny." The partisan struggles surrounding statehood convinced political combatants ranging from newspaper scribblers to the Northwestern states' founding fathers to deploy the ideological weapons that the Revolutionary legacy had put in their arsenals. In short, as Hammond has written: "Competitive democratic politics made slavery a salient issue. It also gave voters a meaningful way to express their opposition to it."[28]

Besides state-level abolition in the nascent free states, the quintessential antislavery exploit of the Revolutionary generation was the abolition of the Atlantic slave trade. On its face, the quick and near-universal execration of a traffic that had provoked only scattered and isolated protests before the Revolution seems to illustrate the straightforward potency of ideas. But this antislavery deed was provoked only in part by the moral repugnance to the trade that Revolutionary ideology created. Economics also helps to explain the ban. Slaveholders in Virginia and Maryland, for example, found themselves with excess slave labor as they transitioned from labor-intensive tobacco cultivation to grain cultivation. They realized that they would be able to sell their excess slaves to buyers in the new territories for a higher price if they could get the government to restrict the foreign supply. Planters in Georgia and the Carolinas, on the other hand, were still trying to "restock" their plantations with slave labor after the disruptions of the Revolutionary War. Economic motives thus help explain why representatives of the Upper but not the Lower South stood with Northerners against the traffic.

National pride constituted another, less tangible, but no less powerful, motive that very quickly mixed in with idealism to create a broad consensus for the abolition of the slave trade. From the beginning of their conflict with Parliament, Americans trumpeted their restrictions and bans on the slave trade as proof of their superior humanity. But when post-Revolutionary Britons spawned their own very public movement against the trade, Americans found they had a competitor for the distinction of being the country most hostile to the commerce in slaves. Worse, their English opponents hoped to demonstrate the superiority of the monarchical institutions that the American experiment in republican government sought to discredit. In the spring of 1807, as both the British Parliament and the United States Congress debated withdrawing from the trade, proponents of abolition in both countries urged their recalcitrant colleagues to win "the glory of being the first in the race."[29] The old-fashioned motive of competitive national pride helped move many on both sides of the Atlantic to action against the African slave trade. The principles of liberty and humanity served not only as the race's prize, but also as its starting pistol.

The South would seem to have been an arena of failure for the antislavery legacy of the American Revolution, but even there Revolutionary ideology made a dent in whites' commitment to slavery when combined with practicalities averse to slavery. Given how powerfully rooted slavery was in Southern society, it took a greater number of practical reasons to move white Southerners to anti-slavery action than it did for white Northerners. But many whites in the Upper South did exert themselves against slavery. In 1782, Virginia passed a law giving slaves easier access to manumission by reducing restrictions on their masters. Between 1782 and 1806 Virginia masters freed between 8,000 and 11,500 slaves.[30] Marylanders evinced even more enthusiasm for manumission, highlighting the distinction between the "Upper" and the "Lower" Chesapeake. In fact, Maryland's manumission laws became so liberalized that some slaves reversed the traditional assumption that African descent conferred slave status by suing (sometimes successfully) for their liberty on the grounds that descent from at least one white person conferred free status.[31]

Ideology and self-interest intermingled in Southern manumission just as they did in Northern abolition. In wills and deeds of manumission, the liberators routinely cited Revolutionary and religious reasons for their actions. One Revolutionary War veteran, for instance, proclaimed that he was freeing sixteen slaves

18

in 1794 because of his "belief that all men by Nature are equally free and independent and that the Holding of Man in a State of Slavery is unjust and oppressive." Most Virginia manumitters were Quakers and evangelicals, but they also acted in a time of unusually prevalent slave resistance, which convinced many that slavery posed a serious security risk. One white Virginian spoke for many when he wrote, "If we will keep a ferocious monster in our country, we must keep him in chains." The "if" spoke volumes: although slaveholders in the Lower South shared both Revolutionary ideals and insurrection anxiety with slaveholders in the Upper South, only the latter group manumitted their slaves in great numbers. The transformation from tobacco to grain agriculture in the Upper Chesapeake encouraged some in that region to embrace manumission. The labor demands of tobacco were more unrelenting than those of grain, and planters turned farmers found that that meant an excess number of slaves and a dangerous increase in their idle time. As the historian Barbara Fields phrased it: "The direction of Maryland's economic development lent an air of commonsense practicality to antislavery ideas." For reasons of ideology, economics, and security, not only individual manumissions but also Southern manumission and abolition societies had their heyday in the late eighteenth century. The wrath they provoked in many planters bore testimony to their effectiveness.[32]

That wrath is worth attending to, because it bespeaks the determination of the majority of white Southerners to keep the "monster" in strengthened chains. This was especially true in the Lower South, where even in the Revolutionary year of 1776 the South Carolinian John Laurens lamented that he had "scarcely ever met with a Native of" South Carolina or Georgia "who did not obstinately" support slavery by any argument at hand. Nothing had changed by 1790, when a Charleston resident attested that it would "be more safe for a man to proclaim through this city that there was no God, than that slave-holding was inconsistent with his holy law." By the early nineteenth century, the few traces of antislavery that had existed in the Lower South had become almost undetectable.[33] By then, the Upper South was also proving to be increasingly unfriendly to abolition. While some families, and even entire counties, developed "a culture of manumission," many Chesapeake manumitters found themselves swimming against the main stream in their neighborhoods and families. In the aftermath of Gabriel's conspiracy in 1800, opponents of slavery in the Upper South became the objects of persecution, and as a result distanced themselves from what they deemed to be the lost cause of Southern emancipation. And in 1806, Virginia passed a law that required freed blacks to leave the state within a year, effectively checking the post-Revolutionary rise in manumissions. Another consequence of the fading antislavery commitment in the Upper South was the rise of the interstate slave trade, by which Chesapeake slaveholders rid their farms of excess slaves by means of sale rather than manumission. One is tempted to conclude that the Revolution nourished only the most ineffectual profession of antislavery senti-ment in most white Southerners—of the sort enunciated by James Monroe when he expressed support for abolition, provided it could be effected "without ex-pense or inconvenience to ourselves."[34]

Worse, Revolutionary principles helped convince others to go beyond even this kind of indecision into the ranks of outright anti-abolitionism. In the mid-1780s, for instance, hundreds of Virginia evangelicals employed both biblical arguments and their reading of Revolutionary ideology when they petitioned the state legislature to repeal the 1782 Manumission Law. The petitioners insisted that they had fought the Revolution to vindicate "our sacred rights of property." They painted antislavery Americans as "Enemies of our Country, Tools of the British Administration." For these and other anti-abolitionists throughout the nation, the Revolutionary War experience had created a strong association of emancipation with British troops and pacifist Quakers. For these Virginians at least, Revolutionary repugnance for emancipation combined with their inter-pretation of the Bible and their economic interests to move them to the sort of organized action that at least matched that of the antislavery societies.[35] Thus, for some white Southerners, Revolutionary and evangelical ideology, economic change, and fear of slave resistance provoked manumissions; for others, this same mix provoked the sale of slaves to domestic slave traders. That difference illus-trates the agency people had in responding to these sea changes, as well as the multivocality of the ideology of the American Revolution.

Tracing the Virginia story deeper into the nineteenth century highlights once again the impact of power politics when mixed with all these other motives. Virginia experienced its strongest antislavery movement in the 1820s, when non-slaveholders centered in the state's western counties campaigned against the power of slaveholders in the state councils. At first, antislavery played a marginal role in the westerners' campaign. It was the resistant slaveholders, claiming that the proposals of the radical westerners posed a threat to their human property, who first brought slavery to bear in this debate. The westerners had in mind equal suffrage and representation for themselves, but easterners' stubborn pro-tection of slave property was what stood in their way. The slaveholders' power and intractability, together with the spectacular slave resistance of Nat Turner's revolt, precipitated a full-scale debate over the place and future of slavery in Virginia society. As the historian Eva Sheppard Wolf has concluded, "Only when antislavery sentiment became tied to the achievement of distinct political ends," did antislavery in Virginia carry "enough weight to spark a sustained and coherent response" from nervous slaveholders. By the end of the debate, "on both sides interest was bound up with culture and morality in a way that made those elements difficult to separate."[36] In that respect, the Virginia slavery debates of the 1820s and early 1830s typified the entire history of antislavery politics in the United States.

In the realm of national politics, antislavery feeling most commonly turned to effective action when partisans attached it to all the passions and loyalties of their electoral struggles. It took both a willingness and an ability to connect slavery to white Northerners' lives for antislavery politics to become a force for change at the polls and in government. The Free Soil Party refined this ability over what the Liberty Party manifested, and then the Republican Party trumped them both. The political acumen of Republican leaders and operatives in appealing to the self-interest of Northern voters created a popular wave that the Republicans rode to power. But the Republicans were not the first party to effectively exploit Northern fear and loathing of slaveholders. For it was the Federalist Party of the early nineteenth century that had showed for the first time the power of Northern sectionalism when Yankees' inert antislavery sentiment mingled with a sense that slavery impacted their lives for ill.

In the years after their party lost national power, the New England Federalist leaders grew both in willingness and ability to pursue a sectionalist course in national politics. Remarkably soon after the Democratic-Republican Thomas Jefferson's inauguration in 1801, New England Federalist leaders began to despair of ever regaining their place at the head of the national government. Therefore, they sought to make their party a sectional powerhouse by rallying "New England men" to defend the specific "interest of the Eastern States" against the rise of the "Virginia influence" that Jefferson's victory represented. Their prime grievance was the Constitution's "three-fifths clause," by which three-fifths of the slave population in a state could be counted toward the apportionment of states' representation in the House of Representatives and the Electoral College. Jefferson would never have been elected in 1800, the Federalists groused, without the extra weight that the clause lent to his Southern base. With the Louisiana Purchase of 1803 such "slave representation" would be expanded, and would shift the sectional balance of power away from the Northeast forever. Thus, Federalist leaders organized to seek repeal of the three-fifths clause, and some even talked of seceding from the Union to form a "Northern Confederacy."[37]

Yet the Federalists learned that a simple appeal to Yankee antislavery sectionalism would not bring success at the polls. In these early efforts, the Federalists had a hard time persuading average citizens to share their outrage. Only Connecticut accepted Massachusetts's call for an amendment abolishing the three-fifths clause, and in 1804 Jefferson carried every New England state except Connecticut. While the Federalist leadership had experienced their ouster from national power in 1801 personally, such blows fell at a distance from the concerns of most ordinary voters. The hard-core Federalists were left to bemoan "the apathy that benumbs" the citizenry.[38]

That apathy, however, did not last beyond 1808, for beginning in that year Jeffersonian policies helped Federalists to convert New Englanders' distrust of Southern slaveholders into a powerful political movement. In 1808, Congress, at President Jefferson's behest, passed an embargo on trade with Great Britain, which ended up hurting America's commerce (especially vital to the New England economy) more than it did Britain's. To the embargo the Democratic-Republicans added the War of 1812, which struck New England Federalists as not only immoral but also the final piece in the Jeffersonian scheme to destroy their section's commerce and political power. "Slave representation" provided a useful explanation for the North's plight. In newspaper editorials, pamphlets, and sermons, Federalists flailed away at the three-fifths clause as enabling Jeffersonians to perpetrate their atrocities, and demanded its repeal as the price of continued union. Especially in newspapers and sermons, some Federalists far exceeded the focus on slave representation, excoriating slavery itself.[39]

As the federal government enforced the embargo and prosecuted the war, Northern voters became more inclined than ever before to rally behind attacks on Southern selfishness. One aggrieved constituent wrote to Daniel Webster in 1813 seething that he "would march at 6 days notice for Washington" if he could rally a body of men to follow him, "and I would swear upon the *altar* never to return till Maddison was buried under the ruins of the capitol." In case Webster missed the sectional content of this rage, the writer added, "All the pleasure I have is anticipating the time when I shall march in armour on the FARTHEST GEORGIA and trample the planters under my feet."[40] One result was a Federalist resurgence at the polls, especially in New England. Another result was a series of resolutions that grew out of town-meeting resolutions in Massachusetts in 1814, most of which listed citizens' desire to see slave representation abolished as a prime reason for holding a New England convention. Under such pressure, both houses of the Massachusetts legislature resolved by wide margins to call such a convention, and four other New England states also agreed to send representatives. The Hartford Convention of 1814–15 followed the town memorials in listing the abolition of slave representation first among the constitutional amendments it proposed. Though it constituted a secret meeting of the Federalist elite, the Hartford Convention—symbol and apex of wartime New England sectionalism—was the result of a grassroots campaign that revealed the depth of Yankee contempt for the slave South.

But in order to tap into those wells of sectional contempt, the Federalists had found it necessary to link an ideological hatred for an otherwise distant Southern slavery to the everyday concerns of average New Englanders. They knew that, absent the war and the accompanying trade restrictions, such a sectional appeal would lose its force. Thus, when the war ended in 1815, most Federalists dropped the issue of slave representation for good. Some individual Federalists would continue to stand against slavery and slave representation up until the Missouri Crisis of 1819–21, but their position was based on individual initiative rather than party policy. This sort of calculated public attention to slavery did not earn the bulk of the New England Federalist leadership many points on any abolitionist scorecard. But the Federalists never claimed to be abolitionists; Massachusetts Federalist chieftain Josiah Quincy spoke for many when he declared later in life that "my heart has always been much more affected by the slavery to which the Free States have been subjected, than with that of the Negro."[41] And so the Federalist wartime campaign can be seen as a big-tent affair, one that did not require purely humanitarian motives from those who joined it.

In the Era of Good Feelings, slavery generated bad feelings in politics when it impinged on Northerners' pocketbooks, and on something less tangible but no less powerful: their identity as proud residents of the free states. When dissident Democratic-Republicans in the Mid-Atlantic states sought federal-government aid after the war to boost that region's economy, they encountered resistance from the Virginia-dominated mainstream of their party. This led to a revived, Federalist-style rhetoric that attacked "Virginia influence." For example, when the administration of Virginian James Monroe failed to embrace protective tariffs, the dissidents wailed that the slaveholders had become "the chief power" in the nation, and wondered out loud whether slavery had not "therefore become dangerous to the liberty, commerce and manufactures of the free states?"[42]

Residents of the Mid-Atlantic of various political stripes now saw slavery as dangerous to more than just their pocketbooks. As the plantation complex expanded into areas that had been conquered during the war, labor-hungry Southern planters bought not only Upper South slaves but also the North's "term slaves," African Americans who were waiting for the gradual process of abolition to free them. Their agents also ranged throughout the Mid-Atlantic, kidnapping free black people and selling them into Southern slavery. In 1818, one Philadelphia editor excoriated a series of kidnappings that had taken place throughout Delaware and Pennsylvania. "Fellow citizens," he cried about one particularly violent example, "these outrages were committed upon a family of free people in Philadelphia, and on the Sabbath day." Should residents of the Mid-Atlantic become implicated in the worst abuses of the slave system, they could bid farewell to their sectional boast of living in the free states. That menace jolted readers from their passive antislavery sentiment into passing legislation against both the sale of term slaves and kidnapping.[43]

The threat of encroachment from the slave states not only produced legislation against the practices in question, but it also hastened the abolition process in New York. "The reputation of the state," Governor Daniel D. Tompkins told legislators in 1817, demanded that "the reproach of slavery be expunged from our statute book" by speeding up the existing process of gradual emancipation. The leaders of the NYMS leveraged this perceived need to firm up New York's free-state credentials. "This one act," they suggested, "is wanting to vindicate and adorn the character of the state." In March 1817, the legislature followed the governor's prodding and passed a law expediting gradual emancipation. The law contained stiff fines for the sale or "transfer" of term slaves, and decreed fines up to $1,000 and prison terms of up to 14 years for the crime of kidnapping.[44]

Northerners in the Mid-Atlantic states bent on preserving their free-state identity got another opportunity to act when Missouri applied for admission to the Union in 1819. They joined Northwesterners in the vanguard of the movement to restrict slavery in Missouri. This was no accident. Residents of both regions came to this debate fresh from defending their respective subregions from the slavery menace—in the Mid-Atlantic, from the worst abuses of the commerce in slaves, and in the Northwest, from slavery itself. In that context, they rather quickly overcame the previous hesitancy of Northern members of Congress to act against slavery expansion. Throughout the Missouri Controversy, congressional debates and voting patterns, and constituent pressure on congressmen, confirmed that ideological opposition to slavery could be turned to powerful political action when slavery struck home to its opponents.[45]

In the antebellum years, antislavery activists proved slow to heed this lesson, and political antislavery on the national level suffered for it. After the Federalists, the next avowedly sectionalist Northern party was the Liberty Party, whose presidential candidate James Birney won only about 7,000 of the 2.5 million votes cast in 1840. "This was true," the historian Frederick Blue has puzzled, "even though Liberty campaigners adopted many of the moral suasion techniques of the Garrisonians, appealing to the consciences of northern voters."[46] But it might better be said that this was true because they appealed *only* to voters' consciences, finding no way to combine conscience and self-interest.

In the years following 1840, antislavery politicians found that both their opportunities and their ability to make that connection increased. By then, thanks to the congressional maneuvers of antislavery Whigs like John Quincy Adams and Joshua Giddings, Congress's gag on antislavery expression had become an issue not of abolitionist agitation or of the rights of black Southern slaves, but of the suppression of freeborn Northerners' free speech in defense of slavery. In 1856, when Representative Preston Brooks of South Carolina entered the U.S. Senate chamber and beat Senator Charles Sumner of Massachusetts nearly to death with a cane, Northerners heard echoes of the Gag Rule fight. The newly founded Republican Party was on hand to help shape the North's response to this incident. In its wake, therefore, the *New York Times* reported that in the North, "the great body of the people, without distinction of party, feel that *their* rights have been assailed in a vital point,— that the blow struck at SUMNER takes effect upon Freedom of Speech in that spot where, without freedom of speech, there can be no freedom of any kind."[47] And as slaveholders endeavored to spread slavery to the western territories, these same Northern sectionalist politicians further honed their ability to link Southern slavery to everyday white Northern lives. Allowing slavery to expand to the territories conquered from Mexico, and especially to Kansas and Nebraska, they successfully argued, would be to deprive the free men of the North and their posterity of the opportunity that the West represented. Northern sectionalist politicians also presented the Fugitive Slave Act of 1850 as further evidence that slavery was reaching its foul hand into freedom's Northern home. Perhaps nothing better dramatized the need for freedom-loving white Northerners to control the coercive power of the state than this draconian law, under which they could be deputized as slave catchers on pain of fines and/or imprisonment. From the 1830s to the 1850s, then, antislavery politicians proved increasingly able to convince white Northerners that their own rights, and even their children's and grandchildren's future, were under siege from the Slave Power in the United States.

And it was this bridging of white Northerners' cherished distance from slavery that ultimately converted the vague antislavery feeling that Northerners had possessed since the American Revolution into organized action. Before the advent of the Gag Rule, one Republican recalled, "abolitionism was but a sentiment, and a mere sentiment is not a sufficient basis for a formidable political organization," unlike "when great principles of constitutional right are violated." The achievement of the Republican Party was its ability to utilize similar turning points to mobilize such "sentiment" into a truly "formidable political organization."[48] The rise of effective free-soil politics illustrated the truth of an observation from the Maine politician F. O. J. Smith. "Divest a subject of *party* interest and *party* excitement," Smith opined, "and it becomes that sort of everybody's business which nobody attends to."[49]

Indeed, it was those who held party interests and other less-than-spotless motives who had converted antislavery sentiment into organized and effective antislavery action. From the Revolution through the antebellum era, the ideology of universal liberty and equality enshrined in the United States' founding documents had proven to be an indispensable starting point for antislavery organization. Together with a humanitarian version of Christianity, that natural rights ideology created and nourished the opposition to slavery that inhabited so many hearts and minds from the Revolutionary generation forward. These ideas also became powerful weapons in the hands of abolitionists of all stripes, and none of them hesitated to use them in their assaults on American bondage.

But the ideas by themselves very rarely moved people from merely wringing their hands over the injustice of slavery to actually picking up those weapons and joining a battalion to storm slavery's citadels. It was only when the enemies of slavery could show that the institution threatened the pocketbooks, political power, civil liberties, claims to national divine providence, national image, sectional identity, and/or security of their recruits, that their ranks swelled. The most effective form of antislavery action took place in the political arena, and there as elsewhere it required the conviction that slavery impacted a voter's life directly to make him act with others to strike against it. This distinction between belief and action, then, offers a richer and more precise understanding of the antislavery impact of the ideals of the American Revolution than the polarized scholarship has produced.

NOTES

1. Bernard Bailyn, *The Ideological Origins of the American Revolution*, enlarged ed. (1967; Cambridge, Mass.: Harvard University Press, 1992), 230–46 (quotations at 245, 231–32).

2. See Winthrop D. Jordan, *White Over Black: American Attitudes toward the Negro, 1550–1812* (Chapel Hill: University of North Carolina Press, 1968), 269–311 (quotation at 289). See also Arthur Zilversmit, *The First Emancipation: The Abolition of Slavery in the North* (Chicago:

University of Chicago Press, 1967); Leon F. Litwack, *North of Slavery: The Negro in the Free States, 1790–1860* (Chicago: University of Chicago Press, 1961); Gerald W. Mullin, *Flight and Rebellion: Slave Resistance in Eighteenth-Century Virginia* (Oxford: Oxford University Press, 1972); Edgar J. McManus, *Black Bondage in the North* (Syracuse, N.Y.: Syracuse University Press, 1973); Duncan J. MacLeod, *Slavery, Race, and the American Revolution* (Cambridge: Cambridge University Press, 1974); William W. Freehling, "The Founding Fathers and Slavery," *American Historical Review* 77 (February 1972): 81–93; Ira Berlin, *Slaves without Masters: The Free Negro in the Antebellum South* (New York: Pantheon, 1974); and Gordon S. Wood, *The Radicalism of the American Revolution* (New York: Vintage, 1991), 7, 186–87. For especially balanced considerations of the impact of Revolutionary ideas, see David Brion Davis, *The Problem of Slavery in Western Culture* (Ithaca, N.Y.: Cornell University Press, 1966); idem, *The Problem of Slavery in the Age of Revolution, 1770–1823* (Ithaca, N.Y.: Cornell University Press, 1975); Ira Berlin and Ronald Hoffman, eds., *Slavery and Freedom in the Age of the American Revolution* (Charlottesville: University Press of Virginia, 1983); Ira Berlin, *Many Thousands Gone: The First Two Centuries of Slavery in North America* (Cambridge, Mass.: Harvard University Press, 1998), pt. 3; and T. Stephen Whitman, *Challenging Slavery in the Chesapeake: Black and White Resistance to Human Bondage, 1775–1865* (Baltimore: Maryland Historical Society, 2007), chaps. 2–3.

3. Gary B. Nash, *Race and Revolution* (Madison, Wis.: Madison House, 1990) (quotations at 4, 6, 34). This interpretation runs throughout Nash's work on this subject: see Nash, *Forging Freedom: The Formation of Philadelphia's Black Community, 1720–1840* (Cambridge, Mass.: Harvard University Press, 1988); Nash and Jean R. Soderlund, *Freedom by Degrees: Emancipation in Pennsylvania and Its Aftermath* (Oxford: Oxford University Press, 1991); and Nash, *The Forgotten Fifth: African Americans in the Age of Revolution* (Cambridge, Mass.: Harvard University Press, 2006).

4. See, for example, Robert McColley, *Slavery and Jeffersonian Virginia* (Urbana: University of Illinois Press, 1964); Staughton Lynd, *Class Conflict, Slavery, and the United States Constitution: Ten Essays* (Indianapolis: Bobbs-Merrill, 1967); Donald L. Robinson, *Slavery in the Structure of American Politics, 1765–1820* (New York: Harcourt Brace Jovanovich, 1971), especially 77–81; Fredrika Teute Schmidt and Barbara Ripel Wilhelm, "Early Proslavery Petitions in Virginia," *William and Mary Quarterly*, 3rd ser., 30 (January 1973): 133–46; Robin Blackburn, *The Overthrow of Colonial Slavery, 1776–1848* (London: Verso Press, 1988), especially 29, 58.

5. See Shane White, *Somewhat More Independent: The End of Slavery in New York City, 1770–1810* (Athens: University of Georgia Press, 1991); idem, *Stories of Freedom in Black New York* (Cambridge, Mass.: Harvard University Press, 2002); Clement Alexander Price, comp. and ed., *Freedom Not Far Distant: A Documentary History of Afro-Americans in New Jersey* (Newark: New Jersey Historical Society, 1980), especially 63–67, 71–73; Graham Russell Hodges, *Slavery and Freedom in the Rural North: African Americans in Monmouth County, New Jersey, 1665–1865* (Madison, Wis.: Madison House, 1997); idem, *Root and Branch: African Americans in New York and East Jersey, 1613–1863* (Chapel Hill: University of North Carolina Press, 1999); Daniel C. Littlefield, "John Jay, the Revolutionary Generation, and Slavery," *New York History* 81 (January 2000): 91–132; Leslie M. Harris, *In the Shadow of Slavery: African Americans in New York City, 1626–1863* (Chicago: University of Chicago Press, 2003); David N. Gellman, *Emancipating New York: The Politics of Slavery and Freedom, 1777–1827* (Baton Rouge: Louisiana State University Press, 2006); Joanne Pope Melish, *Disowning Slavery: Gradual Emancipation*

and "Race" in New England, 1780–1860 (Ithaca, N.Y.: Cornell University Press, 1998); and John Wood Sweet, *Bodies Politic: Negotiating Race in the American North, 1730–1830* (Baltimore: Johns Hopkins University Press, 2003).

6. See, for example, David Waldstreicher, *Runaway America: Benjamin Franklin, Slavery, and the American Revolution* (New York: Hill and Wang, 2004); and Henry Wiencek, *An Imperfect God: George Washington, His Slaves, and the Creation of America* (New York: Farrar Straus Giroux, 2003). I would begin to list the many treatments of Jefferson's confounding relationship with slavery here, but scholars have been known to wade into those murky waters and never be seen again.

7. Simon Schama, *Rough Crossings: Britain, the Slaves, and the American Revolution* (New York: Ecco, 2006) (quotation at 7–8). See also Cassandra Pybus, *Epic Journeys of Freedom: Runaway Slaves of the American Revolution and Their Global Quest for Liberty* (Boston: Beacon Press, 2006).

8. Eva Sheppard Wolf, *Race and Liberty in the New Nation: Emancipation in Virginia from the Revolution to Nat Turner's Rebellion* (Baton Rouge: Louisiana State University Press, 2006). For other works downplaying antislavery sentiment in the early national South, see William W. Freehling, *The Road to Disunion*, vol. 1, *Secessionists at Bay, 1776–1854* (Oxford: Oxford University Press, 1990); T. Stephen Whitman, *The Price of Freedom: Slavery and Manumission in Baltimore and Early National Maryland* (Lexington: University Press of Kentucky, 1997); and Jeffrey Robert Young, *Domesticating Slavery: The Master Class in Georgia and South Carolina, 1670–1837* (Chapel Hill: University of North Carolina Press, 1999).

9. See James A. McMillin, *The Final Victims: Foreign Slave Trade to North America, 1783–1810* (Columbia: University of South Carolina Press, 2004).

10. François Furstenberg, "Beyond Freedom and Slavery: Autonomy, Virtue, and Resistance in Early American Political Discourse," *Journal of American History* 89 (March 2003): 1295–1330.

11. Paul Finkelman, "Slavery and the Constitutional Convention: Making a Covenant with Death," in Richard Beeman et al., eds., *Beyond Confederation: Origins of the Constitution and American National Identity* (Chapel Hill: University of North Carolina Press for the Institute of Early American History and Culture, 1987), 188–225; Finkelman, *Slavery and the Founders: Race and Liberty in the Age of Jefferson* (Armonk, N.Y.: M. E. Sharpe, 1996). For a sampling of recent writings following Finkelman, see Kenneth Morgan, "Slavery and the Debate over Ratification of the United States Constitution," *Slavery and Abolition* 22 (December 2001): 40–65; Akhil Reed Amar, *America's Constitution: A Biography* (New York: Random House, 2005); and Lawrence Goldstone, *Dark Bargain: Slavery, Profits, and the Struggle for the Constitution* (New York: Walker and Company, 2005).

12. See Don E. Fehrenbacher, *The Slaveholding Republic: An Account of the United States Government's Relations to Slavery* (Oxford: Oxford University Press, 2001); Leonard L. Richards, *The Slave Power: The Free North and Southern Domination, 1780–1860* (Baton Rouge: Louisiana State University Press, 2000); and Adam Rothman, *Slave Country: American Expansion and the Origins of the Deep South* (Cambridge, Mass.: Harvard University Press, 2005).

13. This is powerfully illustrated by David Brion Davis in *The Problem of Slavery in Western Culture* and *The Problem of Slavery in the Age of Revolution*. More recently, Christopher Leslie Brown, in *Moral Capital: Foundations of British Abolitionism* (Chapel Hill: University of North

Carolina Press, 2006), has shown the importance of the American Revolution for the rise of organized abolition within Great Britain.

14. This essay is not the first to highlight the importance of such a distinction. For other recent examples, see Brown, *Moral Capital;* and Matthew Mason, *Slavery and Politics in the Early American Republic* (Chapel Hill: University of North Carolina Press, 2006), especially 4–5.

15. See Roger Bruns, ed., *Am I Not a Man and a Brother: The Antislavery Crusade of Revolutionary America, 1688–1788* (New York: Chelsea House, 1977), 3–99 passim; Hodges, *Root and Branch,* 124–25; Nash and Soderlund, *Freedom by Degrees,* chap. 2; Mary Stoughton Locke, *Anti-Slavery in America from the Introduction of African Slaves to the Prohibition of the Slave Trade* (1901; repr., Johnson Reprint Corp., 1968), 21–45; James D. Essig, *The Bonds of Wickedness: American Evangelicals against Slavery, 1770–1808* (Philadelphia: Temple University Press, 1982), especially chap. 2; and Davis, *The Problem of Slavery in Western Culture,* 213–14, 308.

16. Davis, *The Problem of Slavery in Western Culture,* 150–52, chap. 13 (quotation at 151). See also Bruns, *Am I Not a Man,* 278–90.

17. Essig, *The Bonds of Wickedness,* 23–24 (first quotation); Bruns, *Am I Not a Man,* 321, 325–27, 344–48, 358–65, 374–76, 397–400, 423–26, 432–40, 456–61 (second quotation at 362). See also Davis, *The Problem of Slavery in Western Culture,* 370, 438–45, 482–93; Davis, *The Problem of Slavery in the Age of Revolution,* 282–84; Jordan, *White Over Black,* 292–301.

18. See Essig, *The Bonds of Wickedness,* chap. 5; and Kenneth P. Minkema and Harry S. Stout, "The Edwardsean Tradition and the Antislavery Debate, 1740–1865," *Journal of American History* 92 (June 2005): 47–74.

19. See Bruns, *Am I Not a Man,* 268, 274–77, 305, 365–76, 439–40; and John P. Kaminski, ed., *A Necessary Evil? Slavery and the Debate over the Constitution* (Madison, Wis.: Madison House, 1995), 4–5, 10–11, 24.

20. T. H. Breen, "Making History: The Force of Public Opinion and the Last Years of Slavery in Massachusetts," in *Through a Glass Darkly: Reflections on Personal Identity in Early America,* ed. Ronald Hoffman, Mechal Sobel, and Fredrika J. Teute (Chapel Hill: University of North Carolina Press, 1997), 67–95.

21. Nash and Soderlund, *Freedom by Degrees,* 100–14.

22. Gellman, *Emancipating New York,* 5, 33–34.

23. Ibid., 38, 46–55, 68–72.

24. Ibid., 91–95, 130–41, 170–71, 195 (quotation at 131); White, *Somewhat More Independent,* 27–28.

25. Gellman, *Emancipating New York,* 39, 45, 76.

26. John Craig Hammond, *Slavery, Freedom, and Expansion in the Early American West* (Charlottesville: University of Virginia Press, 2007), passim, especially 11, 43; Mason, *Slavery and Politics in the Early American Republic,* 6–7, 25–26, 28.

27. Hammond, *Slavery, Freedom, and Expansion in the Early American West,* 76–95.

28. Ibid., 76–149 (quotations at 98, 135, 121, 78).

29. Matthew Mason, "Keeping Up Appearances: The International Politics of Slave Trade Abolition in the Nineteenth-Century Atlantic World," *William and Mary Quarterly,* 3rd ser., 66 (October 2009): 809–32 (quotation at 809); idem, "The Battle of the Slaveholding Libera-

tors: Great Britain, the United States, and Slavery in the Early Nineteenth Century," *William and Mary Quarterly*, 3rd ser., 59 (July 2002): 665–96.

30. Wolf, *Race and Liberty in the New Nation*, 43. Wolf downplays Revolutionary ideology as a motive for manumission, especially from the 1790s forward (see ibid., x–xi, 39–84). Wolf's estimate also revises downward the numbers in Mullin (see *Flight and Rebellion*, 127) and Berlin (see *Slaves without Masters*, pt. 1).

31. Richard S. Dunn, "Black Society in the Chesapeake, 1776–1810," in Berlin and Hoffman, *Slavery and Freedom in the Age of the American Revolution*, 49–82, especially 52; Mary Beth Norton, Herbert G. Gutman, and Ira Berlin, "The Afro-American Family in the Age of Revolution," in Berlin and Hoffman, *Slavery and Freedom in the Age of the American Revolution*, 190–91.

32. Wolf, *Race and Liberty in the New Nation*, ix (first quotation), chap. 2; Herbert Aptheker, *American Negro Slave Revolts* (New York: Columbia University Press, 1943), 235–38 (second quotation at 235); Barbara Fields, *Slavery and Freedom on the Middle Ground: Maryland during the Nineteenth Century* (New Haven, Conn.: Yale University Press, 1985), 5–6 (third quotation); Locke, *Anti-Slavery in America*, 109–10. For more on the transition from tobacco to grain and its significance, see Berlin, *Generations of Captivity*, chap. 10. For the unusually high incidence of organized slave resistance in the early republic and its political impact, see Mason, *Slavery and Politics in the Early American Republic*, 16–19, 107–9; and the essays by Rob Parkinson and Ed Rugemer in the present volume.

33. Bruns, *Am I Not a Man*, xxviii (first quotation), 264; Kaminski, *Necessary Evil*, 203 (second quotation); MacLeod, *Slavery, Race, and the American Revolution*, 140.

34. Wolf, *Race and Liberty in the New Nation*, chap. 2 (first quotation at 61), 121–27; Louis Morton, *Robert Carter of Nomini Hall: A Virginia Tobacco Planter of the Eighteenth Century* (1941; repr., Charlottesville: University Press of Virginia, 1964), 251–70; Wiencek, *An Imperfect God*, 4–5, 26, 343, 351–61; Gordon Esley Finnie, "The Antislavery Movement in the South, 1787–1836: Its Rise and Decline and Its Contribution to Abolition in the West," Ph.D. diss., Duke University, 1962, especially 143, 212–309; Donald G. Mathews, *Slavery and Methodism: A Chapter in American Morality, 1780–1845* (Princeton, N.J.: Princeton University Press, 1965), 20–61; Essig, *The Bonds of Wickedness*, chaps. 3, 4, 6; Monica Najar, "'Meddling with Emancipation': Baptists, Authority, and the Rift over Slavery in the Upper South," *Journal of the Early Republic* 25 (Summer 2005): 158–86; Merton L. Dillon, *Slavery Attacked: Southern Slaves and Their Allies, 1619–1865* (Baton Rouge: Louisiana State University Press, 1990), 65 (second quotation). For a more famous—and more candid—plea of convenience from Patrick Henry, see Bruns, *Am I Not a Man*, 221–22. Charles F. Irons has expressed doubts about a retreat in the nineteenth century from an antislavery golden age in the eighteenth century; see his *Origins of Proslavery Christianity: White and Black Evangelicals in Colonial and Antebellum Virginia* (Chapel Hill: University of North Carolina Press, 2008), especially 13.

35. Schmidt and Wilhelm, "Early Proslavery Petitions in Virginia," 136–46 (quotations at 139). For other examples that emphasize property rights, see Price, *Freedom Not Far Distant*, 58–61; and Jan Lewis, "The Problem of Slavery in Southern Political Discourse," in *Devising Liberty: Preserving and Creating Freedom in the New American Republic*, ed. David Thomas Konig (Stanford, Calif.: Stanford University Press, 1995), 265–97. For others who sought to tie abolitionists to the British, see Kenneth S. Greenberg, *Masters and Statesmen: The Political Culture of American Slavery* (Baltimore: Johns Hopkins University Press, 1985), 111; David N.

Gellman and David Quigley, eds., *Jim Crow New York: A Documentary History of Race and Citizenship, 1777–1877* (New York: New York University Press, 2003), 35; Hodges, *Root and Branch*, 161–63; and Rob Parkinson's chapter in this volume. See also Wolf, *Race and Liberty in the New Nation*, 88–96; and Irons, *Origins of Proslavery Christianity*. I use the word "anti-abolitionist" here advisedly, for too often the literature conflates opposition to abolition with a truly proslavery position.

36. Wolf, *Race and Liberty in the New Nation*, xii, 225.

37. Mason, *Slavery and Politics in the Early American Republic*, 38–39 (quotations at 38).

38. Ibid., 39.

39. Ibid., chap. 2.

40. *The Papers of Daniel Webster*, ed. Charles M. Wiltse (Hanover, N.H.: University Press of New England, 1974), 1:135–37.

41. Mason, *Slavery and Politics in the Early American Republic*, chap. 2 (quotation at 58).

42. Ibid., chap. 3 (quotations at 78–79).

43. Ibid., chap. 6 (quotation at 140).

44. *Journal of the Assembly of the State of New-York: At Their Fortieth Session* (Albany, 1816), 126–27 (first quotation); *Columbian* (New York City), 3 February 1817; *National Advocate* (New York City), 9 January 1817 (second quotation); *Journal of the Assembly of the State of New York*, 558–62, 568; *Journal of the Senate of the State of New-York: At Their Fortieth Session* (Albany, 1816), 251. The law decreed that no one would be held as a slave in New York after 4 July 1827. For more on this law and its significance, see Zilversmit, *First Emancipation*, 211–14.

45. Mason, *Slavery and Politics in the Early American Republic*, chaps. 6, 8.

46. Frederick J. Blue, *No Taint of Compromise: Crusaders in Antislavery Politics* (Baton Rouge: Louisiana State University Press, 2005), 27.

47. Quoted in William E. Gienapp, "The Crime against Sumner: The Caning of Charles Sumner and the Rise of the Republican Party," *Civil War History* 25 (September 1989): 230.

48. Eric Foner, *Free Soil, Free Labor, Free Men: The Ideology of the Republican Party before the Civil War* (Oxford: Oxford University Press, 1970), 101, 308–9 (quotation at 101).

49. Quoted in Thomas L. Gaffney, "Maine's Mr. Smith: A Study of the Career of Francis O. J. Smith, Politician and Entrepeneur" (Ph.D. diss., University of Maine, 1979), 342. For an especially powerful call to take antislavery politics seriously, despite its intermixture with "impure" motives, see Daniel Feller, "A Brother in Arms: Benjamin Tappan and the Antislavery Democracy," *Journal of American History* 88 (June 2001): 48–74.

Early Free-Labor Thought
and the Contest over Slavery
in the Early Republic

EVA SHEPPARD WOLF

A generation before Adam Smith, in *Wealth of Nations*, criticized slavery as less efficient than free labor, Benjamin Franklin advanced a similar argument. In his 1751 essay, "Observations Concerning the Increase of Mankind...," Franklin claimed that a series of reasoned calculations proved that free labor was economically superior to slave labor. Since he advanced his argument in more of a rhetorical than mathematical way, describing rather than demonstrating the necessary calculations, Franklin seems to have assumed that his readers had arrived with him at the understanding that slaves would "Neglect" their "Business" more than free workers would, because "Neglect is natural to the Man who is not to be benefited by his own Care or Diligence." But most of Franklin's readers probably did *not* accept that conclusion, at least not yet. Conventional wisdom in the mid and late eighteenth century held that slave labor, not free labor, yielded greater production. Americans knew that the wealthiest among them usually held slaves.[1]

In arguing for the benefits of free labor, as in so much else, Franklin rode on—and helped create—the leading edge of a new intellectual and cultural wave. For him, free labor stood as both economically and morally superior to slave labor, because free labor, when supported by "Frugality and Industry," constituted an honorable pursuit. What a complete inversion of centuries of thought that held that only the lowly should labor, that God had punished human beings for Adam and Eve's original sin by making people labor, and that honor redounded to those who made others labor for them! Indeed, Franklin himself had demonstrated his attachment to these traditional ideas when he retired from the working life as soon as he was able, so that he might become a proper English gentleman. But in his 1751 essay, Franklin showed the way toward a new set of ideas.[2]

The new scholarship on the problem of slavery in the early republic takes some cognizance of that new set of ideas, but has not engaged in a sustained way with the crucial topic of the rise of free-labor ideas in the early republic and their connection to Revolutionary-era and early national antislavery thought. While most of the new works on slavery and freedom in the early republic touch on ideas about free labor, many fail to include the topic in the index. Perhaps, to many scholars, the content and nature of free-labor thought seem obvious, in no small part because free-labor ideology has been so intelligently analyzed, though for a later period, by Eric Foner in *Free Soil, Free Labor, Free Men*. But as Eric Foner himself said, in the preface to the 1995 edition of that work, his book "took the free labor ideology as a given, making little effort to trace its ideological origins, social roots, or evolution over time." Similarly, Jonathan Glickstein's thoughtful work, *Concepts of Free Labor in Antebellum America*, focuses on the three decades before the Civil War and only briefly touches on the origins of free-labor ideas before that period. The historical literature on events contemporaneous to early free-labor ideas, particularly the rise of both antislavery thought and capitalism, has also tended to gloss over or ignore ideas about free labor.[3]

An initial examination of the content of and changes in free-labor thought in its nascent phase from the 1750s to the 1810s—and an admittedly selective and incomplete examination at that—nevertheless shows clearly that ideas about free labor in that period underwent several gradual shifts, and also underscores that free-labor ideology did not spring fully formed into the conversations of the antebellum period or the debates over Missouri. To emphasize the extent to which ideas about free labor did not yet cohere into an *ideology*—were not yet part of a coherent, consistent, and widely shared set of assumptions and symbols—I have avoided the word "ideology" when describing early national *ideas* or *thought(s)* about free labor. That is, this essay focuses on culture and ideas in transition. As a consequence, the evidence it examines is not only scattered, but sometimes internally inconsistent.

Still, it is possible to outline the main contours of change, and they are these: Over time, and especially after about 1790, free-labor ideas found a more frequent and central place in antislavery writings, from which they had generally been absent in the 1750s, '60s, and '70s. A corollary to this development was that, in this period, free-labor ideas generally appeared in antislavery writings and not often outside of them. As free-labor arguments grew more central to antislavery discourse, writers began to comprehend slavery as less, not more, productive than free labor. Whereas in the 1770s Quakers had argued that slave owners should give up their slaves despite the economic advantages slavery held, by the time of the Missouri debates Northerners generally viewed the problem as one of two opposing labor systems, with the "barrens of the desert" in slaveholding areas constituting clear evidence of the slave-labor system's failure, particularly when compared to the "verdure and produce" of the free states.[4]

As part of the shift toward seeing free labor as economically advantageous over slave labor, writers began to champion the dignity of that labor, especially free white men's labor, and to link free labor to republicanism. In the early nineteenth century, free-labor arguments often brought together a triad of ideas: the economic superiority of free labor, accompanied by its moral superiority and the importance of personal liberty. The combination of these three emphases lent free-labor arguments much of their power and tied them to a cultural system as well as an economic one. Amidst these changes over time in the frequency and emphases of free-labor arguments, one thing remained relatively constant: early free-labor ideas subsumed women and children's work into that of their husbands and fathers. The rhetoric of free labor was implicitly and highly gendered.

Finally, it should be stated again that this outline of change oversimplifies the history of early ideas about free labor. Between the mid-eighteenth century and the third decade of the nineteenth century, writers' arguments in favor of free labor varied considerably, and sometimes contradicted themselves. But however variable, however protean they were, ideas about free labor's superiority played an important role in antislavery thinking in early national America well before the Missouri Crisis, the Free Soil movement, or the formation of the Republican Party in the 1850s.

Benjamin Franklin's "Observations Concerning the Increase of Mankind" helps us to see both some of what persisted and what changed in early free-labor thinking. On the one hand, later writers adopted many of the arguments Franklin laid out, but other elements of Franklin's essay mark it as an early and unusual example of thought about free labor. For one thing, Franklin's 1751 comments focused most on population growth and not on slavery; unlike so many later essays that dealt with free labor, Franklin's was not primarily an antislavery tract. Also marking his essay as an early example of ideas about free labor was Franklin's view of free labor not as a *system* but rather as a kind of work.

Nevertheless, his essay did constitute an important early statement in the public discussion of how free labor, and, in particular, how a culture championing the dignity of work, affected society. In arguing that age at marriage determined fecundity and that those who could provide materially for a family would marry earlier, he concluded, "If there be a Sect . . . in our Nation, that regard Frugality and Industry as religious Duties, and educate their Children therein, more than others commonly do; such Sect must consequently increase more by natural Generation."[5] In another part of the essay, when noting the increase of whites in the Northern colonies, in contrast to the "diminish'd" whites in the sugar islands, Franklin suggested that, indeed, there *was* a sect whose regard of industry and frugality accounted for their greater fecundity. It was *his* sect, his people: the northern English colonists of America. The slave-owning elite of the sugar islands illustrated what happened when, by contrast, a people spent their wealth on "Foreign Luxuries," and passed the "Habit of those Luxuries" on to their children. Since indulgence in luxuries meant that "the same income is needed for the Support of one that might have maintain'd 100," those who indulged could not afford to support many children. The result was a declining population. "The Whites who have Slaves, not laboring, are enfeebled, and therefore not so generally prolific."[6]

A set of assumptions about gender underlay and sharpened Franklin's analysis, and they also reflected the ideas of the period in which he wrote. In particular, the English of the mid-eighteenth century often understood luxury as an effeminizing force.[7] If slavery encouraged luxury, it followed that slavery diminished the manliness of slaveholders. The numerical decrease among slaveholders as a consequence of their indulging in "luxuries" suggested that slaveholders had become less virile. Slaveholding, rather than increase a man's power, actually made him less potent, "enfeebled." In contrast, free labor's greater reproductive power made it a force of good, a force of creation—and particularly a force of masculine and paternal creation.

In addition, the "Man" so often referred to in Franklin's essay should be understood as a literal man, not as a stand-in for "human." When speaking of slaves—the "Sons of *Africa*," "the Man who is not to be benefited by his own Care or Diligence"—Franklin pictured men. When speaking of free workers or of slaveholders—"a laboring Man," "hired Men"—Franklin and his readers again pictured men.[8]

Indeed, Franklin's analysis would have run into some logical difficulties if it had tried to account for free women's pervasive, but uncompensated, labor. A wife, like a slave or a bound servant, did not earn wages for her labor, did not legally possess the products of her labor, and could not leave her husband/master if she found herself unhappy with her working conditions. She was also subject to reasonable corporal punishment. Was her labor free labor? Did the fact that the family she labored in was partly hers distinguish her labor sufficiently from that of a bound servant or slave? Did marriage endow some sort of emotional, if not legal, ownership over the products of her work in the household economy? Franklin started a trend when he refused to answer, or even to acknowledge, such questions.

The resulting view of free labor, a view that generally persisted, thus tied together ideas about power and manhood with ideas about work. It provided a positive vision, not only a critique of slavery.[9] Free labor, as Franklin understood it, encouraged good personal attributes, such as frugality and industry. Its greater efficiency meant that free laborers would produce more than enslaved ones did. They would also *re*produce more than would the owners of enslaved labor, so free labor promoted manly fortitude and virility —a masculine kind of procreation. Although later commentators on free-versus-slave labor advanced their own particular views of the question, and Franklin in later years did take into account women's labor (as workers, not in childbirth), those who wrote about free labor adhered to the main thesis Franklin laid out in 1751—that, measured in both economic and moral terms, free labor benefited a society better than did slave labor.

But Franklin was ahead of his time in addressing free labor's benefits. And he was also a bit odd in discussing free labor in terms of population growth rather than in terms of slavery per se. It took a while for antislavery writers to come to Franklin's understanding of free labor. In the 1760s and 1770s, for instance, the Quaker abolitionism that dominated antislavery discourse tended to assume that the morality of abolition trumped the economic advantages of slavery.[10] Abolitionists argued, not only in print but face to face in Quaker meetings, that the evil of slavery demanded its end *even though* so many individual Americans found slavery personally and financially beneficial. They did not try to convince their peers that a person could make more money with free laborers than enslaved ones, but rather that one should give up slavery as a matter of morality.

The transition in the American North toward the conviction that free labor held economic advantages over slavery occurred slowly and indirectly, but the Revolutionary period seems to mark an important turning point toward that end. In 1773, just a few years before Adam Smith declared in *Wealth of Nations* that "the work done by slaves . . . is in the end the dearest of any," Benjamin Rush argued in an antislavery pamphlet that economic and moral good supported one another. To convince his audience of the greater productivity of free labor over slave labor, Rush called in an expert witness. He quoted approvingly from one Monsieur Le Poivre, the former French envoy to Cochin-China (present-day southern Vietnam), who had observed free laborers there cultivating sugar. Le Poivre wrote, "I cannot entertain a doubt but that our West-India colonies, had they been distributed, without reservation amongst a free people, would have produced double the quantity that is now procured from the labor of the unfortunate negroes." Le Poivre explained the underlying logic of the free-labor position in terms of a natural order that his Enlightenment cohorts would recognize and appreciate. "Liberty and property," he observed, "form the basis of abundance, and good agriculture. . . . The earth, which multiples her productions with a kind of profusion, under the hands of the free-born labourer, seems to shrink into barrenness under the sweat of the slave." The greater fecundity of earth tilled by free laborers fit the Creator's plan since, according to Le Poivre, "the Author of our Nature" intended that "man" should "cultivate his possession with the sweat of his brow; but still should enjoy his Liberty." As it had for Franklin, a concept of honorable and productive masculine labor animated the scene M. Le Poivre described.[11]

And just as Franklin had set honorable labor in opposition to luxury, so did Benjamin Rush, who emphasized that in addition to its being more productive, free labor, "by diminishing opulence in a few[,] would suppress Luxury and Vice." Free labor would foster a good society in another way too—one championed later by antislavery settlers to the Northwest—since it would "promote the equal distribution of property, which appears best calculated to promote the welfare of Society."[12] Who could oppose a system that united economic productivity with social good?

Still, in 1790, when William Cooper sought to gain support for New York maple sugar over West Indian cane sugar, thus inviting a discussion precisely on that question, free-labor arguments appeared relatively novel. As David Gellman has summarized: "Maple sugar advocates . . . helped to introduce into public dialogue the notion that certain types of labor harmonized better than others with the standards of a just and economically healthy society. They indicated free labor's superiority to slave labor." While William Cooper himself emphasized the high quality of maple sugar and its economic advantages (that it was cheaper than cane sugar, and was literally an untapped resource in maple trees), the editors of the *New York Daily Advertiser* advanced a moral-economic argument. They began by noting that maple sugar was "obtained by the willing labor of freemen." West India sugar, by contrast, "is said to cost four lives" for every hogshead, and is therefore "stained with blood." Writers thus found multiple arguments available as they championed maple sugar, and they used whatever they could; no orthodoxy, and certainly no free-labor orthodoxy, existed.[13]

Another essay of that year showed how the newer belief in free labor's economic power continued to appear alongside the traditionally accepted view that using slaves could make one rich. An essay written by "Rusticus" that appeared in the *New York Daily Advertiser* contained a messy congeries of free-labor arguments typifying the variety of ideas writers advanced in the long period before free-labor thought became standardized as an ideology. In arguing against the slave trade, Rusticus, whose pseudonym apparently referred less to one of the historical personages with that name than to rural simplicity, admitted the economic advantages slavery provided, since "the planter . . . can purchase two Guinea negroes for his [the freeman's] price." Sounding here much like the Quakers who wanted people to give up their slaves, Rusticus emphasized that morality demanded something different than a calculation of profits. It pressed upon human beings to act on behalf of their enslaved fellows and against the "obdurate tyrants" who not only deprived their slaves of liberty but also "punish[ed] them with hunger, nakedness, and wanton stripes." Fighting against the slave trade meant fighting for "the noblest undertaking of men, and christians." At the same time, Rusticus presaged the main theme of later antislavery writing, suggesting, if only briefly, that in fact slavery might prove economically *dis*advantageous. Rusticus noted that a "freeman could indeed do the work [of a slave] and to much better purpose." Rusticus, like Franklin, assumed that those who saw the fruits of their labor in wages or other compensation would work more effectively, "to much better purpose." Believing free labor to be more efficient than slave labor conflicted with his understanding that planters preferred slave labor since it was cheaper—that is, that slavery was more efficient. The contradiction, taken together with the contemporaneous essays about maple sugar, suggests how much ideas about labor were in flux in 1790.[14]

Although the argument for the economic inferiority of slave labor gained traction in the late eighteenth century, assumptions about slavery's economic might persisted a surprisingly long time—well into the nineteenth century. In the second decade of that century many Americans who wrote about slave labor versus free labor still assumed slave labor to be more, not less, efficient than free labor. They thought that where slaves existed they would compete with poor white workers, and white workers would suffer. That only made sense if they thought that when enslaved laborers and free laborers worked side by side, enslaved laborers either produced more or produced the same amount at much lower cost. As one newspaper essayist wrote in 1816, without self-consciousness or further analysis, "The poor laborer will follow the same tract [as the rich Northern emigrants to the Northwest], because the field is fully open to him; there is no competition with the black laborer to lessen the demand for his labor, and lower his wages."[15] Clearly, the writer trusted that his audience would agree with him that slave labor was cheaper than free labor. Similarly, Ohioans in the early years of the nineteenth century fretted that "scornful nabobs surrounded by their miserable slaves" would "condemn those that seek to live by their honest industry."[16] This argument rested on the underlying premise that a slave system generated big profits—that it was economically powerful. But again the economic might of slavery stood in contrast to the moral might of free labor, which here consisted in the "honest industry" of workers. Anti-slavery writers who emphasized the disadvantages with which slavery burdened free white workers simultaneously—if only implicitly and tacitly—recognized that extracted, coerced labor could create more wealth than could free labor.

The halting transition toward seeing free labor as economically advantageous over slave labor coincided in a general way with the transition toward free labor for white people during the Revolutionary and early national eras. In the colonial period, most laborers in America had been bound either as slaves, apprentices, or servants; but by 1830 all forms of bound labor had virtually disappeared from the Northern states, and only slavery remained to any great extent in the Southern ones. In cultural terms, the categories of "bosses" and "employees" replaced those of "masters" and "servants." Americans also created free labor as a legal category in order to accommodate and propel the economic shift away from bound labor, especially in the North. These changes made it easier in the early nineteenth century for Northern Americans to conceive of free labor as a *system* that they could view in contrast to the slave system—an opposition different from the one that the Quakers in the mid-to-late eighteenth century drew between the goodness of freedom and the immorality of slavery. The Swiss immigrant John Badollet, for example, writing in 1806 from Vincennes in the Indiana Territory, felt sure that Indiana would better prosper in the long term if it banned the "odious system" of slavery that Badollet thought would retard settlement.[17]

It should not surprise us that the late-eighteenth-century transition toward free labor coincided with the transition toward free-labor ideology, but it does raise the question of how free-labor thought related to the rise of capitalism. Although clearly some relationship existed, it seems a mistake to view free-labor ideology and practice simply as a natural consequence of the fundamental rearrangement of economic life brought by industrial capitalism. For one thing, the chronology does not always work. The replacement of bound labor by free labor generally preceded rather than followed marketization and industrialization in the American North. Neither did industrialization and the rise of capitalism necessarily doom apprenticeship and servitude, forms of bound labor that persisted in industrializing Britain much longer than in the United States.[18]

Indeed, it seems that by the early years of the nineteenth century—a decade before the wave of industrialization that followed the War of 1812—many Northern Americans had come to believe in the economic might of a free-labor system (although, as argued above, many also still implicitly argued that slavery held great economic power). In discussions over the economic destiny of Louisiana, for example, Republican newspaper editor William Duane, who opposed the expansion of slavery, was certain that "three or four hundred white farmers with their families will produce more sugar than a negro estate with two thousand slaves." As Allan Magruder similarly argued in *Political, Commercial, and Moral Reflections on the Late Cession of Louisiana to the United States,* "In Louisiana, the land can be worked by the real owner of the soil; and the superior care and attention which he bestows on his plantation, will enable him to double its productions," adding, "The free white man who owns the soil he works, will double the quantity [produced by a Negro slave]." These assertions of free labor's vastly superior productivity, which writers offered up to the reader as something needing little justification, indicate the large extent to which Americans in the early nineteenth century had come to share Franklin's assumption that those who worked for themselves labored more effectively and thus produced more.[19]

But productive capacity did not excite people so much as did the idea of freedom. An important part of the story of early free-labor ideas lies in the way Northerners of the early national years began to redefine their localities as "free," and thus as distinct from and superior to the Southern states where slavery persisted. Joanne Melish argues convincingly that in New England, gradual emancipation starting in the 1780s allowed whites to begin to reconceptualize their society as free, and, more particularly, as white and free, and to erase the memory of their slaveholding past. David Gellman notes a similar reformulation of local identity in New York, where as early as the 1790s New York Republicans began to differentiate themselves from their Southern counterparts. In early-nineteenth-century national debates that touched on slavery, Matthew Mason shows, New Englanders made much of their superiority as a free society. The process replicated itself as Americans moved west. Residents of the Northwest began to create an identity as free in the 1810s after they had settled the question of whether slavery would be allowed in the new Northwest states. According to John Craig Hammond, Ohio and Indiana became societies that celebrated freedom, not as a consequence of migration there by Northerners but as a result of lived experience and on-the-ground struggles over slavery.[20]

It is tempting to see Northerners' celebration of freedom and free labor as a natural outcome of the American Revolution and its championing of liberty. But Southern Americans, too, thought of themselves as free. Starting in the 1780s they began to applaud the way slavery could enhance white liberty; by freeing whites from labor's drudgery, slavery allowed white people to cultivate their intellect and culture. Slavery did not necessarily have to figure as an enemy to white liberty.[21]

In the era of the Revolution and early republic, Northerners celebrated more than personal freedom, which white Southerners could extol too. They combined their celebration of personal liberty with the perceived economic as well as moral advantages of free labor in order to explain the goodness of their culture in contrast to another one. Thus combined, their ideas about free labor held much rhetorical and emotional power.

So, rather than serve only as a functional ideology to support capitalist labor relations, free-labor thought in its more mature form—in which free labor was understood in terms of personal liberty, moral superiority, and economic power—worked to impart to those who internalized its tenets a positive sense of self and community. This is not to deny that free-labor ideas and practices *did* serve the new economic arrangements of the early national period: free-labor ideas facilitated the hiring and firing of workers as an employer's needs changed. But free-labor ideas also served as a critique of the new economic forms, since those who championed the dignity of free labor often critiqued the factory and the city, and praised instead the independence of farming and small-town life.[22]

Federalist writers and politicians in the first decade of the nineteenth century demonstrated well how to employ free-labor ideas to celebrate one's own culture and one's own freedom while denigrating those of another. As both Linda Kerber and Rachel Hope Cleves describe, New England Federalist opposition to slavery formed part of their larger opposition to the slave-holding Virginians who dominated the national government. Federalist anti-slavery writers marshaled as many arguments as they could to critique the "Virginia Way of Life." They pointed out that in addition to striking at the dignity of labor and promoting among masters a tyrannical character that threatened republican institutions, slavery tended to yield an impoverished landscape. These three arguments—a version of the triumvirate of personal liberty, moral superiority, and economic power—worked closely together. As one newspaper essayist complained, planters "occupy vast tracts of poor land, and have been accustomed to live among their vassals in a style of feudal hospitality, and mimick grandeur. The poorest among them, consider per-sonal labour a *disgrace.*" A slave-labor system produced "wretchedness and ignorance" on the part of slaves, and "Envy & Jealousy" in the "Bosoms" of the masters. The opposite also held true. Oliver Wolcott noted "Happily" that "in these [Northern] States . . . the employers and the employed, are mutu-ally obliged and mutually dependent," yielding a "spirit of moderation and justice . . . supported by common necessities & obligations." Wolcott and others saw that free labor, as a system, helped create a good society partly because it fostered healthy habits and attitudes, while slavery, as a system, encouraged unhealthy ways.[23]

It is because free-labor ideas came to stand for a whole cultural system, not only an economic one, that they gained increasing importance in discus-sions of slavery's future and especially in early-nineteenth-century discus-sions over the future of the West. Those who wanted to keep slavery out of Louisiana worried about the territory's republican character as well as its economic health. William Duane believed that a free-labor system would better encourage republican habits and would repress the aristocratic, slave-owning ones that did not suit republican society. For Allan Magruder, a Louisiana farmed by free whites rather than slaves would help bring Amer-ica in line with its "republican principles," since he viewed slavery as a "stain upon her [America's] character."[24] (Somewhat paradoxically, Magruder also saw in Louisiana the possibility of abolishing American slavery by colonizing freed slaves there, apparently envisioning that free, white sugar producers would somehow share the territory with black ex-slaves.)

Aligning free labor with republicanism and slave labor against it raised the stakes considerably; the argument became one over which labor system better suited America and which types of American better fulfilled the Revolutionary destiny. For advocates of free labor, the main line of logic went like this: since the makers of the Revolution had fought against the tyranny and corruption that had infected and overtaken the British government, tyranny had no place in the new nation; slavery encouraged tyranny and turned slaveholders into tyrants; thus slavery operated to undermine the goals of the Revolution.

This rhetoric changed little from the 1790s to the 1810s, but it became more forceful over time. When Rusticus in 1790 condemned planters who "exercise[d] . . . unlimited power" and who did not speak the "language" of "mercy," he suggested that slaveholders were ill suited to republican government. Ohio Territorial Governor Arthur St. Clair in 1802 did not suggest; he declared it so. All the men in Ohio territory were republicans, he said, except for "*a few people who wish to introduce negro slavery amongst us.*" Federalists during the War of 1812 went so far as to criticize the president on similar terms, arguing that President Madison could not really demonstrate compassion for American seamen if he "continue[d] the lash of oppression on slaves." Free laborers thus congratulated themselves for being better equipped to carry out the goals of the Revolution and better able to govern the American people than those who compelled the work of slaves.[25]

Free labor supported republicanism—and slavery undermined it—in another way, too. Free labor encouraged a rough economic equality, which better suited republican government. As antislavery Ohioans saw it, "The moment slavery is introduced among us," then "equality of condition is done away." Where "equity reign[ed]," citizens could participate in the polity as peers. By contrast, where slavery dominated, slaveholders would dominate, which was part of the reason antislavery settlers in Indiana so vehemently decried the "Virginia Aristocrats," especially William Henry Harrison, who sought to introduce slavery to Indiana. Antislavery settlers in the Northwest did not want to lose political power on the local level to slaveholders. Echoing Benjamin Rush, they championed a moral economy, one that distributed wealth relatively equally, over an economy that maximized total wealth.[26]

All of these various discussions of free labor's superiority in the early national period focused, as had Franklin's, mostly on the labor of men, and were thus implicitly gendered, part of a conversation about manliness and republican citizenship. William Duane's phrase, "white farmers with their families" who could raise sugar in Louisiana, did not call up an image of white women working in cane fields. Duane saw the male head of household as the main worker, whose family aided in subsidiary ways. Ironically, in defining free labor mostly as a male endeavor, free labor came to include a man's ability to compel work from women and children; that compelled labor still got lumped into the category "free."

Because women did not own their labor as men did, advocates of free labor only rarely discussed women as laborers. One who did, a writer from Schoharie who endorsed William Cooper's maple sugar scheme, revealed how free-labor ideas could subtly shift to take account of women as laborers. Published in the *New York Daily Advertiser,* his letter noted that the work of sapping the trees "is in great measure left to the girls," and formed a "laudable occupation." In New York, "all is freedom—buxom health and voluntary labour." By contrast, the author lamented the debasement of enslaved women, asking his readers to imagine the "famished mother on the parched mountain with her child tied to her back, . . . heavy and dejected, while the unmerciful driver hastens her and her companions forward with the unfeeling cart-whip."[27] But, importantly, the Schoharie letter writer set forced labor in opposition to labor that was "laudable" and "voluntary," not "free." Probably unintentionally, he suggested that at some basic level women could not be free laborers. Truly free labor was more than voluntary and laudable, it was labor one owned oneself. It was masculine.

And in early national America, free labor was also white. By the time of the Missouri Crisis, it was no longer novel to argue that "white men, free laborers, will not, cannot, sit themselves down where labor is dishonored—they feel disgraced by being put upon par with a slave." Northerners of 1820 generally agreed that the white men of the non-slaveholding states possessed an "independent spirit," and that free laborers provided the "stamina of every government, and especially of a republic."[28] Joshua Michael Zeitz argues that the reorientation of the Northern economy toward industry more than commercialism after the War of 1812 accounts in large measure for the shift toward a "free labor synthesis," but focusing on expressions of free-labor ideas from Franklin forward makes the shift appear less sudden and the "centrality" of free-labor arguments in Missouri Crisis debates less "unique."[29]

In highlighting the role and evolution of free-labor thought in the period from 1751 to 1821, I do not mean to suggest that it served as the only or even the main argument slavery's foes marshaled against the institution; free-labor ideas always appeared amongst other attacks against slavery and the slave trade. But arguments about the moral-economic value of free labor and the personal liberty and dignity that free labor nurtured hit closer to home than did antislavery arguments based on empathy or an abstracted sense of evil. When people who identified themselves as free championed free labor over slave labor, they said something about themselves as well as about slaves as people or slavery as a system. They said that their own way of life was good. And more than that, they found a way to feel superior to those (tyrannical planters!) who did not have to labor by the sweat of their brows.

Only a powerful set of ideas could convince people that those who labored themselves were better off than those who could make others do the work for them. If the historians of the contests over slavery in the new republic have tended to assume the obviousness of free-labor logic rather than subject it to sustained analysis or inquiry, the reason may be that we are still in the thrall of free-labor thought. Never has capitalism reigned so supreme as in the years at the turn of the twenty-first century (although that appears to be changing rapidly). If we can step away a bit from our own assumptions so that we might better appreciate free-labor thought as complex, variable, useful, and historically contingent, we will better explain how slavery became an object of contest in the new nation. By focusing more explicitly on free-labor thought, by testing the arguments offered in this essay and extending the study of early free-labor ideas beyond what I have done here, we will better see how economics, ideology, culture, and politics worked together to help Americans understand their place in the world, and we will better comprehend how those self-understandings both bound them together and tore them apart.

NOTES

The author would like to thank the editors of the current volume for encouraging her to write this essay and for offering astute and exceedingly useful suggestions on drafts of it. Thanks also go to San Francisco State colleagues Sarah Curtis, Steve Leikin, Barbara Loomis, and Chris Waldrep, as well as the attendees of the Faculty Colloquium, whose comments moved the essay forward at an early stage.

1. Adam Smith, *An Inquiry into the Nature and Causes of the Wealth of Nations*, 2 vols. in 1, ed. Edwin Cannan (Chicago: University of Chicago Press, 1976), 90–91, 411–13; Benjamin Franklin, "Observations Concerning the Increase of Mankind, Peopling of Countries, &c., written in Pensilvania, 1751," in *The Interest of Great Britain Considered, with regard to her Colonies . . . To which are added Observations Concerning the Increase* (London, 1760; repr., Philadelphia: William Bradford, 1760), paragraph 12.

2. Franklin, "Observations Concerning the Increase of Mankind, Peopling of Countries, &c.," paragraph 20; David Brion Davis, *Inhuman Bondage: The Rise and Fall of Slavery in the New World* (New York: Oxford University Press, 2006), 35, 56, 248; Gordon S. Wood, *The Americanization of Benjamin Franklin* (New York: Penguin, 2004), chap. 1.

3. Eric Foner, *Free Soil, Free Labor, Free Men: The Ideology of the Republican Party before the Civil War* (New York: Oxford University Press, 1970, 1995), ix; Jonathan A. Glickstein, *Concepts of Free Labor in Antebellum America* (New Haven, Conn.: Yale University Press, 1991). Linda Kerber's discussion of Federalist antislavery and anti-Virginia ideas has served as a good treatment of the topic of early free-labor ideas, even though Kerber does not isolate free-labor ideas from other, closely related ideas, and the term "free labor" does not appear in the index of the book (see Kerber, *Federalists in Dissent: Imagery and Ideology in Jeffersonian America* [Ithaca, N.Y.: Cornell University Press, 1970], chap. 2). Joshua Michael Zeitz, in "The Missouri Compromise Reconsidered: Antislavery Rhetoric and the Emergence of the Free Labor Synthesis" (*Journal of the Early Republic* 20 [Fall 2000]: 447–85), does push consideration of free-labor ideas back to the 1820s, but in this essay I wish to examine free-labor ideas in an even earlier period. For an example of an essay that discusses early antislavery thought without raising the issue of free labor, see Thomas Haskell's brilliant work, "Capitalism and the Origins of Humanitarian Sensibility," pts. 1 and 2, *American Historical Review* 90 (April 1985): 339–61, and 90 (June 1985): 547–66. Davis, in *Inhuman Bondage,* does cite free-labor ideas as central in accounting for the ascendancy of antislavery ideas, but does not engage in a sustained or detailed discussion of the topic.

4. Quote is from Senator David Morril of New Hampshire, in *Annals of Congress,* 16th Cong., 1st sess., 152.

5. Franklin, "Observations Concerning the Increase of Mankind, Peopling of Countries, &c.," paragraph 20.

6. Ibid., paragraph 13. Franklin's role as the archetypal Puritan protocapitalist gets its classic treatment in Max Weber's *The Protestant Ethic and the Spirit of Capitalism,* trans. Talcott Parsons (New York: Scribner, 1948; original published in German in 1904).

7. See Drew McCoy, *The Elusive Republic: Political Economy in Jeffersonian America* (New York: W. W. Norton, 1980), 21–32, for a general discussion of luxury; and for luxury as effeminate, see G. J. Barker-Benfield, *The Culture of Sensibility* (Chicago: University of Chicago Press, 1992), 104.

8. Franklin, "Observations Concerning the Increase of Mankind, Peopling of Countries, &c.," paragraphs 24, 12, 6.

9. This view echoes Eric Foner's comment that "political anti-slavery was not merely a negative doctrine," it was "an affirmation of the superiority of the social system of the North" (Foner, *Free Soil, Free Labor, Free Men,* 11).

10. In "Conscience, Interest, and Power: The Development of Quaker Opposition to Slavery in the Delaware Valley, 1688–1780" (Ph.D. diss., Temple University, 1982), Jean Ruth Soderlund writes, "Antislavery reformers in the Society of Friends never contended that slavery was economically unsound in their efforts to convince slave masters to release their blacks" (257). For a sensitive treatment of Quaker antislavery thought, see David Brion Davis, *The Problem of Slavery in the Age of Revolution, 1770–1823* (Ithaca, N.Y.: Cornell University Press, 1975; repr. with a new preface, New York: Oxford University Press, 1999), chap. 5.

11. Smith, *Wealth of Nations,* 411; [Benjamin Rush], *An Address to the Inhabitants of the British Settlements, on the Slavery of the Negroes in America,* 2nd ed. (Philadelphia: John Dunlap, 1773), 5–7.

12. [Benjamin Rush], *An Address to the Inhabitants of the British Settlements, on the Slavery of the Negroes in America.* Rush's free-labor argument appeared amidst other antislavery argu-

ments, including those rejecting the idea that Africans were inferior and that Christianity could support slavery.

13. David N. Gellman, *Emancipating New York: The Politics of Slavery and Freedom* (Baton Rouge: Louisiana State University Press), 93; William Cooper's letter, *New York Daily Advertiser,* 23 August 1790, 14 April 1790.

14. *New York Daily Advertiser,* 30 March 1790.

15. "Slavery," originally published in the *Richmond Compiler,* 11 September 1816, and reprinted in the *Daily National Intelligencer* (Washington, D.C.), 16 September 1816.

16. Quoted in John Craig Hammond, *Slavery, Freedom, and Expansion in the Early American West* (Charlottesville: University of Virginia Press, 2007), 135.

17. Gordon S. Wood, *The Radicalism of the American Revolution* (New York: Random House, 1991), 184; Robert J. Steinfeld, *The Invention of Free Labor: The Employment Relation in English and American Law and Culture* (Chapel Hill: University of North Carolina Press, 1991); John Badollet to Albert Gallatin, 1 January 1806, in *The Correspondence of John Badollet and Albert Gallatin, 1804–1836,* ed. Gayle Thornbrough (Indianapolis: Indiana Historical Society, 1963), 65.

18. Sharon Salinger, "Artisans, Journeymen, and the Transformation of Labor in Late Eighteenth Century Philadelphia" (*William and Mary Quarterly,* 3rd ser., 40 [January 1983]: 62–84), provides one example of a transformation in labor practices that occurred before industrial change. See also Bernard Elbaum, "Why Apprenticeship Persisted in Britain But Not in the United States," *Journal of Economic History* 49 (June 1989): 337–49. In some parts of the United States, however, traditional organization of work by families persisted into the early years of industrialization (see Mary P. Ryan, *Cradle of the Middle Class: The Family in Oneida County, New York, 1790–1865* [New York: Cambridge University Press, 1981], 43–51).

19. "Supply of Sugar," *Federal Republican* (Elizabethtown, N.J.), 29 November 1803 (reprinted from the *Aurora and General Advertiser* [Philadelphia]); Allan Magruder, *Political, Commercial, and Moral Reflections on the Late Cession of Louisiana to the United States* (Lexington, Ky.: D. Bradford, 1803), 113 (quotation), 112. Less easily accepted was that the work traditionally done by slaves could be honorable when performed by whites, but Duane tried to convince his readers that "[those who can clear lands and cultivate Indian corn, vegetables, tobacco, and cotton . . . may with the same industry produce sugar," and Magruder asserted that the hot weather of the West Indies that necessitated slave labor there did not exist in Louisiana, where white people could consequently work (112). "Columbus" also tried to convince whites that growing sugar and coffee was no more difficult than growing corn, beans, and potatoes (see "Arguments in Favor of the Louisiana Purchase, Drawn from a Federal Authority," originally printed in the *Aurora* [Philadelphia], and reprinted in the *Rhode-Island Republican,* 17 September 1803).

20. Joanne Pope Melish, *Disowning Slavery: Gradual Emancipation and "Race" in New England, 1780–1860* (Ithaca, N.Y.: Cornell University Press, 1998), 3, chap. 6; Gellman, *Emancipating New York,* 149; Matthew Mason, *Slavery and Politics in the Early American Republic* (Chapel Hill: University of North Carolina Press, 2006), 27 and passim; Hammond, *Slavery, Freedom, and Expansion in the Early American West,* chaps. 5–7, especially 126–27, 147.

21. Eva Sheppard Wolf, *Race and Liberty in the New Nation: Emancipation in Virginia from the Revolution to Nat Turner's Rebellion* (Baton Rouge: Louisiana State University Press, 2006), 19–20.

22. Foner, *Free Soil, Free Labor, Free Men,* 23–39.

23. Kerber, *Federalists in Dissent,* 23; Rachel Hope Cleves, "'Hurtful to the State': The Political Morality of Federalist Antislavery," this volume; *Boston Repertory,* 2 October 1804, quoted in Kerber, *Federalists in Dissent,* 24n2; Oliver Wolcott, Miscellaneous Notes [1802–3], Wolcott Papers, Connecticut Historical Society, Hartford, quoted in ibid., 34.

24. Hammond, *Slavery, Freedom, and Expansion in the Early American West,* 31; Magruder, *Political, Commercial, and Moral Reflections on the Late Cession of Louisiana to the United States,* 147, 148.

25. *New York Daily Advertiser,* 30 March 1790; "Speech of Governor St. Clair at Cincinnati, [August or September 1802], Arthur St. Clair Papers, Ohio Historical Society, quoted in Hammond, *Slavery, Freedom, and Expansion in the Early American West,* 83; Mason, *Slavery and Politics in the Early American Republic,* 47; Elijah Parish, *A Discourse, Delivered at Byfield, on the Annual Fast, April 8, 1813* (Newburyport, Mass.: E. W. Allen, 1813), 13–14, quoted in ibid., 48.

26. Quotations are from Hammond, *Slavery, Freedom, and Expansion in the Early American West,* 135, 112.

27. *New York Daily Advertiser,* 18 June 1790.

28. Quotations are from Zeitz, "The Missouri Compromise Reconsidered," 472, 474.

29. Ibid., 478–81, 474. "Free labor synthesis" is from the subtitle of Zeitz's article.

"Manifest Signs of Passion"

The First Federal Congress, Antislavery, and Legacies of the Revolutionary War

ROBERT G. PARKINSON

In February 1790, the first United States Congress took up the task of giving life to one of its constitutionally enumerated powers: to establish a uniform rule of naturalization. Delegates debated several provisions of the Naturalization Bill, including the question of how long aliens would be required to live in America before becoming eligible for citizenship. One issue they apparently did not dispute, though, was who could apply. Together, the first American senators and representatives deemed that any alien who was "a free white person" would be suitable for full citizenship in the United States.[1]

All discussion having ended, the Naturalization Bill was ready for President Washington's signature on Monday, March 22, 1790. That afternoon, however, Pennsylvania Senator William Maclay heard a large racket emanating from the House of Representatives and wondered what it was all about. Upon entering that chamber, wide eyed, he recorded the following scene: "The House have certainly greatly debased their dignity. Using base invective indecorous language. 3 or 4 up at a time. Manifest signs of passion. The most disorderly Wandering in their speeches, telling stories, private anecdotes &c &c. I know not what may come of it. But there seems a General discontent among the Members, and many of them do not Hesitate to declare, that the Union Must fall to pieces, at the rate we go on." It seems the important question of who would be eligible to join the new nation had produced more than a little excitement. The ruckus in the House had been triggered by a debate over three separate petitions demanding that the federal government close the twenty-year window that would have allowed the international slave trade to continue in the United States.[2]

Several factors contributed to poison the discourse that spring. First, the House, reticent to reopen what had been a constitutional compromise, had continually tabled the petitions. But their sponsors, the Quaker-led delegations from New York and Pennsylvania, had on that day packed the gallery, "to remind them we are waiting upon them." What for the Quakers was a faithful expression of their resolve was, for Southern members, an ominous sign: the Quaker supporters seemed "like evil spirits hovering over our heads in the gallery." Further complicating matters was the fact that one of the petitions had been introduced under the signature of the president of the Pennsylvania Abolition Society, Benjamin Franklin. It was difficult to ignore that particular imprimatur, as the Quakers well knew. Finally, the question of what, exactly, the petititioners ultimately wanted clouded the discussions. Each petition attacked the slave trade — the "gross national iniquity of trafficking in the persons of fellow-men" — but the petition from Franklin and the Pennsylvania Abolition Society went even further, imploring Congress "to countenance the Restoration of Liberty to those unhappy men," and expressing the hope "that you will devise means for removing this Inconsistency from the Character of the American People." It was unclear to many congressmen whether the Quakers were calling for a halt to the slave trade or for full emancipation.[3]

The debate quickly turned bitter, personal, and, indeed, passionate. Southerners, led by the South Carolinians Aedanus Burke and William Loughton Smith and the Georgian James Jackson, wondered aloud whether the eighty-four-year-old Franklin was in full possession of his faculties. One of them suggested, since Franklin had been a delegate to the convention that had drafted the document, that he "ought to have known the Constitution better." It was "astonishing," William Loughton Smith observed, "to see Dr. Franklin taking the lead in a business which looked so much like a persecution of the southern inhabitants." As one Delaware representative observed, the debate "produced some rather acrimonious animadversions upon the conduct of that venerable philosopher and statesman Dr. Franklin." Franklin was hardly the sole target. The Quakers seated in the gallery listened to other accusations, like that of Aedanus Burke, who suggested that they "and the schemes they are now agitating, put me in mind of Milton's Lucifer, who entered Paradise in the shape of a cormorant." This provocative statement came at the end of a long indictment that painted all Quakers as having been traitors during the Revolution. The South Carolinian's line of attack — utterly discrediting the petitioners by invoking the Revolutionary War — was significant.[4]

It has gone unnoticed by historians. Analysts of the 1790 debate have instead highlighted how many tenets of the antebellum "positive good" defense of slavery were roughly sketched here. Indeed, some of the claims made by Smith and Jackson—that Christianity permitted slavery, that blacks were far better off enslaved in the South than free in Africa, that miscegenation would destroy American society, and that blacks were racially inferior in their intellect and personality—did anticipate the 1830s debates. These justifications, though, were still quite extreme in 1790. Pennsylvania representative Thomas Scott, for one, was taken aback by these arguments. "An advocate for slavery . . . at this age of the world, and on the floor of the American Congress too, is, with me, a phenomenon in politics," he concluded.[5]

But Burke's more subtle tack was not a "phenomenon." Burke appealed to the still fresh memories of the Revolutionary War as a more effective way of impugning the petitions' sponsors. He and other Southerners repeatedly invoked Quaker loyalism during the conflict with Britain. "Are they not the same men," Burke asked, "who, a few short years ago were the avowed friends and supporters of the most abject slavery?" Attacking the Quakers' "base, treacherous character," the South Carolina representative suggested they had operated during the Revolution, "for no other purpose but to rivet the shackles of slavery on their country." "They, in the needful hour, were the enemies of America, but now assume another mask, that of enemies to slavery." Virginia representative John Brown stated that he hoped that his colleagues would not "gratify people who never had been friendly to the independence of America." James Jackson underscored how such anti-Quaker attitudes were hardly limited to the halls of Congress: "Public opinion has declared them, throughout America, to have been enemies to our cause and constitution: Gordon's history declares it; and all others who have written have mentioned that society." Another congressman took this accusation further: "In time of war they would not defend their country from the enemy, and in time of peace they were interfering in the concerns of others, and doing everything in their power to excite the slaves in the southern states to insurrection."[6]

Here was the key connection. What made the recent terrible memories of the Revolution so significant was that now those former Tories were taking on many of the aspects of their British enemy; namely, they were exciting "tumults, seditions, and insurrections" throughout the South. Emancipation, Burke testified, would bring the "greatest cruelty" to the Africans: "Of this we have had experience in South Carolina in 1780." He reminded his colleagues that Lord Cornwallis, "a very intimate old friend of the Quakers," had issued a proclamation giving freedom "to all the Africans who should join his army." Because of Cornwallis's "invitation," Burke argued, "thousands perished miserably by hunger and disease, exhibiting a melancholy example, to shew, how totally incapable *he* is of making a proper use of his new gained liberty, who has been brought up in the habits of slavery." The British had already attempted these "cruel" emancipation schemes during the war, and now, Southern Congressmen argued, Quakers were following right in their footsteps.[7]

Historians of antislavery have underestimated this recall of the Revolutionary War because it seemingly had little to do with slavery. That was true, to a degree. By focusing on the experience of the Revolution, Burke and his Southern colleagues were sidestepping the issue of emancipation and instead indicting antislavery advocates by association. This transference, though, needs to be explained. It represented the continuation of a political argument that was at least fifteen years old—that of the "common cause."

The "common cause" appeal, increasingly put forward by Patriot leaders after 1772, centered on convincing as many colonists as possible to support the Revolution. It was a Janus-faced construction, simultaneously celebrating heroic Americans who recognized tyranny and took steps to destroy it, on one side, and, on the other, denigrating malevolent British leaders and their pitiful, foolish assistants. As soon as the Revolutionary War broke out, Patriot leaders were quick to inform the American public via the press that African Americans had really been British proxies. Rumors circulated throughout the mainland colonies in 1775 that America's slaves—with British backing—would soon commence large-scale insurrections. Quite often it was Patriot leaders, either on the local, provincial, or national levels, who sponsored those stories in the newspapers. The notion that black slaves would act as the king's assistants was a creation of the war, not in small part because thousands of slaves did respond to any possibility that they might be received by royal officers.

The realities and representations of the "common cause" had a profound influence on the course of the American antislavery movement. The language and arguments Burke and his Southern colleagues employed in 1790 were in fact fifteen-year-old artifacts of the Patriots' political campaign to mobilize public support to defeat the British. That campaign, though focused on delegitimizing British "proxies" to win the war, had quickly outlived its usefulness during the Revolution. But in the postwar years, the "common cause" argument provided a ready script—laden with patriotic images and implications—for slaveholders, one they could use to impugn all abolitionists as traitors. Furthermore, it had significant unintended consequences for African Americans themselves. Long after Yorktown, the public campaign to encourage friends and identify enemies during the Revolution would become embedded in the story of the new United States as a racialized narrative that cordoned off those who would not be welcome as American citizens.

To gauge the impact that the war and the "common cause" scenario would have on the antislavery movement, we need only turn to the years immediately preceding the bloodshed. In the early 1770s, something was indeed going on in the courtrooms and legislative chambers of the British empire with regard to slavery. In the spring of 1772 Lord Mansfield ruled in *Somerset v. Steuart* that slavery had no legal basis in Britain. This landmark case deepened the perception that Britain was different from its colonies; unlike its territorial possessions, Britain was seen as "a unique asylum for liberty."[8]

Antislavery activists in the colonies were trying to close that gap. In the early 1770s, several political bodies made plans to decrease the number of slaves in their jurisdictions. The Massachusetts General Court approved a bill in 1771 to prohibit the importation of slaves from Africa. The following year, the Virginia House of Burgesses tried to prohibit the sale of Africans in the Commonwealth, expressing their concerns to the king that if the trade were not prohibited, it would "endanger the very Existence of your Majesty's American Dominions." At the same time, Quaker petitioners were lobbying the New York legislature to approve an import duty on slaves. None of these bills were implemented, since the colonies' royal governors in each jurisdiction refused to accept them. In 1773, at several town meetings in New England, representatives were instructed to work against slavery. One group of individual slaves, citing the "divine spirit of freedom [that] seems to fire every humane breast on this continent," even appealed to the Boston Committee of Correspondence for their freedom.[9]

This wave of antislavery sentiment was ascendant when the First Continental Congress met in the fall of 1774. The Congress included slaves among the enumerated "goods" that would not be imported, in protest to the Coercive Acts. The non-importation plan, known as the Continental Association, put into practice the sentiment Thomas Jefferson had expressed just before the delegates met in Philadelphia. "The abolition of domestic slavery is the great object of desire in those colonies where it was unhappily introduced in their infant state," Jefferson wrote in his widely circulated tract, *A Summary View of the Rights of British Americans.* Apparently stung by Virginia's failure to end the slave trade, Jefferson considered the king's rejection of "our repeated attempts to effect this by prohibitions . . . so shameful an abuse of a power trusted with his majesty," that it became another significant reason to resist Crown authority. A few months later, the town of Darien, Georgia, reinforced Jefferson's sense of the colonies' desire. In the first few days of 1775, the inhabitants of Darien drafted a set of resolutions that included their "disapprobation and abhorrence of the unnatural practice of Slavery in America . . . a practice founded in injustice and cruelty, and highly dangerous to our liberties (*as well as lives*) debasing part of our fellow-creatures below men, and corrupting the virtue and morals of the rest."[10]

Clearly, just before the outbreak of war, a campaign against slavery was building across Anglo-America. Influenced in part by the considerable discussions of political slavery and a deepening discourse of natural rights, by the end of 1774 there was an almost rapturous expectation that slavery would soon disappear from America. At least that was how Benjamin Rush interpreted the events swirling about him. "We have now turned from our wickedness," he wrote just nine days after Congress ratified the Association. "If the same spirit which now prevails in our counsels and among all ranks in every province, continues, I venture to predict there will be not a Negro slave in North America in forty years." Rush continued: "I now feel a *new* attachment to my native country, and I look forward with *new* pleasure to her future importance and grandeur."[11]

Rush's oracular skills were apparently lacking. Predictions that Americans would make their assertions of natural rights apply to Africans would quickly turn out to be hollow. As powerful as that 1770's antislavery wave seemed at the moment, it would crest in 1774 and then recede rapidly. The year 1773 turned out to be the peak year for antislavery publications; according to one historian, "More pamphlets bearing on slavery in this country were published in 1773 than in any year prior to 1819." In fact, the leading writers against slavery would be strangely silent for a decade. Throughout the first several years of the Revolution, only one significant pamphlet, Samuel Hopkins's *A Dialogue concerning the Slavery of the Africans,* published in the spring of 1776, surfaced. Although sentiment against slave imports continued through the 1770s, it did not translate into a consensus for abolition. Just five days before the Battle of Lexington, ten citizens would meet at the Rising Sun Tavern in Philadelphia to organize the "Society for the Relief of Free Negroes Unlawfully Held in Bondage," the first abolitionist society in America. But after only four meetings the group dissolved. During the 1790 petition debate, Massachusetts representative Elbridge Gerry would recall that back in 1774, "the sense of America was against slavery." But something had happened. What had occurred to destroy the "great object of desire"?[12]

It was the war. Colonial unity was not only unfamiliar to the disaggre-gated, jealous colonies, but also very fragile, and by no means assured. One of the ways Patriot leaders were able to keep the colonies together was by taking full advantage of fears of slave insurrections. The Darien Resolutions of January 1775 parenthetically referenced what would become a widespread worry starting that very spring: that slavery was highly dangerous to colo-nists' *lives* as well as liberties. The potential violence of resistant slaves and the willingness of British authorities to sponsor such behavior profoundly altered the "great object of desire." The "common cause" quieted calls—when they should have been loudest—to extend rights to all. But that was not all it did. The threat of slaves attacking their masters had always been one of the darkest nightmares haunting the colonial imagination. When that fear was connected to British schemes, it substantiated arguments that slav-ery needed to be protected and secured—not abolished.

As soon as the smoke had cleared from Lexington Green, stories of British-sponsored slave unrest began to spread throughout the mainland colonies. Although the actions taken by Lord Dunmore would become the most famous, he would not be the only British official to invoke the specter of armed slaves at the outset of the Revolutionary War. In the first months of the war, John Stuart, the British superintendent of Indian affairs for the Southern District, recalled that "the newspapers [in South Carolina] were full of Publications calculated to excite the fears of the People—Massacres and Instigated Insurrections, were words in the mouth of every Child." Stuart's painful comment, penned a year after he had to flee to Florida after the Whigs accused him of being the chief instigator, highlights three impor-tant ideas: the nightmare of slave atrocities, the hand of British agents in agitating violent acts, and the power of the press to stoke popular fears. For the remainder of 1775 shocked colonists in South Carolina and elsewhere did indeed read about rebellions, foiled plots, and rampant rumors of insur-rections in their local newspapers. This was a change in editorial policy; colonial printers in the eighteenth century for the most part censored details about slave rebellions, so as not to inspire future attempts. For example, a few months before the war began, the young Virginia planter James Madison wrote to William Bradford, the printer of the *Pennsylvania Journal,* con-cerning a thwarted slave plot, saying that it was "prudent that such attempts should be concealed as well as suppressed." War with Britain changed this aspect, however. As John Stuart quickly learned, now certain villains could be publicly vilified.[13]

In the summer of 1775, Stuart and other British officials, including the royal governors Josiah Martin, William Campbell, and Lord Dunmore, became the South's first "outside agitators." Newspapers throughout the colonies printed rumors alleging that Martin had offered freedom to North Carolina's slaves. In Charleston, South Carolina, authorities found Thomas Jeremiah, a free black harbor pilot, guilty of "having endeavoured to cause an insurrection" and summarily executed him. It was not exactly Jeremiah's fault; according to one story that circulated widely in Patriot newspapers, this "hellish business doubtless originated either in the British Cabinet or at Head Quarters in Boston."[14]

The most well-publicized and extensive British emancipation scheme of the war's early years was, of course, Lord Dunmore's Proclamation of November 7, 1775, which offered freedom to all able-bodied male slaves of Patriot masters who could reach his camp. Scholars estimate that between 800 and 1,000 Virginia slaves actually reached Dunmore's lines. The perception at the time, however, was that their numbers were decidedly greater. One newspaper report about Dunmore's "Ethiopian Regiment," which appeared in two-thirds of the existing colonial papers, stated: *"Since Lord Dunmore's proclamation made its appearance, it is said he has recruited his army . . . to the amount of about 2000 men, including his black regiment, which is thought to be a considerable part, with this inscription on their breasts:—Liberty to Slaves"* (italics in the original).[15]

A literate person anywhere in the colonies picking up a newspaper during the fourteen months between Lexington and Independence stood a very good chance of reading about blacks aiding the British, slaves running away from their masters, respected royal officials being branded "Negro thieves," or about the previous mechanisms of social control regarding African Americans breaking down. And not just in the South. Runaway slaves sought audiences with British naval officers up and down the coast. A Manhattan newspaper reported that "three Negroes went in a boat with an intent to go on board the Packet," but in this case the officer had replied, "Go about your business, we want no such rascals here." Instead of leaving it there, the Patriot editor of the *New York Constitutional Gazette* invented the runaways' response: *"O Massa* (says the Negroes) *we free men, we Tories, Massa, we King man too"* (italics in the original). The *Pennsylvania Evening Post* documented an unusual encounter on a Philadelphia street. After a white woman reprimanded a black man for getting in her way and insulting her, he replied: "Stay, you damned white bitch, till Lord Dunmore and his black regiment come, and then we will see who is to take the wall." His impassioned response reveals to what degree the possibilities of Revolution had effected the black community.[16]

Whig polemicists tried to lay all of this insurrectionary behavior at the feet of horrible royal governors, corrupt military officers, ministerial schemers, and soon King George himself. Long before Burke expounded this theme against the Quakers in 1790, Patriot publicists focused their attacks on the British for "tampering," "instigating," or "exciting." News accounts depicted African Americans, on the other hand, as passive objects, individuals who had been stolen or seduced by tyrants. Although portraying blacks as devoid of human feeling was nothing new, with all the upheaval of 1775–76 it was increasingly difficult to maintain that fiction.

Nowhere is this more evident than in how the Virginia Whigs responded to Dunmore's Proclamation. When Alexander Purdie printed the emancipation proclamation in his November 24, 1775, issue of the *Virginia Gazette*, it was surrounded with an extraordinary commentary, probably written by the Patriot leader John Page. It was singular because it addressed the slaves themselves. Slaves should not heed the call of Dunmore's "cruel declaration," the writer urged. "But should there be any amongst the negroes *weak* enough to believe that Lord Dunmore intends to do them a kindness, and *wicked* enough to provoke the fury of the Americans against their defenceless fathers and mothers, their wives, their women and children, let them only consider the difficulty of effecting their escape, and what they must expect to suffer if they fall into the hands of the Americans." Do not be weak and wicked: this was the admonition Virginia Patriots gave to their slaves. Dropping the façade that slaves could not think, Page asked blacks to "consider": "Be not then, ye negroes, tempted by this proclamation to ruin yourselves. . . . I have considered your welfare, as well of that of the country. Whether you will profit by my advice, I cannot tell; but this I know, that whether we suffer or not, if you desert us, you most certainly will." This remarkable piece laid bare the Patriot argument. People who were "sincerely attached to the interest of their country," people who "stand forth in opposition to the arbitrary and oppressive acts of any man, or set of men," people who are "moved by compassion and actuated by sound policy": these were the true patriots, the real Americans. They would never be weak or wicked. Those who rejected these lofty principles were subject to suffering. This is the "common cause" argument in its essence, and it was foundational. It was this same formula of friends, enemies, and assistants that Southern congressmen would utilize fifteen years later.[17]

Page was not the only one to connect British behavior, black resistance, and the notion of America's enemies. The Continental Congress included the accusation that British agents were "exciting" slaves, or domestics, in most of its public pronouncements or statements of purpose, and similar language stands at the apex of the Declaration of Independence. While scholars have focused their attention on the philosophical principals outlined in the Declaration's first two paragraphs, the list of twenty-seven grievances registered against the king were far more significant in whether the Declaration would succeed or fail in swaying the "opinions of mankind" throughout a "candid world." Jefferson had assembled those crucial accusations with care; in his rough draft, the final, clinching grievance would also be the longest—and it would be about slavery. Declaring that the king had "waged cruel war against human nature itself" through sponsorship of the African slave trade, Jefferson revived a theme from *A Summary View of the Rights of British Americans,* in which he indicted the Crown for not allowing Virginia to halt slave importations. That this passage could not stand reveals the distance the Patriots had moved in just a matter of months. The war and the demands of union encouraged Jefferson's colleagues in Congress to forget 1774's "great object of desire."

But not completely. While Congress cut the accusation that the king had perpetuated the slave trade's "assemblage of horrors," it retained the substance of Jefferson's secondary indictment, that "he [the king] is now exciting those very people to rise in arms among us, and to purchase that liberty of which he has deprived them, by murdering the people on whom he also obtruded them: thus paying off former crimes committed against the LIBERTIES of one people, with crimes which he urges them to commit against the LIVES of another." After months of reading news reports, hearing whispers, perpetuating stories, and publicizing accounts about the king's men encouraging black resistance throughout the continent, the delegates to Congress could not ignore this part of Jefferson's climactic list of grievances. They pared the accusation down to a few pointed words—"he has excited domestic insurrections"—and fastened it to its twin: the accusation that many of those same British agents were committing similar heinous acts on the frontier, by "endeavour[ing] to bring on the inhabitants of our frontiers the merciless Indian savages, whose known rule of warfare is an undistinguished destruction of all ages, sexes, and conditions."[18]

Here, at the founding moment, Congress was conflating both blacks and the British as un-American. Leaving no room for the thousands of African Americans who supported Independence, the Declaration portrayed them (and Indians) as passive and mindless, and too naive to realize they were being duped by a tyrant king. True Patriots would never fall victim to such crimes. The "We" of "We hold these truths to be self-evident" were neither weak nor wicked. After one year of war, then, the abolitionist beam that Benjamin Rush celebrated as portending the end of all American bondage had dissolved into a penumbra, a narrative put forward by Patriot authorities that all blacks were susceptible to the tyranny of King George, and therefore hostile to American independence.

For the remainder of the conflict, Patriot publicists highlighted British sponsorship of black unrest. From the Mid-Atlantic through the Deep South, the Revolutionary War represented the greatest episode of slave rebellion before the Civil War. After Dunmore, British Army officers, from the commander-in-chief down, periodically experimented with limited emancipation schemes, and African Americans responded, most either escaping to the occupied zone surrounding New York City or following the march of the British army into the Deep South in 1780–81. The near constant presence of British warships in the Chesapeake perpetuated slaveholder anxiety. Long after Dunmore had left the Capes of Virginia, stories about British officers harboring and protecting runaway slaves continued to crop up. In the region around New York City, guerilla warfare involving African Americans often captured public attention. One particularly prominent legend grew around Colonel Tye, an African American partisan whose raids wreaked havoc in New Jersey in 1780. According to one report, "their brave Negro Tye" was a holdover from "Lord Dunmore's crew"; he was one former slave who obviously ignored Patriot pleas not to be "weak" or "wicked."[19]

Just as significant, the definition of the enemy as he who would instigate blacks was also ubiquitous in print throughout the conflict. In the wake of the shock of hearing the news of Benedict Arnold's treason, in the fall of 1780, one widely published poem appeared that created a special "Class of Britain's Heroes," made up exclusively of blacks, Indians, Tories, and Arnold himself. When the infamous turncoat then invaded Virginia at the head of a British force dedicated to the burning of plantations and the "stealing" of slaves, American readers were not surprised to discover that Arnold had been "driven to the old trade of . . . *soul-driving.*" A few months later, as Lord Cornwallis found himself bottled up at Yorktown, the presence of thousands of runaway blacks did not escape attention. When Burke recalled, a decade later, how the slaves had rushed to Cornwallis's lines nine years earlier, his reminiscence could be easily corroborated. Contemporary reports mentioned the work of three thousand blacks who dug entrenchments to protect

Cornwallis's men, while others suggested that the slaves were armed with more than just shovels.[20]

Yorktown ended tragically for most of the African Americans who trailed Cornwallis in hopes of freedom. In a bitter irony, hundreds of hopeful slaves were stricken with smallpox and died on the shores of the York River, five years and two dozen miles removed from where scores of their peers had met a similar fate with Dunmore on Gwynn's Island. But that was not how most Patriots interpreted the wave of smallpox that swept through the camp. For them, Yorktown provided more evidence that an indelible line separated the British and their black auxiliaries from the Americans. After Cornwallis's surrender, stories about what had happened behind the lines reinforced this divide. Rumors surfaced accusing Cornwallis of having spread smallpox in Virginia by ordering that infected blacks be dispersed throughout the countryside. The first issue of Samuel Loudon's *New York Packet,* in January 1776, featured a story about Dunmore's men exhibiting the epithet "Liberty to slaves" on their uniforms. In an ironic circularity, Loudon ended the war by printing a piece that corroborated this rumor about Virginia's resistant slaves. "An Anecdote on Lord Cornwallis," which was subsequently picked up by six other papers, claimed that while marching through Brunswick, North Carolina, Cornwallis had "ordered great numbers of [blacks] to be inoculated with the smallpox, under his immediate inspection, and sent into all parts of the country round about, by which the infection was communicated throughout Virginia, and killed hundreds of innocent men, women, and children." At Yorktown, Americans had finally put an end to such terrible behavior. Just to remind readers of the line separating the heroic Americans from the terrible Britons and their collaborators, Loudon's anecdote concluded with a flourish: "By shewing mercy to the *unfortunate,* demonstrate to the world that you are the *brave, the generous, true-born* sons of LIBERTY."[21]

In the first years of peace, the opponents of slavery sought to pick up where they had left off. In 1784, Philadelphia Quakers revived the antislavery organization that had been abandoned at infancy in 1775. In 1782, Quakers in Virginia helped push that state's legislature to ease restrictions on manumitting slaves. The ground had shifted, however. It was true that the American Revolution had provided antislavery advocates and African Americans with a new stockpile of ideas and symbols to make their case to end the institution in the new nation. But it was also true that the war stories about the sponsors of slave rebellion being the quintessential enemies of America had staying power. The experience of war shaped how the public viewed Quaker political pressure. A couple of years after they had legalized manumission, Virginia's General Assembly received counterpetitions asking them to rescind the act. "A great number of slaves taken by the British Army are now passing in this country," a petition from Hanover County complained, "and therefore to remedy the above evils and prevent their becoming more general . . . your petitioners humbly pray the above recited act may be repealed." Some addressed the problem of free blacks directly—one individual specifically echoing the war, with worries about what "a vast Multitude of unprincipled, unpropertied, revengeful, and remorseless Banditti are capable of perpetrating." Not only should manumission be restricted, opponents argued, but Virginia should keep an eye on suspicious loyalist Quakers. This is an "attempt set on foot, we are informed, by the enemies of our country, tools of the British Administration, and supported by certain men among us of considerable weight, to WREST FROM US OUR SLAVES." In April 1785, when Quakers pressured New York's legislature to abolish slavery gradually, one essayist in Loudon's *New York Packet* accused them of treason as well. The freed blacks, the anonymous writer claimed, "in combination with their friends the Quakers, would give every assistance to our enemies, as we have already experienced their fidelity in the late contest, *when they fought against us by whole regiments,* and the Quakers at the same time supported every measure of Great Britain to enslave us." Aedanus Burke, for one, agreed.[22]

Benjamin Franklin, on the other hand, did not. Or at least it would not seem so. A decade before becoming the first president of the Pennsylvania Abolition Society, however, Franklin was very involved in shaping American perceptions about who they were fighting and why. He was a central figure in how the Patriots justified the "common cause"—and the consequences of that construction.

The war was only a few weeks old when stories about British agents "tampering" with slaves began to unsettle Franklin in Philadelphia. The day after he and his congressional colleagues finished their first public announcement, the "Declaration for the Causes and Necessity of Taking Up Arms," Franklin wrote a friend in England about conspiracy. "Lord Dunmore and Governor Martin have already, taken some steps towards carrying one part of the project into execution by exciting an insurrection among the blacks," he wrote. "This is making war like Nations who never had been friends, and never wish to be while the world stands." After three months passed and more stories about slave unrest heated the atmosphere, Franklin again vented his anger. After cataloging British crimes, which, of course, included "the encouraging our blacks to rise and murder their masters," Franklin ended with a thunderclap: "What would be thought of it, if the Congress should hire an Italian bravo to break into the house of one of your Ministers, and murder him in his Bed? All his Friends would open in full cry against us as assassins, murderers and villains, and the walls of your Parliament House would resound with their execrations! Of these two damnable crimes which is the greatest?" Throughout 1775–76, Franklin's personal correspondence repeatedly denounced British willingness to welcome the aid of African Americans. At the same time, his political activities in Congress centered on turning these stories into opportunities to solidify the "common cause."[23]

Franklin left as ambassador to France a few months after helping draft the Declaration, but even from across the Atlantic he still stayed involved in Patriot perceptions of friends and enemies. In the spring of 1779 Congress asked Franklin to outline a schoolbook that would "impress the minds of Children and Posterity with a deep sense of [British] bloody and insatiable Malice and Wickedness." With the assistance of the Marquis de Lafayette, Franklin drew up a list of twenty-six illustrations to accompany the proposed book. Some of them depicted the activities of "domestic insurrectionists" in lurid detail. A Parisian engraver was to portray one scene of British officers "corrupting Negroes and engaging them to desert from the house, to rob, and even to murder their masters." Another tableau was to show what happened when Patriots did not rally to stop Dunmore and his armed slaves: "master and his sons on the ground dead, wife and daughters lifted up in the arms of the Negroes as they are carrying off." Although this propaganda project never materialized, Franklin cherished it. He envisioned these illustrations "expressing every abominable circumstance of [British] Cruelty and Inhumanity" to adorn the first coinage of the United States. That the Continental Congress thought this was a worthwhile expenditure of time and money, moreover, underscores how important the messages projected by such a book were to the "common cause." When Burke indicted the Quakers by showing them as potential instigators of slave rebellion, he was only following Franklin's lead.[24]

Franklin's contribution to the project of defining America's enemies did not end with Yorktown. One of the most contentious issues during the 1783 Paris peace negotiations centered on British demands that Americans repay debts owed to London merchants. The American position, forwarded by diplomats Franklin and John Jay (who would also go on to take a leading role in the New York Manumission Society), was that the British had already offset many of those debts by impounding American property—that is, slaves—during the war.

Franklin especially bristled when British critics refused to acknowledge the standpoint of American slaveholders on this issue. Rising to increasing British howls that Americans needed to pay their debts, in 1786 he again unleashed his anger. In a sharp rebuttal entitled "The Retort Courteous," Franklin skewered these demands by invoking war stories about British "tampering." Franklin went all the way back to 1775 to remind everyone how the British had already seized plenty of American property. "An order arrives from England, advised by one of their most celebrated *moralists,* Dr. Johnson, in his *Taxation no Tyranny* to excite [the] slaves to rise, cut the throats of their purchasers, and resort to the British army, where they should be rewarded with freedom. This was done, and the planters were thus deprived of near thirty thousand of their working people." As Americans who had read their newspapers during the war already knew, this was only the beginning. Later on, Franklin reminded, the "ingenious and humane" British had "inoculated some of the negroes they took as prisoners . . . and then let them escape, or sent them, covered with the pock, to mix with and spread the distemper among the others of their color, as well as among the white country people, which occasioned a great mortality of both." The future president of the Pennsylvania Abolition Society concluded that Britain "chose to keep faith with its old black, than its new white friends; a circumstance demonstrating clear as daylight, that, in making a present peace, they meditated a future war, and hoped, that, though the promised manumission of slaves had not been effectual in the *last,* in the *next* it might be more successful."[25]

Benjamin Franklin did not like slavery. Although recent revisionist scholarship suggests that his "antislavery credentials have been greatly exaggerated," it is still safe to say that Franklin did not wish to see the institution strengthened in the new nation. His personal opinions about slavery, however, have to be understood in tandem with another of his crusades: the establishment of American unity. The 1790 antislavery petition that bore Franklin's name argued that the "political creed of Americans" dictated that the new nation begin curtailing the institution of slavery. For fifteen years, Franklin had been instrumental in the development of that "political creed." Franklin and his fellow revolutionaries had continually portrayed themselves as liberal, sensitive men of the Enlightenment. They claimed to be men who would extend "mercy to the unfortunate." They believed they were worthy of Loudon's praise as "brave, generous, true-born sons of liberty"— men of action who recognized British tyranny and resisted it with masculine valor. This was, as the historian Nicole Eustace has suggested, the "spirit" that animated the Patriots.[26]

That "spirit"—the core of the "common cause"—had significant racial implications. The notion of a "common cause" also contained a condemnation of the actions taken by both the king's agents and those who were susceptible to their lies. In the public discourse of the Revolutionary War, African Americans fit this description. Patriot propaganda depicted blacks as passive tools of the king. The concept that some men were naturally slaves had been part of western culture as far back as Aristotle, but the Revolutionary War gave such ideas a new grounding. Nearly without exception, throughout the Revolution newspapers ignored African Americans who supported the Patriots, and instead offered images of blacks either embracing the king or willingly going along with his troops. When the conflation of British and black intersected with colonial racial prejudices and fears about slave rebellions, it dampened the universalist, inclusive potential of the revolutionaries' rhetoric. Over the long term, Quakers, lacking much of this baggage, could recover from being tarred as Tories, but blacks could not. African Americans, slave and free, would suffer deep wounds from the specific ways Patriots reacted to and shaped the public's perception of the war. François Furstenberg has recently argued that nineteenth-century civic texts put forward narratives that simultaneously showed "white Americans choosing to risk their lives to fight for their liberty," and slaves who "refused to risk their lives fighting for their own freedom." They chose to render themselves "incapable of citizenship," Furstenberg contends. That vital construction did not wait for Parson Weems, though. It was first crafted by Franklin, Jefferson, and their Patriot colleagues at the founding moment itself.[27]

In sum, the arguments made by Southern congressmen in 1790 were not a "phenomenon." When Georgia representative James Jackson argued that Quaker efforts "would excite tumults, seditions, and insurrections," he too carried forward what the Patriots had loudly proclaimed was the cornerstone of British tyranny from 1775 on. Recalling these war memories produced the "base invective, indecorous language," and "manifest signs of passion" that Maclay recorded in his diary.[28]

One more interested party fired a parting shot. After hearing his sanity questioned on the floor of Congress, Benjamin Franklin fought back with satire. Only five weeks away from death, the ailing Franklin published an essay that was a dazzling act of ventriloquism: he repeated South Carolina's arguments in the voice of an imaginary African Muslim slaveholder. Noting that Southern speeches "put me in mind of a similar one made about 100 years since by Sidi Mehemet Ibrahim," he then quoted the "speech," which decimated the proslavery arguments made by Smith, Jackson, and their colleagues. "Let us then hear no more of this detestable proposition, the manumission of Christian slaves," Franklin mocked, speaking as Ibrahim, "the adoption of which would, by deprecating our Lands and Houses, and thereby depriving so many good citizens of their properties, create universal discontent, and provoke insurrections, to the endangering of government, and producing general confusion."[29]

No matter how brilliant, this satire contradicted many of the images Franklin had helped publicize over the past fifteen years. This clever inversion would be Franklin's last bagatelle, and as such, it has been held up as proof of his antislavery convictions. Perhaps so. But as much as Franklin and the other Founding Fathers might have wished slavery away, by the end of the eighteenth century it was increasingly secure, and race was embedded in the new nation. To be sure, the revolutionaries provided a linguistic template which African American activists and abolitionists would use to expose American hypocrisy to that same "candid world." Yet, at the same time, with Revolutionary shovels and pick-axes, Franklin, Jefferson, and their Patriot colleagues had also buried race deep in the political structure of the new republic. Hardly a conspiracy, it was accomplished to achieve a wholly different goal: to maintain unity and defeat the world's strongest military. All the propaganda that played on fear did more than just mobilize Americans to defeat the British, though. The campaign the Patriots waged to garner support for the Revolutionary War had tragic consequences. At one level, it armed slaveholders with a new rhetorical weapon with which they could defend slavery: attack any abolitionists as enemies of the Revolution. That device would become a staple of American politics for more than a generation.

Yet there was even more damage. The values inherent in the "common-cause" appeal helped reify race in the new nation and gave it a whole new valence. Given the "passion" that resounded through the House in 1790, the conception of blacks and their defenders as threats to the republic was obviously neither hegemonic nor consensual, but it was nevertheless a crucial part of the American Founding. It cannot be denied that, as one congressman stated that March, the "language of America in the day of distress" featured concepts of equality and universal rights. At the same time, American unity was achieved by showing how the people who "seduced," "excited," and "instigated" passive slaves were truly enemies of independence. "Race words were war words," the historian John Dower has written about World War II. In the case of the American Revolution, war images further deepened and grounded colonial stereotypes about black's inferiority and their inherent incapability of acting as full-fledged republican citizens.[30]

So when the new federal government debated the future of America's connection to the international slave trade and set about making rules about who could become a citizen and who could not, these old war stories mattered. The Naturalization Act of 1790 stipulated that a "person of good character" who would "support the Constitution of the United States" could become an American citizen. After all the proclamations, newspaper reports, children's books of atrocities, peace treaties, and declarations of independence that connected "black" and "enemy," the Congress hardly needed to include the words "free" and "white" when defining who really constituted "We the people." They were well understood.

NOTES

1. *Documentary History of the First Federal Congress of the United States of America, 4 March 1789–3 March 1791*, ed. Linda Grant De Pauw et al. (Baltimore: Johns Hopkins University Press, 1972–), 6:1516 (hereafter cited as *DHFFC*).

2. *DHFFC*, 9:226. The 1790 petition episode is covered in David Waldstreicher, *Runaway America: Benjamin Franklin, Slavery, and the American Revolution* (New York: Hill and Wang, 2004), 235–39; Howard A. Ohline, "Slavery, Economics, and Congressional Politics, 1790," *Journal of Southern History* 46 (August 1980): 335–60; William C. diGiacomantonio, "'For the Gratification of a Volunteering Society': Antislavery and Pressure Group Politics in the First Federal Congress," *Journal of the Early Republic* 15 (Summer 1995): 169–97; and Richard S. Newman, *The Transformation of American Abolitionism: Fighting Slavery in the Early Republic* (Chapel Hill: University of North Carolina Press, 2002), 39–49.

3. John Pemberton to James Pemberton, 2 March 1790, Pennsylvania Abolition Society Papers, Historical Society of Pennsylvania, Philadelphia; *DHFFC*, 12:719; "Memorial of the Philadelphia Yearly Meeting, October 3, 1789," *DHFFC*, 8:322–23; "Memorial of the Pennsylvania Abolition Society, February 3, 1790," *DHFFC*, 8:324–26.

4. *DHFFC*, 12:302, 813, 825. One New York newspaper suggested that the animosity was reminiscent of a terrible moment from Franklin's past: "Franklin, with the whole body of Quakers, have received such abuse, as would make even a Wedderbourn blush!" (*New York Daily Advertiser*, 23 March 1790). See also the *Federal Gazette* (New York), 26 March 1790; and *DHFFC*, 12:749.

5. *DHFFC*, 12:819–20.

6. *DHFFC*, 12:748, 762, 800 (Jackson is referring to William Gordon's *History of the Rise, and Establishment of the United States of America*, 4 vols. [London, 1788]); *DHFFC*, 12:754. For more on colonial attitudes toward the Quakers before the Revolution, see Peter Silver, *Our Savage Neighbors: How Indian War Transformed Early America* (New York: Norton, 2008), 191–215.

7. *DHFFC*, 12:648, 747.

8. Christopher Leslie Brown, *Moral Capital: Foundations of British Abolitionism* (Chapel Hill: University of North Carolina Press, 2006), 101.

9. *Revolutionary Virginia: The Road to Independence*, comp. William Van Schreeven, ed. Robert Scribner (Charlottesville: University Press of Virginia, 1973–83), 1:87; petition by Peter Bestes, Sambo Freeman, Felix Holbrook, and Chester Joie to Boston Committee of Correspondence, 20 April 1773, in American Antiquarian Society, *Catalogue of Early American Imprints, 1639–1800: Including the Microform Series "Early American Imprints, First Series, 1639–1800 (Evans)."* (New Canaan, Conn.: Readex, 1993), Evans no. 42416.

10. Thomas Jefferson, *A Summary View of the Rights of British Americans*, in *The Papers of Thomas Jefferson*, ed. Julian P. Boyd (Princeton, N.J.: Princeton University Press, 1950), 1:130; Darien (Ga.) Resolutions, 12 January 1775, in *American Archives*, 4th ser., by Peter Force, Prepared and Published under Authority of an Act of Congress (Washington, D.C.: Clarke and Force, 1840–46), 1:1136.

11. Benjamin Rush to Granville Sharp, 1 November 1774, in John A. Woods, ed., "The Correspondence of Benjamin Rush and Granville Sharp, 1773–1809," *Journal of American Studies* 1 (April 1967): 13–14.

12. Winthrop Jordan, "An Antislavery Proslavery Document?" *Journal of Negro History* 47 (January 1962): 54; Gary B. Nash and Jean R. Soderlund, *Freedom by Degrees: Emancipation in Pennsylvania and Its Aftermath* (New York: Oxford University Press, 1991), 80; *DHFFC*, 12:796.

13. John Richard Alden, "John Stuart Accuses William Bull," *William and Mary Quarterly*, 3rd ser., 2 (July 1945): 320; James Madison to William Bradford, 26 November 1774, in James Madison, *Papers*, ed. William T. Hutchinson and William M. E. Rachal (Chicago: University of Chicago Press, 1962), 1:130.

14. *South Carolina and Country Journal* (Charleston), 3 June 1775, and eight others; *Providence Gazette*, 29 July 1775, and sixteen others.

15. These figures, first proposed by Benjamin Quarles almost half a century ago, have stood the academic test (see Quarles, *The Negro in the American Revolution* [Chapel Hill: University of North Carolina Press, 1961], 19–32). See also the *Virginia Gazette* (Dixon & Hunter), 2 December 1775, and nineteen others.

16. For "Negro thieves," see the *Pennsylvania Journal* (Philadelphia), 17 January 1776, and eight others. See also the *New York Constitutional Gazette*, 20 September 1775; the *Newport Mercury*, 2 October 1775; and the *Pennsylvania Evening Post* (Philadelphia), 14 December 1775, and two others.

17. Nicole Eustace, *Passion is the Gale: Emotion, Power, and the Coming of the American Revolution* (Chapel Hill: University of North Carolina Press, 2008), 70–75; *Virginia Gazette* (Purdie), 24 November 1775.

18. *Thomas Jefferson: Writings*, ed. Merrill D. Peterson (New York: Library of America, 1984), 22.

19. The most famous of these emancipation schemes, Commander Henry Clinton's Philipsburg Proclamation, mirrored Dunmore's emancipation deal. It was issued in the summer of 1779, just before the British began their invasion of the Deep South (see Sylvia Frey, *Water from the Rock: Black Resistance in a Revolutionary Age* [Princeton, N.J.: Princeton University Press, 1991], 113–21. See also the *Virginia Gazette* (Dixon & Hunter), 19 December 1777, and four others; and Graham Russell Hodges, *Slavery and Freedom in the Rural North: African Ameri-*

cans in Monmouth County, New Jersey, 1665–1865 (Madison, Wis.: Madison House, 1997), 96–104. For news accounts of Tye's raids, see the *New Jersey Gazette* (Trenton), 12 April 1780, and nine others; and the *Pennsylvania Packet* (Philadelphia), 3 October 1780, and four others.

20. *New York Journal* (Poughkeepsie), 9 October 1780, and six others; *Pennsylvania Packet* (Philadelphia), 19 June 1781, and four others. For digging trenches, see the *Maryland Journal and Baltimore Advertiser*, 21 August 1781, and four others. For "1000 armed negroes," see the *Freeman's Journal* (Philadelphia), 8 October 1781, and fifteen others.

21. *New York Packet*, 15 November 1781, and six others.

22. Fredrika Teute Schmidt and Barbara Ripel Wilhem, "Early Proslavery Petitions in Virginia," *William and Mary Quarterly*, 3rd ser., 30 (January 1973): 133–46 (quotations at 138–39); *New York Packet*, 4 April 1785 (emphasis added).

23. Benjamin Franklin to Jonathan Shipley, 7 July 1775, in *Letters of Delegates of Congress, 1774–1789*, ed. Paul Smith (Washington, D.C.: Library of Congress, 1976–2000), 1:606–7; Franklin to Shipley, 13 September 1775, ibid., 2:7.

24. Benjamin Franklin to David Hartley, 2 February 1780, in *The Papers of Benjamin Franklin*, ed. Leonard W. Labaree et al. (New Haven, Conn.: Yale University Press, 1959–), 31:439; "Franklin and Lafayette's List of Prints to Illustrate British Cruelties," ibid., 29:590–93; Franklin to Edward Bridgen, 2 October 1779, in *Benjamin Franklin: Writings*, ed. J. A. Leo Lemay (New York: Library of America, 1987), 1011–12; Charles Ritcheson, *Aftermath of Revolution: British Policy toward the United States, 1783–1795* (New York: Norton, 1971 [1969]), 70–87.

25. "The Retort Courteous," in *Benjamin Franklin: Writings*, 1127–28.

26. Waldstreicher, *Runaway America*, xii; Eustace, *Passion Is the Gale*, 397.

27. David Brion Davis, *The Problem of Slavery in Western Culture* (New York: Oxford University Press, 1966), 69–72; François Furstenberg, *In the Name of the Father: Washington's Legacy, Slavery, and the Making of a Nation* (New York: Penguin, 2006), 22.

28. *DHFFC*, 12:648.

29. *Federal Gazette* (New York), 25 March 1790, reprinted in *Benjamin Franklin: Writings*, 1157–60.

30. *DHFFC*, 12:815; John W. Dower, *War without Mercy: Race and Power in the Pacific War* (New York: Pantheon Books, 1986), 148.

"Good Communications Corrects Bad Manners"

The Banneker-Jefferson Dialogue and the Project of White Uplift

RICHARD NEWMAN

Although it marked the only semi-official contact between a federal govern-ing official and a black reformer in the early national period, the exchange of letters between Thomas Jefferson and Benjamin Banneker in 1791 still flies under the scholarly radar. Perusing recent titles on the ever expanding shelf of Jefferson studies, for instance, reveals little extended discussion of Banneker—a rather strange thing considering the explosion of literature on black abolitionism and emancipation in Jefferson's and Banneker's world.[1] For many scholars, the Hem-ings affair takes center stage in the saga of Jeffersonian race relations.[2] Here, the inner Jefferson's struggle with racial intimacy—his longtime sexual relationship with enslaved family member Sally Hemings, the half-sister of his deceased wife Martha—encapsulates the public man's contradictory nature as both advocate of universal freedom and opponent of black liberty. If he could not acknowledge his own enslaved lover Sally Hemings, with whom he had several children, how could Jefferson surmount American racism?

Yet because of its private nature, the Hemings affair does not illuminate public debates over black freedom at the close of the eighteenth century. A new look at the Banneker-Jefferson dialogue, however, with a focus on Banneker's motives, illuminates perhaps the central issue for statesmen and reformers con-sidering emancipation at both the state and federal levels: the prospect of black moral and intellectual improvement.

Indeed, when approached as part of a broader series of dialogues over racial uplift in early national culture—and not simply an intriguing but ultimately limited conversation between Banneker and Jefferson—the correspondence becomes much more ramifying. For one thing, it exemplifies black abolitionists' early and continued attempt to turn cultural forms (writing and publishing) into political weapons that also proved their fitness for freedom.[3] Lacking a voice in the formal political realm, Banneker confronted Jeffersonian racial ideology— defined as a wall of doubt about black intellectual abilities and therefore the efficacy of emancipation itself—through the medium of personal correspondence; he then turned that dialogue into an often-reprinted pamphlet and the inspiration for "Banneker's Almanac": the first antislavery calendars in American culture. Banneker's work also inspired the creation of an interracial and intersectional alliance of white reformers who themselves used print culture to challenge Jeffersonian doubts about blacks' educational abilities. Finally, and perhaps most importantly, both Banneker and his white allies attempted to reverse the definition of moral crisis at the heart of the Jeffersonian racial dilemma, arguing that white masters, and not enslaved people, desperately needed moral uplift for emancipation to succeed. If Banneker and his allies' antislavery moralism did not succeed during the early republic, the project of swaying white hearts and minds would nevertheless remain a defining feature of racial reform movements throughout the nineteenth century and well into the twentieth.

Banneker's Dialogue with Jefferson

The Banneker-Jefferson dialogue began in August 1791 in the federal capital of Philadelphia when Thomas Jefferson received a note requesting the celebrated Virginian's immediate attention. A member of Washington's famed first cabinet, Jefferson had been living in the City of Brotherly Love for almost a year, accompanied by his enslaved chef James Hemings. The letter, penned by a free black man from Maryland with whom Jefferson was already familiar (for he had approved of Banneker's appointment to the survey of the District of Columbia), asked the Sage of Monticello to embrace the egalitarianism he had once promised as the birthright of all human beings. "Sir," Banneker began, "I am fully sensible of the greatness of that freedom, which I take with you on the present occasion; a liberty which seemed to me scarcely allowable, when I reflected on the distinguished and dignified station in which you stand, and the almost general prejudice . . . which is so prevalent in the world against those of my complexion."[4] Though the two men were separated by color, status, and early American racial history itself, Banneker asked Jefferson to become black freedom's great champion. To prove black educational ability, Banneker even enclosed a draft version of his soon-to-be-published almanac.

Jefferson offered a courteous though brief reply, both thanking Banneker for the almanac and assuring him, "Nobody wishes more than I do, to see such proofs as you exhibit, that nature has given to our black brethren talent equal to those of other colors of men."[5] The Virginian did not, however, rise to Banneker's challenge. Indeed, even though Jefferson forwarded the almanac to French reformers, he subsequently expressed doubts about the black writer's abilities. Convinced that enslaved people were morally degraded, and that liberated blacks threatened American democracy itself, Jefferson only deepened his colonizationist convictions over the next decade. As far as Jefferson was concerned, there could be no dialogue, as yet, over black equality within American culture; rather, any racial dialogue must focus on eradicating the twin evils of slavery and free(d) blacks.

What were Jefferson's objections to egalitarian emancipation (the belief that black equality within American culture would follow slave liberation)? As Ari Herlo and Peter Onuf have perceptively argued, Jefferson believed that people of color were morally degraded. The "ultimate obstacle to the integration of emancipated slaves into republican society," Herlo and Onuf conclude, "was their retarded moral development after generations of unjust captivity and brutal exploitation. In moral terms, they were still children, yet to be raised to even a rudimentary understanding of the requirements of a free society." Jefferson's brief exchange with Banneker put these concerns succinctly: although an opponent of slavery, he viewed blacks as the equivalent of "imbeciles."[6]

In fact, because republics were by nature fragile and dependent on a morally virtuous citizenry, Jefferson believed that free people of color threatened the very viability of the new American nation. In *Notes on the State of Virginia,* his report to a French diplomat about the political, economic, and natural landscape of Virginia, Jefferson let loose his essentialized notions of both race and the American Republic, sharply condemning bondage as a school of tyranny for white masters while also envisioning blackness as a barrier to mass emancipation. Because blacks had never produced art, literature, or philosophical discourses of any note, Jefferson asserted, they could never be integrated into a political culture that demanded citizen virtue, morality, and education. Of course, slavery's inherent violence also created an equally fearsome barrier, Jefferson believed, for even if virtuous slaves were to be emancipated en masse, they would seek vengeance on their former masters.[7]

Jefferson was far from the only public persona who expressed such concerns. As a flood of recent scholarship has shown, even Northern statesmen debating emancipation shared his doubts about free blacks. Though they had debated the matter since the mid-1780s, New Yorkers would not adopt a gradual abolition statute until 1799, largely because they could not agree on what to do with emancipated people of color. By the early national period, anti-abolitionists' concerns about racial difference overtook their concerns about labor throughout the Mid-Atlantic and Northeast. Now egalitarian emancipation was viewed as inherently problematic.[8]

Of course, early abolitionists also recognized that Jefferson had given powerful voice to the very idea of emancipation by declaring universal liberty both a human birthright and the cornerstone of American society. A multitude of black writers paid homage to Jefferson's liberationist phraseology. Black Philadelphians who authored the first draft petition to Congress (ca. 1792) seeking gradual emancipation echoed Jefferson's phraseology: "We have with other men . . . an unalienable right to life, liberty and the pursuit of happiness."[9] Similarly, James Forten's 1813 pamphlet, "Series of Letters by a Man of Color," written in opposition to a proposed Pennsylvania law that would have required migrating free blacks to prove their freedom by registering with local officials, also began with allusions to Jefferson. "We hold this truth to be self evident," he declared, "that God created all men equal[, including] the white and black man."[10] Some early national slaveholders offered a backhanded compliment to Jeffersonian liberalism by criticizing the notion that everyone was inherently equal. Masters in South Carolina cringed at the notion that "their" bondmen and bondwomen might view themselves as even theoretically equal to white masters.[11]

As he so often did, then, Jefferson expressed the American mind on race and emancipation—or, one might say, the divided American mind. Slavery was unjust, he believed, but emancipation perhaps more worrisome. What could be done? Until and unless reformers created "a system" for elevating blacks' moral sense to that of whites, Jefferson (again like many others) would remain both theoretically against bondage and passionately anti-abolitionist.

If Jefferson's paradoxical racial thought—a belief that blacks were born free and equal yet remained so morally degraded that they must remain in chains—placed the abolitionist burden on blacks themselves, then African Americans offered a none too subtle reply that put the moral burden back on white slaveholders. Banneker's letter to the Virginian remains one of the key moments in this moral counterattack. Through the 1850s, free black activists would cite the Banneker-Jefferson dialogue as evidence of African Americans' intellectual confidence and educational abilities. The Providence African Union Society reprinted excerpts of Banneker's appeal to Jefferson in a short history of the group in 1821, viewing it as an epigram of black uplift. And a correspondent to the *Colored American* put the matter more bluntly in 1837, arguing that Banneker's challenge to Jefferson "should be published [often, so] that it may remain an everlasting witness against those who assert that the African is not capable of rising in the scale of intelligence with other men."[12]

Displaying his own learning and moral sense, Banneker, did not overtly condemn Jefferson as a hypocrite. Rather, he attempted to reconcile Jefferson's (and America's) warring selves by celebrating the Virginian's principled antislavery stand, noting that Jefferson had expressed "just apprehensions of the horrors" of bondage in *Notes on the State of Virginia* (selections of which Banneker later reprinted in his almanac). Moreover, Jefferson had recognized the Declaration of Independence as an "invaluable doctrine" to abolitionists everywhere. Yet Banneker also pointedly reminded Jefferson of the contradictions at the heart of the Virginian's own life. "Sir, how pitiable is it to reflect, that although you were so fully convinced of the benevolence of the father of mankind, and of his equal and impartial distribution of these rights and privileges . . . you should at the same time contract his mercies . . . detaining by fraud and violence so numerous a part of my brethren, under growing captivity and cruel oppression." It is a stunning accusation, as Banneker's anger bubbled up to the surface—he even labels slaveholders like Jefferson "criminals"—before receding under the weight of polite and reasoned discourse. Indeed, Banneker then moved beyond anger by asking Jefferson to spur a moral reformation among Southern slaveholders. "Wean yourselves from those narrow prejudices which you have imbibed with respect to [us]," he called out, and become a "most active" proponent of schemes designed to uplift blacks "from any state of degradation, to which the unjustifiable cruelty and barbarism of man may have produced them."[13]

A retiring and bookish personality (ironically, somewhat like Jefferson himself), Banneker is not now viewed as a leading black abolitionist. Yet his antislavery appeal was clearly indebted to, and helped propel, an emerging black protest tradition. Like other Afro-Christians in the late-eighteenth-century Atlantic world, Banneker asked Jefferson to reconsider slaveholding in light of Scripture.[14] Following the lead of the famed slave narrator Olaudah Equiano, he used Acts 17:12 to conjure an image of interracial brotherhood. There is, Banneker observed, "one universal father [who] has given being to us all; and . . . he has not only made us all one flesh, but . . . he hath also, without partiality, afforded us all the same sensations and endowed us all with the same faculties."[15] Borrowing from Revolutionary-era black writers, Banneker also highlighted Exodus, reminding Jefferson that a just God had already intervened in the affairs of men to destroy oppression. If that God had protected white Americans oppressed under the British, and ancient Israelites enslaved by Egyptians, would He not render divine judgment against recalcitrant American masters too?

Like other early racial reformers, Banneker also favored the literary dialogue as a preferred route to white moral uplift. As a rhetorical form, dialogues were a common feature of Enlightenment-era discourse. Caleb Bingham's *The Columbian Orator,* perhaps the most famous rhetorical primer in early national educational circles, featured several dialogues as examples of great oratory. Bingham claimed that dignified exchange was an essential aspect of republican society, for the art of persuasion allowed Americans divided by region, status, and political persuasion to surmount their differences. By printing "Dialogue Between a Master and Slave," for example, Bingham hoped to inculcate the virtues of empathy and universalism in his readers by giving voice to the ostensibly silent people of color inhabiting America. The sketch imagines a conversation between a runaway slave and his angry master, who, rather than beating the bondman, seeks a dialogue about the black man's actions. "Now villain!" the master thunders, "What have you to say for this failed attempt to run away?" When the slave replies that his servile condition should explain everything, the master counters, "I am not content with that answer." The master's attempt to explain his position—he has treated the slave kindly and asks for loyalty in return—elicits a more thoughtful explanation from the enslaved man. "Since you condescend to talk to me, as man-to-man, I will reply," the bondman states, discoursing, in turn, on slaves' universal desire for liberty.[16]

A Bostonian with antislavery convictions, Bingham hoped to undermine mainstream Americans' beliefs that people of African descent were uncultured and amoral beings. In fact, the genius of this imagined dialogue is not merely that the enslaved man gains his freedom, but that it is a black person's artful use of language that carries the day. It is little wonder that Frederick Douglass would later hail Bingham's morality play as one of his great inspirations. The dialogue allowed white society to see blacks' humanity as well as their potential for moral and intellectual progress.

By Bingham's time, not only had Banneker produced a factual counterpart to this fictionalized dialogue, but a host of black and white abolitionists had long since attempted to create real exchanges with slaveholders. The

New Divinity Preacher Samuel Hopkins published one of the most famous examples in 1776: *A Dialogue Concerning the Slavery of the Africans*. Nearly two decades later, Kentuckian Gilbert Imlay blasted Jeffersonian racial ideology by writing that African Americans were "essentially the same in shape and intellect" as whites.[17] In the 1790s, the black minister Richard Allen addressed federal officials over the prospect of national emancipation. In language that eerily prefigured Bingham's imagined dialogue between white and black characters, Allen asked "those who keep slaves and approve the practice" meeting in the nation's temporary capital of Philadelphia to "consider how hateful slavery is in the sight of that God, who has destroyed Kings and princes, for their oppression of the poor slaves." Displaying a keen moral sense which many slaveholders feared bondmen had lost to a life of toil, Allen recognized that slavery "debased [blacks'] spirits." But no more so than indentured servitude had delayed white European moral and educational progress. Indeed, he challenged, if white society "cleared its hands of slaves" and treated liberated people of color as true family members who might someday become useful citizens, then blacks would surely rise within American culture. As Allen put it in a nod to interracial brotherhood, "it is in our posterity enjoying the same privileges with your own that you ought to look for better things."[18]

As Allen's words indicate, first-generation black abolitionists often used appeasing discourse to illustrate their moral development, thereby answering one of Jefferson's main objections: that African Americans were educationally and ethically stunted. Through a similar deployment of probing yet moderate language, Banneker sought to counter Jefferson's racial essentialism. By engaging Jefferson in the literate realm, he hoped to challenge the masters' view that African Americans were so morally degraded as to be beyond the pale of American civic integration. By then publishing his correspondence with Jefferson, Banneker also showed that moral enlightenment was a double-edged sword: white masters, who were themselves morally obtuse for refusing to solve a problem they had created, must now embrace racial reform. The gift of Banneker's almanac was in a sense a peace offering from black to white: *I have read your work and will show you how much I have learned*, Banneker seemed to be saying to Jefferson. The accompanying essay of roughly fifteen paragraphs effectively asked Jefferson to return the favor by illustrating his own capacity to grow as an egalitarian abolitionist. (Like some early national politicians, Banneker may also have been linking black moderation to the manly virtue of reason, as opposed to the unmanly trait of passion.[19]) Far from being a hastily sketched letter, Banneker's appeal to Jefferson reflected an acute sense of learning and perception that might enable the very creation of an emancipation dialogue with the greatest slave-holding exponent of universal freedom in the world.

Of course, Jefferson did not see things this way, and so it is little wonder that he later dismissed Banneker's attempt to create a dialogue. In fact, he came to believe that white reformers had probably assisted Banneker with the production of his antislavery appeal and almanac. As Jefferson told Banneker himself, he still awaited evidence of a "systematic" transformation of enslaved people into moral beings. Questionable exceptions like Banneker proved little.[20]

Why did Jefferson remain so skeptical? Blacks' seemingly childlike moral obtuseness was only one of his concerns. As Alexander Boulton has argued, Jefferson' racial doubts also flowed from trans-Atlantic scientific debates over nature and society. Just as Jefferson believed that the mammoth and the elephant were different species, so too did he regard white and black as "polygenetic" (or separate) creations. By defining blacks into the landscapes they inhabited, Jefferson created his own sense of racial environmentalism: blacks' separate "African" natures were unequal, degraded, and, for the foreseeable future, fixed. This conception of blackness differed markedly from most early abolitionists' versions of environmentalism: the belief that one's character was not fixed through time or space, and could actually be changed depending on one's social and educational circumstances. Jefferson simply did not believe, as these racial reformers did, that nurture transcended nature—that American society could indeed cultivate black talent.[21]

As revealing as this scientific interpretation is, it does not illuminate the matter fully. For Jefferson received Banneker's letter not at his beloved Monticello, where he was surrounded by slaves, nor in a European salon while debating scientific theories, but rather in the North American capital of abolitionism: Philadelphia. Though this fact is often noted in passing, it may be a critical part of Jefferson's continued emphasis on black "imbecility" as an obstacle to emancipation. Philadelphia in the early 1790s was a cauldron of racial debate, with both black and white abolitionists battling slavery's ardent defenders, including congressmen and members of Washington's cabinet who worriedly brought slaves north of the Mason-Dixon Line and into free territory. For Jefferson, emancipating Philadelphia offered a glimpse of the world turned upside down. Here abolitionists enjoyed a public listing in the city directory, courts ruled against slaveholders' absolute property rights in man, and free black communities surged. Less than two decades after passing the gradual abolition act of 1780, Pennsylvania's enslaved population had dropped from roughly seven thousand to just a few hundred. And soon after Banneker contacted Jefferson in 1791, the Pennsylvania Abolition Society began pushing for an immediate abolition law. Though that effort was unsuccessful, Pennsylvania nevertheless became freedom's northern borderland for both slaves and free blacks throughout the Mid-Atlantic. Philadelphia's free black population had surpassed two thousand by the time the federal government moved there in 1790; it would more than triple over the next decade.[22]

Even in a Northern context, black freedom raised alarms among white citizens. But enlightened Pennsylvanians had an answer for this concern too: the creation of an abolition society dedicated to black oversight, education, and eventually uplift. The Pennsylvania Abolition Society began publicizing its educational initiatives in 1789 when Ben Franklin, a longtime Northern slaveholder who became an abolitionist convert and president of the group in his last years, signed a handbill posted around Philadelphia announcing the expansion of black schools. For those worried that emancipation would threaten American democracy by unleashing black freedmen unprepared for life beyond bondage, the new Society headed up by Franklin offered reassuring words about white paternalism in the new nation's temporary capital. Echoing Jefferson, Franklin characterized ex-slaves as "machines," and noted that they were probably not ready to face freedom alone. Yet Franklin also favored the Society's schools and committees (including those that examined the moral condition of free people of color) as a middle way to future black equality.[23]

Though not a vanguard abolitionist by any means, Franklin did believe that people of color would slowly but surely rise within American society.[24] By the early 1790s, the Pennsylvania Abolition Society allowed interested reformers to visit their schools, where black pupils copied out such phrases as "Quote great authors" and "Humility is a virtue." A census of the free black community conducted by Pennsylvania abolitionists in 1790 offered a statistical analog to black uplift; it found stable black families, hard-working people of color, and a desire among free blacks and newly liberated enslaved people to master both literacy and marketable skills. This was probably why Banneker contacted Jefferson when and where he did—in abolitionism's home and the site of America's first racial reconstruction. Banneker had already cultivated abolitionist contacts in Philadelphia; he evidently thought Jefferson would have too—and that he surely would have embraced black freedom, being surrounded by such hopeful abolitionists.[25]

When Jefferson mapped Northern abolitionist trends onto the South (with its much larger enslaved populations), however, he saw no glorious interracial future. Few Virginians did. The burst of Southern manumissions at the close of the eighteenth century had actually surpassed those in such Northern states as Pennsylvania. Between 1782 and 1806, private emancipations in Virginia alone liberated as many as 10,000 people of color, according to Eva Sheppard Wolf's terrific research.[26] Nevertheless, few Virginia statesmen publicly supported abolitionism (and many free people of color faced expulsionary laws). When Ben Franklin asked Virginia governor Edmund Randolph in 1788 to support abolitionism, Randolph replied that he could do no more than speak as a private citizen; public discussion of black freedom was simply unacceptable. Virginia Quakers who founded the first schools for people of color during the 1790s discovered the same thing: they were viewed as anathema among slaveholders. By the early 1800s, as Glenn Crothers has reported, even diehard Quaker abolitionists had either curtailed their activities altogether or had simply departed the Old Dominion.[27]

For many Virginians (Jefferson included), the flight of blacks to British lines during the Revolution had precluded any possible civic integration of free people of color. Whereas abolitionists used the prevalence of runaway slaves and slave violence as ominous signs of blacks' desire to go free at virtually any cost, Jefferson and many others viewed black rebellion as evidence of blacks' base morality. Until his dying days, Jefferson remembered the black runaways who had responded to Lord Dunmore's emancipation edict in the 1770s as having betrayed both their masters and the American nation. During the 1790s, Jefferson watched with horror as Haitian slaves watered the tree of liberty with white blood, going so far as to refer to Francophone race rebels as "the cannibals of the terrible republic."[28] (It could not escape Jefferson's attention that Pennsylvania refused to allow fleeing Haitian masters entry into the Quaker State with their slaves.)

If there was a moral lesson about black uplift at the close of the eighteenth century, Jefferson did not see it—not in Banneker's missive, not in Northern abolitionism, not even in individual Southern emancipations. The lessons of history surged in the other direction, as black revolutionary actions at home and abroad provided the clearest possible evidence that neither enslaved people nor free blacks could be a part of Western culture, Western governing institutions, or Western society. Add to this a Lockean belief in the moral degradation of enslaved people (for being locked in a war with their masters) and it is clear that Jefferson deeply feared black freedom. Tellingly, whenever he spoke of slavery and emancipation, Jefferson did so in conditional phraseology, using the extreme future tense. As he essentially told

Banneker, this was not the time to embrace black equality, whether in Pennsylvania, the Caribbean, or in his own cradle of liberty: Virginia.

Continuing the Dialogue with Jefferson: Banneker's Antislavery Network

Just as slave rebels in St. Domingue offered their own response to recalcitrant French planters, so too did Banneker and an emerging antislavery alliance attempt to transcend Jeffersonian racial doubts in the United States. Though excited that Jefferson would reply to him, Banneker was far from satisfied with a brief doff of the cap from the famous Virginian. Throughout the 1790s, he used his almanac to argue against racial essentialism—to prove both that black uplift was possible and that white masters needed to undergo a moral reformation for abolitionism to work.

Banneker's first order of business was to get his almanac published, antislavery commentary included. Although twenty-eight editions of his almanac would be printed by the late 1790s, publication initially proved more difficult than he thought.[29] Even reform-minded printers wanted either confirmation of Banneker's authorship or an introduction by a well-known white figure in order to legitimize the new almanac. Banneker believed that his correspondence with Jefferson, in which Jefferson tacitly acknowledged Banneker as the almanac's creator, had facilitated its publication. More importantly, Banneker saw Jefferson's imprimatur (his reply) as a rationale for entering the public realm as an antislavery advocate. Banneker shrewdly approached his Maryland sponsors about placing the Jefferson correspondence in either the almanac itself or in "the public papers." Not coincidentally, the dialogue soon appeared as both a separate pamphlet (in Philadelphia) and as part of "Banneker's Almanac . . . for 1792." As Silvio Bedini argued long ago, Banneker clearly saw the almanac as "propaganda for the antislavery movement," with Jefferson playing a starring role. The Virginian was, simply, "a natural target for any timely expression on the subject."[30]

Banneker had more than abolitionism in mind. He had also asked his patrons to publish a poem on black uplift: "Behold ye Christians! And in pity see / those Afric sons which nature formed free; / behold them in a fruitful country blessed / of nature's bounties see them rich possest." Somehow lost in the debate over the inaugural printing of his almanac, these unpublished lines expressed Banneker's core belief that people of color were endowed with the same faculties as whites, and could, as he himself had already demonstrated, rise above slavery's "doom." But the poem also made clear that racial redemption required support from white figures, like Jefferson—slaveholders who had consciously, and "relentlessly," in Banneker's words, accepted the benefits of "cruel" bondage but who had not truly expressed "remorse" about it. Now, Banneker implied, they must demonstrate their own ethical evolution by fully embracing black uplift and equality.[31]

In this way, Banneker saw his life as part of a constant dialogue with white Americans over racial progress. The free-born Banneker routinely emphasized the connection between his sober moral philosophy and his daily living habits. Ready for public scrutiny after word spread of his almanac-making prowess and mathematical abilities, he welcomed to his Maryland farm a steady stream of inquisitive people who sought to test the alleged Black Genius. The person they discovered, as one white acquaintance recalled, did not disappoint, displaying "gentlemanly manners" and a "habitually industrious" nature. Dedicated to "improving the knowledge he had gained at school," he would "dive into his books" at every opportunity. He was, in the words of his first white biographer (a Maryland women whose mother had often met with Banneker), cognizant of his status as "a pioneer . . . for the improvement of his race."[32]

Banneker's black moralist persona pervaded the almanacs as well. Even in places where slavery was not mentioned per se, he represented (or emphasized himself) themes of virtuousness, universalism, and equality that correlated to debates over racial equality and emancipation. In "Epitaph on a Watchmaker"—included in several 1797 editions—Banneker rather ingeniously imagined himself as a timekeeper steadily taking America's moral pulse. Riffing on Benjamin Franklin's famous epitaph—which compared the Philadelphia printer to a book whose future editions would be published without "errata"—Banneker used watchmaking (his original talent) as a metaphor for his life: "Here lies, in a horizontal position, the outside case of Peter Pendulum, watchmaker, whose abilities were an honor to his profession. Integrity was the main spring, and prudence the regulator. Of all the actions of his life, humane, generous and liberal, his hand never stopped till he relieved distress. So nicely regulated were all his motions, that he never went wrong except when set going by people who did not know his key: even though he was easily set right again."[33]

Read against the antislavery pronouncements lining his almanacs, the clockmaker epitaph takes on a distinct abolitionist shape. Much like the black abolitionists emerging around him, Banneker saw himself as providing the nation's true moral beat of universal liberty, not unending slavery. His final lines, imagining the afterlife, flowed from black sacred history, particularly the story of Exodus. Having "departed this life wound up in hope, of being taken in hand by his maker, and having been thoroughly cleaned, repaired and set going in the world come," Banneker comes into contact with a righteous God, who recognizes his virtuousness and rewards him with grace. The lesson? Those who ignored the moral beat of the universe—that is to say, slaveholders—would suffer a much harsher fate by its ultimate timekeeper.[34]

In the almanac, seemingly innocuous "ephemera"—scattered poetry, brief philosophical discussions, snippets of prose—assumed a similarly moralistic tone, pointing to the fallacies of a hierarchical worldview and the illiberal perspectives that underwrote racial supremacy (among other things). Banneker's 1793 Philadelphia almanac placed British abolitionist Thomas Cowper's "On Liberty, and In Praise of Mr. Howard" immediately after Jefferson's meditations on the destructiveness of the master-slave relationship. Cowper's image of "a captive bird" released "into the boundless sky" captured the proto-romantic sacralization of natural freedom valued by both Banneker and his abolitionist supporters: "Oh, could I worship aught beneath the skies / that Earth hath seen, or fancy could devise / Thine altar, sacred liberty, should stand / built by no mercenary vulgar hand." "A Burlesque on Genealogy," printed in the 1796 almanac, satirized "two men disputing one day upon their genealogy, each of them pretend[ing] to be better than the other." As each man tries to outdo the other with respect to family roots and cultural status, one of them finally declares that he can prove that his family existed before the great flood of Genesis. Unimpressed, his opponent replies that he can prove a lineage preceding Adam! The first man's reply serves as the punchline—one that undermines all sacred genealogies: "You're in the right . . . for before Adam, there were no animals but brutes, and it is very certain you are descended from them."[35]

This cheeky bit of commentary had very real analogues in Banneker's antislavery world of print. More than a few examples of racial burlesque floated through the press during the early 1790s, doubtless fueled by debates over America's first emancipation statutes. In New York, black and white writers dueled over the stereotypical image of Africans as apes, or as the missing link between premodern brutes and humankind. In Philadelphia, a free black man named Henry Moss was ogled as a racial curiosity because of a skin condition that turned him "white." For some white commentators, blackness was viewed as a scientific conundrum, a philosophical dilemma, and a barrier to emancipation. Banneker's almanac consistently satirized such thinking: in a republican society where everyone was supposedly born free and equal, how could certain people be set in stone as "imbeciles" undeserving of freedom?[36]

Because almanac-making involved not only the compiler (or author) of meteorological calculations, but the publisher as well, who might add supplementary material to bolster the document's marketability, scholars will never be sure exactly who produced what. Did Banneker organize the bulk of the material appearing in his nearly thirty almanacs? Or did each printer improvise from Banneker's template? Banneker's almanacs were published by a variety of printers in the Mid-Atlantic region, with slight variations defining these many publications. Yet Banneker made clear that, with his name as the author, the almanacs were vehicles of antislavery sentiment, not merely meteorological instruments. Publishers usually complied with his wishes. In fact, while the 1793 edition published by the Quaker abolitionist Joseph Crukshank remained the most stridently abolitionist of all the almanacs, all of them contained material that pictured Banneker as a formidable opponent of racial degradation. Both editions of the 1793 almanac, one published in Philadelphia and the other in Baltimore, featured Banneker's dialogue with Jefferson. Thus, whether or not he remained in touch with each new printer, Banneker was the guiding force—the muse—behind the almanacs' broader antislavery moralism. As he scribbled on one of his own almanacs: "Evil communications corrupt good manners. I hope to live to hear, that good communications corrects bad manners."[37]

Banneker's antislavery network encompassed a range of printers, reformers, and even politicians interested in joining his dialogue over emancipation and racial uplift. Daniel Lawrence, a Quaker printer from New Jersey who moved to Philadelphia at virtually the same time that Banneker initiated his correspondence with Jefferson, became one of his first allies. In 1792, Lawrence reprinted Banneker's correspondence with Jefferson in a separate pamphlet, which included a brief biographical sketch of Banneker from a well-known Maryland politician. While Lawrence did not add his own prefatory thoughts on the Banneker-Jefferson correspondence, he clearly took Banneker's abolitionist position to heart: in 1792, he also reprinted a British anti-slave-trading pamphlet.[38]

Southern reformers saw Banneker as the perfect embodiment of racial uplift. Baltimore printers William Goddard and James Angell offered the first edition of Banneker's almanac, having already printed material for several gradual abolition societies in Maryland. Even though they shared many of the racial biases of late-eighteenth-century America—double-checking to see if Banneker had authored the almanac—Goddard and Angell viewed bondage as an anomalous part of the new republic. In 1789, they printed the constitution of the Maryland Society for Instituting the Gradual Abolition of Slavery, a group modeled on the Pennsylvania Abolition Society. A few years later, they published the constitution of the Chestertown Society for Promoting the Abolition of Slavery. Banneker personified their understanding of the antislavery movement: if liberated and given access to education, African Americans would become industrious and sober members of the republic.[39]

Goddard and Angell's public support of Banneker should not be taken for granted. In 1792 they printed a defense of the Maryland Abolition Society that illuminated the dangers of vociferously supporting black freedom claims below the Mason-Dixon Line. Responding to a lawsuit filed by two slaveholders against Maryland abolitionists (charging them with improperly interfering with masters' property rights), the printers hailed abolitionists as virtuous and civic-minded. The case revolved around the freedom suits of two blacks who eventually wound up in the abolition society's care. After the group refused to relinquish them, their Maryland masters sought compensation, going so far as to alert the Maryland General Assembly. Ultimately, the slaves were freed, though not without dour warnings about the perils of abolitionist meddling in a master's property rights. Banneker's almanac offered Southern reformers a less direct way to attack slavery.

Unsurprisingly, Philadelphia printers with abolitionist sympathies published several versions of Banneker's almanac during the 1790s. The Quaker printer Joseph Crukshank, a Pennsylvania Abolition Society member who had vied with Goddard and Angell for publication rights to Banneker's first almanac, printed three editions between 1792 and 1794. Crukshank had a long and distinguished tradition of antislavery publication dating to the early 1770s, when he had printed John Wesley's "Thoughts on Slavery." Philadelphian Daniel Humphreys's edition of Banneker's almanac built upon his 1787 publication of the black New Yorker Jupiter Hammon's "Address to the Negroes," which, by calling on blacks to remain pious and morally upright, served as an example of both racial uplift and black literary accomplishment.

Like Goddard and Angell, Crukshank, and Humphreys, many of Banneker's other printers were tied in to regional, national, and even trans-Atlantic reform networks. The Philadelphian William Gibbons, who issued an edition of Banneker's almanac in 1795, also printed Mary Wollstonecraft's "Vindication of the Rights of Women." Philip Edwards of Baltimore published both Bannaker's almanac and the antislavery address of a white Maryland reformer named George Buchanan. While Edwards became known as a maverick publisher of antislavery tracts, Buchanan became one of Maryland's most visible racial reformers. A physician and member of the Philadelphia-based American Philosophical Society, Buchanan was also a founding member of the Maryland Society for Promoting the Abolition of Slavery. The group's constitution declared that a "common father created all mankind free and equal," and that "it is the duty and interest of nations and individuals, enjoying every blessing of freedom, to remove the dishonor . . . from amongst them."[40] By treating abolitionism as the masters' moral imperative, the Maryland Abolition Society attempted, like Banneker, to find a way beyond the Jeffersonian conundrum which posited that slavery was wrong but that abolitionism was even worse.

Like Banneker, Buchanan desperately sought a dialogue with Jefferson. Not only did he publicly dedicate his antislavery oration and pamphlet "to the Honorable Thomas Jefferson . . . Secretary of State, Whose patriotism, since the American Revolution, has been uniformly marked, by a sincere, steady and active attachment to the interest of this country," Buchanan also peppered his document with allusions to the celebrated Virginian. Critiquing bondage from historical, ideological, and moral perspectives, Buchanan noted that "an impartial view" of humanity proved that the "white, swarthy and black [must] all be linked together." Buchanan further argued that slavery drained the moral sense from all masters, and, by extension, the societies they ruled: "To deprive a man of his liberty, has a tendency to rob his soul of every spring to virtuous actions." Using Montesquieu (one of Jefferson's heroes) as his guide, Buchanan declared that "slavery clogs the mind, perverts the moral faculty, and reduces the conduct of man to the standard brutes." For Buchanan, American masters' tenacious hold on slavery represented a moral decline. His message was clear: "Exterminate the pest of slavery from your land."[41]

Did Banneker influence Buchanan's decision to publish so direct a challenge to Jefferson and American slaveholders? While the white Maryland abolitionist initially delivered his antislavery oration on July 4, 1791, Buchanan did not actually publish his address until after Banneker's almanac had debuted. That fact alone may have inspired Buchanan to turn his oratory into a pamphlet on slaveholders' moral degradation. More broadly, Banneker and Buchanan shared a sense of moral urgency about slaveholders' seeming obliviousness to the divine reckoning that was sure to come. Using lines from Exodus, Buchanan declared that, "He that stealeth a man and selleth him, or if he be found in his hand, he shall surely be put to death." Arguing that bondage "wantonly abused the rights of man, and willingly sacrifices our liberty at the altar of slavery," Buchanan, like Banneker, even alluded to Jefferson's fear of divine retribution: "Know, my countrymen these things are not to be expected—heaven will not overlook such enormities! She is bound to punish impenitent centers, and her wrath is to be dreaded by all."[42]

The black almanac-maker's most ardent public defender was better known than even Buchanan. He was Maryland doctor and politician James McHenry. Author of an often-reprinted biographical sketch and testimonial of Banneker, McHenry depicted Banneker as the archetypal American self-made man. A student of Benjamin Rush, who was not only America's leading physician during the early 1790s but one of its best-known abolitionists, the Irish immigrant McHenry had served in the Continental Army as a surgeon before returning to his adopted home of Maryland. Although he owned five slaves by the 1790s, McHenry also supported abolition, going so far as to back a failed gradual emancipation statute in Maryland (modeled on Pennsylvania's law). When he assumed a position in Washington's presidential cabinet and moved to Philadelphia in 1796, McHenry and his wife did what Jefferson would not do in his lifetime: they offered indenture contracts to several of their slaves on condition that the slaves would travel to emancipating Pennsylvania as well. After a series of negotiations—and a failed attempt by some enslaved people in the McHenry clan to both claim freedom and remain with their families in Baltimore—three of the bondpeople accepted the offer and traveled to Philadelphia; two of these slaves remained with the McHenry family, gaining liberty only decades later, long after McHenry himself had passed away in 1816.[43]

As a statesman in a slaveholding polity who publicly supported emancipation, McHenry was precisely the type of figure that late-eighteenth-century racial reformers like Banneker hoped to win over. McHenry, in turn, believed that Banneker's life offered a great lesson to slaveholders: people of color did indeed seek moral uplift, and would happily trade bondage for freedom and educational opportunities. Banneker's well-known work with the famed Ellicott family on the survey for the District of Columbia attracted McHenry's notice. But McHenry's commitments to the ideals of the American Revolution, as well as his connections to abolitionists in and beyond Pennsylvania, helped underwrite his racial egalitarianism as well. As an Irish immigrant, McHenry knew well the meaning of English oppression and quasi-slavery. As a Federalist, he also registered little fear over government programs designed to enhance America's moral standing, including gradual abolitionism.

McHenry's biographical account of Banneker emphasized those virtuous qualities and habits of mind that Jefferson saw missing in people of African descent. McHenry described Banneker not as a savant—an autodidact or an exception to the Jeffersonian rule of black incompetence—but as a product of individual, family, and communal uplift: the embodiment of the American spirit. "His father and mother having obtained their freedom," he observed, "were able to send him to an obscure school, where he learned, when a boy, reading writing and arithmetic . . . and to leave him, at their deaths, a few acres of land, upon which he has supported himself ever since, by means of economy and constant labor." For McHenry, Banneker had earned "a fair reputation" through a diligent use of "leisure time"—that is, through "acquiring knowledge" that was useful and practical to those around him. McHenry told the story of Banneker's quick mastery of mathematics, and of his concern that scientific and mechanical knowledge be put to use, not just for himself but for his "neighbors." Banneker's almanac, in McHenry's eyes, was not merely a productive tool, but a moral one as well. It provided lessons to all those who doubted blacks' virtue and educational abilities.[44]

As McHenry's words illustrate, Banneker had become not merely a tool of the antislavery cause, but a rejoinder to doubts about racial uplift. Philadelphia Quakers had inaugurated the tradition of using black biography to legitimate abolition in the 1780s. "Are greater degrees of virtue and native Wisdom more requisite in black Men than in white, to give them an equal Title to Liberty?" members of the Philadelphia Yearly Meeting asked rhetorically in an address to London abolitionists in October 1787. Arguing that clear evidence of moral degradation among white citizens did not diminish their claims to freedom, Quaker abolitionists wondered why blacks had to prove so much to attain liberty. Nevertheless, to bolster the abolitionist cause, the Philadelphia Meeting on Sufferings forwarded a pamphlet of emancipation success stories to English reformers then building a case against the African slave trade.[45]

London Quakers had actually requested just such a pamphlet, one that would illustrate the moral "Benefit from Liberating [slaves]." Not only would justice be done to blacks, they asserted, but white consciences would be soothed by the matching of good deeds to their own "liberal" words. Interestingly, British reformers worried that Pennsylvania emancipation would not be "so striking" in international eyes. What they wanted were examples of Southern abolition—that is, for a Jefferson to step forward and speak positively about black uplift from deep within slave society. "As some Parts of Maryland & Virginia are within the limits of your Yearly Meeting," they wrote to the Pennsylvania Quakers, "and you have Correspondence with the more southern Districts[,] we thought [you could give] . . . satisfactory general Accounts . . . of the good Effects of Manumission in some parts of the Continent; to which, it seems, an Increase of Industry, a superior Cultivation, and even the Acknowledgements of the more candid Negro Masters, bear ample Testimony." If Jefferson or some other major Virginian would publicly sanction abolition, it would make a great difference in trans-Atlantic debates over black uplift. But no one could be found in Virginia.[46]

By highlighting Banneker's educational and moral excellence, then, his publishers filled that void, creating a glowing image of black freedom that was rare in Southern locales. In fact, Banneker's almanac and biography allowed Southern abolitionists to publicly raise consciousness about emancipation in the heart of slave country. The example of Richmond publisher Samuel Pleasants, who printed a 1797 edition of Banneker's almanac covering "Virginia, Pennsylvania, Delaware, Maryland and Kentucky," remains a powerful one. The well-known publisher of the *Virginia Gazette* and the brother of one the state's most visible abolitionists—Robert Pleasants—Samuel was sympathetic to the cause of racial reform. During the 1780s the Pleasants brothers had liberated twelve enslaved people who had been bequeathed to them by their father. Still, none of the other almanacs that Samuel Pleasants printed had expressed antislavery sympathies, until Banneker himself came along. Yet, by 1796, Pleasants' other calendar—entitled the *Virginia Almanack*—contained two new antislavery excerpts that had not appeared in any previous edition. The next year, he published Banneker's almanac itself. For Pleasants, it seemed, Banneker had illustrated a new way to combine antislavery moralizing with daily discourse.[47]

Other publishers saw Banneker as the antidote to Jeffersonian racial doubts—a sure sign of the Black Genius emerging in American culture. An anonymous poem published in a 1795 Philadelphia almanac took aim at anti-abolitionists by celebrating racial redemption, and not racial regression, as the lesson of Banneker's success. Referring to him as the "sublime" and "great" Banneker, the poem conjured a world where black "talents" and "greatness" would flow unimpeded: "How large the field! How wide its vast domain! / which got off thy ideas, Banneker, contain! / My muse, too painted, must to regions soar, / where genius, like Newton's, to explore." Mentioning Newton two more times, the poet argues that Banneker's gifts are not exceptional—or "peculiar," in the parlance of the day—but rather stem from "nature's self." Nature and nature's God, which Jefferson saw as erecting a wall of separation between black and white, becomes in this poem, as in Banneker's almanacs themselves, the wellspring of black genius. By championing the equality of all, "no matter what complexion they boast," Americans would adhere to "nature's plan." Fittingly, nature is invoked again in the final stanzas, to prove that racial hierarchies remain the creation of man alone. "How clear the proofs exhibited in thee," the poet observes of Banneker, "that black men talents have as well as we, / whom nature gives us another hue to wear, / a hue we boast to be than yours more fair?" This allusion to "fairness" refers not only to skin color, but to egalitarianism—suggesting that Banneker remained a more exemplary democrat than did slaveholders like Jefferson.[48]

For his antislavery alliance, the lesson of Banneker's life was clear: he had a moral standing that exceeded that of many white figures. And his almanac pictured an egalitarian future that was sure to come. Indeed, like the seasons and the stars, all things must cycle and change, including white conceptions of black inferiority. If slaveholders did not understand this elemental celestial rule—if they remained morally obtuse and committed to antiquated notions of racial difference—then they would be reduced to dust by nature and nature's God.

A Dialogue That Might Have Been

In 1810, a few years after Benjamin Banneker had passed away on the Maryland farm he had once owned but had been forced to sell in order to survive (he then paid rent to live there), a black writer living a few miles away conjured a new dialogue with recalcitrant Chesapeake masters. The black Baltimorean Daniel Coker's "Dialogue between a Virginian and an African Minister" recounted a debate between a black preacher and a slaveholding grandee that was clearly indebted to Banneker's correspondence with Jefferson. Yet Coker's tale never actually happened. The story featured a black preacher whose moral sense and reasoning ability far surpassed that of white planters, though its central white figure also displays a moral learning curve that far surpassed that of the still-living Jefferson. Arguing that emancipation was justified by both sacred Scripture (the Bible) and American ideology (the Declaration of Independence), Coker's African minister methodically picks apart the Chesapeake master's rigid defense of bondage, leaving white power (force) as the only justification of slavery. In a rousing final scene, the white Virginian concedes the morality and utility of emancipation. "Sir," he tells the delighted black preacher, some form of abolitionism "ought to be done."[49]

Though pure fantasy, one can imagine Coker sitting down to rewrite the exchange that inspired it, as if to say, *Had Jefferson and other planters responded in this way to Banneker, perhaps Southern emancipation might succeed!* In another sense, though, Coker was commenting on a critical theme within the early emancipation struggle, at least from the perspective of vanguard racial reformers like Banneker: the necessity of white citizens' moral development. Literally borrowing a page from Banneker, Coker hoped that his dialogue would spur a new wave of reflection and moral growth among Southern planters (and perhaps white citizens throughout the United States), who would then champion egalitarian emancipation.

His hopes came to naught. By the 1810s a hardening of racial lines had set in—what the historian James Stewart has insightfully labeled "racial modernity."[50] Defined by a rigid view of the color line, racial modernity found both black and white activists pessimistic about racial reform. Over the next few decades, Southern emancipation dwindled and colonization became the only way to even think about mass abolitionism. Yet, as black writers from Banneker to Coker had illustrated, there was another tradition, one that espoused a progressive view of racial uplift among white as well as black citizens. Like Banneker, many early black activists had hoped that their persuasive literary productions would demonstrate African Americans' moral improvement, fomenting a corresponding educational development among slaveholding whites that would lead to national emancipation. Steeped in the language of evangelical religion and black prophecy, this discourse linked the fate of the American nation itself to slaveholders' moral choices. If they embraced abolitionism and equality, then God would be pleased. Otherwise, a dark fate awaited unrepentant slaveholders and the grand republic they controlled.

As Michael Vorenberg has pointed out, many antebellum statesmen, slaveholders included, remained unmoved by these prophetic calls, in large part because they viewed human constitutions (like the federal Constitution itself) as fixed and unchangeable.[51] For slaveholders like Jefferson, innate black degradation was the racial law of the land. Antebellum abolitionists would use condemnation rather than subtle persuasion to counter masters' beliefs, to little avail. Only the chaos of Civil War and its aftermath would compel slaveholders and anti-abolitionist Northerners to confront the morality of racial oppression. And even that attempted reconstruction failed, leaving to twentieth-century civil rights reformers Banneker's original task of uplifting white souls.

Notes

I would like to thank Matt Mason and Craig Hammond for their expert editorial guidance, David Waldstreicher for illuminating discussions of the black protest tradition in the era of the Constitution, and the great folks at the Library Company of Philadelphia for research help, particularly Jim Green, for his insights on almanacs in early national print culture.

1. See, for example, Kevin Hayes's much-praised recent book, *The Road to Monticello: The Life and Mind of Thomas Jefferson* (New York: Oxford University Press, 2007), which does not even consider Banneker. Joseph Ellis's well-regarded and award-winning biography, *American Sphinx* (New York: Vintage, 1997), considered the significance of race, but not Banneker; indeed, Ellis subsequently addressed race through a reconsideration of the Hemings affair.

2. Annette Gordon-Reed's monumental and prize-winning new biography, *The Hemingses of Monticello: An American Family* (New York: Norton, 2008), briefly examines the Banneker-Jefferson correspondence but uses the Jefferson-Hemings family saga as a better window for understanding race in early America. Jan Lewis and Peter Onuf's terrific book, *Sally Hemings and Thomas Jefferson: History, Memory, and Civic Culture* (Charlottesville: University Press of Virginia, 1999), has a brief reference to Banneker vis-à-vis Jefferson's racial thought. R. B. Bernstein's generally good short biography, *Thomas Jefferson* (New York: Oxford University Press, 2003), refers briefly to Banneker but shines the light on Jefferson as an antislavery man.

3. On the growth of free black society in the North, see especially James Horton and Lois Horton, *In Hope of Liberty* (New York: Oxford University Press, 1997); James Oliver Horton, *Free People of Color: Inside the African American Community* (Washington, D.C.: Smithsonian, 1993), 43–46; and Patrick Rael, *Black Identity and Black Protest in the Ante-Bellum North* (Chapel Hill: University of North Carolina Press, 2002). See also Hosea Easton, *"To Heal the Scourge of Prejudice": The Life and Writings of Hosea Easton,* ed. George Price and James Stewart (Amherst: University of Massachusetts Press, 1999).

4. Banneker to Jefferson, 21 August 1791, reprinted in Benjamin Banneker, *Copy of a Letter from Benjamin Banneker to the Secretary of State, With His Answer* (Philadelphia, 1792), 3.

5. Ibid., 11–12.

6. See Ari Helo and Peter Onuf, "Jefferson, Morality, and the Problem of Slavery," in Peter Onuf's essential book, *The Mind of Thomas Jefferson* (Charlottesville: University of Virginia Press, 2007), 236–70.

7. See David Waldstreicher's fine edition of *Notes on the State of Virginia* (New York: Bedford, 2002).

8. See, for example, David Gellman, *Emancipating New York* (Baton Rouge: Louisiana State University Press, 2006). See also Joanne Pope Melish, *Disowning Slavery: Gradual Emancipation and "Race" in New England, 1780–1860* (Ithaca, N.Y.: Cornell University Press, 1999); and Bruce Dain, *A Hideous Monster of the Mind: American Race Theory in the Early Republic* (Cambridge, Mass.: Harvard University Press, 2002).

9. See Richard S. Newman, Roy Finkenbine, and Douglass Mooney, "Philadelphia Emigrationist Petition, circa 1792: An Introduction," *William and Mary Quarterly*, 3rd ser., 64 (January 2007): 161–66.

10. James Forten, *Series of Letters by a Man of Color* (Philadelphia, 1813), 1.

11. Masters in the Deep South may have helped construct an antislavery Jefferson by condemning his reply to Banneker, worrying as they did that it legitimized black humanity—

and therefore claims to black freedom. According to the literary scholar Dickson Bruce, the viciously anti-abolitionist South Carolina statesman William Loughton Smith even chided Jefferson for his rather naive acknowledgment of a black man's ostensible claim to equal treatment in public. Nevertheless, the dominant Jefferson remained the one who doubted blacks' moral abilities. At no point between 1791 and the 1820s did Jefferson support abolitionism without colonization, or change his essentialist views on race (see Dickson Bruce Jr., *The Origins of African American Literature, 1680–1865* [Charlottesville: University Press of Virginia, 2001], 151–52). On Jefferson and early national slaveholders, see also William W. Freehling, *The Road to Disunion*, vol. 1, *Secessionists at Bay, 1776–1854* (New York: Oxford University Press, 1989).

12. *The Colored American* (New York), 20 May 1837.

13. Banneker to Jefferson, 19 August 1791, reprinted in *Copy of a Letter from Benjamin Banneker to the Secretary of State, With His Answer*, 3–10.

14. For an extended treatment on emerging black protest traditions, see Richard S. Newman and Roy Finkenbine, "Black Founders in the New Republic: Introduction," *William and Mary Quarterly*, 3rd ser., 64 (January 2007): 83–94.

15. Banneker to Jefferson, August 21, 1790, reprinted in *Copy of a Letter from Benjamin Banneker to the Secretary of State, With His Answer*, 3–4.

16. See "Dialogue Between a Master and a Slave," in the *Columbia Orator* (Boston, 1797), reprinted in part 2 of David Blight's edition of *Narrative of the Life of Frederick Douglass*, 2nd ed. (New York: Bedford, 2003).

17. On Imlay's observations from the early 1790s, see Gary Nash and Graham Russell Gao Hodges, *Friends of Liberty: Thomas Jefferson, Tadeusz Kościuszko, and Agrippa Hull: A Tale of Three Patriots, Two Revolutions, and a Tragic Betrayal of Freedom in the New Nation* (New York: Basic Books, 2008), 133–36. I am indebted to John Craig Hammond for pointing out this work.

18. Richard Allen, "An Address to Those Who Keep Slaves and Approve the Practice," part of Absalom Jones and Richard Allen's *Narrative of the Late Awful Calamity . . . in 1793* (Philadelphia, 1794), reprinted in *Pamphlets of Protest: An Anthology of Early African American Protest Literature, 1790–1860*, comp. Richard Newman, Patrick Rael, and Philip Lapsansky (New York: Routledge, 2001), 42.

19. I am indebted to Matthew Mason for making this fine point. See also Peter Knupfer, *The Union As It Is* (Lawrence: University Press of Kansas, 1991).

20. Interestingly, both Banneker and subsequent generations of abolitionists attributed to Jefferson egalitarian sympathies that the Sage of Monticello simply did not have, or they manipulated Jefferson's egalitarian views to bolster their own abolitionist claims on the American Republic. Not only did Banneker see Jefferson's return note as evidence of Jefferson's abolitionist evolution, others did too. In the 4 January 1855 edition of *Frederick Douglass' Paper*, Douglass picked up a story from an Albany paper that highlighted Jefferson's alleged antislavery beliefs—particularly the 1791 reply to Banneker—which supposedly disproved the Virginian's fears that blacks could not be educated. The abolitionist William Allen similarly asserted that anti-abolitionists who used Jefferson as an anti-black figurehead "sadly missed their figure"; his correspondence with Banneker clearly showed otherwise. This anti-slavery Jefferson whose reply to Banneker legitimized black humanity—and therefore their claims to freedom—certainly angered vehemently proslavery Southerners. Nevertheless, the dominant

Jefferson remained the one who doubted blacks' moral abilities. At no point between 1791 and the 1820s did Jefferson support abolitionism without colonization, or change his essentialist views on race.

21. Alexander Boulton, "The American Paradox: Jeffersonian Equality and Racial Science," *American Quarterly* 47 (September 1995): 467–92.

22. Gary Nash still offers the best overall treatment of racial debates in early national Philadelphia; see his *Forging Freedom: The Formation of Philadelphia's Black Community, 1720–1840* (Cambridge, Mass.: Harvard University Press, 1988).

23. See the following broadsides from Franklin and the Pennsylvania Abolition Society: "Address to the Public" (Philadelphia, November 1789); and "A Plan for Improving the Condition of the Free Blacks" (Philadelphia, October 1789) (*Digital Early American Imprints*, Series I, Evans [1639–1800], available online at http://www.readex.com/readex/product.cfm?product =4 [access by subscription]).

24. See David Waldstreicher's trenchant study of Franklin and slavery, *Runaway America* (New York: Hill and Wang, 2004), particularly chaps. 7–9.

25. See Richard S. Newman, *Freedom's Prophet: Bishop Richard Allen, the AME Church, and the Black Founding Fathers* (New York: New York University Press, 2008), chaps. 3–4.

26. Eva Sheppard Wolf, *Race and Liberty in the New Nation: Emancipation in Virginia from the Revolution to Nat Turner's Rebellion* (Charlottesville: University of Virginia Press, 2006). The figure of 10,000 manumissions in Virginia is at the higher end of Wolf's estimates, but plausible.

27. See A. Glenn Crothers, "Quaker Merchants and Slavery in Early National Alexandria," *Journal of the Early Republic* 25 (Spring 1995): 47–77.

28. Jefferson quoted in George F. Tyson, ed., *Toussaint L'Ouverture* (Englewood Cliffs, N.J.: Spectrum/Prentice Hall, 1973), 93.

29. Silvio A. Bedini nicely collects all these editions in his biography of the publisher, *The Life of Benjamin Banneker* (Baltimore: Maryland Historical Society, 1972) (see especially 379–84).

30. Ibid., 164.

31. On Banneker's undated poem (ca. 1790), see ibid., 164.

32. Martha Tyson, *A Sketch of the Life of Benjamin Banneker, from Notes Taken in 1836* (Baltimore, 1854).

33. Silvio Bedini wonders if Banneker simply copied these lines from a printer in the British Isles, though even if he did, it tells us much about his mindset (see Bedini, *The Life of Benjamin Banneker*, 197–98).

34. Ibid.

35. *Banneker's Virginia, Pennsylvania, Delaware, Maryland and Kentucky Almanack and Ephemeris, for the Year 1797* (Richmond, 1796).

36. On Henry Moss, see Harriet A. Washington, *Medical Apartheid: The Dark History of Medical Experimentation on Black Americans From Colonial Times to the Present* (New York: Anchor Books, 2006), 80.

37. See Tyson, *A Sketch of the Life of Benjamin Banneker, from Notes Taken in 1836*.

38. In addition to *Copy of a Letter from Benjamin Banneker to the Secretary of State, With His Answer*, see Daniel Lawrence's publication of William Crafton Bell's *A Short Sketch of the Evidence for the Abolition of the Slave Trade* (Philadelphia, 1792).

39. See Goddard and Angell's twin antislavery publications, *The Constitution of the Mary-*

land Society, for Instituting the Gradual Abolition of Slavery* (Baltimore, 1789) and *The Constitution of the Chester-Town Society, for Promoting the Gradual Abolition of Slavery* (Baltimore, 1791).

40. John Thomas Scharf, *A History of Maryland from the Earliest Period to the Present Day* (Baltimore, 1879), 306.

41. George Buchanan, *An Oration Upon the Moral and Political Evil of Slavery* (Baltimore, 1793), 7–20.

42. Ibid.

43. Karen Robbins, "Power among the Powerless: Domestic Resistance by Free and Slave Women in the McHenry Family of the New Republic," *Journal of the Early Republic* 23 (Spring 2003): 47–68.

44. See McHenry's open letter dated 20 August 1791 to the Baltimore publishers Goddard and Angell, regarding Banneker's life, which is reprinted in *Banneker's Almanac . . . for 1792* (Baltimore, 1791), 2–4.

45. See Philadelphia Yearly Meeting, Meeting of Sufferings, October 1787, Pemberton Papers, Historical Society of Pennsylvania, Philadelphia.

46. London Meeting of Sufferings to Philadelphia Yearly Meeting, 3 November 1786, Pemberton Papers, Historical Society of Pennsylvania, Philadelphia.

47. See "On Negro Slavery and the Slave Trade" and "An Extract of an Address to the Citizens of the United States [on Domestic Slavery," in the *Virginia Almanack . . . 1796* (Richmond, 1795), printed by Samuel Pleasants. The *Virginia Almanack . . . 1795* (Richmond, 1794) contained neither of these antislavery excerpts. Yet, by 1796, Pleasants was preparing to publish *Banneker's Virginia, Pennsylvania, Delaware, Maryland and Kentucky Almanack . . . 1797* (Richmond, 1796), which by then had a strong antislavery reputation.

48. "Addressed to Benjamin Banneker," in *Banneker's Almanac, for the Year 1795 . . .* (Philadelphia, 1794), frontmatter.

49. Daniel Coker, *Dialogue between a Virginian and an African Minister* (Baltimore, 1810), 38.

50. See James Brewer Stewart, "The Political Meanings of Color in the Free States, 1776–1840," in *Abolitionist Politics and the Coming of the Civil War* (Amherst: University of Massachusetts Press, 2007).

51. See Michael Vorenberg's fine book, *Final Freedom: The Civil War, the Abolition of Slavery, and the Thirteenth Amendment* (Cambridge, Mass.: Harvard University Press, 2001), especially part 1: "Slavery's Constitution."

Caribbean Slave Revolts
and the Origins of the Gag Rule

A Contest between Abolitionism
and Democracy, 1797–1835

EDWARD B. RUGEMER

O n December 18, 1835, when Congressman William Jackson of Massachusetts presented a petition from his constituents for the abolition of slavery
in Washington, D.C., James Henry Hammond of South Carolina countered with
a unique response. He moved that the petition "be not received." House Speaker
James Polk replied that such a motion had never been voiced, and off and on for
several weeks the House discussed the procedural issues at stake.[1] Hammond did
not participate in most of this debate, but on February 1, when Congressman
Caleb Cushing (again of Massachusetts) presented another petition for the abolition of slavery in the capital, Hammond was ready. In a prepared speech, Hammond reviewed the sordid history of abolitionism and the danger of its recent
success in the British Empire. Hammond sought to make it absolutely clear why
Congress could not accept petitions from the abolitionists. It was a matter of
Southern security. Abolitionist fanatics aimed to "excite a servile insurrection."
This goal lay behind their meetings, publications, lectures, and missions that had
proliferated in the North over the past few years. Unless Congress wanted to see
fire and bloodshed lay waste to the slaveholding states, it would reject these
petitions outright. They should not even be considered.[2]

No one responded directly to Hammond, but three days later Henry Pinckney
of South Carolina proposed a series of resolutions. Pinckney softened Hammond's gag, probably in concert with presidential aspirant Martin Van Buren,
who wanted the issue buried. Pinckney's resolutions called for the creation of a
select committee in the House with very specific instructions to consider the
abolition petitions. The committee would not discuss the merits of the petitions;

rather, it would report that "Congress possesses no constitutional authority to interfere . . . with the institutions of slavery in any of the States," and "ought not" to interfere with slavery in Washington, D.C. Pinckney's resolutions passed by a wide margin, and a committee was formed that consisted of five Northerners and four Southerners; seven of the nine committee members were Democrats. Pinckney's resolutions backed off from the extreme constitutional strictures that Hammond had sought, but the report of the select committee accepted Hammond's assertion that abolitionist agitation threatened servile war and that abolitionist "machinations" would "overthrow the whole system of civil society in the slaveholding portions of the Union." The abolition of slavery in the capital would lead "directly and inevitably to insubordination and revolt throughout the South." Has anyone forgotten, asked the committee, "the history of St. Domingo, or the insurgent attempt at Charleston, or the tragical scenes at Southampton?"[3] While they disagreed on the constitutional solution, Hammond and the moderates agreed that abolitionism would cause insurrections and therefore had to be silenced. Where had this assumption come from?

Historians have not explored this question with much rigor. Most note, correctly, that James Henry Hammond proposed the gag, and some argue that the idea actually originated with John C. Calhoun. But why did these men demand a gag? Russel Nye wrote of the widespread charges of "incendiarism" leveled against the abolitionists in connection with the mail campaign during the summer of 1835. But Nye believed that the charges were without basis and that the fear of insurrection was "more imaginary than real." William Shade agrees, and claims that the Calhounites were "playing upon the anxiety" of insurrection scares. Charles Sellers, Leonard Richards, Sean Wilentz, and Daniel Walker Howe simply point to the political extremism of Hammond and the Calhounites, as if that is explanation enough.[4] William Lee Miller, following the argument of William Freehling in his landmark *Prelude to Civil War*, takes Southern fears seriously, and observes that by 1835 it had become a "staple of southern polemic" to accuse abolitionists of trying to instigate servile war. Miller quotes James Garland of Virginia, from the debates that followed Hammond's motion, who described the abolitionist as an "instigator of midnight murder and assassination." Miller rightly looks to the Haitian Revolution, Denmark Vesey's conspiracy in Charleston, and to Nat Turner's rebellion as recent events that explained Southern vitriol. But this begs another question: why did Southern militants assume that abolitionist agitation would lead to insurrection?[5] Denmark Vesey's conspiracy and Nat Turner's rebellion were just two of the five insurrections or conspiracies that seemed to demonstrate a pattern of abolitionist agitation followed by revolutionary activity among slaves. By 1835, many white Americans readily identified abolitionist agitation as the cause of insurrection. This had happened in Barbados in 1816, in Demerara (now Guyana) in 1823, and in Jamaica in 1831, just months after the rebellion in Virginia. In 1815, British abolitionists began agitation for a Registry Bill to enforce the abolition of the trans-Atlantic slave trade. The next year, in Barbados, enslaved people rose in rebellion. In the summer of 1822, just months after the tense debates over the future of Missouri had ended, Charleston slaveholders discovered the conspiracy organized by Denmark Vesey. The very next year, in Demerara, a rebellion led by the slave preacher Quamina followed a petition campaign led by Thomas Fowell Buxton to force the West Indian Assemblies to ameliorate their slave codes. Turner's rebellion followed the circulation of David Walker's incendiary *Appeal to the Colored Citizens of the World*, as well as the appearance of William Lloyd Garrison's *Liberator*. And the rebellion in Jamaica followed the most vigorous campaign British abolitionists had ever launched, complete with mass petitions and traveling lecturers. By 1833, the struggle over slavery had come to a head in Britain's Atlantic empire, and Parliament abolished slavery that August. Americans paid careful attention to these developments, and militant Carolinians led the attempt to stifle abolitionism in the United States. Ironically, recent Caribbean history enabled their cause.[6]

The historian John Brooke has encouraged scholars of the early American republic to engage with the later writings of Jürgen Habermas, whose 1996 *Between Facts and Norms* offers an unromantic conception of how democracy works. Habermas's model of democracy provides historians with a valuable tool for tracing the impact of public opinion with more precision than is customary. He argues that democratic practice consists of two interdependent and overlapping processes, "opinion-formation" and "will-formation." Opinion-formation is an informal process that takes place in the chaotic public sphere and results in public opinion. Will-formation occurs in legislatures, courts, or bureaucracies that wield political power, and it results in laws, decisions, or rules that govern society. Public opinion emerges from the accretion of information and arguments that become accepted by a majority of citizens. It is shaped by "mass media," in Habermas's formulation, which for the early republic means newspapers, pamphlets, and books. Opinion-formation in the public sphere preceeds (and continues during) will-formation in government, since in democratic practice, those who hold positions in government are held accountable to public opinion. The moment of will-formation means that a majority has reached a decision and acted with the political power of an institution. Nevertheless, the decision only "represents a caesura in an ongoing discussion," as there is usually a minority that does not subscribe to the dominant public opinion.[7]

In this essay I argue that for the majority of white men, whose representatives directly controlled the levers of power in the federal government, the democratic process, as Habermas describes it, worked. The establishment of the gag rule was a moment of will-formation that followed a long process of opinion-formation on the issue of the relationship between slave rebellions and abolitionism. From 1797 through 1835 white Americans had absorbed the lessons of Caribbean writers that abolitionist agitation caused slave rebellion. The news of West Indian rebellions, which most newspapers presented as black rebels killing whites at the instigation of radical abolitionists, shaped public opinion in the United States. This interpretation of West Indian events set Denmark Vesey's Charleston conspiracy and Nat Turner's rebellion in a particularly disturbing light for American slaveholders. The assumption that abolitionism caused rebellion explains the fierce rhetoric of legislators like James Henry Hammond, and while his colleagues may not have gone to such extremes, the repetition of this understanding of rebellion had appeared enough in print to become a "fact" that justified votes in favor of a significant violation of civil rights supposedly guaranteed by the Constitution.

Governor John Floyd of Virginia thought he knew precisely what had happened in Southampton during the summer of 1831. Just as abolitionists had been agitating throughout Great Britain, the radical Northerner William Lloyd Garrison had started publication of his *Liberator* in January 1831. Garrison's paper called, in strident terms, for the immediate abolition of American slavery, and some of Floyd's constituents had sent him issues they had found in Virginia. Floyd noted in his diary that the Boston newspaper had "the express intention of inciting the slaves and free negroes . . . to rebellion." He further explained to Governor James Hamilton of South Carolina that the rebellion had originated from a convergence of "Yankee" influences. First, Northern preachers had taught the slaves that "God was no respecter of persons—the black man was as good as the white—that all men were born free and equal—that they cannot serve two masters—that the white people rebelled against England to obtain freedom, so have the blacks a right to do." This dangerous message had been compounded by the naive religiosity of women, who had taught "the negroes to read and write" in order that they could comprehend the Scriptures for themselves. Literate slaves had then come upon "the incendiary publications of Walker, Garrison and Knapp of Boston," brought by "Yankee peddlers." Rebellion had been the inevitable result.[8]

Governor Floyd had inherited a trans-Atlantic slaveholding tradition that dated back to the first interpretations of the Haitian Revolution. The charge that abolitionists instigated slave rebellions had its genesis in slaveholder responses to the insurrection in Saint-Domingue that began in 1791. Saint-Dominguan slaveholders in the National Assembly accused the Amis des Noirs, the French abolitionist society, of instigating the rebellion, and the West India interest in London translated and reprinted these speeches in a pamphlet.[9] The accusation was popularized and given its fullest elaboration by the Jamaican planter and historian Bryan Edwards, whose 1797 *An Historical Survey of the French Colony of St. Domingo* also laid the violence of Haiti at the feet of the Amis des Noirs. Edwards was well known to Americans of the early republic. His three-volume history of the British empire in the West Indies, first published in 1793, was definitive in its time. Edwards had been a member of the Jamaican Assembly, and during the Revolutionary War he defended the rebellious North Americans and argued against Britain's military efforts to suppress the colonial rebellion. In 1791, when the slaves rebelled in French Saint-Domingue, Edwards was on his plantation in Jamaica. He visited the stricken island on behalf of the colonial government of Jamaica, which ultimately assisted French slaveholders.[10]

By 1797 when Edwards penned his *Historical Survey,* Toussaint L'Ouverture and an army of ex-slaves had defeated military forces from Spain, France, and Great Britain, with the occasional assistance of the John Adams administration. Edwards wrote his *Historical Survey* as a lesson for slaveholders. The Haitian Revolution, he argued, "had one . . . origin. It was not the strong and irresistible impulse of human nature, groaning under oppression, that excited [the slaves] to plunge their daggers into the bosoms of unoffending women and helpless infants. They were driven into those excesses—reluctantly driven—by the vile machinations of men calling themselves philosophers."[11] Edwards alleged a causal relationship between the writings of French abolitionists, the Amis des Noirs, the plotting of literate free blacks, and the insurrection of the slaves. Edwards warned his fellow planters in the British West Indies that their lives too were threatened by abolitionism. As Christopher Brown has elegantly shown, British abolitionists had begun to agitate against the slave trade in the aftermath of the American Revolution, and for Bryan Edwards this meant that English-speaking slaves would soon learn "ideas of their own natural rights and equality of condition," which would lead to a "general struggle for freedom through rebellion and bloodshed." Foreshadowing the proponents of the gag rule, Edwards demanded that the abolitionists end their agitation out of concern for the personal security of West Indian whites. British abolitionists did not listen, of course, and the rebellions in Barbados, Demerara, and Jamaica seemed to provide substance for his accusation.[12]

We can be fairly sure that Americans read Bryan Edwards. After going through three editions published in Great Britain, Edwards's *Historical Survey of the French Colony* (which now appeared as the fourth volume in his *History of the British Colonies in the West Indies*) went through five more printings in the United States—three times in Philadelphia (1805, 1806, 1810), as well as Charleston (1810), and Baltimore (1810). As early as 1800, Edwards's thesis on the origins of slave rebellions had become a rhetorical staple in the politics of slavery. In the aftermath of Gabriel's Rebellion in Richmond, Virginia, for example, many whites pointed to what William Vans Murray described as "the eternal clamour about liberty" that resounded in the election of that year. An anonymous writer to the *Fredericksburg Herald* ascribed the revolt to "vile French Jacobins, aided and abetted by some of our own profligate and abandoned democrats." In a land where "every white man is a master and every black man is a slave," the doctrines of liberty could only produce "general insurrection." This tragic reality had been proven, the author opined, by the "horrors of St. Domingo." Such accusations may have been driven by the partisanship of a hard-fought election, but for slaveholders they revealed the same fearsome truth described by Bryan Edwards.[13]

Caribbean rebellions influenced the politics of American slavery through the close-knit web of communication that linked North America to the Caribbean. Commerce between the mainland and the islands began with the earliest settlements and, while the independence of the United States restructured this trade, it never stopped.[14] Newspapers began to connect the Anglo-Atlantic over the first half of the eighteenth century, and they were political organs from the start.[15] The Post Office Act of 1792 allowed newspapers to be shipped to subscribers through the mail system at extremely low rates, which Richard John has likened to a subsidy for editors. The Act also mandated the delivery of "exchange papers," whereby printers received at very low cost the newspapers of other regions. John argues that such policies began to unify the United States along a nationwide network of information, where, in Toqueville's famous rendering, the newspaper could put "the same thought at the same time before a thousand readers."[16]

The nexus between the newspaper system of the United States and the broader Atlantic was described by Achille Murat, the Sicilian prince who became an American citizen. In his account of westward expansion, Murat portrayed both the post office and the newspaper as essential elements in the development of the quintessential "American" town. The post office enabled average citizens to receive a newspaper, generally more than one. "Everyone" subscribed to the newspaper from "the village from which he [had] emigrated," and usually another from "Washington, or from some Atlantic town." Murat boasted that Americans were remarkably well informed, receiving "reviews and magazines, literary journals, novelties of every sort, [which] come to us from New York, Philadelphia, and England, at a moderate price, and a month or two after their publication over the Atlantic."[17]

Reports on the insurrection in Barbados began to appear in American newspapers in the middle of May 1816, first in New York, where the commercial links with the West Indies were the strongest, and then spreading throughout the country through exchange papers. On May 11, the *Evening Post* of New York learned from one Captain Thompson that "insurrection had broken out among the blacks of Barbadoes." Forty plantations had been set afire and troops were on the way.[18] The reports linked the rebellion to British abolitionists. On the 27th of May, for example, the *New York Commercial Advertiser* disclosed the rebellion's cause, as well as its bloody end. The rebels had been "deluded" into believing "that their *friends* in England, had obtained their freedom." They had "demanded . . . payment for their labour," and when this was refused, they had set fire to the estates, destroying eighty. In the end, 2,000 slaves had been killed in the suppression, along with "two whites who were ringleaders."[19] Several newspapers printed the comments of Barbados assemblyman James Bovell, who directed his ire at the "African Institution," the new organization of British abolitionists, which had successfully campaigned for the Registry Bill. The Institution claimed philanthropy for its inspiration, said Bovell. It alleged to have the moral well-being of the colonies in mind, and merely sought the "amelioration" of the slaves' condition. But such advocacy displayed a dangerous ignorance of history, for the Amis des Noirs had also been philanthropists. Had Britons forgotten the horrors of Saint-Domingue? Bovell had not: "We who have been enlightened by the history of the Antilles know too well the confidence that is due to these lofty pretensions." The rebellion recalled the "example of St. Domingo," and Bovell accused the African Institution of dangerously treading where history taught men not to go.[20]

Another widely reprinted article penned by Thomas Ritchie, editor of the *Richmond Enquirer*, employed the familiar trope of British tyranny to expound upon the meaning of the rebellion. Ritchie was an influential player in

Southern politics and his opinions had clout. "The insurrection of the slaves in Barbadoes is distressing to every generous heart," he wrote, "but is it possible to forget that the butchered planters are only the victims of those misfortunes which their countrymen would have brought upon us?" The rebellion in Barbados was a lesson in the benefits of independence. The horrors faced by Barbadian planters were the responsibility of their own "countrymen" in Britain, and had the South still been a part of the British empire, they too would now suffer. To elaborate the metaphor, Ritchie compared Parliament's antislavery meddling in the West Indies to Lord Dunmore's emancipatory proclamation during the Revolutionary War: "It was they who would have taught our slaves to rebel, to desert, and to massacre their masters—it was they who wove them into regiments, landed them upon our shores, and taught them to lure away their fellows."[21] Pauline Maier has observed that during these same years Americans began to emphasize the preservation of the Revolution's history.[22] Ritchie's allusion to the Revolution bears this out, but with an agenda for his own time. British tyranny linked West Indian planters with the Revolutionary generation, and abolitionism echoed Lord Dunmore's proclamation. American independence protected Southern slaveholders from the threats of agitation.

News of the insurrection in Demerara began to appear in October 1823, when memories of conspiracy in Charleston were still quite fresh. There had been a "general uprising" in the interior of Demerara; troops were on the way from Barbados, and martial law had been proclaimed. By mid-October, readers of *Niles' Weekly Register* and Richmond's *Enquirer* had learned that "a fanatic preacher, a white man" had caused the revolt by misleading the slaves into believing they had been freed by Parliament. Ritchie's comment that this was "one of the unhappy fruits of the misdirected zeal of the British philanthropists," made clear the accusation of abolitionist responsibility.[23]

As the story of the rebellion continued to unfold, the connection between the rebellion and the abolitionist movement appeared repeatedly in American newspapers. In mid-October, a widely disseminated excerpt from the *Demerara Royal Gazette* reported that "evidence and confessions" demonstrated that the organization of the rebellion was too complex to have been developed by black slaves. There was little doubt that a "superior order of people" had planned the insurrection. "Perhaps the intriguing Saints at home had a hand in it—if so, they will hear with disappointment and pain that a superintending and just Providence has frustrated their diabolical intentions . . . to make Demerara a second St. Domingo!" The accusation was direct.[24]

In a November article entitled "The Curse," Baltimore editor Hezekiah Niles returned to the news from the West Indies and linked it to the insurrection scare in Charleston. "The people of one of the southern states," he observed, "have hardly recovered from their agitation at the discovery of a plot among the slaves to effect a general rising . . . [and] we now hear of fearful apprehensions in another quarter on a similar account." Niles reported unrest in nearly all of the West Indian colonies, especially Barbados, where it appeared that some colonists believed the Methodists intended to raise another insurrection. The belief proved so pervasive that a white mob destroyed the Methodist Chapel in town and forced the minister to flee for his life. In Jamaica, a meeting of colonists resolved that abolitionism was nothing less than "MEDITATED ROBBERY." Echoing a common American argument, white Jamaicans protested that slavery was a "curse entailed on the people of her American colonies, on the continent and in the West Indies" by Britain, and that pure hypocrisy moved British writers to "blame us because we have slaves!" These Jamaicans admitted slavery was a curse— upon themselves and upon their cousins in the United States. Not only had it brought upon them unfair moral censure by their countrymen in Britain, that very censure had threatened their lives by instigating their slaves to rebel.[25]

In December 1823, Thomas Ritchie reprinted a piece on the West Indies from the *Charleston Patriot*. West Indian whites "from Barbados to Jamaica" had roundly protested Parliament's measures to ameliorate colonial slavery. As he had during his coverage of the rebellion in Barbados in 1816, Ritchie turned to the familiar parallels of the West Indian experience with the American Revolution. He reported that the language of writers in the islands' newspapers was "precisely the tone and character of that used in this country previous to the revolution."[26] Ritchie also reprinted the *Bermuda Gazette*'s accounts of West Indian planters who were "all in arms against the regulations which the Saints of the African Institution have induced Ministers to propose, relative to the future treatment of the slave population."[27] The sarcastic and derogatory term "Saints" had been applied to the abolitionists by their conservative critics in Britain and the West Indies. Appearing in Richmond's *Enquirer*, the anecdote suggested an analogy between British abolitionists and the oppressions of an odious, meddling Parliament on the eve of the American Revolution. Such comparison provided a potent frame of reference for American readers, and conveyed the British West Indian colonial struggle against Parliament as a just cause reminiscent of the American Revolution.

While the themes in newspaper coverage of the rebellions in Barbados and Demerara were remarkably consistent, a comparison of these two spans of coverage reveals some important distinctions that illustrate the opinion-formation process. In 1816, news of the rebellion in Barbados appeared in the American political press through twenty-two reports, and spread around the country through thirteen identifiable exchange papers. The infrastructure of the United States–British West Indian information network did not change between 1816 and 1823, and news from Demerara reached American readers through thirty-one reports, which spread through fourteen identifiable exchanges of American newspapers. The change in the newspaper coverage lies in the extent of time editors devoted to the story of abolitionism and rebellion in the West Indies. In 1816, American editors continued coverage for as long as thirty-eight days (*Niles' Weekly Register*) to as few as twelve days (Charleston's *Mercury*), for an average news cycle of twenty-six days. In 1823, American newspapermen followed the rebellion for an average of ninety-seven days, more than three times as long, with coverage lasting as long as one hundred and sixty-five days in New York's *Evening Post,* to as little as the one lonely report offered by Henry Pinckney of the Charleston *Mercury.*[28]

The relative silence of the *Mercury* should not surprise us. The Denmark Vesey conspiracy had been discovered just a year before, and South Carolina was the only state that approximated the racial composition of the West Indies.[29] The *Mercury*'s sole report on the 1823 rebellion conveyed that a "Preacher" had been arrested and would probably be hung, but there was no discussion of the "Saints." The report ended on a sobering note for any slave or free black who harbored subversive ideas: "Many of the Negroes had been killed by the troops sent against them, and several executions had taken place."[30] The contrast of the *Mercury*'s sole report in 1823 with the intensification of newspaper coverage nationally from 1816 to 1823 can be attributed to three developments in the struggle over slavery in the United States: the emergence in the North of abolitionism (moderate though it was); the debates over the statehood of Missouri; and the Denmark Vesey Conspiracy, especially the white panic it created. While space does not allow for an exploration of these developments, two series of essays penned in 1823 and 1827 by Robert J. Turnbull shed light on their import.

Beginning in late August, 1823, Turnbull published in the *Mercury* a series of essays above the pseudonym "Caroliniensis." He leveled sharp, personal criticism at Supreme Court Justice (and Carolinian) William Johnson for publishing his obiter dictum on South Carolina's Negro Seamen

Laws. The laws had been passed as a response to the Vesey Conspiracy, but in July 1823 they faced a challenge in the Supreme Court when the British consul in Charleston sued for a writ of habeus corpus on behalf of Henry Elkison, a free black Jamaican sailor who had been arrested on his arrival in Charleston port. Johnson dismissed the suit on a legal technicality (the Negro Seaman Laws were state laws, and as a federal judge he did not have jurisdiction), but Johnson nevertheless argued that the laws were unconstitutional and should be revised. Johnson caused quite a sensation when he read his opinion from the bench and had it published as a pamphlet. Robert Turnbull was the key author of the Negro Seaman Laws, and his response to Johnson's critique revealed the powerful influence of recent Caribbean history.[31]

Central to Turnbull's argument was the Edwards thesis on slave rebellion. In light of the "occurrences of the past summer," Turnbull argued, Johnson should not have published his opinion. Writers in a slave society must be wary of ideas that were "liable from the very nature of [their] subject, to be misunderstood by one class of our population." This was particularly true for their own moment in history, when the careful observer could see "the progress of opinions in other countries on this subject . . . societies, and plans . . . striking at the vital interests of the States of the South." The danger was nowhere more apparent than in the West Indies, where "the colonial interests of the British Empire [were] about to be immolated on the altars of folly . . . surrendered to the fanaticism of a thousand Wilberforces." And was Johnson not aware that this "self same spirit" was abroad in his own country? "Go over the sections of this confederacy," Turnbull suggested, and Johnson would realize that "fanaticism, false charity, fashionable humanity . . . are in dreadful operation, and array against the State, which gave him birth."[32]

Turnbull accused Johnson of risking insurrection in Charleston by printing his pamphlet. He conceded that the framers of South Carolina's constitution had not excluded free black seamen, but argued that developments over the last twenty years had transformed the slaveholding world. The fundamental issue was not a matter of legal precedent; it was a matter of the safety of the white population. At the moment of independence, "there were then afloat no doctrines of African emancipation . . . the *Abolition Society* of Philadelphia, the *British Association* in London, and the *Amis des Noirs* in Paris, had not yet formed . . . and the Abbé Gregoire had not written that celebrated letter, which was afterwards the torch, which lighted up the insurrection of St. Domingo."[33] Turnbull warned his readership that South Carolina must keep in mind the recent past and not forget the lessons of former generations. His account came straight from Edwards's *Historical Survey,* but Turnbull blended this familiar history with the recent organization of the Pennsylvania Abolition Society to warn his readers of the current threats that faced South Carolina. The parallels were profoundly disturbing. French Saint-Domingue had been sacrificed by the abolitionists in Paris; the British West Indies were under mortal threat from abolitionists in London; and abolitionists were on the move in Philadelphia. Fanatical abolitionism had emerged on both sides of the Atlantic, and the South was threatened by potential insurrections.[34]

In response to trans-Atlantic abolitionism and its demonstrated effects, Turnbull developed the rationale by which South Carolina could exert power in its own right as a sovereign state in order to protect its interests, despite the possibility that this action might conflict with the policy or law of the federal government. The threat was clear enough. Abolitionist ideas were afloat, free blacks were known to disseminate abolitionist ideas, and slave rebellions were known to result. As a sovereign state, South Carolina had the right to "self-preservation," a political truth attested by the great political philosophers, of whom Turnbull cited Vattel, Grotius, and Pufendorf, who had all defended slavery as well. He quoted specifically from Vattel: "A nation or state has a right to every thing which can secure it *from threatening danger, and to keep at a distance whatever is capable of causing its ruin*" (italics in the original). The emphasis alluded to free black seamen, of course, and the Negro Seamen Act that kept them "at a distance," beyond the earshot of South Carolina's slaves. But the political concept at the heart of this law, and Turnbull's argument, was that South Carolina could act in any way it wished on the question of slavery and abolitionism.[35]

Caroliniensis echoed the lessons of Bryan Edwards, the reports from Barbados, and the panic of Charleston in the summer of 1822. But during the summer of 1827 Turnbull published another series of essays, *The Crisis,* which reflected the persistence of West Indian tumult and the example it posed for slaveholders in the United States. Turnbull compared the colonial relationship between the West Indies and Parliament to the relation between the Southern states and the federal government. The "unfortunate fate of the people of the West Indies may be our lot," he wrote, if the southern states did not assert their power as "Sovereign and Independent States." If the South remained "patient and submissive before Congress," their similarities with the "weak colonists" in the British Caribbean would become painfully evident.[36] With rhetoric that foreshadowed the fire-eaters of later decades, Turnbull warned the South that one potential future of their section of the country was visible in the ruins of the British West Indian colonies. In Turnbull's estimation the abolitionism manifested in the North posed the direst threat to the slaveholding states. He mentioned by name Benjamin Lundy's *Genius of Universal Emancipation,* which he mistakenly located in New York, and an unnamed paper recently established in Philadelphia. "Sooner or later," he predicted, emancipation would be discussed in the halls of Congress, giving Congress the opportunity "officially to express its opinion against slavery as an evil, and the profession of a desire to eradicate it from the land." The dissemination of such opinions filled Turnbull with the "DEEPEST apprehensions," as he feared the "discontent and uneasiness which might thereby be produced in the minds of those, who are now contented and happy."[37] Any discussion of slavery in Congress would cause "DEATH and DESTRUCTION" in the South. Turnbull made an ominous prediction: "Discussion will be equivalent to an act of emancipation, for it will universally inspire [that hope] amongst the slaves. It will be to teach the slave, that for a gradual amelioration of his condition, he is not to look to his master . . . but . . . to Congress alone." After all, it had been "the discussions in the British Parliament, which have caused from time to time, the insurrectionary movements in the West Indies, and brought the colonists from wealth to despondence, and from despondence almost to despair; and it will be discussion of the subject by Congress, which will bring us, one and all, to complete ruin."[38] Repeating the lessons of Bryan Edwards, which had reappeared for a broad audience in newspaper reports of the rebellions of 1816 and 1823, Turnbull endowed mere "discussion" with the ability to *cause* a slave rebellion.

The insurrections of 1831 brought the Anglo-Atlantic world of slavery and abolitionism to a tipping point. We have already observed the assumptions of Governor John Floyd on the origins of the rebellion in Southampton, Virginia. As the news of Nat Turner gave way to stories from Richmond on the historic debates on the gradual abolition of Old Dominion slavery, news reports of insurrection in Jamaica began to arrive in Atlantic ports. Most newspapers began coverage of the slave revolt in Jamaica in late January 1832 when their readers learned of an "insurrection among the slaves of the island" that had resulted in the establishment of martial law. By the next month the whole island was reported "in confusion," and the next weeks' papers saw Jamaica's plight as serious indeed. While "the leaders in the late insurrection ha[d] principally been taken, and great numbers executed . . . more than five hundred had fled to the mountains, and were still in a state of rebellion." The rebellion at its peak, Americans learned, had involved "thirty thousand [armed] negroes . . . two thousand [of whom] had been killed [and] who had destroyed the entire stock of one hundred and fifty plantations . . . valued at *fifteen millions of dollars."*[39]

The reports made it clear that Jamaican planters blamed the missionaries, whom they took to be abolitionist proxies. The proclamation of Major General Willoughby Cotton to the rebels, for example, was widely reprinted in American newspapers. Cotton led the military effort against the rebellion, and he demanded that the rebels return to the plantations, asserting that "wicked persons have told you that the King has made you free. . . . I come among you to tell you, you are misled." Reports made it clear that those "wicked persons" were the missionaries. A letter from a Kingston merchant written to a correspondent in New York and reprinted in New York's *Gazette* and Baltimore's *Patriot* argued that most Jamaican planters "ascribe the revolt to the seditious and rebellious conduct on the part of the Baptist and Methodist Missionaries, sent among us by the infernal Anti-Colonial Society of the Mother Country." There was no "Anti-Colonial Society," of course, but for Jamaican planters "anti-slavery" had precisely the same meaning. When the Jamaican Assembly made its report to Parliament on the causes and effects of the rebellion, it attributed the insurrection to "the measures of the parent government in favor of the slaves, and the conduct of the missionaries."[40]

Coming after Haiti, Barbados, Charleston, and Demerara, the Virginia and Jamaica rebellions now gave American slaveholders evidence that abolitionist agitation led to insurrection. Moreover, this news spread throughout the United States with great breadth. American editors devoted much more attention to the insurrection in Jamaica than they had to the rebellions in Barbados and Demerara. Thirty-nine reports of the insurrection appeared in the newspapers studied, and editors followed the news from Jamaica for a significantly longer period of time, averaging 148 days, almost two months longer than the Demerara rebellion had been covered in 1823. Moreover, many papers also followed the impact of the rebellion into Parliament, where debates on the rebellion led to debates on abolition.[41]

Sectional difference in American coverage of West Indian rebellions had been evident in 1823 with the exceptionally sparse coverage of the Charleston's *Mercury*. In 1832, as the South still reeled from the reports from Southampton, the sectional distinction was far deeper. Southern papers *began* with the news that "tranquility" had been restored, and Thomas Ritchie's *Enquirer* and the *Maryland Gazette* printed only one report on the rebellion. While Ritchie simply cataloged the destruction of property and slaves, the *Gazette* noted the similarity to the rebellion in Southampton, reporting that "a negro preacher was at the head of the whole plot." The *Mercury* dismissed the rebellion as "local disturbances" in its first report, in February, and only returned to the story in April to report on the Jamaican Assembly's determination to resist the abolitionism of Parliament. Such limited coverage was certainly due to fear of the possible spread of rebellious tendencies by word of mouth, via the newspapers.[42]

Three years later, Henry Pickney's resolutions placing a gag on abolitionist petitions to Congress won easy majorities and, as we have seen, Hammond's emphasis on the connection between abolitionism and insurrection was retained. Abolitionism had grown in the North despite the warnings of a series of rebellions. For white Southerners, control over the flow of news in their own localities—as exercised in Richmond and Charleston—was no longer adequate. Abolitionism had to be silenced at the national level.

Hammond had learned this lesson from Bryan Edwards, Robert Turnbull, and a concerned reading of the newspaper reports from the Caribbean. But the dangerous link between abolitionism and rebellion had also been reported in the Northern press, and evidence suggests white Northerners absorbed the same lesson. An anti-abolitionist broadside printed in 1835 in Hartford, Connecticut, for example, condemned the "rash and reckless measures" of the abolitionists, which threatened the South with "the evils and horrors of insurrection, massacre, and a servile war." In a similar condemnation of the abolitionists, a "subscribers" statement from South Kingston, Rhode Island, found in the papers of the Democrat Elisha R. Potter Jr., claimed that abolitionist agitation had "the tendency to excite . . . insurrection on the part of the slaves and will perhaps result in a war of extermination." Martin Van Buren, in his famous letter to the North Carolina committee describing his position on slavery in Washington, D.C., accepted the Southern belief that abolitionist petitions had "the tendency to provoke a general assassination of the white population in the Slaveholding States." Among Northern Democrats, the slaveholders' claim that abolitionist agitation led to insurrection had become the dominant public opinion. The gag rule represented a democratic response to this dangerous public issue.[43]

Newspaper coverage of Caribbean slave rebellions cultivated the opinion-formation process described by Habermas and shaped the beliefs of Americans throughout the country about the relationship between abolitionist agitation and slave rebellion. Carolinians such as Hammond were naturally most affected by this belief, as their own lives and livelihoods were directly subject to the ramifications of this connection. But Northerners such as

Van Buren, and those who expressed their opinion in Hartford, Connecticut, and South Kingston, Rhode Island, also accepted the connection between abolitionism and rebellion, even though their own lives were not threatened. Thus, even though the constitutional right to petition was clearly undermined by the gag rule, enough Northern congressmen believed that Southern slaveholders had a very good reason to treat abolitionist petitions differently than all others: abolitionist petitions could be deadly. If white Northerners allowed abolitionism to flourish, insurrections would terrorize the South and Southerners would have no choice but to break their ties to the Union as a matter of self-preservation. As the select committee argued, the choice at hand was to "determine between the suppression of abolition, and the destruction of the Union." Patriotism demanded the suppression of abolitionism.[44]

The process of will-formation that resulted in the gag rule, then, was shaped by a process of opinion-formation. The insurrections of 1831, British abolition in 1833, and the abolitionist petition drive of 1835 had been the precipitant events that brought the issue to the surface, but opinion-formation about abolitionism had gradually unfolded over a period of about forty years, beginning with the first interpretations of the Haitian Revolution. There was more to Northern support of the gag rule than party ties. Through books and newspapers, the proslavery understanding of abolitionism had spread from the Caribbean throughout the United States, shaping the next phase of the trans-Atlantic struggle over slavery.

NOTES

I would like to thank the editors, Matt Mason and John Craig Hammond, as well as David Gellman, for their close reading and commentary on this essay. The arguments expressed here receive fuller treatment in Edward B. Rugemer, *The Problem of Emancipation: The Caribbean Roots of the American Civil War* (Baton Rouge: Louisiana State University Press, 2008).

1. *Register of Debates*, 24th Cong., 1st sess., 1966–91.

2. *Register of Debates*, 24th Cong., 1st sess., 2448–62 (quotation at 2456). See also *Remarks of Mr. Hammond of South Carolina on the Question of Receiving Petitions for the Abolition of Slavery in the District of Columbia* (Washington City: Duff Green, 1836), 12. Richard Newman has investigated the origins of a similar gag in the first Congress in 1790. But in this period before the Haitian Revolution, Southerners never deployed the argument that antislavery petitions would cause slave insurrections; only constitutional arguments were made (see Richard S. Newman, "Prelude to the Gag Rule: Southern Reaction to Antislavery Petitions in the First Federal Congress," *Journal of the Early Republic* 16 [Winter 1996]: 571–99).

3. *Register of Debates*, 24th Cong., 1st sess., appendix, 104, 111. The committee included Henry L. Pinckney (S.C.), Thomas L. Hamer (Ohio), Franklin Pierce (N.H.), Benjamin Hardin

(Ky.), Leonard Jarvis (Maine), George W. Owens (Ga.), Henry A. Muhlenberg (Penn.), George C. Dromgoole (Va.), and Joel Turrill (N.Y.). All were Democrats, except for Pinckney, who was elected on the Nullification ticket, and Hardin, who identified with the opposition to Jackson. Party affiliations for members of Congress can be searched at http://bioguide.congress.gov/biosearch/biosearch.asp.

4. Russel B. Nye, *Fettered Freedom: A Discussion of Civil Liberties and the Slavery Controversy in the United States, 1830–1860* (East Lansing: Michigan State College Press, 1949), 33, 58–59, 61 (quotation); William Shade, "The Most Delicate and Exciting Topic": Martin Van Buren, Slavery, and the Election of 1836," *Journal of the Early Republic* 18 (Autumn 1998): 475; Charles Sellers, *The Market Revolution: Jacksonian America, 1815–1846* (New York: Oxford University Press, 1991), 403; Leonard L. Richards, *The Slave Power: The Free North and Southern Domination, 1780–1860* (Baton Rouge: Louisiana State University Press, 2000), 129; Sean Wilentz, *The Rise of American Democracy: Jefferson to Lincoln* (New York: W. W. Norton, 2005), 451; Daniel Walker Howe, *What Hath God Wrought: The Transformation of America, 1815–1848* (New York: Oxford University Press, 2007), 513.

5. William Lee Miller, *Arguing about Slavery: The Great Battle in the United States Congress* (New York: Knopf, 1996), 29–30; William W. Freehling, *Prelude to Civil War: The Nullification Controversy in South Carolina, 1816–1836* (New York: Harper and Row, 1965). In his *Road to Disunion,* vol. 1, *Secessionists at Bay, 1776–1854* (New York: Oxford University Press, 1990), Freehling narrows his argument to the fear inspired by Denmark Vesey and Nat Turner, excluding Caribbean influences. He has also clearly demonstrated that Hammond acted on his own (see especially 308–36).

6. I have explored the historical links between agitation and rebellion in Rugemer, *The Problem of Emancipation,* chaps. 2–4. For the impact of African American resistance to slavery in an earlier period, see Matthew Mason, *Slavery and Politics in the Early American Republic* (Chapel Hill: University of North Carolina Press, 2006), chap. 5.

7. Jürgen Habermas, *Between Facts and Norms: Contributions to a Discourse Theory of Law and Democracy,* trans. William Rehg (Cambridge, Mass.: MIT Press, 1996), 171, 179 (quotation), 306–7, 362–63. John Brooke's essays on Habermas are particularly helpful; see "Reason and Passion in the Public Sphere: Habermas and the Cultural Historians," *Journal of Interdisciplinary History* 29 (Summer 1998): 43–67; and "Consent, Civil Society, and the Public Sphere in the Age of Revolution and the Early Republic," in *Beyond the Founders: New Approaches to the Political History of the Early American Republic,* ed. Jeffrey L. Pasley, Andrew W. Robertson, and David Waldstreicher (Chapel Hill: University of North Carolina Press, 2004): 207–50.

8. "Excerpts from the Diary of Virginia Governor John Floyd, 1831–1832," reprinted in *The Confessions of Nat Turner and Related Documents,* ed. Kenneth S. Greenberg (Boston: Bedford, 1996), 110. Isaac Knapp was a Boston publisher who often worked with Garrison.

9. *A Particular Account of the Commencement and Progress of the Insurrection of the Negroes in St. Domingo, which began in August, 1791: Being a Translation of the Speech Made to the National Assembly, the 3d of November, 1791 by the Deputies from the General Assembly of the French Part of St. Domingo,* 2nd ed. (London, 1792). See also Lowell B. Ragatz, *The Fall of the Planter Class in the British Caribbean, 1763–1833* (New York, 1933), 268. A variation on the accusations of Saint-Dominguan slaveholders—blaming William Wilberforce for the insurrection—filtered into the New York press from London as early as 1792; see David Gell-

man, *Emancipating New York: The Politics of Slavery and Freedom, 1777–1827* (Baton Rouge: Louisiana State University Press, 2006), 133.

10. For more on Edwards, see Olwyn M. Blouet, "Bryan Edwards and the Haitian Revolution," in *The Impact of the Haitian Revolution in the Atlantic World,* ed. David Geggus (Columbia: University of South Carolina Press, 2001): 44–57.

11. Bryan Edwards, *An Historical Survey of the French Colony in the Island of St. Domingo,* vol. 4 of his *The History, Civil and Commercial, of the British Colonies in the West Indies,* 4 vols. (Philadelphia: Printed and Sold by James Humphreys, 1806), xv–xvi (quotation); see also ibid., 9, 65–69.

12. Ibid., 89; Christopher L. Brown, *Moral Capital: Foundations of British Abolitionism* (Chapel Hill: University of North Carolina, 2006). For intriguing evidence of an antislavery interpretation of the Haitian Revolution that points toward the end of slavery rather than its perpetuation, see Gellman, *Emancipating New York,* 140–44.

13. Both Murray and the *Herald* are quoted from Winthrop D. Jordan, *White Over Black: American Attitudes Toward the Negro, 1550–1812* (Chapel Hill: University of North Carolina Press, 1968), 395–96. For more on the connections between Gabriel's Rebellion and the election of 1800, see Douglas R. Egerton, *Gabriel's Rebellion: The Virginia Slave Conspiracies of 1800 and 1802* (Chapel Hill: University of North Carolina Press, 1993), chap. 3.

14. *Freeman's Banner* (Baltimore), 14 April 1832; F. Lee Benns, *The American Struggle for the British West India Carrying Trade, 1815–1830* (1923; repr., Clifton, N.J.: Augustus M. Kelley, 1972), 46–188.

15. Charles E. Clark, "Early American Journalism: News and Opinion in the Popular Press," in *The Colonial Book in the Atlantic World,* ed. Hugh Amory and David D. Hall (Cambridge: Cambridge University Press, 2000), 354–55.

16. Richard John, *Spreading the News: The American Postal System from Franklin to Morse* (Cambridge, Mass.: Harvard University Press, 1995), 36–37; Alexander de Toqueville, *Democracy in America,* 2 vols. (1840; repr., New York: Vintage, 1990), 2:111.

17. Achille Murat, *The United States of North America* (London: Effingham Wilson, 1833), 63.

18. *Evening Post* (New York), 11 May 1816.

19. *Commercial Advertiser* (New York), 27 May 1816.

20. *Commercial Advertiser* (New York), 26 June 1816; *Daily National Intelligencer* (Washington, D.C.), 24 June 1816; *Enquirer* (Richmond), 16 July 1816.

21. Quoted in *Niles' Weekly Register,* 1 June 1816; and in the *Daily National Intelligencer* (Washington, D.C.), 31 May 1816. Both papers cite the *Enquirer* (Richmond), but the particular issue in which this writing appeared has not survived. As exchange papers, these three newspapers were used by editors throughout the country. For more on Dunmore's proclamation, see Benjamin Quarles, *The Negro in the American Revolution* (1961; repr., New York: W. W. Norton, 1973), 19–32. It is also possible that Ritchie alluded to the War of 1812, when Britain again protected runaway slaves and made some into soldiers in the West Indian regiments (see Frank A. Cassell, "Slaves of the Chesapeake Bay Area and the War of 1812," *Journal of Negro History* 57 [April 1972]: 144–55).

22. Pauline Maier, *American Scripture: Making the Declaration of Independence* (New York: Knopf, 1997), 177.

23. *Niles' Weekly Register,* 11 October 1823; *Enquirer* (Richmond), 7 October 1823; *Christian Repository* (Wilmington, Del.), 10 October 1823; *Evening Post* (New York), 8 October 1823.

24. *American & Commercial Advertiser* (Baltimore), 16 October 1823; *Albion* (New York), 18 October 1823; *Enquirer* (Richmond), 24 October 1823.

25. *Niles' Weekly Register,* 29 November 1823.

26. *Enquirer* (Richmond), 16 December 1823, reprinted from the *Patriot* (Charleston).

27. *Enquirer* (Richmond), 20 December 1823.

28. Few newspapers in the early republic enjoyed longevity, making systematic analysis of the change in press coverage difficult. The newspapers chosen to analyze American press coverage of the rebellions represent influential regions or editors in the United States during this period. For the rebellion in Barbados, the following newspapers were thoroughly investigated from 1 May 1816 to the end of that year: *Niles' Weekly Register,* the *City Gazette & Commercial Advertiser* (Charleston), the *Evening Post* (New York), the *Enquirer* (Richmond), and the *Daily National Intelligencer* (Washington, D.C.). For the rebellion in Demerara, the following newspapers were thoroughly investigated from 1 July 1823 to the end of that year: *Niles' Weekly Register,* the *American & Commercial Daily Advertiser* (Baltimore), the *Mercury* (Charleston), the *Evening Post* (New York), and the *Enquirer* (Richmond).

29. Lacy Ford, *Origins of Southern Radicalism: The South Carolina Upcountry, 1800–1860* (New York: Oxford University Press, 1988), 123. In the Low Country parishes, blacks could exceed 90 percent of the population. The South Carolina press had also neglected to cover Gabriel's Rebellion in 1800 (see Jordan, *White Over Black,* 395).

30. *Mercury* (Charleston), 9 October 1823.

31. Alan F. January, "The South Carolina Association: An Agency for Race Control in Antebellum Charleston," *South Carolina Historical Magazine* 78 (July 1977): 194–97.

32. [Robert J. Turnbull and Isaac Edward Holmes], *Caroliniensis* (Charleston: A. E. Miller, [1824]), 20, 24, 40.

33. Ibid., 45.

34. On the Pennsylvania Abolition Society, see Richard S. Newman, *The Transformation of American Abolitionism: Fighting Slavery in the Early Republic* (Chapel Hill: University of North Carolina Press, 2002), 39–59.

35. Turnbull and Holmes, *Caroliniensis,* 40.

36. *The Crisis,* 128–29.

37. [Robert Turnbull], writing in *The Crisis,* 13, 121, 129. Lundy's paper was printed in Baltimore.

38. Ibid., 132.

39. Quotations are from some of the earliest reports of the insurrection, several of which were widely reprinted in the United States. See, for example, the *Albion* (New York), 21 January 1832, and 18 and 25 February 1832; the *Recorder* (Boston), 15 February 1832; the *Statesman* (Boston), 28 January 1832, 25 February 1832; the *Mercury* (Charleston), 14 February 1832; the *Christian Advocate and Journal & Zion's Herald* (New York), 17 February 1832; the *Christian Watchman* (Boston), 27 January 1832, and 17 and 24 February 1832; the *Connecticut Courant* (Hartford), 24 January 1832, and 14, 21, and 28 February 1832; the *Enquirer* (Richmond), 24 February 1832; the *Mercury* (Newport, R.I.), 18 February 1832; *Niles' Weekly Register,* 11, 18, and 25 February 1832; the *Maryland Gazette* (Annapolis), 26 January 1832; and the *Vermont Gazette* (Bennington), 29 February 1832.

40. Willoughby's proclamation was quoted in the *Patriot & Mercantile Advertiser* (Baltimore), 7 February 1832; *Niles' Weekly Register,* 11 February 1832; and the *Connecticut Courant*

(Hartford), 14 February 1832. The letter in the *Gazette* (New York) was reprinted in the *Patriot & Mercantile Advertiser* (Baltimore), 25 February 1832. The Jamaica Assembly report was quoted in *Niles' Weekly Register*, 21 July 1832. For the role of the missionaries in the Jamaica insurrection, see Mary Turner, *Slaves and Missionaries: The Disintegration of Jamaican Slave Society, 1787–1834* (Urbana: University of Illinois Press, 1982).

41. These figures are based on a thorough investigation of the following papers for all of 1832: *Niles' Weekly Register*, the *Mercury* (Charleston), the *Evening Post* (New York), the *Enquirer* (Richmond), and the *Patriot & Mercantile Advertiser* (Baltimore).

42. *Enquirer* (Richmond), 24 February 1832; *Maryland Gazette* (Annapolis), 26 January 1832; *Mercury* (Charleston), 14 February 1832 and 2 April 1832.

43. "A Declaration of the Sentiments of the People of Hartford, Regarding the Measures of the Abolitionists, October 1835," Broadsides Collection, John Hay Library, Brown University, Providence, R.I.; "Abolition Paper" [South Kingstown, R.I., 22 January 1836], Elisha Reynolds Potter Jr. Papers, box 6, Rhode Island Historical Society, Providence, R.I.; Martin Van Buren to Junis Amis et al., 4 March 1836, *Martin Van Buren Papers* [microfilm] (Washington, D.C.: Library of Congress, 1960), reel 15, frame 5161.

44. *Register of Debates*, 24th Cong., 1st sess., appendix, 104.

PART II

The State and Slavery

Founding a Slaveholders' Union,
1770–1797

George William Van Cleve

During the Lincoln-Douglas debates of 1858, Abraham Lincoln argued that "our fathers" had created a Union whose Constitution and founding principles envisioned that slavery would be "placed . . . in the course of ultimate extinction" when possible. Stephen Douglas disagreed vehemently, and their epic contest over the issue resounded throughout the nation.[1] In our time, historians continue to debate both the validity of Lincoln's historical claim and slavery's implications for our understanding of the Revolution and early national history.[2] This essay argues that Lincoln's historical account of "the Founders'" intent was flawed. Some of them may well have wanted to set slavery on a course of ultimate extinction, but they lacked the power to achieve that end without compromising their far stronger desire to create a federal union that possessed sufficient power to govern a continent.

Historians of slavery agree that it played a central role in early American political development, but they disagree in some respects about precisely why this occurred. Some of them argue that the Declaration of Independence and the Constitution either supported abolition or were "open-ended" regarding slavery, a position not supported by the historical evidence. Others argue instead that many contemporaries did not intend the Declaration to apply to blacks or to end slavery, and that the Constitution was heavily "proslavery." They regard constitutional choices as having strongly influenced slavery's growth.[3]

But the "proslavery" Constitution historiography in turn raises methodological problems. Is it possible to identify a unitary Founders' intent on slavery? Different meanings have been ascribed to the term "proslavery." Undue emphasis on one set of events, such as the adoption of the Constitution, may mistakenly gloss over the remarkable divisiveness of slavery, which led to disputes about it that continued with varying force over many decades. Finally, the typical focus of historiography on the politics of slavery on American history, as opposed to British imperial history, leads to underestimation of slavery's "staying power" as an institution.

To avoid these methodological issues and provide a stronger foundation for understanding slavery's history, this essay examines continuity and change in the transition from British imperial support for slavery to a new American regime governing it during the formative era from 1770 to 1797. Revolutionary-era Americans made contested political choices that had fundamental implications for slavery. Abolition occurred at the state level where slavery was politically and economically marginal, but major slave states rejected abolition and instead sought slavery's expansion. During the same period, at the federal level Americans embraced a form of constitutional federalism far weaker than British parliamentary federalism; they rejected natural law as a basis for federal constitutional interpretation where slavery was concerned; and they agreed to treat slaves as property equivalent to other forms of property for important purposes such as compensation and fugitive rendition. These framework choices were important steps toward the creation of a "slaveholders' Union," that is, a union where protection of slavery was an integral part of law and governance. Instead of setting slavery on a "course of ultimate extinction," the new Union permitted it to expand markedly in the early republic.

British Slavery Policy on the Eve of the Revolution

During the eighteenth century, Britons were the world's largest slave traders, and slaveholders were a wealthy and powerful "interest" in the British empire. For most of the century, British law and policy viewed slaves primarily as a form of property. In addition to providing powerful military protection to slaveholders, Britain supported slavery by imposing uniform policies on it.[4] Due in part to British support, by 1770 there were about 470,000 slaves in mainland colonies and slavery was a major economic institution there. But British protection of slavery became increasingly controversial in the last third of the eighteenth century. Just before the American Revolution, the legality of slavery in England itself became a prominent issue. In response, Britain appeared poised to alter its policies in ways damaging to slavery.

 In 1729, the Crown's Law Officers had decided that slaves remained enslaved when they were brought to England, treating them as a form of "imperial," not just colonial, property. This was followed by a "sweeping statute" adopted in 1732 to protect British investors, which guaranteed uniform imperial treatment of slave property for debt-recovery purposes in

England and its colonies. Under that law, "Negroes" were explicitly declarea a form of property. Overriding all contrary colonial laws, creditors throughout the empire were given powerful remedies to protect their interests in such property. The evidence suggests that colonial slave imports expanded as a result.[5]

Under British policy, American colonies could not abolish slavery or prohibit slave imports. Various colonies, including Pennsylvania and Virginia during the 1760s and early 1770s, tried to limit or bar slave imports by taxing them heavily, but the Privy Council rejected those efforts. King George III specifically instructed his Governor General of Virginia in late 1770 not only to disallow any increase in slave import taxes but to veto any other proposed law "by which the Importation of Slaves shall be in any respect prohibited or obstructed." But just before the American Revolution, British imperial policy appeared to be on the verge of important changes adverse to slavery.[6]

In mid-1772, Lord Mansfield, Chief Justice of the English Court of King's Bench, freed a slave from captivity in the case of *Somerset v. Stewart*.[7] The case nominally involved the freedom of one slave from Virginia, James Somerset, who had unsuccessfully attempted to flee his owner, Charles Steuart (or Stewart), after being brought to England. But the Court was advised that as many as 14,000 blacks in English servitude might be affected by its decision. West Indian slaveholders' association attorneys (who controlled the Virginia slave owner's defense) vigorously asserted that it could also adversely affect colonial slavery. In the American colonies, twenty-two out of twenty-six operating newspapers for which a full year's editions survive reported arguments in the case, the decision, or both.[8] Although the precise legal significance of Mansfield's decision has been disputed, certain points about it are clear.

Mansfield conceived of a slave primarily as a person whose legal status was slavery, not as a form of property. Because slavery was a status, it could change as a slave moved from one jurisdiction to another. Mansfield held that Somerset's status in England was governed by English and not colonial law. The status concept of slavery rejected a major aspect of British policy created by the 1729 Law Officers' decision and supported by Mansfield's mentor, Lord Hardwicke. In 1749, as Lord Chancellor, Hardwicke had reaffirmed that colonial slave status did not change in England, in the course of a decision holding that English law itself authorized claims to recover slaves as a form of property.[9] Mansfield's decision devalued slave property by rejecting the idea that slavery had a uniform character throughout the empire.

Mansfield also concluded that slavery had no foundation in natural law, holding that it could be authorized solely by positive law (statute or very long-standing custom). Finally, Mansfield held in *Somerset* that English law did not permit anyone held in servitude to be taken forcibly out of the country. If colonists possessed English rights (as they increasingly asserted), the decision implied that a fugitive slave could not legally be recaptured by a slave owner unless the positive law of the colony to which the slave had fled specifically permitted the slave to be recaptured. This meant that in some cases successful flight might transform a colonial slave into a free person, an alarming prospect for slave owners.

Mansfield's decision adopted a federalist approach for slavery, implying that slavery could be made legal in colonies through positive law though unauthorized in England. But Mansfield's decision also removed any doubt that if Parliament chose to end the slave trade or colonial slavery, it could do so. Under Mansfield's reasoning, colonial slaveholders could not argue that their property or contract rights prevented such action.[10] The political impact of *Somerset* spread throughout the empire. Although many historians conclude that it was intended only to apply to slavery in England, the decision ignited a substantial controversy in the American colonies. Colonists from Massachusetts to South Carolina thought that *Somerset*'s principles might well bar slavery in their colonies.[11]

Attorneys in Massachusetts quickly asserted in slave freedom lawsuits that *Somerset* barred slavery there. They contended that residents of Massachusetts possessed English rights, and thus that slavery was illegal there since no statute authorized it. In Pennsylvania, Benjamin Rush wrote a widely circulated pamphlet arguing that *Somerset* meant that England was about to change its policy to oppose slavery. Meanwhile, a pamphleteer in South Carolina asserted that it would be disastrous if South Carolinians continued to assert that they possessed English rights, because this meant that the *Somerset* decision would apply to the colony, threatening slave property.[12]

Slave owners and their representatives attacked the decision in pamphlets and newspapers, not just in England and the West Indies, but in Rhode Island, Connecticut, New York, Massachusetts, and Virginia. Some claimed that it would ruin "our African Trade." Others argued that it would occasion "a greater ferment in America (particularly the islands) than the Stamp Act," because of the instability in property rights it would create. Still others heatedly attacked the decision for disregarding established property rights by varying them according to "climate" (jurisdiction).[13]

Henry Marchant, a prominent Rhode Island attorney, represented a slave purchaser there in a heavily contested slave freedom suit pending at the time of *Somerset*. In 1771, Marchant went to London as Rhode Island's colonial agent. He concluded, after he attended a key London court hearing in the *Somerset* case, that the arguments made for Somerset's freedom in England would apply equally well in the colonies. Marchant's conclusion would have been deeply disturbing to any American slave owner.[14]

The *Somerset* decision divided Americans just before the Revolution. While it encouraged antislavery activity in Northern states, slave owners were concerned about future British policy after *Somerset*. They thought that the decision abandoned key aspects of Britain's support for slavery, and strongly challenged others. During and after the Revolution, Americans debated whether to adopt British government principles, including *Somerset*'s conception of slavery as a status. Slaveholders' representatives were deeply involved in such debates. Often acting in response to slaveholder concerns, Americans made choices about federalism, natural law, and property rights that strengthened slavery in the new Union. At the same time, the major slave states rejected abolition.

AMERICAN FEDERALISM, SLAVERY, AND ABOLITION, 1770–1797

Slavery was lawful in each of the American colonies when the Revolution began. Many Americans were willing to reconsider slavery's status in individual states. But this did not happen at the federal level; instead, federal power over slavery was limited from the Articles of Confederation onward. Some historians suggest that this occurred because of slavery's established legal status, but it appears that political factors played a predominant role.[15]

Federalism was a central principle of both the Articles of Confederation and the Constitution. The Constitution's version of federalism divided authority between levels of government and reinforced that division by giving states political representation in the Senate. Constitutional federalism was in part a result of the strongly held belief that maintaining the strength of local government would protect freedom against possible central government tyranny. But federalism was also a virtue born of political necessity. Federalism permitted constitutional drafters to avoid very divisive, indeed probably unresolvable, disputes between the states over a variety of controversial social issues, such as the separation of church and state, the extent of suffrage, and slavery. In the case of slavery, federalism also constituted an effort to finesse persistent sectional political divisions.[16]

No Union would have been possible unless federalism had been applied to slavery. This was evident from the Confederation's experience. Sectional divisions over slavery prevented it from creating even a workable taxation system. In 1785, Congress had rejected without debate efforts to legislate nationwide against slave imports based on objections by "southern and eastern" congressmen.[17]

However, American federalism differed radically from British "imperial federalism," because under American federalism Congress had limited powers over slavery, unlike Parliament. The Constitution's slave wealth representation and enumerated powers provisions strongly buttressed its federalism regarding slavery. Constitutional protections for slavery were also insulated against change by a powerful sectional veto, since amendments could be prevented by a slave state bloc. From the outset, American federalism provided substantial legal and political protection to slavery that would not have been available within the British empire, especially after *Somerset*.

American federalism also strongly favored slavery in practice, despite its nominal neutrality (states could abolish slavery if they chose). The fundamental result of applying federalism to American slavery was to leave the major slave states, which collectively had contained 87 percent of the 1770 slave population, free to maintain and expand slavery for a generation after the Revolution. None of the major slave states chose to begin gradual abolition during the Revolutionary era, and they supported its expansion instead.

Most states north of the Mason-Dixon Line had begun gradual abolition of slavery by 1797, and the remaining Northern states would soon follow. The overall effects of state abolition efforts were limited. On the positive side, the combined actions of states that undertook gradual abolition or liberalized manumission during the formative era freed about 11 percent of the total American black population in 1800. But from 1770 to 1800, the slave population nearly doubled, growing to almost 900,000. By 1797, if not earlier, it became clear that major slave states had no plans for gradual abolition, as shown by the 1790 congressional slavery debate and by events in Virginia, the largest slave state at the time.[18]

The intense 1790 congressional debate about federal power to control slavery ended by confirming, and indeed strengthening, the Constitution's federalism on that issue, construing the federal government's powers (as opposed to state authority) very narrowly. But the debate also demonstrated that abolition would not occur in several major slave states in the foreseeable future. Representatives of the Deep South states made unmistakably clear that their states were committed to slavery. They vigorously asserted that their states had a constitutional right to continue and to expand slavery. They contended that the Constitution would never have been agreed to if it had not sufficiently protected slavery. And they made many of the affirmative "proslavery" arguments in favor of maintaining slavery that became more prominent in American political discourse from the 1830s onward. These congressmen ridiculed claims by Northern representatives that the Declaration of Independence had been intended to lead to the abolition of slavery. They challenged antislavery congressmen to demonstrate how the new country could afford to buy out slave owners or to colonize the rapidly growing slave population, and found no takers.[19]

Virginians' actions in the 1790s confirmed that the Deep South was not alone in its continued commitment to slavery. In part because Virginia had taken the lead in liberalizing its slave manumission law in 1782, it was commonly thought of as the most progressive of the major slave states on slavery issues. However, a careful recent study provides strong evidence that liberalized manumission in Virginia did not portend abolition there. It shows that post-Revolutionary Virginia manumissions were "many fewer" than previously estimated. Manumissions motivated by antislavery sentiment (as opposed to economic reasons) fell off sharply by the early 1790s, more than a decade before Virginia law began to force curtailment of manumission. The study concludes that "on the whole white Virginians remained committed to" slavery throughout the eighteenth century. Slave manumission did not pose a significant threat to the continuation of slavery there. Contemporaneous political developments support those conclusions.[20]

In 1797, the Virginia legislature rejected without debate an important gradual abolition proposal made by a prominent judge, St. George Tucker. Tucker's proposal was remarkably progressive because it was designed to result in abolition without colonization, which Tucker believed was both wholly impracticable and inhumane. After its rejection, he wrote bitterly that his proposal had been defeated by the "blind fury of the enemies of freedom," and that he had no hopes that Virginia would move toward gradual abolition in the foreseeable future. The offhanded rejection of Tucker's proposal demonstrated that whatever the level of "conditional antislavery" sentiment and rhetoric in Virginia had been in the early 1780s, both had weakened markedly since then. At this time, Virginians also changed their laws to impede antislavery forces' efforts to aid slaves' freedom claims in court. Other slave states were unlikely to abolish slavery after Virginia declined even to debate the issue.[21]

Federalism also had important effects on slavery's expansion. From the outset, it affected how citizens thought about the bonds created by the Union. During the constitutional ratification debate in Massachusetts, citizens vigorously debated slavery's relation to the Union. Anti-federalists argued that the Constitution should be rejected because it would require citizens to enter into a union with evil slaveholders. Federalists contended in response that the Constitution was a political and not a moral union: "Their [the South's] consciences are their own, tho' their wealth and strength be blended with ours." They also argued that the view that the Union needed to satisfy moral criteria on slavery had no historical foundation, since Massachusetts had allied with slaveholding jurisdictions such as France. Despite this anti-federalist attack, Massachusetts narrowly ratified the Constitution.[22]

Finally, federalism became the foundation of the "equal footing" doctrine, which protected slavery's expansion. In the late eighteenth century, there was a conflict within American political thought between the Jeffersonian Republican position that political rights were collective rights, and the view that such rights were individual rights.[23] For Jeffersonians, the citizens of states had a right to determine collectively their political destiny on various matters, including slavery. Leaders such as Thomas Jefferson and James Madison sought to extend federalism to the creation of new political communities. They argued that new territories and states should enter the Union on an equal footing with the original states. Because each new jurisdiction had the right to decide its own political fate, it could not be dictated to by Congress on an issue such as slavery.[24]

By the late 1790s, with Congress's acquiescence, slavery was spreading rapidly to the West in new slave territories and slave states. By 1800, there were more than 50,000 slaves in Kentucky and Tennessee alone, or more than the entire 1770 slave population in all of the Northern states combined. During the formative era, slavery grew sufficiently through natural increase, imports, and territorial acquisitions to neutralize any adverse effects of the 1808 federal slave import prohibition on its ability to expand further. Northern state opposition to slavery's western expansion before 1800 was either limited or ineffectual.[25]

NATURAL RIGHTS AND POSITIVE LAW

A second important area where Americans were divided about a principle central to Mansfield's *Somerset* decision was the proper relationship between natural law and natural rights, on the one hand, and positive law (including written constitutions), on the other. Under the dominant tradition in British law, positive law, such as parliamentary statutes, could "trump" natural law. Before the Revolution, Americans such as James Otis had contended instead that natural law should always govern both constitutions and laws. Particularly after *Somerset* held that slavery was contrary to natural law, their view had important implications for slavery.

Natural rights thought influenced certain areas of early American law, such as contract and property law. More broadly, some Founding-generation leaders thought that Nature rather than History should be a guide to political action as well as law, rejecting the traditional reliance of British constitutional law and policy on historical precedent and custom. Some scholars argue that the natural law tradition also applied to slavery.[26]

But at least where slavery was concerned, the evidence suggests that early Americans were sharply divided on the proper relationship between natural law and positive law. It also suggests that natural law advocates were not politically strong enough to incorporate their views explicitly into the Constitution itself where slavery was concerned through some form of rights declaration. As a result, many contemporaries thought that the Constitution derived its authority over slavery only from the republican principle of popular sovereignty, not from natural law. This becomes clear if one traces the course of the debate over natural rights and slavery from the controversy over the Virginia Declaration of Rights of 1776 through the drafting of the Constitution and early republic court decisions on slavery.

Virginia's Declaration of Rights reflected slavery's powerful influence. In the Declaration's preamble, its drafters had originally asserted that "all men are by nature equally free and independent" and that consequently all men possessed certain rights—such as life, liberty, and property. But several leaders objected to this language. They asked, "Why couldn't this same language be used by slaves to claim their freedom?" Why couldn't it also be used to demand universal suffrage for all men—or even women, for that matter? In response, the Virginia legislature—at Edmund Pendleton's suggestion—qualified the idea that rights could not be alienated, providing that men could not alienate rights "when they enter into a state of society." This provision was apparently intended to exclude slaves (and perhaps women) from the coverage of the rights provisions. The drafters of the Declaration also acknowledged that positive law could supersede their statement of natural rights (though this would be unjust, they said). The final Declaration appeared to be a retreat from British philosopher John Locke's view that rights were inherent and unalienable, instead recognizing popular will as a governing republican principle.[27]

In the 1780s, the Massachusetts courts faced a similar question about the relation between slavery and that state's constitutional "free and equal" clause. Although historians disagree about precisely how abolition occurred in Massachusetts, one view is that slavery was abolished in 1783 by a court decision that the "free and equal" clause of the state constitution necessarily meant that slavery could not exist there.[28] The intimate connection between "free and equal" declarations like those in Virginia and Massachusetts and the legal status of slavery meant that slavery would pose an inexorable obstacle to any effort to include a declaration of rights like that contained in the Declaration of Independence in the 1787 federal Constitution.

At the 1787 Constitutional Convention in Philadelphia, delegates Edmund Randolph of Virginia and John Rutledge of South Carolina opposed inclusion of any natural rights statement in the Constitution. Randolph and Rutledge played leading roles in defending the interests of slave states. As members of the convention's Committee of Detail, which produced the first draft of the Constitution, they argued that its preamble should avoid the type of general statements of "natural rights of men not yet gathered into society" found in the "the first formation of state governments." In light of their vigorous efforts to protect slavery, their argument can appropriately be viewed as in part an attempt to finesse a potentially irresolvable conflict over how such a rights statement would affect slavery. The Randolph-Rutledge position prevailed; the Constitution as adopted lacked any rights statement.[29]

A candid explanation of the reason for avoiding such natural rights statements in the Constitution was offered shortly afterwards by General Charles Cotesworth Pinckney, speaking to the South Carolina House of Representatives. Pinckney, a lawyer trained in the Middle Temple in London, had been a major spokesman on slavery-related issues in Philadelphia. As he said: "Another reason weighed particularly, with the members from this state, against the insertion of a bill of rights. Such bills generally begin with declaring that all men by nature are born free. Now, we should make that declaration with a very bad grace, when a large part of our property consists in men who are actually born slaves."[30]

During ratification, Philadelphia convention delegate William Pierce of Georgia defended the absence of a bill of rights in the Constitution to Virginia attorney St. George Tucker by pointing to slavery as an insurmountable obstacle to any agreement on one. Pierce wrote that it would have been nearly impossible for the convention to have adopted a bill of rights, because it would "have been difficult in the extreme to have brought the different states to agree in what probably would have been proposed as the very first

principle, and that is, 'that all men are born equally free and independent.'"
He argued that no Virginian would have accepted such a principle. To
protect slavery, a Virginian would instead have insisted on modifying "some
of the expressions in such a manner as to have injured *the strong sense of
them,* if not to have buried them altogether in *ambiguity and uncertainty*"
(italics in the original).[31]

This evidence suggests that slave state delegates to the Philadelphia convention could not have agreed to any constitutional statement of human
rights equality without insisting on major qualifications to shield slavery
from its effects. The solution chosen by the convention was to avoid entirely
the issue of incorporating the Declaration of Independence. This meant
that, as Abraham Lincoln later acknowledged, the Declaration's pledge of
equality was not "one of legal obligation" in our "frame of government."[32]

When the Bill of Rights was adopted in the First Congress, Congress
made no effort to incorporate the Declaration's egalitarian claims. Congress rejected even James Madison's proposed prefatory rights declaration,
though it omitted egalitarian language. Instead, Congress included in the
Bill of Rights protections for property rights that at least some contemporaries thought were intended to apply to slaves equally with other property.[33]

The Constitution's failure to incorporate natural law principles explicitly
was a victory for slave owners. In its slavery cases during the early republic,
the Supreme Court declined to interpret the Constitution to bar or limit
slavery based on either the Declaration or natural law principles.[34] Similarly,
state courts that imposed substantial limitations on slavery during the formative era did so by relying on positive law—a state statute or constitutional
provision. Post-Revolutionary American courts were fairly consistent in de-
ferring to clearly expressed legislative and popular choices about slavery,
which left the largest part of slavery intact and growing in response to
market forces.[35]

PROPERTY RIGHTS

A final area in which Americans were divided about whether to follow the
principles of the *Somerset* decision involved the protections given to property rights in slaves. Americans proved willing to treat slaves as property in
significant respects not just under state but under federal law, to that extent rejecting Mansfield's view that slavery should instead be regarded as a
changeable status of human beings who might still possess other legal rights.
Slaveholders received important protections as a result.

Protection of property rights was a major purpose of the Constitution. For slave owners, the critical question was whether slaves would be treated as a form of property entitled to the same kind of legal protection as any other form of property. As General Pinckney expressed their concern during the Philadelphia convention, "Property in slaves should not be exposed to danger under a Govt. instituted for the protection of property."[36] Ultimately, Marshall-era Supreme Court decisions on slavery applied this equivalence principle in important contexts, such as slave freedom cases.[37]

During the formative era, though, Americans were divided about the issue. It could be argued that the Constitution is ambiguous on this point for various reasons, among which is that it uses the word "persons" to describe fugitive slaves. But state and federal laws and judicial interpretation of the Constitution provided protection to slave property *qua* property in important respects. A profoundly significant long-term effect of providing such protection was to create persistent uncertainty about whether slave property was entitled to similar protection during national expansion. These points can be illustrated by analyzing developments in two areas: slave owners' rights to compensation for slaves, and rendition of fugitive slaves.

During the 1790 congressional debate about federal authority over slavery, antislavery congressmen apparently conceded that a compensated slave buyout would be necessary if slavery were abolished by federal law. Yet well before then, antislavery advocates in both England and the United States had argued that slave property should not be entitled to protection like that given to other forms of property. They argued (often basing their contentions on *Somerset's* principles) that slave owner rights to slave property could never become "vested rights" (entitling owners to compensation) because title to slaves was necessarily founded on force, fraud, or theft via the slave trade. But most early Americans disagreed. Even leading antislavery advocates accepted the need for slave owner compensation if abolition occurred.[38]

Economic historians have shown that, as a result, almost every state that engaged in gradual abolition before 1804 effectively compensated slave owners for their existing slaves (and their future offspring) at nearly 100 percent of their market value. Legal claims that abolition of slavery for existing slaves could occur without compensation were rejected everywhere except Massachusetts. Slave property was deemed equivalent to other forms of property where government compensation was concerned.[39]

The adoption of the "just compensation" clause of the Fifth Amendment to the Constitution provided another significant indication that slave property would receive federal law protection equivalent to that of other property. The amendment was debated and adopted in 1789 during the same Congress which engaged in the first major post-Constitutional debate on federal powers over slavery, including a discussion of a compensated buyout for slave owners. If there had been any significant federal-level political support for limiting compensation to slave owners, or for treating slaves as a form of property different than other forms of property, the process of considering the amendment would have been a logical place to raise that issue. Yet as far as can be determined from the sketchy legislative history of the Fifth Amendment, no one advocated any distinction between forms of property in determining what property should be provided with just compensation. One lawyer advised the Pennsylvania Abolition Society in 1794 that the federal Constitution would bar uncompensated taking of slave property even at the state level.[40]

Another important respect in which Americans agreed to treat slaves as a form of property under federal law was the rendition of fugitive slaves. The *Somerset* principle that slavery was a legal status had important implications for fugitives. It meant that although for some legal purposes slaves were deemed a form of property, for other purposes English law would regard them as human beings with rights that the law would protect. For example, Lord Mansfield had made clear during the *Somerset* hearings that under English law, using brutal force against a slave of the kind then permissible in Virginia would be regarded as criminal conduct if the same slave were in servitude in England. In the United States, however, the idea of slavery as a changeable status was rendered largely inapplicable to rendition of fugitive slaves by federal law. Instead, Americans agreed to protect slave owner property rights in laws governing rendition, even in newly organized territories.[41]

Slavery's strength in the early republic is vividly demonstrated by the fact that federal legislation assumed that slavery was legal except where it was prohibited by law. That premise went unchallenged, even in areas with few if any slaves. Thomas Jefferson proposed unsuccessfully in 1784 that slavery be prohibited in all Western territories of the United States after 1800. Jefferson's proposal assumed that unless Congress prohibited territorial slavery, it would be legal there. The drafters of the Northwest Ordinance of 1787, which prohibited slavery, also worked from the premise that slavery needed to be prohibited explicitly in the new territory, because otherwise it would be legal there. This premise provided part of the justification for Northwest Territory Governor Arthur St. Clair's 1790 decision that the Northwest Ordinance should be interpreted as prospective only, which Congress did not challenge. The view that slavery was legal until prohibited in territories and new states was the "accepted rule" behind all of the territorial legislation adopted by the United States through at least 1800 (though the issue is clouded somewhat by existing rights).[42]

When federal or state laws barred slavery, creating areas of freedom, American slaveholders believed that they needed to protect slavery against the "example of the fugitives becoming contagious," as Henry Clay later put it. Colonial slaveholders had experienced chronic problems with runaway slaves, which had intensified during the Revolution, and also had to contend with jurisdictions such as Spanish Florida, a "magnet for Carolina slaves" (which notoriously freed fugitives who converted to Catholicism). They concluded that the creation of free jurisdictions to which slaves could readily flee would significantly increase slave flight unless steps were taken to enable their recapture at reasonable cost. They were able to take a major stride toward this goal during the formative era by establishing that fugitive slaves would continue to be treated functionally as property no matter where they were found.[43]

The Northwest Ordinance of 1787 contained a fugitive slave clause, which provided in substance that fugitive slaves must be delivered up to the person entitled to their labor. The ordinance could not have included its bar on slavery within the territory and still have been adopted with slave state support unless it included such a clause. The political indispensability of such a slave recapture provision was so widely accepted that it had been included voluntarily in draft ordinance legislation since 1785 by Massachusetts congressman Rufus King, its lead sponsor.[44]

Concerns about protecting slave property against flight led slave state representatives to seek to add the Fugitive Slave Clause to the Constitution. Historians differ about why the Constitutional Convention unanimously agreed to their proposal.[45] A particularly interesting historical question is why the clause—and the legislation Congress adopted to implement it in 1793—provided very little protection for the rights of fugitive slaves.

At the Philadelphia convention, states that had already begun gradual abolition could have insisted that fugitive slaves who fled to free jurisdictions should be treated as free men until it was proven that they were legally slaves. Since most American states had explicitly adopted English common law, under the principles of *Somerset* they could have asserted, for example, that the rights of such fugitive slaves in free states should include the right not to be physically seized by a slave owner. Free states could also have insisted that an alleged fugitive slave should have a statutory right to testify, or be entitled to a jury trial. Lord Mansfield had permitted an alleged slave to testify in a jury trial of an English slave freedom case decided just before *Somerset*.[46] But that was not what happened.

Instead, as earlier historians have noted, both the Northwest Ordinance and the Fugitive Slave Clause of the Constitution made largely inapplicable to fugitives the *Somerset* principle that the law of the state or territory where a fugitive slave was found would govern the slave's status. Both used federal law to prevent that result by overriding state law. They treated the fugitive slave functionally as property whose recapture and re-enslavement had to be permitted by a free state because the slave (or the practical equivalent, rights to the slave's labor) remained property there.[47]

Historians have given considerable attention to the proper interpretation of the Fugitive Slave Clause.[48] The clause received very little debate in state ratifying conventions. In the Virginia ratifying convention, where ratification was sharply contested and anti-federalists argued vociferously that the Constitution did not sufficiently protect slavery, the clause was described by James Madison as a victory for the protection of slave property that overrode existing state laws. Modern historians conclude, however, that the clause was passively voiced and did not authorize Congress to implement it. They contend that it was intended to be "self-executing" by the states. Yet Congress soon agreed to pass a federal law to implement the clause, which became known as the Fugitive Slave Act of 1793.[49]

The Act had been requested in late 1791 by President George Washington to resolve a dispute between Pennsylvania and Virginia over the criminal prosecution of several men who had allegedly kidnapped a fugitive slave in Pennsylvania and returned him to Virginia. Briefly, the Act provided that a fugitive slave who had been captured could be seized by the slave owner or his agent and then returned to his or her slave state based on an ex parte affidavit sworn to by the slave owner and presented to a court in the state where the fugitive was captured. Stiff statutory penalties were imposed against efforts to hinder or obstruct a slave owner seeking to capture or return a fugitive slave to slavery. According to a leading account of the fugitive slave legislation, the Senate "bitterly" debated the legislation before adopting it. But the circumstances surrounding the law's passage suggest there was limited controversy over its basic provisions, and none regarding its constitutionality.

The bill that became the Fugitive Slave Act passed the House of Representatives by a vote of 48–7, and the Senate by a voice vote. In House delegations from states that had already begun gradual abolition, the vote on the legislation was 18–4 in its favor. No member of Congress opposed the legislation on the ground that Congress lacked constitutional authority to adopt it, so far as we know. In sharp contrast, in the years just before 1793, congressmen had often argued that Congress had no constitutional power to adopt particular legislation, such as the law creating the first Bank of the United States.

The exceptionally capable lawyers for the Pennsylvania Abolition Society do not seem to have believed that the Act was an unconstitutional exercise of Congress's powers, although they were well aware that the proposed Act compromised the rights of fugitives in various respects. The Society later declined to represent fugitive slaves in cases where it believed that they were covered by the Act and had no legitimate defense to recapture, rather than challenging the law's constitutionality. There was no significant controversy about the passage of the Act in newspapers in several major cities located in states where abolition had begun by 1793.[50]

Fugitive slaves were members of a strongly disfavored group during the formative era, owing both to their race and to their poverty. Yet during that period there were individual efforts to aid fugitive slaves, and in at least one case, an entire community provided protection. One of George Washington's own slaves became a fugitive in the late 1790s and was effectively protected by the New Hampshire community to which she fled. But in an apparent paradox, Congress was able to establish a nationwide system for the recapture of fugitive slaves that operated through state and federal officials without engendering any serious national—or even major state-level—controversy before 1800. The sources suggest that one important reason for this was that, at the time, most citizens in states that began gradual abolition of slavery conceived of their responsibilities to slaves and freed blacks as limited to their own residents.[51]

In 1779, for example, five years before it began abolition, Rhode Island passed a law providing that resident slaves could not be sold outside of the state. Pennsylvania's 1780 gradual abolition law, on the other hand, specifically preserved the rights of out-of-state slaveholders to recapture their slaves in Pennsylvania, and permitted Pennsylvania slave owners to re-enslave their own fugitive slaves if they could recapture them within five years after the law was passed. These examples (to which others could be added) suggest that Northern states did not protest against the Fugitive Slave Act of 1793 because, at the time, their white majorities thought either that protection of fugitive slaves was not their concern or that permitting slaves' recapture by their owners was desirable social policy.

In rendition of fugitive slaves, slaveholders were therefore enabled by federal law in important respects to treat slaves as property much like any other form of property. The profound conflict between the concept of slavery as a status, and slavery as a form of property, was addressed in federal law in a manner that diverged sharply from the direction of English law after *Somerset*, and created an important part of the foundation for later slaveholder claims that slaves were property everywhere.

CONCLUSION

During the formative era, Americans made critical choices about the new nation's slavery policies. These choices effectively protected slavery as an institution, especially when compared to evolving British law and policy. Federalism freed the slave states to pursue their economic interest in preserving and expanding slavery. The principle that Constitutional interpretation regarding slavery should be based on positive law meant that federal courts concluded they lacked authority under the Constitution to challenge slavery without explicit statutory or constitutional authorization. Treating slaves as property for key purposes under federal law protected the economic basis of slavery as a highly mobile source of forced labor and liquid capital. During this same period, slave states rejected abolition and sought to expand slavery.

These pivotal choices were important steps in creating a slaveholders' Union. The Early Republic saw genuine progress against slavery in some parts of the Union. But Americans created a Union in which slave labor markets could operate freely and respond to growing world demand for slave labor products without significant national political or judicial restraint. Early American legal and political institutions were well adapted to permit slavery to grow apace with the new nation, and it did.

NOTES

I thank Peter Onuf, Matthew Mason, and John Craig Hammond for their perceptive and helpful comments on this essay.

1. Lincoln's Rejoinder, Sixth Debate with Stephen A. Douglas, October 13, 1858, in *The Collected Works of Abraham Lincoln*, ed. Roy P. Basler (New Brunswick, N.J.: Rutgers University Press, 1953), 3:275–83 (quotation at 276).

2. The historiography on slavery and formative-era law and politics includes sources cited in the introduction to this volume, particularly notes 2 and 3; and Mark A. Graber, *Dred Scott and the Problem of Constitutional Evil* (Cambridge: Cambridge University Press, 2006); Robin L. Einhorn, *American Taxation, American Slavery* (Chicago: University of Chicago

Press, 2006); Staughton Lynd, *Class Conflict, Slavery, and the United States Constitution: Ten Essays* (Indianapolis: Bobbs-Merrill, 1967); and William M. Wiecek, *The Sources of Antislavery Constitutionalism in America* (Ithaca, N.Y.: Cornell University Press, 1977). Slavery's powerful role in shaping early American law and politics is analyzed in George William Van Cleve, *A Slaveholders' Union: Slavery, Politics, and the Constitution in the Early American Republic* (Chicago: University of Chicago Press, 2010).

3. For differing views on the significance of the Constitution in slavery's history, compare the works of Don Fehrenbacher (*The Dred Scott Case: Its Significance in American Law and Politics* [New York: Oxford University Press, 1978], and *The Slaveholding Republic: An Account of the United States Government's Relations to Slavery* [New York: Oxford University Press, 2001]), with those of Paul Finkelman (*Slavery and the Founders: Race and Liberty in the Age of Jefferson*, 2nd ed. [Armonk, N.Y.: M. E. Sharpe, 2001]), and Staughton Lynd (*Class Conflict, Slavery, and the United States Constitution*). For further discussion of the historiography, see David Waldstreicher, *Slavery's Constitution: From Revolution to Ratification* (New York: Hill and Wang, 2009), 10–19.

4. For British colonial slavery policy, see Robin Blackburn, *The Making of New World Slavery* (London: Verso, 1997), especially 383–92; and David Richardson, "The British Empire and the Atlantic Slave Trade, 1660–1807," in *The Oxford History of the British Empire*, ed. P. J. Marshall (Oxford: Oxford University Press, 1998), 2:440–64.

5. The text of the 1729 opinion is quoted in full in *Knight v. Wedderburn* (Scottish Court of Civil Session, 1778); that decision is printed in Great Britain, Court of Session, *Decisions of the Court of Session* (Edinburgh: Bell & Bradfute, & E. Balfour, 1791), 8:5–9, 7. The 1732 statute is "An Act for the more easy Recovery of Debts in His Majesty's Plantations and Colonies in America," 5 George 2, chap. 7 (1732) (Eng.), text in *The Statutes at Large, From the Second to the 9th Year of the Reign of King George II*, ed. Danby Pickering (Cambridge: Joseph Bentham for Charles Bathurst, 1765), 16:272–74. It is analyzed in Claire Priest, "Creating an American Property Law: Alienability and Its Limits in American History," *Harvard Law Review* 120 (December 2006): 385–458, 423–25, 435–36 (quotations at 385, 423–24).

6. See Eva Sheppard Wolf, *Race and Liberty in the New Nation* (Baton Rouge: Louisiana State University Press, 2006), 21–23; Arthur Zilversmit, *The First Emancipation: The Abolition of Slavery in the North* (Chicago: University of Chicago Press, 1967), 48, 91; and George III, King of Great Britain, "Instructions to Lieutenant Governor William Nelson" (1770), MSS 3195, Albert and Virginia Small Special Collections Library, University of Virginia, Charlottesville.

7. *Somerset v. Stewart*, Lofft 1, 98 English Reports 499, 20 State Trials 1 (Court of King's Bench [U.K.], 1772). For one report of the proceedings and Lord Mansfield's oral decision in *Somerset v. Stewart*, see Great Britain, Courts, *The English Reports* [full reprint ed.] (Edinburgh: William Green and Sons; London: Stevens and Sons, 1909), 98:499–510. Leading analyses of the decision, which cite and analyze other case reports, are James Oldham, *English Common Law in the Age of Mansfield* (Chapel Hill: University of North Carolina Press, 2004), 305–23; and William M. Wiecek, "*Somerset*: Lord Mansfield and the Legitimacy of Slavery in the Anglo-American World," *University of Chicago Law Review* 42 (Autumn 1974): 86–146. And see George Van Cleve, "Somerset's Case and Its Antecedents in Imperial Perspective," *Law and History Review* 24 (Fall 2006): 601–45.

8. For a detailed account of *Somerset* colonial press coverage, see Patricia Bradley, *Slavery, Propaganda, and the American Revolution* (Jackson: University of Mississippi Press, 1998), 66–80.

9. *Pearne v. Lisle*, Amb. 75 (Court of Chancery [England], 1749), reprinted in Great Britain, Courts, *The English Reports* [full reprint ed.] (Edinburgh: William Green and Sons; London: Stevens and Sons, 1903), 27:47−49.

10. Van Cleve, "Somerset's Case," 636, 643n200.

11. Ibid., 642−45; Bradley, *Slavery, Propaganda, and the American Revolution*, 81−82.

12. Wiecek, *The Sources of Antislavery Constitutionalism in America*, 44. And see *Caesar v. Greenleaf*, Essex Inf. Ct., Newburyport, Mass. (1774), in *The Legal Papers of John Adams*, ed. L. Kinvin Wroth and Hiller B. Zobel (Cambridge, Mass.: Harvard University Press, 1965), 2:64−67; Benjamin Rush, *An Address to the Inhabitants of the British Settlements in America, upon Slave-Keeping*, 2nd ed. (Philadelphia, 1773), 19, 49; and Back Settler [pseud.], *Some Fugitive Thoughts on a Letter Signed Freeman, Addressed to the Deputies, Assembled at the High Court of Congress in Philadelphia* (Charleston, S.C., 1774), Evans no. 13630, 25.

13. *Providence Journal & Country Gazette*, 10 October 1772; *Virginia Gazette* (Rind), 12 November 1772; *Connecticut Courant* (Hartford), 31 July 1772; *Newport Mercury*, 3 August 1772; *Boston News-Letter*, 23 July 1772; *New York Journal, or the General Advertiser*, 27 August 1772.

14. Henry Marchant, Diary, 1:123, Papers of Henry Marchant (typescript version), American Philosophical Society, Philadelphia (original, Rhode Island Historical Society, Providence).

15. Sally E. Hadden, "The Fragmented Laws of Slavery in the Colonial and Revolutionary Eras," in *The Cambridge History of Law in America*, ed. Michael Grossberg and Christopher Tomlins (Cambridge: Cambridge University Press, 2008), 1:263. See also Earl M. Maltz, "Slavery, Federalism, and the Structure of the Constitution," *American Journal of Legal History* 36 (October, 1992): 466−98.

16. For this line of thought I am indebted to the work of Peter Onuf, especially "Federalism, Republicanism, and the Origins of American Sectionalism," in *All Over the Map: Rethinking American Regions*, ed. Edward L. Ayers et al. (Baltimore: Johns Hopkins University Press, 1996), 11−37.

17. Einhorn, *American Taxation, American Slavery*, 118−38; Joseph DeLaplaine to Friends Meeting, 10th month 1785, Society of Friends, Miscellaneous Documents, Philadelphia Meeting for Sufferings, Friends Historical Library, Swarthmore, Penn.

18. See Ira Berlin, *Many Thousands Gone: The First Two Centuries of Slavery in North America* (Cambridge, Mass.: Harvard University Press, 1998), 369−71 (table 1).

19. For an account of this debate, see Richard S. Newman, "Prelude to the Gag Rule: Southern Reaction to Antislavery Petitions in the First Congress," *Journal of the Early Republic* 16 (Winter, 1996): 571−99. For its broader implications, see Joseph J. Ellis, *Founding Brothers: The Revolutionary Generation* (New York: Alfred A. Knopf, 2000), 81−119.

20. Eva Sheppard Wolf, *Race and Liberty in the New Nation* (Baton Rouge: Louisiana State University Press, 2006), x−xi, 39−84.

21. St. George Tucker to Jeremy Belknap, 13 August 1797, in Massachusetts Historical Society, "Letters and Documents Relating to Slavery in Massachusetts," in *Collections of the Massachusetts Historical Society*, ed. Charles Deane, 5th ser. (Boston: Massachusetts Historical Society, 1877), 3:375−442, 428; Richard S. Newman, *The Transformation of American Abolitionism: Fighting Slavery in the Early Republic* (Chapel Hill: University of North Carolina Press, 2002), 34−35.

22. Landholder VI (Oliver Ellsworth), in the *Connecticut Courant* (Hartford), 10 December 1787 (reprinted several times in Massachusetts), in *The Documentary History of the Ratification of the Constitution*, ed. Merrill Jensen, John P. Kaminski, and Gaspare J. Saladino (Madi-

son: State Historical Society of Wisconsin, 1976–), 14:398–404; Philanthrop, in the *Northampton Hampshire Gazette*, 23 April 1788, ibid., 7:1743–46.

23. James W. Ceaser, *Nature and History in American Political Development: A Debate* (Cambridge, Mass.: Harvard University Press, 2006), 29–30.

24. Peter S. Onuf, *The Mind of Thomas Jefferson* (Charlottesville: University of Virginia Press, 2007), 89–94; Onuf, *Statehood and Union* (Bloomington: Indiana University Press, 1987), 46–66 (for the early history of "equal footing").

25. John Craig Hammond, *Slavery, Freedom, and Expansion in the Early American West* (Charlottesville: University of Virginia Press, 2007), 3–7.

26. For a leading history of natural rights in early American law, see G. Edward White, *The Marshall Court and Cultural Change, 1815–1835*, abridged ed. (Oxford: Oxford University Press, 1991), 674–740. See also Ceaser, *Nature and History in American Political Development*, passim; and Robert Cover, *Justice Accused: Antislavery and the Judicial Process* (New Haven, Conn.: Yale University Press, 1975).

27. Ralph Ketcham, *James Madison: A Biography* (Charlottesville: University Press of Virginia, 1990), 71–72.

28. See Emily Blanck, "Seventeen Eighty-Three: The Turning Point in the Law of Slavery and Freedom in Massachusetts," *New England Quarterly* 75 (March 2002): 24–51.

29. *Supplement to Max Farrand's "The Records of the Federal Convention of 1787,"* ed. James H. Hutson (New Haven, Conn.: Yale University Press, 1987), 183n1.

30. Jonathan Elliot, *The Debates in the Several State Conventions on the Adoption of the Federal Constitution, as Recommended by the General Convention at Philadelphia, in 1787*, 2nd ed. (Washington: Taylor & Maury, 1836), 4:316.

31. William Pierce to St. George Tucker, 28 September 1787, in *Letters of Delegates to the Continental Congress, 1774–1789*, ed. Paul H. Smith (Washington, D.C.: Library of Congress, 1996), 24:445–49.

32. Abraham Lincoln to James N. Brown, 18 October 1858, in *The Collected Works of Abraham Lincoln*, 3:327–28.

33. *Creating the Bill of Rights: The Documentary Record from the First Federal Congress*, ed. Helen E. Veit, Kenneth R. Bowling, and Charlene Bangs Bickford (Baltimore: Johns Hopkins University Press, 1991), 11–12.

34. In 1825 the Supreme Court ruled that positive law—not natural law—governed the interpretation of the law of nations with respect to the slave trade, in *The Antelope*, 23 U.S. (10 Wheat.) 66 (1825), in U.S. Supreme Court, *Reports of Cases Ruled and Adjudged in the Supreme Court of the United States*, vol. 10, *February Term 1825* (New York: R. Donaldson, 1825), 66–133, commonly cited as *United States Reports*, 23:66. By inference, the Court would have adopted the same view of slavery (see *Mima Queen v. Hepburn*, 11 U.S. [7 Cranch] 290 [1813], in U.S. Supreme Court, *Reports of Cases Argued and Adjudged in the Supreme Court of the United States*, vol. 7, *February Term, 1812, and February Term, 1813* [Washington, D.C., 1813], 290–99, commonly cited as *United States Reports*, 11:290; and White, *The Marshall Court and Cultural Change*, 694–740).

35. See *Pirate, alias Belt v. Dalby*, 1 Dall. (U.S.) 167 (Pa. 1786), in Alexander James Dallas, *Reports of Cases Ruled and Adjudged in the Courts of Pennsylvania before and since the Revolution* (Philadelphia: Printed for the Reporter, by T. Bradford, 1790), 167–69, commonly cited as *United States Reports*, 1:167–69 (law governing status of slave brought to Pennsylvania). *Negro*

Flora v. Executors of Joseph Graisberry (Pennsylvania Court of Errors and Appeals, 1802) is unreported and its records reportedly lost. However, the court's unanimous decision that slavery was constitutional under the 1790 Pennsylvania Constitution (despite a constitutional "free and equal" clause) is reported in the *Gazette of the United States* (Philadelphia), 30 January 1802, and in the *Oracle of Dauphin & Harrisburg (Pa.) Advertiser*, 8 February 1802. The case background is discussed in Edward Raymond Turner, "The Abolition of Slavery in Pennsylvania," *Pennsylvania Magazine of History and Biography* 36, no. 2 (1912): 129–42.

36. U.S. Constitutional Convention (1787), *The Records of the Federal Convention of 1787*, ed. Max Farrand, rev. ed. (New Haven, Conn.: Yale University Press, 1966), 1:593–94.

37. See sources in n. 34.

38. Joanne Pope Melish, *Disowning Slavery: Gradual Emancipation and "Race" in New England, 1780–1860* (Ithaca, N.Y.: Cornell University Press, 1998), 50–59.

39. Robert William Fogel and Stanley L. Engerman, "Philanthropy at Bargain Prices: Notes on the Economics of Gradual Emancipation," *Journal of Legal Studies* 3 (June 1974): 377–401. New York's 1827 abolition occurred after owners had received de facto compensation.

40. Opinion of Jos. [Joseph?] Thomas on abolition of slavery by 1790 Pennsylvania Constitution, box 4, Papers of William Rawle, Historical Society of Pennsylvania, Philadelphia.

41. The leading comprehensive study of the law of fugitive slavery is Paul Finkelman, *An Imperfect Union: Slavery, Federalism, and Comity* (Chapel Hill: University of North Carolina Press, 1981).

42. For an account, see Fehrenbacher, *The Slaveholding Republic*, 255–60 (quotation at 260).

43. Ibid., 103 (quotation); Ira Berlin, *Generations of Captivity: A History of African American Slaves* (Cambridge, Mass.: Harvard University Press, 2003), 44.

44. Robert Ernst, *Rufus King: American Federalist* (Chapel Hill: University of North Carolina Press, 1968), 54–55.

45. Cf. Wiecek, *The Sources of Antislavery Constitutionalism in America*, 79, and Fehrenbacher, *The Slaveholding Republic*, 44.

46. *Rex v. Stapylton* (Court of King's Bench [U.K.], 1771) was an unreported Middlesex County (England) criminal indictment for false imprisonment of an alleged slave. The case is discussed and some substantive trial proceedings are quoted in sources about the work of the British abolitionist Granville Sharp, particularly in Prince Hoare, *Memoirs of Granville Sharp, Esq.* (London: Printed for H. Colburn, 1820). The decision is analyzed in Oldham, *English Common Law*, 308, 310–13.

47. Finkelman, *An Imperfect Union*, 38–42.

48. See, for example, Paul Finkelman, "The Kidnapping of John Davis and the Adoption of the Fugitive Slave Law of 1793," *Journal of Southern History* 56 (August 1990): 397–422.

49. U.S. Constitutional Convention (1787), *The Records of the Federal Convention of 1787*, 3:325; Fehrenbacher, *The Slaveholding Republic*, 44. For legislative history, see Finkelman, "The Kidnapping of John Davis and the Adoption of the Fugitive Slave Law of 1793."

50. Finkelman, "The Kidnapping of John Davis and the Adoption of the Fugitive Slave Law of 1793," 416–17.

51. John Wood Sweet, *Bodies Politic: Negotiating Race in the American North, 1730–1830* (Baltimore: Johns Hopkins University Press, 2003), 259–62; Henry Wiencek, *An Imperfect God: George Washington, His Slaves, and the Creation of America* (New York: Farrar, Strauss and Giroux, 2003), 321–34.

"Uncontrollable Necessity"

The Local Politics, Geopolitics, and Sectional Politics of Slavery Expansion

JOHN CRAIG HAMMOND

In one of the most oft-repeated statements from the early republic, Thomas Jefferson likened the Missouri Controversy to an unexpected "firebell in the night." Jefferson knew better. In November 1818, New Yorker James Tallmadge tried to block the admission of Illinois into statehood because slavery was "not sufficiently prohibited" in its constitution. Six months earlier, New Hampshire Republican Arthur Livermore had proposed amending the U.S. Constitution to prohibit slavery "in any State hereafter admitted to the Union." Over the previous twenty years, Northern Republicans had repeatedly fought to limit slavery's growth in the Southwest and to keep it out of the Northwest entirely. Hardly a startling "firebell in the night," the Missouri Crisis was the culmination of twenty years of Northern efforts to restrict slavery's Western expansion. Jefferson also charged that the "firebell in the night" was a false crisis, the work of crypto-Federalist Clintonians who schemed to use slavery to unite the North behind their bid to gain power. Again, Jefferson knew better. Loyal Northern Republicans initiated the crisis and provided solid support for the Tallmadge Amendment, fighting, as they had always done, against slavery and its expansion. Finally, Jefferson warned that the sectional passions unleashed by the Missouri Crisis heralded a "knell to the Union." In that, Jefferson was more right. Yet the threat that slavery restriction might sunder the Union along geographical lines was not entirely new either. Previous Northern efforts to rein in slavery expansion had been defeated by the very real fear that restrictions on Western slavery might lead to disunion—not along Northern and Southern lines, but between the Atlantic states and the Trans-Appalachian West.[1]

With the publication of Glover Moore's *The Missouri Controversy,* Jefferson's interpretation of events would enter the historiography of politics and slavery in the early republic.[2] And there it would remain, in one form or another, for the next fifty years. Moore, of course, modified the specifics of Jefferson's interpretation, and historians have systematically challenged Moore's main points. Yet Moore's conclusions—and Jefferson's interpretation—still remain generally accepted in the historiography. As recently as 2001, a leading political historian could charge that the Missouri Crisis had been "a kind of surrogate presidential politics," played by New Yorkers seeking to take power from the Virginia dynasty. Similarly, a distinguished historian of sectional politics could conclude that the Missouri Controversy arose out of Northerners' sudden "realization that under the 'Virginia dynasty' . . . the national prospect had been weighted heavily in favor of slavery."[3] But the recent outpouring of scholarship on the politics of slavery in the early republic, coupled with long-standing challenges to the Moore-Jefferson interpretation, beg for a new interpretation of the conflicts over slavery expansion that culminated in the Missouri Controversy.[4]

In the three decades preceding the Missouri Controversy, Northern Republicans repeatedly sought to halt slavery expansion. These efforts failed because of the weaknesses of the American Union in the early American West. Through 1815, the main sectional conflicts over slavery expansion were fought between the Atlantic states and the Trans-Appalachian West. Rather than battling Southern slaveholders, Northern opponents of slavery expansion contended with fervently proslavery Western planters, farmers, speculators, and merchants. This polyglot group of expatriated Americans, British loyalists, French planters, and "men of no country" threatened disunion whenever Congress considered restrictions on Western slavery. Through 1812, local circumstances in Kentucky, the Southwest Territory, the Mississippi Territory, and the Louisiana Purchase assured that white settlers already there would favor the continuation of slavery under American rule. Imperial struggles for the Trans-Appalachian West, the uncertain loyalties of white Westerners, and the weaknesses of the American Union in the West meant that Congress was forced to accept these decisions.

The year 1815, however, marked a dramatic turning point in the struggle over slavery's growth in the West. The Napoleonic Wars had destroyed any European designs for a mid-continent empire, and the end of the War of 1812 solidified Western loyalties and consolidated the place of the West in the American Union. The years after 1815 also witnessed the emergence of a more aggressive antislavery politics at the local, state, and national levels, much of it led by obscure Northern Republicans. By 1819, it seemed all but certain that Northern Republicans would make some type of move to restrict the growth of slavery in the West. When Missouri applied for statehood, Northern restrictionists saw their chance, seeking to halt the growth of slavery in what would become the new state of Missouri. More importantly, and almost entirely overlooked, they expected that restrictions on Missouri slavery would serve as the first step toward prohibiting the "further extension of slavery into all states and territories hereafter admitted to the Union."[5] Northern restrictionists failed, however, to anticipate the unyielding opposition of slaveholders from the Atlantic states. Prior to 1815, Eastern slaveholders had opposed restrictions on the grounds that they would provoke disunion in the West. But after 1815, slaveholders from the Atlantic states made expansion into the West inseparable from the well-being and survival of slavery in the East. In laying claim to the West, Southern slaveholders fundamentally changed the orientation of the problem of slavery expansion. With the Missouri Crisis, what was once a conflict between Eastern federal power and local Western interests now became an intractable sectional contest between the free states of the North and the slave states of the South.

I

Historians have considered the consolidation of the American Union in the West, and the growth and expansion of slavery between 1790 and 1815, as two separate topics. One account focuses on the creation of a "union of interests" that eventually gained the loyalty of white Westerners by protecting and promoting their interests.[6] The other focuses on how slaveholding "founding fathers" protected the interests of Chesapeake and Carolina slaveholders by opening the bulk of the Trans-Appalachian West to slaveholders and the domestic slave trade from the East.[7] The first account underestimates the importance of slavery in binding white Westerners to the fledgling United States; the second, by focusing on the "founders," overstates the power of the federal government to restrict slavery's Western growth, and incorrectly treats the early American West as "virgin territory."

The Trans-Appalachian West possessed a long history of settlement, slavery, and non-American governance that predated any federal decision to permit or prohibit slavery. White settlers, Native Americans, African Americans, state governments, and European powers had all left their imprint on the West long before Congress enacted the territorial ordinances that would permit or exclude slavery. From 1787 through the Missouri Controversy,

Congress never independently established slavery in an unsettled, virgin West. In every case—the Southwest Territory in 1790, Kentucky in 1792, the Mississippi Territory in 1798, and Louisiana and Missouri in 1804 and 1805—Congress ratified a decision that had already been made by the territory's white inhabitants and the state or foreign governments that had preceded federal possession of a territory. Indeed, all of these territories possessed thriving slave societies prior to American possession or the advent of federal governance. Rather than establishing slavery in the Western territories, the federal government had acquired Western domains where slavery was an entrenched, postcolonial institution, ubiquitous and expanding long before American possession or governance. Rather than opening a virgin West to American slaveholders from the Atlantic states, the federal government repeatedly found itself accommodating Western slaveholders, in the interest of securing an American Union in the West.[8]

A narrow focus on the "founders'" failure to prohibit slavery expansion also assumes the existence of a powerful nation-state capable of compelling the obedience of Westerners. At the time of the Missouri Controversy, the federal government clearly possessed the power to prohibit the expansion of slavery, even if Southern politicians denied that it possessed the authority to do so. Before then, however, something like the reverse situation held sway. Neither Southern politicians nor Western settlers had questioned the federal government's constitutional authority to prohibit slavery in federal territories. Instead, debates in Congress centered on whether the government possessed the real, effective power needed to implement meaningful restrictions on slavery, and whether restricting slavery would weaken the prospects for a lasting American Union in the West. Whenever the possibility of restricting slavery in a territory had been raised, white Westerners and American officials in the West warned that disunion might follow. Indeed, Western farmers, slaveholders, merchants, and speculators made clear their preference for living under European powers who would protect slavery, rather than under an American empire whose commitment to Western slavery seemed questionable.[9]

Their threats proved effective because of the unique geopolitical circumstances in the West. Between the 1780s and 1815, the future of Western slavery was entangled in what François Furstenberg has labeled "the Long War for the West": a critical period in North American and Atlantic history between 1754 and 1815 when "native, imperial, and settler actors" struggled to determine the fate of the Trans-Appalachian West. This "Long War for the West" created what Jeremy Adelman and Stephen Aron have termed the "power politics of territorial hegemony": the determination of imperial powers, Native Americans, and white settlers to establish territorial hegemony in the contested borderlands of North American. Through 1815—the critical period of slavery expansion in the early republic—the United States was a weak, overextended republic. In the West, it contended with white settlers determined to protect their parochial interests, Native Americans intent on stopping American expansion, and European powers still interested in a mid-continent empire. The inability of the government to compete in the "power politics of territorial hegemony" forced Congress to permit slavery where the white population demanded it.[10]

The "power politics of territorial hegemony," and the presence of slavery prior to American possession, influenced the expansion of slavery as early as the First Congress. In 1789, Congress re-passed the Northwest Ordinance of 1787 and its Article VI prohibition on slavery. Later in that same session, however, Congress voted to permit slavery in the Southwest Territory. Congress's failure to extend Article VI to the Southwest Territory certainly reflected the demands of Chesapeake and Carolina planters that some portion of the West be open to them. But Congress's exclusion of Article VI from the Southwest Ordinance also reflected the differing realities of settlement, slavery, federalism, and geopolitics north and south of the Ohio River. The Northwest contained few white settlers, the Confederation Congress had settled state claims to the region, and slavery had only the barest presence there. In addition, American settlement in the Northwest was led by a cadre of loyal army officers and settlers from New England. Both groups remained committed to upholding American authority in the Northwest and to maintaining the exclusion of slavery. Furthermore, the British in Canada preferred to exclude American settlers from the Northwest rather than gain their loyalty. In 1789, then, Article VI promised to strengthen an American presence in the Northwest.[11]

The situation in the Southwest Territory was starkly different. By 1790, white settlers there had already grown frustrated with the inability of American governments to address their concerns. To gain American assistance in prosecuting Indian wars and securing access to the Mississippi River, leading men in Tennessee deliberately spread rumors that settlers were plotting to make the region a Spanish protectorate. The leading American official in the West feared that Western Americans were already becoming "Spaniards for all intents and purposes," and James Blount—a United States senator and a future British and Spanish conspirator—went so far as to name the main area of settlement there the "Mero District," after the Spanish governor of Louisiana. Complicating these geopolitical worries, the government of North Carolina had already provided the legal basis for slavery in the territory, and at least 3,400 slaves already resided in the Southwest Territory in 1790. Furthermore, thousands of North Carolinians possessed wartime warrants for land in the Southwest: they had obtained them under the presumption that slavery would be permitted there, and they fully expected to be able to settle the Southwest Territory with the benefit of slave labor. The government of North Carolina defended these claimants—among them, secessionists from the "lost state" of Franklin—by refusing to cede the region unless Congress dropped the Article VI exclusion of slavery from the Southwest Ordinance. Even if Congress could have overcome North Carolina's objections to Article VI, it could not ignore the tenuous loyalties of slaveholders and aspiring slaveholders already in the region. The Spanish were actively enticing men such as Blount with promises of access to the Mississippi River, and Spain would never impose anything akin to the Northwest Ordinance's Article VI. Congress understood that there would be no faster way to drive men like Blount into Spanish arms than to extend the Northwest Ordinance's Article VI prohibition on slavery to the Southwest.[12]

Similar circumstances—weak or nonexistent federal power and popular local support for a long-established institution—inhibited any federal attempt to restrict slavery in Kentucky. Virginia law and slaveholding settlers had established slavery in Kentucky beginning in the 1770s, and by 1790 there were nearly 12,000 slaves there. Because Kentucky never was a federal territory (Virginia governed Kentucky as its westernmost counties until 1792), only the government of Virginia or the people of Kentucky could abolish slavery there. Twice in the 1790s, Kentucky held constitutional conventions in which gradual abolition proposals were proposed. Both times, planters and farmers overwhelmed the small antislavery factions led by evangelicals. In the 1790s, both Kentucky and Tennessee were admitted to statehood with constitutions that protected slavery. But in neither case was the federal government instrumental in either establishing slavery there or in permitting its expansion. Rather, Congress merely affirmed decisions that had already been made by the thousands of slaveholding settlers and the state governments who had established slavery there in the 1770s. Given their preexisting history of slavery and the lack of federal power to do anything about it, both Kentucky and Tennessee were admitted to statehood with nary an objection based on slavery.[13]

The same federal weaknesses, geopolitical concerns, and settler demands that allowed slavery's expansion into Kentucky and the Southwest Territory would thwart federal efforts to halt expansion in the strategically vital postcolonial borderlands of the Lower Mississippi Valley. In an extraordinary period of territorial acquisition, the United States acquired the bulk of the Lower Mississippi Valley through the Treaty of San Lorenzo (1795) and the Louisiana Purchase (1803). Policymakers in the East understood that the entire Trans-Appalachian West would remain in the American Union only if the Lower Mississippi Valley and New Orleans remained securely in American hands.[14] But the future of the Lower Mississippi Valley rested in the hands of an untrustworthy lot of land speculators, slaveholders, and "men of no country" who were loyal to whichever imperial power promised to best protect their interests—interests inextricably bound to the region's growing "system of slavery."[15]

Complicating any American effort to restrict slavery expansion, the United States had acquired possession of the Lower Mississippi Valley at the very moment that the region was being remade by plantation revolutions. Though slavery had existed in Louisiana and the Natchez Country since the early 1700s, both had long been on the margins of the Atlantic plantation complex. It was only in the 1770s that Spain began devoting resources for the development of a plantation economy in the Lower Mississippi Valley. Then, in the 1790s, the introduction of the cotton gin in the Natchez Country and the flight of Saint-Domingue sugar planters to Louisiana set off a plantation revolution that transformed the region's languishing "societies with slaves" into full-blown "slave societies." Historians have typically framed the problem of slavery in the Old Southwest as one of permitting or prohibiting the expansion of American slavery from the Atlantic states into that region. The situation appeared starkly different to contemporaries. In the Lower Mississippi Valley in the late 1790s it was not American slavery, fed by the domestic slave trade, that was expanding into a "virgin West." It was Caribbean slavery, fed by the international slave trade, expanding into the disputed borderland domains of France, Spain, and Britain. In the area that would later become the Louisiana and Mississippi Territories, the United States did not so much create an empire for slavery, as much as it acquired two strategically located slave societies in the midst of Caribbean-style plantation revolutions. Congress would permit the continued expansion of slavery in the Lower Mississippi Valley, not so much as a means to open the Southwest to American slaveholders, but to accommodate the slaveholders already there.[16]

In 1795 Spain ceded its claims to the Natchez Country, the disputed border region that would be organized as the Mississippi Territory in 1798.

The Washington administration dispatched Andrew Ellicott, a Pennsylvania Quaker, Federalist, and surveyor, to protect American interests in Natchez. Ellicott was given the seemingly impossible task of securing American rule until Congress could frame a territorial ordinance and send officials to govern its newest possession. Once in Natchez, Ellicott despaired at the prospects of gaining the support of the white inhabitants: a motley collection of British loyalists, expatriated Americans, Spanish officials, "men of no country," "enemies of my country," and numerous "banditti." Ellicott contended for their loyalty, along with a British officer seeking to regain British possession of the Natchez Country and with a Spanish governor who hoped to prevent American possession, all against the backdrop of rumors of what became the Blount Conspiracy. Ellicott's "enemies" knew exactly how to destroy popular support for American rule: they circulated rumors that Ellicott and the United States government believed that slavery "ought to be prohibited here, as in the Northwestern Territory." To counter these rumors, Ellicott—an antislavery Quaker and Federalist from Pennsylvania—unexpectedly found himself issuing circulars pledging that, under American rule, slavery would be permitted, "upon the same footing, that it is in the southern states."[17] After issuing this pledge, Ellicott and the few loyal American planters in Natchez pleaded with Secretary of State Timothy Pickering to ensure that Congress permit slavery when it created a territorial government. Pickering obliged, recommending in his report on the state of affairs in the Mississippi Valley that Congress immediately create a territorial government that sanctioned slavery in the Natchez Country.[18]

Pickering's recommendation seemed poised to sail through Congress until Federalist George Thatcher proposed applying Article VI of the Northwest Ordinance to the Mississippi Territory. In the course of the ensuing debate, two stark options emerged. Congress could permit slavery in Mississippi, placating slaveholders there and securing a strategic American presence in the Lower Mississippi Valley. Or Congress could prohibit slavery, all but ensuring that the white inhabitants of the Natchez Country would rebel against American authority. Even the most stridently proslavery South Carolinians devoted the bulk of their objections to warning that a prohibition on slavery would drive, not South Carolina, but the Natchez Country out of the Union. With even reliably antislavery congressmen such as the Philadelphia abolitionist Thomas Hartley distancing themselves from Thatcher's proposal, only twelve representatives voted to apply Article VI to the Mississippi Territory.[19] Immediately following passage of the Mississippi Ordinance, Pickering dashed off two identical letters that demonstrated how closely the sanction for slavery and the creation of a union of interests were tied together in the Southwest. The letters instructed Ellicott to inform the white inhabitants of the territory that Congress had made it official: they "may keep slaves." A few months later, Pickering informed the designated governor, Federalist Winthrop Sargent, that Congress had permitted slavery in Mississippi because "almost all of the inhabitants are possessed of slaves." The connection between slavery expansion and securing the American Union came together one last time in Sargent's inaugural address, in which he explained that the United States had permitted slavery, "in special indulgence to the people of this territory."[20]

Five years later, the Louisiana Purchase brought the conflict between limiting Western slavery and securing the Lower Mississippi Valley to a head. At the time of the Purchase, Louisiana was in the midst of an unprecedented plantation boom. As every planter, farmer, merchant, and American agent in Louisiana understood, the plantation boom could be sustained only with uninterrupted access to the slave trade. In Natchez, Congress had granted local whites' demands that the United States sanction slavery. Yet with the Louisiana Purchase, Congress sought to strangle the budding plantation revolution by cutting off access to slave labor entirely. In 1804, a Republican-controlled Congress placed severe restrictions on slavery in the Louisiana Purchase. The 1804 Territorial Ordinances outlawed both the international and domestic slave trades and placed strict conditions on the expansion of American slavery into Louisiana. The 1804 Ordinances only permitted American citizens, "removing into said Territory for actual settlement, and being, at the time of such removal, *bona fide* owner of such slave or slaves," to carry slaves into Louisiana. While Americans could settle in Louisiana with the slaves they already owned, they were prohibited from selling their slaves in or into Louisiana, with violations punishable by immediate freedom for the slave. These intricate regulations balanced an intent to end the plantation revolution in Louisiana with Congress's desire to encourage American settlement as a means of securing Louisiana.[21]

The restrictions proved to be a resounding failure. Louisiana planters, farmers, and merchants, along with American officials in Louisiana, all warned that disunion and reunification with France would ensue if Congress insisted on restricting white Louisianans' right to "an unlimited slavery." By the summer of 1804, the situation in Louisiana had grown so desperate that American newspapers reported that "the French at New Orleans" were "discontented, troublesome," and on the verge of rebellion. The flurry of letters sent from American officials in New Orleans to policymakers in Washington all identified the same source of discontent and trouble: the prohibitions on the slave trade. Indeed, one American official in New Orleans counseled that repeal of the slavery restrictions "would go farther with them, and better reconcile them to the Government of the United States, than any other privilege." Congress took this advice. The 1804 Ordinances expired after one year, and in 1805 Congress quietly declined to renew the bulk of the restrictions on slavery in Louisiana. And although Congress maintained the ban on the international slave trade, slave traders skirted this restriction by having slave ships touch port at Charleston, thus "domesticating" the international slave trade before the ships moved on to New Orleans. As was the case in Natchez, Congress found itself facing a stark choice, between permitting slavery and gaining the loyalty of the white population, or prohibiting slavery and inviting disunion.[22]

Historians have pointed out that the Missouri Controversy might have been avoided if Congress had opted to permit slavery in Louisiana, at the same time banning it in what would become Missouri.[23] But in 1804 the "Missouri Country" constituted a booming, if small slave society, not "virgin territory" whose future could be determined by "founding fathers" in Washington. The French, British, and Native American inhabitants of Missouri had long used slave labor in their mixed-agricultural and fur-trading economy. In the 1790s, Article VI had driven French slaveholders from Illinois into the Missouri Country, increasing the number of slaves in the region. After 1800, a substantial number of Americans seeking generous Spanish land-grants had begun crossing the Mississippi River into Missouri, adding to the number of slaveholders and aspiring slaveholders. The expansion and consolidation of slavery in the Missouri Country was also spurred by the plantation revolutions downriver, as Missouri's new and old slaveholders gladly met the increased demand for foodstuffs and other commodities in those regions. Slaveless farmers who hoped to cash in on the boom added to the clamor for more slave labor. By 1804, Missouri's was a small, but thriving, slave society, with slaves accounting for up to one-third of the population in the main settlements at St. Louis, St. Genevieve, and Cape Girardeau.[24]

As soon as rumors of the Louisiana Purchase reached the Missouri Country, the white inhabitants there expressed concerns that the status of slavery in the territory not be changed under American rule. American agents there immediately sent letters east warning that, "even among the Americans not slaveholders," the white inhabitants of the Missouri Country were universally "averse" to American rule if it came with restrictions on slavery. Congress ignored these warnings, placing stiff restrictions on slavery and appointing the officers of the Indiana Territory to govern the Missouri Country, setting off fears that Congress would soon prohibit slavery entirely by extending the Northwest Ordinance and Article VI to Missouri. Outraged white Missourians responded by insisting that the United States recognize their right "to the free possession of our slaves," along with "the right of importing" more. Congress then quietly repealed the restrictions on slavery in 1805.[25] As had happened elsewhere, the presence of slavery prior to American possession, and the ongoing expansion of Missouri's slave society, combined with geopolitical realities to defeat Congress's attempt to restrict the growth of Western slavery. Northerners would twice more attempt to "prohibit the admission of slaves" into the Missouri Country, with no success. In 1811, Pennsylvania Republican Jonathan Roberts would voluntarily withdraw his proposal to ban slavery in Missouri, because, "on the eve of war," much of the Western "country" was "infatuated with the spirit of opposition to the Government." And one year later, with the Trans-Appalachian West already embroiled in the War of 1812, only seventeen congressmen would support an identical effort by Pennsylvania Republican Abner Lacock.[26]

If the defeat of these proposals exemplified the conflict between restricting slavery and securing the American Union in the West, it also suggested the conditions under which the United States could enact effective restrictions on slavery. The impending War of 1812 had doomed Roberts's and Lacock's proposals. And though the United States had failed to win the War of 1812, it did emerge victorious in the more important "Long War for the West." The victors would soon fall out over the spoils, and slavery would prove central to that falling out. But before then, Northerners, Southerners, and Westerners would have to come to terms with the realities of a more secure Union, a more powerful federal government, and passions and interests that the tremendous growth of slavery over the previous twenty-five years would unleash.

II

The years after 1815 saw a renewed Northern interest in attacking slavery and a renewed interest in the West. Within four years, these would converge in the Missouri Controversy. In the immediate postwar period, antislavery literature poured out from Northern presses. From Philadelphia to Ohio, more aggressive and more numerous antislavery societies distributed tracts, sermons, and pamphlets. Widely-read English travel narratives condemned the continuation of slavery in the United States. *Niles' Weekly Regis-*

ter printed long, detailed proposals for gradual emancipation. And in Philadelphia, Republican William Duane's *Aurora* took a decidedly antislavery stance.[27]

The new antislavery literature was accompanied by a rising number of conflicts between Southern slaveholders who demanded greater protections for slavery, and white Northerners who demonstrated a growing unease with both slavery and slaveholders. As an increasing number of runaway slaves found refuge in Pennsylvania and Ohio, Southern slave catchers encountered hostile mobs, charges of kidnapping, and state judges who freed slaves on legal technicalities. When Southern slaveholders demanded a new fugitive slave law, Northerners insisted that the right of habeas corpus should be extended to all alleged fugitives. Another controversy erupted when free blacks and "term-slaves" (slaves who were slated to be freed under the North's gradual abolition laws) found themselves kidnapped or sold into Deep South slavery, prompting Northern states to seek federal enforcement of state laws that prohibited the sale of slaves out of Delaware and the Middle Atlantic states. At the same time, abolitionist societies sought new legal protections for free and kidnapped blacks, new regulations on the burgeoning domestic slave trade, and the acceleration of the North's gradual-abolition laws. Finally, the expansion of the illegal international slave trade which fed the cotton and sugar regimes in the Southwest attracted the attention of Virginia slaveholders, prompting Congress to pass a series of ever-stiffer penalties on trade.[28]

The years after 1815 also saw a dramatic change in the West's place in the American Union. The War of 1812 and the Napoleonic Wars had destroyed any lingering European ambitions for a mid-continent empire. White Western Americans had demonstrated their loyalty by scoring celebrated victories over the Northwest Indian alliance, the Red Sticks, and the British at New Orleans. They could now also count on having their interests better represented in Congress, as Westerners such as Henry Clay were gaining prominence in Washington. The great postwar migration to the West and an ambitious program of internal improvements similarly promised a fuller integration of the West into the Union. Rapid political consolidation also followed victory in the "Long War for the West": by late 1818, six western territories had either received or applied for statehood; Britain had agreed to joint occupation of the Oregon Country; Spain stood ready to cede Florida; and some Southern politicians were insisting that the Louisiana Purchase also included at least part of Spanish Texas. By 1819, the United States stood cautiously but confidently on the verge of securing a continental empire.[29]

Postwar expansion and consolidation also renewed Easterners' interest in Western slavery. Indiana's 1816 Constitution contained the strictest antislavery provisions of any state constitution in the country, including a provision that Article VI could never be repealed from the state constitution. Indiana's exclusion of slavery received extensive coverage in the national press, and Northern newspapers celebrated the demonstrated efficacy of Article VI. Northern enthusiasm for restricting Western slavery soon manifested itself in Congress. In April 1818, New Hampshire Republican Arthur Livermore proposed a constitutional amendment that would have prohibited slavery "in any State hereafter admitted into the Union," though the House voted down his proposal because of the impending admission of Alabama. Six months later, New York Republican James Tallmadge again raised the issue when he tried blocking Illinois statehood, because slavery was "not sufficiently prohibited" in its constitution.[30]

The debate over Illinois slavery prefigured the Missouri Crisis in important ways. Slavery had existed in the Illinois Country since the early 1700s. Even after the Northwest Ordinance excluded slavery, American settlers, and even government officials, had carried slaves into the territory. By the 1810s, an elaborate system of indentured servitude ensnared Illinois's 1,200 African Americans in a system of bondage that differed little from slavery. As Illinois moved toward statehood, leading politicians and a majority of white settlers favored the full legalization of slavery. Nonetheless, they recognized that Congress would require that Illinois adopt Article VI as a condition of statehood. Their proposed constitution thus included Article VI, but contained an elaborate set of exceptions that permitted slavery in all but name. Illinois politicians expected that once they gained statehood, they would fully legalize slavery in a new state constitutional convention to be held in a few years. Until then, their labor needs would be met by a system of indentured servitude and numerous exceptions to Article VI. What Illinois's proslavery politicians presented to Congress in 1818, then, was the constitution of a proto–slave state wrapped in free-state garb.[31]

Spotting the subterfuge, James Tallmadge proposed that Illinois remove the protections for slavery and indentured servitude and that, like Indiana, it adopt a clause forever prohibiting the repeal of Article VI. Yet the debate took an unexpected turn when a Southern representative defended the "antislavery" provisions of the Illinois constitution. According to George Poindexter of Mississippi, the Illinois constitution promised to eradicate slavery in a Western territory with a long history of slavery but a comparatively small number of slaves and a climate unsuitable for plantation agriculture. In Poindexter's formulation, Illinois had struck a balance that protected the rights of slaveholders already in place while providing for the gradual abolition of the slavery that had existed in the territory prior to statehood. While most Northern congressmen seem to have agreed with Poindexter, thirty-three representatives—a full third of the representatives from the Northern states—still saw fit to vote against admission. More telling, during the debate, Tallmadge stated his conviction that "the interest, honor, and faith of the nation, required it scrupulously to guard against slavery's passing into a territory where they have power to prevent its entrance." Tallmadge understood that the key issue was power, and there was little doubt that Congress now possessed the power needed to restrict slavery's Western expansion. Less than three months later, he would set off the Missouri Controversy by introducing his own gradual abolition plan for Missouri, a territory, like Illinois, with a comparatively small slave population and a climate unsuitable for plantation agriculture. This time, the House would approve Tallmadge's proposal with near-unanimous Northern support.[32]

In retrospect, by 1819, it was probably inevitable that something like the Missouri Controversy would come to pass. The emergence of a more secure West and the prospect of a continental republic; new sectional conflicts over slavery and increased Northern interest in restricting Western slavery; and, finally, the emergence of a federal government whose power increasingly matched its authority—all suggested that Northern Republicans would support any practical measure to restrict slavery expansion. What occurred in 1819, then, amounted to more than Northerners having "awakened quite suddenly to a realization" that "the national prospect had been heavily weighted in favor of slavery."[33] If Northern politicians awoke to anything, it was to the realization that the federal government now possessed the real, effective "power" needed to halt slavery's expansion in a continental republic.

Politicians also realized that the lack of power had been the deciding factor in their earlier decisions to permit slavery's expansion. In the heat of the Missouri Controversy, James Tallmadge declared that it was "an old principle," that "whenever the United States have had the right and *power,* they have heretofore prevented the extension of slavery." While Northern politicians conceded that previous Congresses had permitted slavery elsewhere, they maintained that Congress had done so only out of "uncontrollable necessity." Geopolitical rivalries, patterns of settlement, state claims to the Old Southwest, and the presence of slavery there had all meant that the federal government lacked the "power" to prohibit slavery in Kentucky,

Tennessee, the Mississippi Territory, and Louisiana. Yet Congress's inability to halt the growth of slavery in the Old Southwest did not diminish its right to do so in Missouri, nor to prohibit its expansion into the Trans-Mississippi West. Indeed, now that the federal government possessed the power needed to prohibit slavery's further extension, Northern restrictionists concluded that Congress was obligated to use it.[34]

Though historians have often focused their studies on the overly broad question of slavery in the United States, or on the narrow issue of sectional political strength, Northern Republicans who led the fight against Missouri slavery focused their arguments on the future of slavery in the Western portions of an expanding American Union. Throughout the Missouri Controversy they insisted that slavery in the Trans-Mississippi West was a national problem that required a comprehensive solution—one that began with restricting slavery in Missouri. By 1819 both Northerners and Southerners understood that American expansion had entered a new phase. Post-Revolutionary expansion into the Trans-Appalachian West, followed by the Louisiana Purchase, had created an enormous but unstable Union. Now, the existing Union seemed secure and many white Americans anticipated a new round of territorial acquisition and incorporation that would carry the American Union all the way to the Pacific. The outcome of the Missouri Controversy would set the "authority of precedent" for slavery in the remainder of the Louisiana Purchase and in the expected American expansion into Texas and on to the Pacific Coast. In order to prohibit slavery in the Far Western reaches of an expanding empire, Congress would have to halt slavery's expansion now, in Missouri. As Northerners—Republicans and Federalists—insisted, this would be the first step toward prohibiting slavery "in all new states and territories hereafter admitted to the Union." At the same time, however, most Northerners disclaimed any intentions of interfering with slavery in the Southern states. Much like Abraham Lincoln three decades later, Northern restrictionists sought to exclude slavery from the West rather then to emancipate slaves in the South.[35]

Southern slaveholders would have none of it. By 1819, restrictions on Western slavery menaced slavery in the East in ways that they never had in 1798, 1804, or 1811. Eastern slaveholders' unbridled opposition to the Tallmadge restrictions marked a significant change in the way that slaveholders understood the relationship between Eastern and Western slavery. Prior to 1810, slaveholders from the Atlantic states rarely tied the future of slavery in the East to its continued expansion in the West. Their claims to the West generally did not extend past the Carolina Upcountry, the Georgia interior,

Kentucky, and Tennessee, and they had expressed no concerns that restrictions on slavery in a place such as Louisiana would menace slavery in an Eastern state like Virginia. Except for a few visionaries such as Thomas Jefferson, they rarely imagined the far-off plantations of Natchez and Louisiana as a destination for the Chesapeake's growing population of slaves, slaves who were already being sold in vast numbers to "Georgia traders" who fed the demand for slave labor in the Carolina Upcountry and the Georgia interior.[36]

It was only during the crucial decade leading up to the Missouri Crisis that slavery in the Atlantic states became powerfully tied to its continued expansion in the West. The great expansion of the domestic slave trade in the 1810s created powerful new ties between slavery in the East and in the West. Perhaps 5,000 Chesapeake slaves had been sold into plantation slavery in the Lower Mississippi Valley in the period between 1790 and 1810. But between 1810 and 1820, over 120,000 Chesapeake slaves were either sold into the new domestic slave trade that fed Louisiana's and Mississippi's nearly insatiable appetite for slave labor, or were forced west with migrating slaveholders. In the decade leading up to the Missouri Controversy, the West became a vast outlet for the Eastern states' "excess" slave population. Northern proposals to exclude slavery from "all state and territories hereafter admitted to the Union" thus threatened to leave white Southerners "damned up in a land of Slaves," cutting off Eastern planters' most ready source of cash and leaving them increasingly vulnerable to slave rebellions.[37]

Slavery in the Atlantic states became further tied to its continued expansion into the West as thousands of Easterners flooded the Western country after 1815. Postwar, "Missouri fever" and "Alabama fever" set off an extraordinary mass migration, as settlers and slaves from the Atlantic states swelled the population of the Old Southwest. Between 1810 and 1820, the non-Indian populations of Mississippi and Louisiana doubled, and the population of Alabama increased twelvefold. Further west, the non-Indian population of Missouri tripled, from under 20,000 to over 60,000, of which perhaps 10,000 were enslaved blacks. After 1815, Western settlement offered Southern white families opportunities that were increasingly hard to come by in the Eastern slave states, and even in such recently settled states as Tennessee and Kentucky. After 1815, nearly every Southern community and family, black and white, was touched by this mass migration to the West. After 1815, Eastern slavery and the Southern social order became tied to the West in a way that it never had been at the time of the acquisition of the Natchez Country and the Louisiana Purchase.[38]

With Eastern and Western slavery connected in new ways, and with Southern politicians accepting the permanence of slavery, slaveholders defended their "rights" to Missouri and a vast, but ill-defined, West in a manner that had been absent from previous debates. Slaveholders now insisted that unrestricted access to the West was inseparable from the well-being and survival of slavery in the East. Slavery "will most probably continue to exist through all succeeding time," explained the widely-read essayist, "An American." Having accepted slavery's permanence, slaveholders now had to provide for "the proper and effectual management of slaves" through unrestricted access to the West. As Philip Barbour of Virginia noted at the height of the Missouri Controversy: "The real question is, what disposition shall we make of those slaves [in the existing slave states]? Shall they be perpetually confined on this side of the Mississippi, or shall we spread them over a much larger surface by permitting them to be carried beyond that river?" Only by gaining free access to the vast regions "beyond the river" could Eastern slaveholders preserve an institution they now accepted as permanent. With Western expansion so closely tied to the preservation of slavery in the East, Southern slaveholders could only understand the Tallmadge restrictions and a prohibition on slavery "in all states and territories hereafter admitted to the Union" as a direct threat to slavery where it already existed. To allow Congress to restrict expansion in the West amounted to ceding power over slavery's future in the East. Indeed, as one slaveholder remarked, prohibiting expansion was tantamount to "a declaration that slavery does not exist within the United States; but if it does, that Congress may abolish it, or confine it to narrow limits." With the preservation of slavery in the East tied to its continued expansion in the West, any distinction between restricting the institution in the West and abolishing it in the East was now a distinction without a difference.[39]

Though the early republic's most divisive sectional conflict ended with a compromise that temporarily solved the problem of slavery in the Louisiana Purchase, it also permanently sectionalized expansion, an especially foreboding development in a republic intent on conquering a continent.[40] In the 1820s, the sectional disunionism displayed during the Missouri Controversy squelched Unionist Southern politicians' desire for the acquisition of new territories suitable for slavery's expansion, especially Texas. Cautious expansionists could only hold back Southern expansionism for so long. Whig dislike for expansion, and Democratic sensitivities to the sectional implications of the acquisition of Texas, managed to put off annexation until well into the 1830s. But the death of the anti-annexationist William Henry Harrison allowed the anti-Whig Whig John Tyler to put Texas back on the national agenda. Democrats seized the opportunity offered by Tyler, turning the sectional policy of Texas annexation into the nationalist agenda of Manifest Destiny. But Democrats could not shroud the rankly proslavery annexation of Texas and the Mexican War under the mantle of Manifest Destiny for long. David Wilmot's Proviso made manifest the sectional underpinnings of annexation and war, revealing a new destiny for the ever-expanding republic.

The Compromise of 1850 would address the immediate problems of slavery in the territory acquired in the Mexican War, but like the Missouri Compromise, it would solve an immediate problem by putting off the larger issue. After the Compromise of 1850, four years of uneasy sectional harmony reigned before Southerners demanded repeal of the Missouri Compromise. That was followed by ever more strident calls for the annexation of Cuba, the creation of a new slave state in southern California, and finally, the acquisition of the entire "Golden Circle"—the rich plantation lands that stretched from Mexico through Central America and the northern rim of South America, and into the Caribbean. The Republican Party of Lincoln— like its forebears in the Missouri Controversy—responded by promising a definitive end to slavery's expansion. Like their forebears, too, Southern disunionists would have none of it. In the end, it would not be Southern slavery that led to disunion, civil war, and the destruction of slavery, but Southerners' insistence that the preservation of their cherished institution required unending expansion.

NOTES

1. Thomas Jefferson to John Holmes, 22 April 1820, Thomas Jefferson Papers, Library of Congress, Washington, D.C.; *Annals of Congress*, 15th Cong., 2nd sess., 305; ibid., 15th Cong., 1st sess., 1675. For Republicans and slavery expansion, see John Craig Hammond, *Slavery, Freedom, and Expansion in the Early American West* (Charlottesville: University of Virginia Press, 2007); and Sean Wilentz, "Jeffersonian Democracy and the Origins of Political Antislavery in the United States: The Missouri Controversy Revisited," *Journal of the Historical Society* 4 (Fall 2004): 375–401.

2. Glover Moore, *The Missouri Controversy, 1819–1821* (Lexington: University of Kentucky Press, 1953).

3. Ronald P. Formisano, "State Development in the Early Republic: Substance and Structure, 1780–1840," in *Contesting Democracy: Substance and Structure in American Political*

History, 1775–2000, ed. Byron E. Shafer and Anthony J. Badger (Lawrence: University Press of Kansas, 2001), 7–36 (quotation at 20). Don Fehrenbacher, *The Slaveholding Republic: An Account of the United States Government's Relations to Slavery* (New York: Oxford University Press, 2001), 263.

4. For the most significant challenges to Moore's interpretation, see Richard H. Brown, "The Missouri Crisis, Slavery, and the Politics of Jacksonianism," *South Atlantic Quarterly* 65 (Winter 1966): 55–72; Donald Robinson, *Slavery in the Structure of American Politics, 1765–1820* (New York: Harcourt Brace Jovanovich, 1971), 378–400; Major L. Wilson, *Space, Time, and Freedom: The Quest for Nationality and the Irrepressible Conflict, 1815–1861* (Westport, Conn.: Greenwood Press, 1974), 22–48; Leonard Richards, *The Slave Power: The Free North and Southern Domination, 1780–1860* (Baton Rouge: Louisiana State University Press, 2000), 52–82; Robert Pierce Forbes, *The Missouri Compromise and Its Aftermath: Slavery and the Meaning of America* (Chapel Hill: University of North Carolina Press, 2007); Wilentz, "Jeffersonian Democracy and the Origins of Political Antislavery in the United States"; and Hammond, *Slavery, Freedom, and Expansion in the Early American West.* For slavery and politics in the early republic, see Matthew Mason, *Slavery and Politics in the Early American Republic* (Chapel Hill: University of North Carolina Press, 2006).

5. For a sample of the widespread Northern calls for Congress to prohibit slavery "in all states and territories hereafter admitted into the Union," see "Wilmington Meeting" and "Resolutions of the Delaware General Assembly," *Niles' Weekly Register,* 22 January 1820; "Resolutions of the Pennsylvania Legislature," *Niles' Weekly Register,* 1 January 1820; "Resolutions of the New Jersey Legislature," *Niles' Weekly Register,* 22 January 1820; "Resolutions of the House of Assembly of New York," *Niles' Weekly Register,* 5 February 1820; "Resolutions of the New Hampshire Legislature," *Niles' Weekly Register,* 8 July 1820; "Town Meeting," *Liberty Hall and Cincinnati Gazette,* 21 December 1819; "Petition & Memorial, of . . . the Republican Electors of Woodbridge . . . ," *Washington Whig* (Bridgeton, N.J.), 22 November 1819; "Meeting at Camden," *Washington Whig* (Bridgeton, N.J.), 20 December 1819; "Meeting at Keene, New Hampshire," *Concord Observer,* 20 December 1819; Ohio, *Senate Journal, 1820,* 145–47, 154, 169; and Ohio, *House Journal, 1820,* 166, 176, 198–99. See also Hammond, *Slavery, Freedom, and Expansion in the Early American West,* 150–68.

6. For the literature on the relationship between expansion and the American Union, the uncertain future of the Trans-Appalachian West, and the West's eventual incorporation into the American Union polity, see François Furstenberg, "The Significance of the Trans-Appalachian Frontier in Atlantic History," *American Historical Review* 113 (June 2008): 647–77.

7. Fehrenbacher, *The Slaveholding Republic,* 255–63; idem, *The Dred Scott Case: Its Significance in American Law and Politics* (New York: Oxford University Press, 1978), 82–100; William W. Freehling, *The Road to Disunion,* vol. 1, *Secessionists at Bay, 1776–1854* (New York: Oxford University Press, 1990), 138–43; idem, *The Reintegration of American History: Slavery and the Civil War* (New York: Oxford University Press, 1994), 12–33; Paul Finkelman, *Slavery and the Founders: Race and Liberty in the Age of Jefferson,* 2nd ed. (Armonk, N.Y.: M. E. Sharpe, 2001); Adam Rothman, *Slave Country: American Expansion and the Origins of the Deep South* (Cambridge, Mass.: Harvard University Press, 2005), 18–34.

8. For the presence of slavery in the West prior to American possession, see Hammond, *Slavery, Freedom, and Expansion in the Early American West.* For the federal government's

inability to confront long-standing colonial practices and institutions, see Jack P. Greene, "Colonial History and National History: Reflections on a Continuing Problem," *William and Mary Quarterly*, 3rd ser., 64 (April 2007): 235–50.

9. Hammond, *Slavery, Freedom, and Expansion in the Early American West*, 1–75.

10. Furstenberg, "The Significance of the Trans-Appalachian Frontier in Atlantic History," 650; Jeremy Adelman and Stephen Aron, "From Borderlands to Borders: Empires, Nation-States, and the Peoples In Between in North American History," *American Historical Review* 104 (June 1999): 814–41. Like Furstenberg, Thomas Bender, in *A Nation among Nations: America's Place in World History* (New York: Hill and Wang, 2006), 61–115, places the struggle for the Trans-Appalachian West within an extended period of continental and trans-Atlantic conflict between imperial powers, Native Americans, and local settlers. Imperial powers in North America understood that they could govern Western settlers and local elites only by addressing the often conflicting interests of these groups see Eric Hinderaker, *Elusive Empires: Constructing Colonialism in the Ohio Valley, 1673–1800* (New York: Cambridge University Press, 1997); and Patrick Griffin, *American Leviathan: Empire, Nation, and Revolutionary Frontier* (New York: Hill and Wang, 2007). For the ways that the federal government accommodated the interests of Western slaveholders, and for the important exceptions in the Northwest, see Hammond, *Slavery, Freedom, and Expansion in the Early American West*.

11. Hammond, *Slavery, Freedom, and Expansion in the Early American West*, 9–11, 76–123; Andrew R. L. Cayton, " 'Radicals in the Western World': The Federalist Conquest of Trans-Appalachian North America," in *Federalists Reconsidered*, ed. Doron Ben-Atar and Barbara B. Oberg (Charlottesville: University Press of Virginia, 1998), 77–96.

12. "An Act for the Government of the Territory South of the Ohio River," in *The Territorial Papers of the United States*, ed. Clarence E. Carter, 28 vols. (Washington, D.C.: Government Printing Office, 1934–75), 4:3–19; *Annals of Congress*, 1st Cong., 2nd sess., 988; Arthur St. Clair to the Secretary of Foreign Affairs, 13 December 1788, in *The Territorial Papers of the United States*, 2:168–69; John R. Finger, *Tennessee Frontiers: Three Regions in Transition* (Bloomington: Indiana University Press, 2001), 99–131; Kevin T. Barksdale, *The Lost State of Franklin: America's First Secession* (Lexington: University Press of Kentucky, 2009).

13. Hammond, *Slavery, Freedom, and Expansion in the Early American West*, 9–12; Stephen Aron, *How the West Was Lost: The Transformation of Kentucky from Daniel Boone to Henry Clay* (Baltimore: Johns Hopkins University Press, 1996), 89–95.

14. For the importance of the Lower Mississippi Valley in securing the Trans-Appalachian West, see Furstenberg, "The Significance of the Trans-Appalachian Frontier in Atlantic History."

15. Andrew Ellicott to Sarah Ellicott, 17 February 1799; and Daniel Clark Sr. to Andrew Ellicott, 18 March 1798, both in Andrew Ellicott Papers, Library of Congress; "Memorial to Congress by Permanent Committee of the Natchez District," 23 October 1797, in *The Territorial Papers of the United States*, 5:9–11.

16. For the comparatively late development of a plantation society in the Lower Mississippi Valley, see Ira Berlin, *Many Thousands Gone: The First Two Centuries of Slavery in North America* (Cambridge, Mass.: Harvard University Press, 1998), 77–90, 195–215, 325–57; and Hammond, *Slavery, Freedom, and Expansion in the Early American West*, 31–36.

17. Andrew Ellicott, Circular Letter to the Inhabitants of the Natchez District, 13 October 1797; and Ellicott to Captain Green, 19 October 1797, both in Andrew Ellicott Papers, Library of

Congress. Ellicott had already concluded that the United States would have to permit slavery in the Natchez Country (see Ellicott to Pickering, 24 September 1797, in *The Territorial Papers of the United States,* 5:5).

18. Ellicott to the Permanent Committee, 26 September 1797; and Ellicott to Pickering, 26 September 1797, both in Andrew Ellicott Papers, Library of Congress; "Memorial to Congress by Permanent Committee of the Natchez District," 23 October 1797, in *The Territorial Papers of the United States,* 5:9–11; *Message from the President of the United States . . . Relative to the Affairs of the United States on the Mississippi . . . January 23, 1798* (Philadelphia, 1798); Pickering to Ellicott, 12 February 1798, Andrew Ellicott Papers, Library of Congress. For concerns that Britain, France, or Spain might seize the Natchez Country, see Andrew Ellicott, Circular Letter to a Member of Congress, 25 September 1797, Andrew Ellicott Papers, Library of Congress.

19. *Annals of Congress,* 5th Cong., 2nd sess., 1305–13 (quotation at 1309).

20. Pickering to Ellicott, 27 March 1798, 1 April 1798, in *The Territorial Papers of the United States,* 5:16–18; Pickering to Winthrop Sargent, 4 May 1798, Winthrop Sargent Papers, Ohio Historical Society, Columbus; "Governor Sargent's Address to the Inhabitants of this Territory," 18 August 1798, in *Mississippi Territorial Archives, 1798–1819,* ed. Dunbar Rowland (Nashville: Brandon Printing, 1905), 1:26.

21. *Annals of Congress,* 8th Cong., 1st sess., 1186; *National Intelligencer* (Washington, D.C.), 16 March 1804; "An Act for the Organization of Orleans Territory and the Louisiana District," 26 March 1804, in *The Territorial Papers of the United States,* 9:209; Hammond, *Slavery, Freedom, and Expansion in the Early American West,* 36–46.

22. "Remonstrance of the People of Louisiana," in *American State Papers,* 10, *Miscellaneous* 1:399; *National Intelligencer* (Washington, D.C.), 4 September 1804; "Discontent in Louisiana," *National Intelligencer* (Washington, D.C.), 24 August 1804; John W. Gurley to the Postmaster General (forwarded to Jefferson), 14 July 1804, in *The Territorial Papers of the United States,* 9:305.

23. Freehling, *The Road to Disunion,* 1:141–42; Fehrenbacher, *The Slaveholding Republic,* 260–61; Finkelman, *Slavery and the Founders,* 151.

24. Hammond, *Slavery, Freedom, and Expansion in the Early American West,* 32–33, 51–57; Thomas Jefferson, "Queries on Louisiana, 1803," and Benjamin Stoddert, Notes on Louisiana, 3 June 1803, both in Thomas Jefferson Papers, Library of Congress; "Description of Louisiana," in *Annals of Congress,* 8th Cong., Appendix, 1576; Stephen Aron, *American Confluence: The Missouri Frontier from Borderland to Border State* (Bloomington: Indiana University Press, 2006).

25. Thomas T. Davis to Thomas Jefferson, 5 November 1803, in *The Territorial Papers of the United States,* 13:7–8; "Remonstrance of the Representatives elected by the Freemen of their Respective Districts in the District of Louisiana," *American State Papers,* 10, *Miscellaneous* 1:401–4; "An Act for the Government of Louisiana Territory," 3 March 1805, in *The Territorial Papers of the United States,* 13:92–95.

26. *Annals of Congress,* 12th Cong., 1st sess., 1248; *Annals of Congress,* 16th Cong., 1st sess., 336–37.

27. For Northerners' "defending against slavery" and the profusion of antislavery literature that appeared after 1815, see Mason, *Slavery and Politics in the Early American Republic,* 75–176.

28. For Northern mobs and judges' freeing of fugitive slaves, see Hammond, *Slavery, Free-*

dom, and Expansion in the Early American West, 143–45. For the Fugitive Slave Law debates, see *Annals of Congress,* 15th Cong., 1st sess., 225–26, 231–38, 241–54, 257–58, 825–40. For the sale of "term-slaves" out of the Middle Atlantic states, see the *Annals of Congress,* 15th Cong., 2nd sess., 75–76, 336; and the *National Intelligencer* (Washington, D.C.), 21 December 1818. For antislavery societies' efforts to secure black freedom, see Richard S. Newman, *The Trans- formation of American Abolitionism: Fighting Slavery in the Early Republic* (Chapel Hill: Uni- versity of North Carolina Press, 2002). For controversies over the domestic slave trade, see Robert Gudmestad, *A Troublesome Commerce: The Transformation of the Interstate Slave Trade* (Baton Rouge: Louisiana State University Press, 2003). For the international slave trade, see Fehrenbacher, *The Slaveholding Republic,* 150–52.

29. Furstenberg, "The Significance of the Trans-Appalachian Frontier in Atlantic History"; Hammond, *Slavery, Freedom, and Expansion in the Early American West,* 152–54.

30. *Annals of Congress,* 15th Cong., 1st sess., 1675–76. For the interest in slavery and expansion prompted by Indiana statehood, see, "From the Richmond *Compiler,*" in the *Na- tional Register* (Washington D.C.), 28 September 1816; and the *National Intelligencer* (Wash- ington D.C.), 16 September 1816.

31. James Simeone, *Democracy and Slavery in Frontier Illinois: The Bottomland Republic* (Dekalb: Northern Illinois University Press, 2000); Hammond, *Slavery, Freedom, and Expan- sion in the Early American West,* 120–23; *Annals of Congress,* 15th Cong., 2nd sess., 305–11.

32. *Annals of Congress,* 15th Cong., 2nd sess., 308–10.

33. Fehrenbacher, *The Slaveholding Republic,* 263.

34. *Annals of Congress,* 15th Cong., 2nd sess., 1208 (emphasis added); A Philadelphian [Robert Walsh], *Free Remarks on the Spirit of the Federal Constitution, the Practice of the Federal Government, and the Obligations of the Union, Respecting the Exclusion of Slavery from the Territories and New States* (Philadelphia, 1819), 6; Hammond, *Slavery, Freedom, and Ex- pansion in the Early American West,* 150–68.

35. *Niles' Weekly Register,* 14 August 1819. Resolutions adopted in Northern public meetings and Northern state legislatures calling on Congress to prohibit the "further extension of slavery in all states and territories hereafter admitted to the Union" abounded throughout the North; see n. 5 for a small sampling. For congressional proposals "prohibiting by law the introduction of slaves into the territories of the United States west of the Mississippi," see *Annals of Congress,* 16th Cong., 1st sess., 158, 732, 733–34, 801–4, 1566–67; and James Barbour to Spencer Roane, 13 February 1820, Misc. Collection, W. L. Clements Library, University of Michigan, Ann Arbor.

36. For changing Southern interest in the West between the 1790s and the Missouri Con- troversy, see Hammond, *Slavery, Freedom, and Expansion in the Early American West,* 13–54, 161–68; and Lacy Ford, "Reconfiguring the Old South: 'Solving' the Problem of Slavery, 1787– 1838," *Journal of American History* 95 (June 2008): 95–128. For patterns of migration and the domestic slave trade between the East and the West, see Steven Deyle, *Carry Me Back: The Domestic Slave Trade in American Life* (New York: Oxford University Press, 2005), 17–38; and Allan Kulikoff, *The Agrarian Origins of American Capitalism* (Charlottesville: University Press of Virginia, 1992), 226–38.

37. Spencer Roane to James Monroe, 16 February 1820, in "Letters of Spencer Roane, 1788– 1822," *Bulletin of the New York Public Library* 10 (1906): 175. For concerns that restrictions on expansion would lead to slave rebellions in the Atlantic states, see, for example, *Annals of*

Congress, 15th Cong., 2nd sess., 1189. For the expansion of the domestic slave trade, see Deyle, *Carry Me Back,* 17–38; and Kulikoff, *The Agrarian Origins of American Capitalism,* 226–38.

38. For "Missouri fever," see Hammond, *Slavery, Freedom, and Expansion in the Early American West,* 57–75. For "Alabama fever" and the explosive growth of the white and black populations in Alabama, Mississippi, and Louisiana, due mainly to the emigration of whites from the Atlantic states, Kentucky, and Tennessee, see Rothman, *Slave Country,* 181–85. The growth of indigenous slavery in the Mississippi Territory and Louisiana through 1810, followed by the expansion of slavery from the Atlantic states, Kentucky, and Tennessee into the lower Mississippi Valley, is evident from a close reading of Rothman, *Slave Country,* 35–117.

39. "An American," *Richmond Enquirer,* 13 and 30 November 1819; *Annals of Congress,* 15th Cong., 2nd sess., 1189; ibid., 16th Cong., 2nd sess., 1344. For the new emphasis on the permanence of Southern slavery and its relationship with Western expansion, see, in addition to the essays of "An American," "Cato," in the *National Intelligencer* (Washington, D.C.), 4 December 1819; "Limner," in the *National Intelligencer,* 3 November 1819 and 29 January 1820; and "From the National Intelligencer" and "State of Missouri," in the *Richmond Enquirer,* 25 February 1819. For changes in Southern thinking about the "management" of slavery in the Atlantic states, see Mason, *Slavery and Politics in the Early American Republic,* 158–76; and Berlin, *Many Thousands Gone,* 217–356.

40. For the politics, pressures, and compromises that went into forging the Missouri Compromise, see Wilentz, "Jeffersonian Democracy and the Origins of Political Antislavery in the United States." For a more thorough but questionable account, see Forbes, *The Missouri Compromise and Its Aftermath,* 69–120.

Positive Goods and Necessary Evils

Commerce, Security, and Slavery in the Lower South, 1787–1837

Brian Schoen

Situating the region most committed to slavery, the Lower South, within the politics and history of the early United States remains a difficult task. Much of the literature makes the region the exception to most rules. As the rest of America transformed the Revolutionary spirit into a liberal-capitalist nation, Georgians, and particularly South Carolinians, supposedly took another path, drifting and eventually sprinting into a counterrevolutionary, even pre-modern, mindset. In short, the rest of the world passed the Lower South by, leaving it as a marginalized region on the fringes of the allegedly greater story of American political and economic development.[1]

Not all historians have accepted this view. Indeed, several recent scholars provide a starkly different trajectory that places racism, slavery, and the Lower South at the center of the national story. In this narrative, far from shrinking to the fringes of mainstream American political development, Lower South planter-politicians and their Virginia allies emerge as leaders of a "slave power" that hijacked or perverted the principles of freedom to make the United States a "slave nation." The precise timing of this transformation remains unclear, though increasingly the Constitutional Convention—that vexing "compact with the Devil" —appears to mark the moment that supposedly determined the outcome. This newer narrative turns the more traditional one on its head, making the Lower South's devotion to slavery the national rule rather than the regional exception.[2]

While both accounts are compelling, neither does justice to the complicated political story of the Lower South during the first half-century of the "politics of slavery." Both narratives jump teleologically from one slave-related debate to the next, often seeking to explain the origins of secession, rather than explaining particular developments on their own terms. As the present volume illustrates, however, the issue of slavery seldom entered early national politics predictably or in an isolated manner—even for those hypersensitized Lower South politicians who were willing to use almost any political tactic to prevent interference with their institution. More frequently, the debates over slavery were ill-defined, the unintended byproducts of other policy discussions, including the nature of national political economy, the entrance of new states into the Union, or debates over the contours of federalism. Understanding the politics of slavery thus requires not just appreciating how its institutional presence affected American society and politics; it also requires accepting that the politics of slavery was reshaped by seemingly unrelated developments. Lower South politicians' commitments to bettering their economic and geopolitical positions in an ever-changing Atlantic world indelibly shaped how they understood and approached their defense of slavery.

This essay looks forward from the Revolution, rather than backwards from nullification or the Civil War, to trace the Lower South's deeply pragmatic—and thus often turbulent—relationship with the federal government. It examines how Southerners linked their essential commitment to slavery with other political issues—some of them only partly related to the issue of slavery—such as regional security, or the region's transition from a languishing, eighteenth-century, Caribbean-focused economy, to a vibrant, nineteenth-century one based around the coastal and trans-Atlantic trade in cotton. In this "big picture" approach, no clear trajectory emerges. For one thing, Lower South politicians did not have to work their way toward a marginal political position within the Union. They began the national period hyperconscious of their peripheral economic position, and believed that the federal Constitution would be essential to remedying it. After successfully deflecting antislavery proposals in the First Congress, Southern politicians relied heavily on federal power to secure and extend their region's borders, enhance trade, and protect slavery from external threats. The strides they, and other Americans, made in creating a relatively secure and commercially integrated polity by the 1820s, however, unintentionally created the very circumstances that made the region less reliant on—and, with the bursting forth of protectionism and Northern anti-slavery measures, more suspicious of—the federal government, particularly with regard to its handling of trade policy and the situation of free blacks. If we situate the Lower South, then, within a broader and more fluid economic and political context, its leaders appear less as ideology-driven reactionaries and more as shrewd calculators. They willingly deployed federal power when it protected their broad array of interests, but sought to curtail it when changing circumstances threatened to undermine their robust cotton business and the still fragile system of slavery undergirding it.

I

The devastation of America's first "civil war" (and the Revolutionary War had been an especially bloody one in the Lower South), not the horrors of its second, guided the thoughts and actions of the post-Revolutionary generation. A humiliating wartime occupation ended only after the British fleet had departed from Charleston and Savannah. During the war, as many as 25,000 slaves had been confiscated or had emancipated themselves under the fog of war, and many of them had willingly removed themselves permanently from America's shores, with the help of the British Royal Navy. In their wake they left a deeply Anglophobic white population and a once prosperous colonial economy that was now largely cut off from traditional markets and that still faced significant threats. The return of Florida to America's Spanish rivals renewed a century-old rivalry, one that escalated concerns about the still formidable Native American nations in that region. Within the states, inflation was up, real estate values down. Even the resumption of trade—aided by Tory merchants who remained after the war—brought only slight relief, while generating a general debt crisis that by 1785 threatened, in one governor's estimation, to "transfer the whole Property of a large part of your Own Citizens, into the Hands of Aliens."[3] Making matters worse, new Navigation Acts passed by Britain severely restricted access to previously profitable markets, leading Low Country planter Ralph Izard to lament that "the present state of the commerce of America with the West Indies certainly cannot be added to the advantages . . . derived from the Revolution."[4] This, along with low rice and tobacco prices and an end of bounties for indigo production, dealt a significant blow to Lower South planters and merchants.[5]

The traditional measures for the eighteenth-century economy—imports and exports—indicate the disproportionately negative impact of the Revolution on the economy of the Lower South. In the early 1770s, the combined figures for Carolina and Georgia represented roughly 18 percent of the value of all imports and 38 percent of all exports to and from the thirteen mainland colonies. By the early 1790s, these two southernmost states provided only 9 percent of all taxable imports and roughly 15 percent of national exports. White residents around the regional metropolis, Charleston, which had once boasted the highest per capita wealth in North America, lived with great uncertainty about their postwar economic future. The situation in the backcountry, where brutality had been worse and economic opportunities less, looked even bleaker. Far from fretting that commerce would bring moral decay, proud coastal elites and desperate inland farmers shaped a political agenda aimed at gaining greater access to markets.[6]

The ideals of the Revolution and economic dislocation that accompanied it might have provided an opportunity for the Deep South to rethink slavery's utility. Instead, Georgia and South Carolina planters, farmers, and merchants redoubled their efforts to rebuild their plantation system, keeping the slave trade open for much of the 1780s, despite the fact that doing so deepened the problem of debt. In 1784 alone, planters and backcountry farmers purchased—mostly on credit—an estimated 10,000 slaves, which revealed considerable faith in the institution's long-term viability. Only in 1787 did concerns over specie drain and the Low Country's unique fears of a black population majority lead South Carolina to suspend slave importations. Backcountry residents, desirous of greater slave holdings for themselves, opposed the action. Similar motives led Georgia to continue to legally import slaves directly from Africa until 1799. Unlike patriots elsewhere during and after the Revolution, in the Lower South planters never lost their conviction that economic growth required Atlantic commerce, and that staple-production required more slaves. Thus, the delegates from the Lower South who arrived in Philadelphia in 1787 were desirous of a federal system that would be capable of protecting their states' unique commitment to slavery. Hard-earned compromises on issues like the three-fifths clause, the international slave trade, and fugitive-slave laws provided significant assurances that the new Constitution would protect slaveholders' property. However, shortsightedness—perhaps intentional—left considerable ambiguity regarding the domestic slave trade and what the "privileges and immunities clause" might mean for slaveholders' "right" to carry human chattel through free territory, or for the right of free blacks to travel through states that restricted or prohibited their movement.[7]

Mollified enough, South Carolina and Georgia voters enthusiastically embraced a new government they believed critical for securing a precarious geopolitical situation and restoring international commerce. Despite some posturing to the contrary while in convention, Georgia and South Carolina federalists demonstrated a deepening conviction that the new government would positively protect the region by stabilizing financial markets and negotiating trade agreements, hopefully remedying what Charles Pinckney referred to as the greatest of South Carolina's concerns: the "destruction of our commerce."[8] If resurrecting trade topped Carolinians' aspirations for the new government, the hope of securing its vast border against incursions from Native Americans and other occupants of Spanish-controlled Florida largely explains Georgia's quick and unanimous ratification of the new Constitution. The residents of both states celebrated the creation of a new polity which they believed would be more conducive to the pursuit of shared economic interests and security, and more likely to prevent potential conflicts, including over slavery.[9]

The following decade would test the faith of many residents of the Lower South, but primarily on issues other than slavery. By responding to antislavery petitions in language that James Madison described as "intemperate beyond all example and even all decorum," congressmen from the Lower South effectively blunted antislavery efforts at the federal level, forcing slavery's critics to delay targeting the slave trade and to focus their efforts on laws in the Northern states.[10] The rise of a powerful Jeffersonian-Republican opposition, nationally and within the Lower South, emerged primarily out of a frustration with international and domestic policies that were seen as neglecting agrarian interests. Hamiltonian-inspired commercial and foreign policies, like the Jay Treaty, enhanced the nation's dependence on British markets and merchants, but Georgians were especially angered by the administration's land policies and its attempts to deal fairly with Native Americans in the Old Southwest, who claimed sovereignty over western lands stretching to the Mississippi. By 1800, discontented Southerners were inclined to throw their support behind those state politicians who had tied their own ambitions to Jefferson's and Madison's national political agenda. Once the dust had settled, the election of 1800 demonstrated that what had been a previously murky regional politics had now tilted into a solidly Republican voting bloc. The prospect of having a fellow slave owner back in the White House had helped ease the concerns of planters in the Lower South, but more importantly, it was Jefferson's pro-expansionist policies and his promises to prioritize the interests of Southern agrarians that had attracted Southern voters increasingly consumed by "cotton fever."[11]

On balance, the Republican leadership in the White House and Congress did not disappoint. Jefferson accelerated diplomatic efforts to obtain New Orleans and East and West Florida, and he ratcheted up efforts to peaceably coerce Native Americans off of lands east of the Mississippi. Signaling its restored faith in the federal government, in 1802 Georgia entrusted its western lands to the national reserve, in exchange for $1.25 million and promises to pressure Native Americans to relinquish claims within the state. A year later, the diplomacy of Secretary of State James Monroe had secured New

Orleans and the vast Louisiana Territory. Ratification of that treaty and the subsequent enabling legislation, both opposed most forcefully by Northern Federalists, permitted slavery's extension there. As Lower Louisiana rapidly advanced toward statehood, the Republican-dominated territorial legislature and Jefferson's appointed governor opened the region to the interstate trade in slaves. Even a territorial ban on the Atlantic slave trade benefited South Carolinians, whose reopening of the trade in 1803 allowed them to "domesticate" African captives before shuttling them off to fresh lands in the Southwest. Less controversially, Jefferson and his successors used federal powers to create land offices, build roads, fortify the Southwest, and smooth the settlement of the Deep South.[12]

To the delight of Southern slaveholders, Jefferson's administration also turned back the racially progressive foreign policy of John Adams by cutting commercial and political ties with black Haitian revolutionaries who now ruled the old French colony of Saint-Domingue. As early as the late 1790s, concerns about the escalating violence in that colony, the flow of black and white refugees, and an alleged "conspiracy of French Negroes to fire" Charleston had led Georgians and South Carolinians to restrict or prohibit the entrance of free blacks into their ports.[13] Continued anxiety that developments in the Caribbean might lead to race warfare in the United States, along with increased confidence in Jeffersonian leadership, led Southern slaveholders to actually broaden the duties of federal officials within their states. In early 1803, the apparent ineffectiveness of North Carolina's acts against foreign black migrants led Wilmington residents to ask Congress for assistance against the "brigands from the French West Indian islands." The proposed legislation, strongly supported by Lower South representatives, levied stiff federal fines and tasked federal officials with enforcing state laws restricting the admission of "any negro, mulatto, or other persons of colour."[14]

The largely unstudied bill, vaguely entitled "An Act to Prevent the Importation of Certain Persons into Certain States," generated some anxiety from Northeasterners, who contended that it illustrated Virginia's "despotic sway" over national politics and violated the "privileges and immunities" of black sailors and white shipmasters.[15] The exemption of black "natives, citizens, or registered seamen of the United States," however, cleared the way for the act's easy passage, by a 48–15 vote. Some earlier critics even supported it, noting that the law would also put federal officials to work curtailing the international slave trade. Contrary to historians' assumptions, however, the act had emerged out of a desire to restrict the movement of

Caribbean blacks to the United States, not primarily to further curtail American participation in the international slave trade.[16] Indeed, South Carolina and Georgia officials welcomed the presence of federal officials to assist in preventing the entrance of potentially dangerous blacks, free or slave. The 1803 federal law revealed that Republicans could craft national legislation regarding slavery and free blacks with minimal controversy, so long as they remained cognizant of local differences and were able to skirt any possible constitutional problems.

The Jeffersonian-Republican alliance proved even more willing to use the tools of the federal government to protect commercial agrarian interests, including those of planters in a regional economy that had been transformed by the expanding production of cotton. Driven by increased global demand, cotton had quickly outstripped traditional crops and naval supplies as the region's primary export commodity. With the help of optimistic backcountry growers (mostly Jeffersonians), the value of all exports from Georgia and South Carolina had grown by 212 percent and 78 percent, respectively, between 1795 and 1800, compared to a national average of 48 percent.[17] This badly needed growth had helped to reverse the relative economic decline of the previous quarter-century, compensating for the dramatic reduction of the region's once profitable West Indian trade and tying the region's economy to direct trade with Britain and Northern ports. Profits from cotton also gave slavery new economic life, as inland cotton growers siphoned off surplus slaves from less profitable tobacco, indigo, and rice plantations. The domestic slave trade redistributed labor with tragic efficiency, helping to preserve slavery's profitability nationally and better harmonizing the interests of slaveholders from both the Upper and Lower South.[18]

These economic changes had unforeseen and subtle political ramifications, especially when Britain once again targeted American shippers in 1806. Trapped between defending American commerce to the West Indies and Continental Europe, and risking the increasingly critical direct cotton trade for which Great Britain was the chief consumer, Lower South planter-politicians consciously decided to support "free trade and sailors' rights" by entering into a commercial war. That choice allowed them to paint themselves as self-sacrificing patriots who were leveraging their access to cotton markets for the benefit of Northeastern interests. Yet the tools employed by Jefferson to accomplish this end—the embargo against British trade, new navigation acts, and draconian enforcement mechanisms—would end up greatly expanding national and executive regulatory powers, setting precedents the Southern planter-politicians would later regret. More immediately, the failure of commercial warfare to win timely redress, coupled with British efforts to monopolize American cotton, culminated in a war with the region's chief trading partner. Protecting national interests in the Atlantic came with a price.[19]

The commercial and military warfare that dominated national politics from 1806 to 1816 had little to do with slavery directly. These external threats may even have muted political disagreement (or at least public awareness) over the decision of Congress to halt participation in the international slave trade. For the Republican Party in particular, the proclaimed military victory over the British, and political victory over the Federalists, marked a high point in interregional cooperation—which was later cemented in policy, with the virtual exclusion of foreign ships from the coastal trade, the institution of a second National Bank, and the introduction of moderately protective tariffs beneficial to American industry. Yet amidst the euphoria, the period had ushered in forces that promised to dramatically, if gradually, transform the politics of slavery. Frustrated with Southern-led policies and their own shrinking influence, some Federalists sought to challenge the very underpinnings of Southern power: the three-fifths clause. The "rebirth of freedom" that emerged out of the war also reenergized an ascendant group of Northern Republicans, who intensified their antislavery efforts by accelerating state emancipation, cracking down on the illegal slave trade, and supporting the antislavery potential of the American Colonization Society.[20]

The war and its aftermath reshaped the Lower South's outlook in a different direction. Except for the case of a small number of Old Republicans, faith in the national government had been enhanced by events and the region's heightened economic power. Andrew Jackson's military exploits had forced large land cessions from the Red Sticks, Creeks, Chickasaws, and Choctaws, thus reducing the Indian threat and opening up new land for cotton. Commercial conventions signed with Britain in 1815 and 1818 had brought the resumption of direct trade with Britain on better terms, allowing planters to finally capitalize on high cotton prices and bumper crops. Alabama's and Mississippi's statehood petitions generated little opposition. Even the official end of the international slave trade had the salient effect of removing the tensions between the Lower South and other American regions over that issue, instilling further hope that an era of good feelings might yet emerge. Regional challenges remained, in the form of Maroon communities, fugitive slaves, slave insurrections, and the continued presence of Seminole warriors and their Spanish allies, but especially after James

Monroe's election in 1816, Lower South Republicans had every reason to believe that the federal government would help meet these challenges.

II

Basking in a major postwar cotton boom and in the Republicans' triumphal and self-congratulatory version of events, prominently placed Lower South politicians temporarily dropped their guard against the potential implications for slavery of freer Northern states and a stronger federal government. In fact, some continued to turn to federal legislation to buffer them from the effects of a growing free-black population. Responding to isolated Northern state-court decisions awarding personal freedom to slaves, in December 1817 William Smith became the most vocal proponent of a new fugitive-slave law that would have curtailed Northern personal-liberty laws and suspended habeas corpus, by forcing federal and free-state courts and officials to return suspected fugitive slaves merely upon the presentation of a certificate issued by a Southern magistrate. Enough pliable Northern votes had helped pass competing House and Senate versions of the bill, but the apparent unwillingness of Southern congressmen to guarantee greater protections for free blacks had thwarted a final compromise. More successfully, and in hindsight more surprisingly, Carolina representative Henry Middleton co-sponsored a bill that stiffened federal penalties against the international slave trade and gave the president the authority and federal funds necessary to recolonize black captives. In what would later be seen as an alarming precedent, William Crawford, an Old Republican from Georgia who served as Monroe's treasury secretary, urged the president to make use of this broadly defined executive power to begin resettling former slaves in Liberia.[21]

Even the fuse lit when James Tallmadge proposed banning slavery from Missouri, in February 1819, proved to be a comparatively long one for most Lower South residents. Nine months into the controversy, Charles Pinckney observed that in Charleston, "scarcely a word was said of the Missouri question; no man there ever supposed that one of such magnitude was before you."[22] As compromise efforts resumed in early 1820, the anti-restrictionist Pennsylvania senator Jonathan Roberts contrasted the position of representatives from Virginia, "the spoild child of the Union," with that of such "reasonable men" and willing compromisers as Pinckney and Lowndes. Although both Georgia's and South Carolina's senators opposed the restriction of slavery above the 36°30" parallel, almost half (7 of 16) of the states' representatives (and a majority of South Carolina's delegation) nevertheless voted for the amendment, which appeared to end the controversy.[23] Afterwards, Pinckney would declare the compromise "a great triumph." By October, Secretary of War John C. Calhoun was assuring Southern correspondents that there was "no reason to expect a storm."[24] South Carolinians and Georgians were as concerned with economic and geopolitical security in an uncertain Atlantic world as they were with the possible introduction of slavery into the more northern territories of the Trans-Mississippi West.

By mid-1820, regional newspapers had turned their attention back to where it had been before the Missouri debate: to frustration over Spain's unwillingness to ratify the Adams-Onís Treaty of 1819 that would cede Florida to the United States, and to concern over attempts to raise the duties on textiles in the wake of the 1819 Panic. Even Congress's late-session failure to raise tariffs did not prevent "a very numerous and respectable" body of concerned Charleston residents from organizing against future protectionist efforts. In a remonstrance sent to Congress in December, State Attorney Robert Hayne and Stephen Elliot detailed the likely redistributive effects of such protectionism, claiming that slave-based cotton production gave the South a "peculiar interest" in ensuring "that our interchange with the world should be free."[25] These and other free traders' efforts, perhaps aided by the firestorm created when Northern congressmen objected to a clause in Missouri's constitution that banned the entrance of free blacks, had the effect of postponing any serious tariff revision, which would have to wait nearly four years.

Why such a large number of congressmen cited the "privileges and immunities" clause against Missouri's ban remains something of a mystery, especially given that both Northern and Southern states had a long history of restricting the movement of free blacks. To Lower South politicians like Pinckney, however, the "unexpected and inexcusable opposition" initially seemed a desperate attempt to block the hard-earned entrance into the Union of another slave state. As the stalemate continued, however, Northern recalcitrance suggested an ominous shift, advancing well beyond earlier concerns that federal laws (such as the 1803 federal law supporting state bans and the Fugitive Slave Act of 1818) might discriminate against the movement of free blacks to now suggest that even slave states had no right to do so.

The argument was especially worrisome to South Carolinians, who, as recently as December, had debated the constitutional parameters of such a measure before reinstating their own prohibition upon the entrance of free blacks into the state, "unless it be in consequence of shipwreck . . . or as a seaman on board."[26] Pinckney now leapt to Missouri's defense. Claiming to have drafted the relevant portion of the federal Constitution on the issue, he brazenly dismissed even the possibility of "a black or colored citizen," suggesting that "the silence of Congress on the antecedent laws of the Southern and Western States, on this very subject ought to be considered as full proof that" the Founders "knew the imminent danger there was in the Southern and Western States admitting such persons."[27] After what Robert Forbes has accurately described as "a quasi-historical exegesis, relying on . . . flexible principles of logic," Pinckney turned to present interests, hoping that an Atlantic- and cotton-centered economic analysis might make Northerners reconsider.[28]

Using recently released Treasury reports and the flood of petitions lamenting post-Panic conditions, he highlighted the Northeast's dependence on exporting Southern produce, particularly cotton, and on carrying foreign and domestic goods to Southern markets. "In this state of things," it seemed "almost superfluous to ask if it is not of much greater consequence to the Northern and Eastern States to preserve an Union from which they derive such very important benefits, than to risk it to give to a few free negroes and mulattoes the right to settle in Missouri contrary to the declared unanimous wish of the people of that State?" Pinckney's efforts may have strengthened the spine of Southerners, but they did not end the impasse. It was only with the release of Henry Clay's Joint Senate and House Committee Report, which illogically accepted the prohibition on free blacks while declaring that it should not be construed to impede the "privileges and immunities" guaranteed to citizens under the United States Constitution, that the gridlock was finally broken.[29] Observers made what they wanted of the clause, demonstrating that legal obfuscation again proved expedient for diffusing the crisis.

Even as Clay's final compromise hung in the balance, the news that Spain's new liberal government had finally accepted Adams's transcontinental treaty brightened the political picture, especially for South Carolinians and Georgians. Though Clay's opposition to the terms of the treaty has recently been cited as evidence that "Southerners" opposed the treaty because of its failure to include Texas, Southeasterners, some already lined up for the anticipated Florida land bonanza, generally praised it for acquiring Florida, "a country" that the Charleston *City Gazette* deemed "of more value to us" than Texas. Indeed, correspondence from the U.S. minister to Spain, John Forsyth, reveals that he used reports of American interest in Texas not to reopen negotiations, but as leverage to compel the new liberal government to complete the sale of East and West Florida lands closer in proximity to his home state of Georgia.[30] By removing a long-standing bone of contention with Spain, the treaty also reduced the likelihood of conflict with Britain and France.

Continued peace paved the way for commercial policies favorable to cotton planters, including, ultimately, an end to French discriminatory duties on American ships in June 1822. Waning external threats justified reductions in military expenditures, thus aiding Treasury Secretary Crawford's efforts at fiscal retrenchment, a policy seen as necessary to deal with a national debt without raising tariffs. The period from 1819 to 1821 portended some ominous signs of things to come, but with few exceptions, the region's faith in the federal government had survived the tumult, not least because, amidst the fury, the actions of national officials had actually advanced regional security and achieved freer trade. Yet these successes had the unintended effect of lessening Georgians' and South Carolinians' reliance on the federal government just when developments at home and in Washington suggested how deeply federal efforts to form and protect an "American System" of trade could threaten slavery and the international cotton trade.

III

The first Missouri controversy temporarily removed the question of slavery's expansion from national political discourse, but the issue at the crux of the second Missouri controversy, the status of free blacks, could not be so easily suppressed. Different understandings of that multifaceted subject, along with the eventual political success of protectionism in 1824, forced a growing number of Lower South slaveholders to perceive powers they had previously conceded to the federal government in a more threatening light. Crises over free black sailors, nationalist economic policy, and colonization proposals led them to believe that a more robust states' rights constitutionalism might provide the only solution to future political challenges.

Denmark Vesey's Charleston conspiracy reminded slaveholders of the daily threats they faced, while their response unintentionally triggered a crisis that struck at the legal and economic premises of National Republican efforts to create a more self-sufficient economy. Vesey's previous time as a sailor, and rumors of a Haitian component to his plan, heightened alarm over incoming sailors. Accordingly, one of many laws targeting free blacks that legislators passed called for any "free negroes or persons of color" employed on ships arriving in port to be jailed, with the captains of such vessels being forced to pay for detention expenses and to "carry away" the sailor, or face a one thousand dollar fine and two months' imprisonment. Sailors not removed could be "deemed and taken as absolute slaves."[31]

The growing presence of free black sailors in Southern ports had been the flip side of the greatly accelerated cotton business that Lower South residents so proudly boasted had become critical to the nation. Despite making up only 2.5 percent of the Northeast's population in 1820, African Americans, with limited opportunities and willing to accept comparatively low wages, comprised between 16 percent and 23 percent of berths from key Northern cities.[32] Though black sailors had always been important to the Atlantic trade, the progress of emancipation in the Northern state now meant that most had experienced freedom. Such sailors had generally been exempt from state and local regulations. Now South Carolina legislators sent a resounding message that free black outsiders would no longer be considered necessary evils, but "moral contagions." Though expressing concern about Caribbean-born black sailors, the South Carolina Association, an organization made up of over three hundred prominent residents formed to enforce the act, focused especially on the need to prevent "most of the vessels coastwise" from being "manned principally by free negroes and persons of colour from the Northern and Eastern States." That "evil increased of late" threatened to "inveigle away our slaves" and introduce among them "pernicious principles and opinions."[33]

At first glance, this drastic action seems ill conceived, especially given the languishing Atlantic economy, record low cotton prices, and the adverse effect on native ship owners. The act, however, represented a calculated risk by Low Country proponents who apparently believed that the law conformed to federal standards, and that the economic downturn had made Northern carriers even more desperate than Southern planters. Intentionally draconian penalties would, it was hoped, "compel" ship masters "to employ white men only on board such vessels as traded to this port." Even as the act came under attack, its supporters suggested that "strict execution of the act was producing the happiest effects" and "would in a few months" end the threat.[34] Nor, despite the inconvenience to ship owners, did custom house records indicate that the act was negatively affecting commerce. The total American and foreign tonnage entering South Carolina ports actually increased by 16 percent during the first year of the new law's enforcement.[35]

While supporters highlighted the law's necessity as a deterrent, victims quickly seized on its questionable constitutionality, reopening the broad debate over the parameters of federalism and of free blacks' place within the Union. One month into enforcement, a Philadelphia ship captain asked a state court for a writ of habeas corpus for two black sailors jailed under the act. When denied, he and forty-two other American masters petitioned Congress for "energetic measures" against an act they argued "destroys the liberty of freeman" and unconstitutionally "interferes with the freedom of navigation."[36] Alarmed with the jailing of British citizens, the British consul appealed directly to the State Department, contending that the law violated the terms of the 1815 Commercial Convention that guaranteed reciprocal commerce. The debate over a state's right to prevent the entrance of free blacks, hypothetically raised by the second Missouri Controversy, had been reengaged on a grander stage and with much higher stakes.

An unanticipated court ruling from a native son brought the issue to a head and forced a more carefully crafted response. Before ultimately concluding that the limits of the 1789 Judiciary Act prevented him from granting relief to a British citizen in a state criminal case, the Charlestonian William Johnson—who had been appointed to the Supreme Court by Jefferson— enthusiastically endorsed the complainants' arguments, ruling that ships and black sailors had a "right" to enter port. Johnson, revealing a strongly National Republican view of political economy and the Constitution, argued that the act had disunionist tendencies, interfered with international treaties, and violated the federal government's exclusive right over international or interstate commercial regulation. Though the "privileges and immunity" clause did not specifically apply to the sailor's situation, Johnson noted that the racial standard applied set a very slippery slope.[37]

In a protracted newspaper war, critics excoriated Johnson for venturing outside the facts and ruling "extra-judicial," but finding a constitutional argument applicable against both foreign and U.S. sailors proved more difficult. Respondents hoped that federal laws, including the 1803 one, would provide ample precedent, but as Johnson retorted, those laws, having expressly exempted American sailors, "cut both ways."[38] As a result, defenders of the act continually returned to the contention that Johnson had overlooked "the inherent rights of the individual states," which had always included, they claimed, the police "regulation of a black population found within her limits." After cataloguing state laws revealing their willingness to assert those "rights," one defendant then claimed that states had not been expressly granted such authority only because "no man at that time doubted her right, or her power." To bolster their case, they turned to international law asserting a people's right to "self-preservation," and cited well-established quarantine laws as well as Britain's recent passage of an Alien Act allowing removal of foreigners deemed "dangerous to the peace and tranquility of the country." Very precise circumstances surrounding a quite unexpected legal debate—not a deep states' right tradition—forced those supporting the acts, including former Federalists, into a strident states' rights constitutionalism that few would have envisioned necessary even a few years earlier. Johnson's ruling also created a deep distrust of the federal courts and federal magistrates, who in 1803 had been asked to enforce state laws against free blacks, but who now stood poised to undermine them.[39]

Despite indirect appeals from Secretary of State Adams, and Attorney General William Wirt's ruling against the law in 1824, state politicians refused to relent, amending it only to exempt sailors on board military ships. Narratives of the so-called Negro Seamen's controversy sometimes end here, exaggerating South Carolina exceptionalism and propelling us toward the Nullification Crisis.[40] Congress refused to take up the ship master's petition. Cabinet officials (most with presidential aspirations) proved unwilling to force its repeal. Even Chief Justice Marshall privately admitted that the issue was too contentious to handle, and mused that "Brother Johnson has hung himself on a democratic snag in a hedge composed entirely of thorny state rights."[41] Though they had a solid case against the constitutionality of South Carolina's position, federal officials feared reopening the fresh wounds from 1821.

As that crisis remained unresolved, intervening political developments suggested that the Lower South Republicans' earlier acceptance of the tools of commercial warfare against Britain (including high duties) had created a dangerous precedent that now threatened the region's ever-growing need for freer international trade. In early 1824, Henry Clay pushed a revised tariff schedule, which would have raised average duties to around one-third of the value of imports, onto the floor of the Senate. While recent historians have been quick to read anti-tariff arguments as merely masks for proslavery defenses, the flood of early anti-tariff petitions from the Lower South cautions against such an interpretation. Protests from backcountry counties like Putnam County, Georgia, and Low Country communities around Charleston scarcely even allude to slavery. Instead, the memorialists remained narrowly fixed on the tariff's disproportionately negative economic effects in the short run, and on longer-term fears that Europe might respond by finding alternative sources of cotton. Though future nullifiers drew a relatively straight line between the tariff and slavery, the immediate and wide-ranging implications of these understudied tariff debates on slavery remained elusive, partly because free-traders and protectionists found it politically expedient to keep the issues separate. The passage of higher tariffs did, however, ominously suggest a powerful political alliance between the Northeast and the West, a concern that the progress of such Northern projects as the Erie Canal and Adams's and Clay's allegedly "corrupt bargain" only furthered.[42]

Other indications of the Lower South's troubles occurred in early 1825 when two competing proposals regarding slavery met with very different reactions. The previous December, Georgia had proposed a constitutional amendment that would have expressly permitted states to ban free blacks. In January 1825, Ohio—a state with its own concerns about free-black immigrants—proposed a dramatically different plan, suggesting that slavery was a national evil that required federally funded colonization. The Cotton States, joined by Missouri but not by the rest of the slave states, followed Georgia's lead in bluntly rejecting the idea as "calculated to infringe the rights of the states."[43] By summer, however, eight state legislatures had endorsed Ohio's plan, while nine states had rejected Georgia's. Congressional action on behalf of colonization and Adams's insistence on sending delegates to a Pan-American conference further rankled slaveholders, the latter also raising concerns that the nation might be drawn into alliances that could threaten conflict with essential trading partners. Though Adams took special care to avoid consciously alienating Southern slaveholders, developments, closely scrutinized by politically opportunistic opponents, could not help but have that effect.

While a few radicals in the region—an odd mix of former Federalists, inconsolable Crawfordites, and repentant Calhounites—pointed toward nullification, most others sublimated their anger within a Jacksonian opposition they believed would, as Jefferson had in 1800, rebalance the federalist system and protect slavery and cotton. Jackson's first term made significant but not complete strides in accomplishing both of these goals. Though Southeastern free-traders remained severely frustrated with Jackson's hesitancy to move against the so-called "Tariff of Abominations" that helped place him in office, slaveholders found other decisions more to their liking. In addition to his Maysville Road veto and the withdrawal of federal support for Liberia, Jackson's administration brought federal Native American policy in line with Georgians' long-standing desire for removal, promising reduction of the last non-slave threat from the Southeast and perhaps staving off nullification in that state.[44]

Possibly hoping to blunt nullification, Jackson's administration accepted South Carolina's position on the seamen's controversy, a significant boon to other states considering following their lead. Already, a lack of federal boldness—coupled with the publication of David Walker's fiery *Appeal* in September 1829, the continued circulation of calmer anti-slavery Quaker tracts, and specific instances of slave unrest—had led Georgia and North Carolina to follow suit by placing "such obstacles in the way of vessels bringing" free blacks that would "induce their owners & officers to desist from their employment." Though attempting to better shield the laws from federal scrutiny by conforming them to quarantine laws, these laws shared the same punitive mechanisms as South Carolina's, including threats of imprisonment or even enslavement and steep fines for ship captains.[45] In 1830, the U.S. Attorney General, Georgian John Berrien, gave them and other states, including eventually Alabama, Florida, and Louisiana, the political, diplomatic, and legal cover they needed. Going out of his way to embarrass Wirt for his earlier opinion, Berrien defended such measures as internal police laws, then opined that "there is a perfect harmony between the legislation of South Carolina and the United States."[46] South Carolina's policy remained the harshest, in terms of jail time and fines, but empowered by Jackson's position, other states manned the turret with her.

The unwillingness of the federal government to touch the matter speaks volumes about slavery's semi-sacred place within the early Second Party System, and provides further evidence for what Donald Ratcliffe sees as a "racist consensus that most Northerners had come to share" by the late 1820s.[47] No executive official prior to Lincoln took significant action against the Negro Seamen Acts. Some domestic victims appealed to their elected official in Congress, but not until the early 1840s did they even receive a hearing, and then primarily as part of a larger fight against Texas annexation. The pro-Southern bent that Jackson gave to the Supreme Court all but assured that the nation's top court would not interfere. Chief Justice Roger Taney, who as Attorney General had issued an unofficial opinion supporting the acts' constitutionality, strengthened the legal edifice for the acts by supporting a broad construction of state policing power in the quite unrelated case of *New York v. Milne.*[48] With victims, black and white, trapped in federalism's Gordian knot, merchants either had to cajole local officials to look the other way or conform to the intentions of the act. The precipitous decline in the percentage of African Americans onboard ships doing business in Savannah and New Orleans in the years after enforcement began strongly suggests that the legislation had a powerful effect.[49] Despite these inconveniences, the profits derived from carrying cotton continued to lure merchants and their increasingly white crews to Southern ports. Northern economic nationalists, who accommodated Lower South sensibilities because they needed their cotton, did not generally find the favor returned, as Lower South planters' and politicians' desire for free trade prevented them from embracing an "American System."

Georgians and South Carolinians who reflected back on their first half-century under the Constitution had reason to be cautiously optimistic about their future within the Union. Their borders had never been more secure, allowing some to conceive of more ambitious territorial gains in the Trans-Mississippi West. Predictions of economic catastrophe had proven short-sighted. Cotton prices and production had returned to high levels by the mid-1830s, and British and Northern dependence on slave-grown cotton had deepened. Despite fears that they might not be achieving the same economic growth as their Northern or Western neighbors, their position within the national and global economy had matured considerably since the 1790s. While nullification had been defeated as a constitutional principle, it had created the political pressure to force a gradual tariff reduction and a more sympathetic executive and judicial position on the Seamen's Acts. Even the mass petitioning and mailing campaign of Northern abolitionists offered a political silver lining. Enough Northern representatives and senators had joined an increasingly united Slave South to gag antislavery petitions and prohibit delivery of abolitionist mails.

Though never complete, such partial victories, whether tacit or acknowledged, ultimately allowed many slave owners in the early 1840s to again embrace a more expansive view of the federal government's role in protecting slavery, just as a deep economic depression also left many thinking they needed federal action to aid in economic recovery. With their state police power generally secured from federal intervention and their fugitive slaves running away at alarming rates, slaveholders felt increasingly comfortable urging, and ultimately receiving, a stronger fugitive-slave act that gave federal judges the authority to temporarily deputize a state's citizens and compel them to act on slaveholders' behalf.[50] Such a strong "nationalist" position would have been much harder to imagine at a time prior to the tacit acceptance of their ability to control black travelers within their own states. Yet whereas the early politics of slavery had been about suppressing, obscuring, or harmonizing conflict, the later one functioned more like Newton's laws of physics. In part because the nation's diverse populations had become more interconnected, every success on one front created an equal and opposite reaction elsewhere in the extended republic. Southern slaveholders' efforts to pursue and protect their own material interests increasingly limited the rights not only of blacks, but of whites, be they manufacturers, abolitionist petitioners, ship captains, or farmers seeking a future in Western lands. Northern white politicians faced the same question that countless white ship owners traveling to and from Southern ports did. How much inconvenience would they accept in exchange for doing business with a South that controlled the most lucrative commodity of the day? Until the rise of a free-soil Republicanism, more often than not, they grudgingly succumbed to the politics of commerce and cotton.

NOTES

1. See William Freehling, *Prelude to Civil War: The Nullification Controversy in South Carolina, 1816–1836* (New York: Oxford University Press, 1965); *The Road to Disunion*, vol. 1, *Secessionists at Bay, 1776–1854* (New York: Oxford University Press, 1990); Manisha Sinha, *The Counterrevolution of Slavery: Politics and Ideology in Antebellum South Carolina* (Chapel Hill: University of North Carolina Press, 2000); and the many works of Eugene Genovese.

2. See, for example, Lawrence Goldstone, *Dark Bargain: Slavery, Profits, and the Struggle for the Constitution* (New York: Walker and Co., 2005); Paul Finkelman, *Slavery and the Founders: Race and Liberty in the Age of Jefferson* (New York: M. E. Sharpe, 2001); Donald Robinson, *Slavery in the Structure of American Politics, 1765–1820* (New York: Harcourt Brace Jovanich, 1971); Leonard Richards, *The Slave Power: The Free North and Southern Domination, 1780–1860* (Baton Rouge: Louisiana State University Press, 2000); Robin Einhorn, *American Taxation, American Slavery* (Chicago: University of Chicago Press, 2006); and, perhaps with the most sophistication, Robert E. Bonner, *Mastering America: Southern Slaveholders and the Crisis of American Nationhood* (Cambridge: Cambridge University Press, 2009). A work that avoids either extreme is Matthew Mason's *Slavery and Politics in the Early American Republic* (Chapel Hill: University of North Carolina Press, 2006).

3. "Message from Moultrie to House of Representatives," 23 September 1785, in South Carolina, General Assembly, House of Representatives, in *Journals of the House of Representatives, 1783–1794,* ed. Lark Emerson Adams (Columbia: University of South Carolina Press, 1979), 313–14.

4. Ralph Izard to Thomas Jefferson, 1 July 1786, in *The Papers of Thomas Jefferson*, ed. Julian Boyd (Princeton, N.J.: Princeton University Press, 1954), 10:83–84.

5. Sylvia Frey, *Water from the Rock: Black Resistance in a Revolutionary Age* (Princeton, N.J.: Princeton University Press, 1991); Jerome Nadelhaft, *The Disorders of War: The Revolution in South Carolina* (Orono: University of Maine at Orono Press, 1981); George R. Lamplugh, *Politics on the Periphery: Factions and Parties in Georgia, 1783–1806* (Newark: University of Delaware Press, 1986).

6. For the colonial success of the plantation system, see S. Max Edelson, *Plantation Enterprise in Colonial South Carolina* (Cambridge, Mass.: Harvard University Press, 2006); and Peter A. Coclanis, *The Shadow of a Dream: Economic Life and Death in the South Carolina Low*

Country, 1670–1920 (New York: Oxford University Press, 1991). On net wealth, see Alice Hanson Jones, *Wealth of a Nation To Be* (New York: Columbia University Press, 1980), app. A, 357. For colonial trade, see U.S. Bureau of the Census, *Historical Statistics of the United States* (Washington, D.C.: Government Printing Office, 1975), ser. Z213–26. For postwar trade, see "Duties Collected" and "Value of Exports from October 1, 1790 to September 30, 1810," in *American State Papers,* Class IV, *Commerce and Navigation,* 1:140, 927. The import values are approximations based on the percentage of duties collected in Georgia and South Carolina.

7. Paul Finkelman, *An Imperfect Union: Slavery, Federalism, and Comity* (Chapel Hill: University of North Carolina Press, 1981), 44–45; David Lightner, *Slavery and the Commerce Clause: How the Struggle against the Interstate Slave Trade Led to the Civil War* (New Haven, Conn.: Yale University Press, 2006), chap. 2; David Waldstreicher, *Slavery's Constitution: From Revolution to Ratification* (New York: Hill and Wang, 2009).

8. Jonathan Elliot, *Debates in the Several State Conventions on the Adoption of the Federal Constitution, as Recommended by the General Convention at Philadelphia in 1787* (Washington, D.C., 1836), 4:253.

9. David C. Henderickson, *Peace Pact: The Lost World of the American Founding* (Lawrence: University Press of Kansas, 2003), 213, 234–35.

10. James Madison to Benjamin Rush, 20 March 1790, in *The Papers of James Madison,* ed. Charles F. Hobson (Charlottesville: University Press of Virginia, 1981), 13:109.

11. Joyce Chaplin, "Creating a Cotton South," *Journal of Southern History* 57 (May 1991): 171–200; Rachel Klein, *Unification of a Slave State: The Rise of the Planter Class in the South Carolina Back Country, 1760–1808* (Chapel Hill: University of North Carolina Press, 1990).

12. Jed H. Shugerman, "The Louisiana Purchase and South Carolina's Reopening of the Slave Trade in 1803," *Journal of the Early Republic* 22 (Summer 2002): 263–90; Adam Rothman, *Slave Country: American Expansion and the Origins of the Deep South* (Cambridge, Mass.: Harvard University Press, 2005), especially 22–72.

13. Robert Alderson, "Charleston's Rumored Slave Revolt of 1793," in *The Impact of the Haitian Revolution in the Atlantic World,* ed. David Geggus (Columbia: University of South Carolina Press, 2001), 93–111 (quotation at 105); Ira Berlin, *Slaves without Masters: The Free Negro in the Antebellum South* (New York: New Press, 1992), 92–99.

14. *Annals of Congress,* 7th Cong., 2nd sess., 459, 467–72, 534.

15. Ibid. See also *Congressional Gazette,* 23 February 1803.

16. Paul Finkelman, "Regulating the African Slave Trade," *Civil War History* 54 (December 2008): 399.

17. "Value of Exports from October 1, 1790 to September 30, 1810," in *American State Papers,* Class IV, *Commerce and Navigation,,* 1:927.

18. Brian Schoen, *The Fragile Fabric of Union: Cotton, Federal Politics, and the Global Origins of the Civil War* (Baltimore: Johns Hopkins University Press, 2009), 13–60; Michael Tadman, *Speculators and Slaves: Masters, Traders, and Slaves in the Old South* (Madison: University of Wisconsin Press, 1989); Steven Deyle, *Carry Me Back: The Domestic Slave Trade in American Life* (New York: Oxford University Press, 2005).

19. Brian Schoen, "Calculating the Price of Union: Republican Economic Nationalism and the Origins of Southern Sectionalism, 1790–1828," *Journal of the Early Republic* 23 (Summer 2003): 173–206.

20. Matthew Mason, *Slavery and Politics in the Early American Republic*, 42–74. See also Donald Ratcliffe in this volume.

21. Thomas Morris, *Free Men All: The Personal Liberty Laws of the North, 1780–1861* (Baltimore: Johns Hopkins University Press, 1974), 35–41; Donald Fehrenbacher, *The Slaveholding Republic: An Account of the United States Government's Relations to Slavery* (New York: Oxford University Press, 2002), 151–52; Chase Mooney, *William H. Crawford, 1772–1834* (Lexington: University Press of Kentucky, 1974), 188–90.

22. *Annals of Congress*, 16th Cong., 1st sess., 1310.

23. *Annals of Congress*, 16th Cong., 1st sess., 428, 1587–88. For the initial "lack of fervor over Missouri," see Robert Pierce Forbes, *The Missouri Compromise and Its Aftermath: Slavery and the Meaning of America* (Chapel Hill: University of North Carolina Press, 2007), 50–51 (Robert and Pinckney quotes at 79); Glover Moore, *The Missouri Controversy, 1819–1821* (Lexington: University of Kentucky Press, 1953), 218; and Freehling, *Prelude to Civil War*, 108.

24. Samuel Eliot Morison, *The Life and Letters of Harrison Gray Otis, Federalist, 1765–1848* (Boston: Houghton Mifflin, 1913), 2:233n21; John Calhoun to Charles Tait, 26 October 1820, in *The Papers of John C. Calhoun*, ed. W. Edwin Hemphill (Columbia: University of South Carolina Press, 1971), 5:414.

25. *Charleston Courier*, 30 August and 7 September 1820; "Remonstrance against an Increase of Duties on Imports," in *American State Papers*, 3, *Finance*, 3:563–67. For the Panic's role in exacerbating sectional tension, see Daniel S. Dupre, "The Panic of 1819 and the Political Economy of Sectionalism," in *The Economy of Early America: Historical Perspectives and New Directions*, ed. Cathy Matson (University Park: Pennsylvania State University Press, 2006), 263–93.

26. South Carolina, *The Statutes at Large of South Carolina* (Columbia: A. S. Johnston, 1838–41), 7:459.

27. *Annals of Congress*, 16th Cong, 2nd sess., 1139.

28. Forbes, *The Missouri Compromise and Its Aftermath*, 109–18 (quotation at 114).

29. Ibid.; *Annals of Congress*, 16th Cong., 2nd sess., 1141–43.

30. *City Gazette* (Charleston), 3 April 1821; John C. Calhoun to Charles Tait, 29 January 1820, in *The Papers of John C. Calhoun*, 4:617; Mr. Forsyth to the Duke of San Fernando and Quiroga, 18 October 1819, 16th Cong., 1st sess., serial 80, 27:93. This problematizes Matthew Crocker's conclusions in "The Missouri Compromise, the Monroe Doctrine, and the Southern Strategy," *Journal of the West* 43 (Summer 2004): 45–52.

31. South Carolina, *The Statutes at Large of South Carolina*, 7:461; Lacy Ford, *Deliver Us from Evil: The Slavery Question in the Old South* (New York: Oxford University Press, 2009), chap. 9.

32. W. Jeffrey Bolster, *Black Jacks: African American Seamen in the Age of Sail* (Cambridge, Mass.: Harvard University Press, 1998), 235–36.

33. Petitions to the General Assembly, n.d., reel ST1466, no. 1415, South Carolina Department of Archives and History, Columbia.

34. *Charleston Mercury*, 23 and 18 August 1823.

35. "Report of the Secretary of the Treasury," 11 February 1824, 18th Cong., 1st sess., serial 38.

36. *Memorial of Sundry Masters of American Vessels Lying in Charleston, S.C.* (Washington, D.C.: Gales and Seaton, 1823), 4–5.

37. William Johnson, *The Opinion of the Hon. William Johnson . . . ex parte Henry Elkison, a subject of His Britannic Majesty, vs. Francis G. Deliesseline, sheriff of Charleston District* (Charleston, 1823).

38. *Charleston Mercury,* 26 September and 7 October 1823; "Philo Charoliniesis," in *Charleston Mercury,* 18 September 1823.

39. *Charleston Mercury,* 6 September, 29 August, and 17 September 1823.

40. Freehling, *Prelude to Civil War,* passim; Alan January, "The First Nullification: The Negro Seamen Acts Controversy in South Carolina, 1822–1860," Ph.D. diss., University of Iowa, 1976. A partial exception is the superb account offered in Forbes, *The Missouri Compromise and Its Aftermath,* 155–73.

41. John Marshall to Joseph Story, 26 September 1823, in *The Papers of John Marshall,* ed. Herbert Johnson, (Chapel Hill: University of North Carolina Press, 1998), 9:338.

42. Though otherwise insightful, Robert Forbes's analysis goes too far in stating that tariff opponents "feared the *revenues*" generated by tariffs more than their "expense" (Forbes, *The Missouri Compromise and Its Aftermath,* 167). These petitions are discussed in Schoen, *The Fragile Fabric of Union,* chap. 3.

43. In Senate, 19 November 1824, in *Acts of the General Assembly of the State of Georgia, 1824,* 1:158–59, http://neptune3.galib.uga.edu/ssp/cgi bin/legis-idx.pl?sessionid—7f000001& type=law&byte=6915106.

44. Donald J. Ratcliffe, "The Nullification Crisis, Southern Discontents, and the American Political Process," *American Nineteenth Century History* 1 (Summer 2000): 1–30.

45. "Report of the Joint Select Committee on . . . the Subject of Slaves, Etc.," North Carolina General Assembly Session Records, November 1830–January 1831, Joint Committee Reports, North Carolina State Archives, Raleigh; *Acts of the State of North Carolina at the Session of 1830–1831* (Raleigh: Lawrence and Lemay, 1831), chap. 30, 49–50; *Acts of the State of Georgia, 1829* (Milledgeville, 1830), 168–71.

46. *Official Opinions of the Attorney General of the United States, 1825–1835* (Washington, 1852), 2:421–42 (quotations at 428, 433).

47. Ratcliffe, in this volume. Bonner's work also suggests the growing dominance of Southerners' understanding of nationalism within the American mindset (see Bonner, *Mastering America,* especially 81–148).

48. Lightner, *Slavery and the Commerce Clause,* 69–71.

49. Bolster, *Black Jacks,* 237 (table 1).

50. Gautham Rao, "The Federal *Posse Comitatus* Doctrine: Slavery, Compulsion, and Statecraft in Mid-Nineteenth-Century America," *Law and History Review* 26 (Spring 2008): 1–56.

Slave Smugglers,
Slave Catchers, and Slave Rebels

Slavery and American State
Development, 1787–1842

DAVID F. ERICSON

The 1860 Democratic Convention fractured over the demand of the Southern Democrats for a federally imposed territorial slave code. The Northern Democrats refused to accede to this demand, which they saw as an unprecedented intrusion of the federal government on a traditional state and local function. Their principle was their candidate's principle as well. Illinois Senator Stephen A Douglas championed "popular sovereignty," the power of the territories themselves, rather than the federal government, to enact territorial slave codes.

The Northern Democrats were historically correct, at least on the specific point in dispute. Congress had not been in the practice of enacting territorial slave codes. On the broader relation between the federal government and slavery, however, it was the Southern Democrats who were correct. State actors had engaged in actions that were supportive of the institution of slavery from the very origins of the federal government. A federally imposed territorial slave code would not have been unprecedented in light of that prior history.[1]

The literature of politics and history has largely adopted the position that the continuing presence of slavery on American soil had little to do with the development of the federal government.[2] It contends that, if anything, the presence of slavery depressed the development of the federal government, because of fears that a strong central state would act to abolish the institution. The Southern-based "Old Republicans," such as Nathaniel Macon (North Carolina) and John Randolph (Virginia), had adopted this position in opposing the "American System" policies in the post–War of 1812 years. Scholars of politics and history have often noted how the demand of Southern Democrats for a federally imposed territorial slave code in 1860 was inconsistent with their traditional states' rights position. They have not often noted how that demand was consistent with the past practices of the federal government.[3]

The presence of slavery powerfully affected the development of the federal government. This relationship was particularly strong during the antebellum period, but slavery also had significant effects on state development during earlier periods of American history. Slavery was not the sole engine of state development before the Civil War. Other factors, such as the market revolution, frontier settlement, and wars with Great Britain and Mexico, also had major effects.[4] Yet the relationship between slavery and the development of the federal government remains relatively unexplored, especially in the years prior to the Mexican-American War.

Slavery had significant effects on the development of the federal government during this earlier period in at least three policy areas.[5] In the slave-trade policy area, Congress enacted laws and executive officials (eventually) engaged in coordinated efforts to interdict activities in violation of those laws. In the fugitive-slave policy area, Congress enacted one major piece of legislation and executive officials engaged in a variety of efforts to recover fugitive slaves and secure compensation for slave losses. Finally, in the military-deployment policy area, the army deployed troops in response to (potential) slave revolts as well as to remove Native Americans from Southern states and territories in order to facilitate slavery expansion. In each policy area, the presence of slavery placed the federal government on a particular path of development. Those paths were conspicuously military paths.

THE SLAVE TRADE

This policy area had two tracks. The first track featured the federal ban on slave imports. Federal efforts to interdict slave smuggling into the United States in violation of that ban characterized its implementation. The second track featured the federal laws against the participation of American citizens, ships, and flags in the international slave trade. Federal efforts to interdict slave trading outside the territorial limits of the United States in violation of those laws characterized its implementation. The first track was the more successful one because, unlike the second, it was largely self-enforcing. The frontier for the international slave trade was much larger than for slave smuggling into the United States, and the profits to be made from the trade were much greater. This difference meant that the second track had the more significant effect on the development of the federal government.[6]

After much debate, the delegates to the Constitutional Convention added a slave-trade clause to their plan of government. The clause authorized Congress to enact a federal ban on slave imports, with an earliest possible effective date of January 1, 1808. The delegates thus contemplated a major shift in governing authority from the state to the federal level in this policy area, but delayed its implementation until at least 1808. In his 1806 Message to Congress, President Thomas Jefferson (Virginia) urged Congress to enact such a ban as soon as it was constitutionally authorized to do so. Jefferson anticipated proscribing "all further participation in those violations of human rights which have been so long continued on the unoffending inhabitants of Africa, and which the morality, the reputation, and the best interests of our country, have long been eager to proscribe." By an overwhelming 103–5 margin, Congress enacted a federal slave-import ban on March 2, 1807, with a January 1, 1808, effective date.[7]

The federal government would now regulate slave imports as part of its broader responsibility for controlling the nation's borders. Federal officials were relatively successful in accomplishing this task. Following military raids on slave-smuggling operations in the two frontier areas where they had been most prominent—Florida and Louisiana—slave smuggling into the United States virtually ceased in the early 1820s. From 1821 to 1842, the only documented cases of slave smuggling were one in New Orleans involving fifteen slaves in 1826 and another along the Louisiana-Texas border involving four slaves in 1833.[8]

United States marshals, customs collectors, and military officers arrested slave smugglers and seized smuggled slaves pursuant to the federal ban on slave imports. The resources devoted to interdicting slave smuggling were, however, too small to significantly affect the development of the federal government. There were simply not enough cases.

Yet the slave-import ban was the first federal law that successfully attempted to control the movement of people into the United States. In a very real sense, it was the nation's first immigration law. The slave-trade clause had conjoined slave imports and immigration as movements of people that Congress could not prohibit until 1808, at least not within existing states. Congress did not enact a law specifically prohibiting immigration into the United States until 1875, when it acted to exclude criminals and prostitutes.

Then, in 1882, it enacted legislation to exclude Chinese immigrants, which was the more comparable case to the slave-import ban in targeting a specific ethnic or racial group.[9]

Both before and after 1808, Congress attempted to control the movement of slaves into areas under its exclusive jurisdiction. The first Mississippi (1798) and Louisiana (1804) territorial constitutions contained slave-import bans, but neither was enforced. The first Louisiana territorial constitution went further in also limiting the movement of slaves into the territory from other states and territories, but Congress, in reaction to local protests against the restrictions, allowed them to lapse when it reorganized the territory in 1805. The Northwest Ordinance (1787) contained similar restrictions, but, at least initially, enforcement efforts were left to unsympathetic territorial governors who were themselves slaveholders, such as Ninian Edwards in Illinois and William Henry Harrison in Indiana. Even the first territorial governor of Ohio, Arthur St. Clair, interpreted the ordinance article as "a prohibition to any future introduction of them [slaves] but not to extend to the liberation of those the people already possessed of, and acquired under the sanction of law." After 1808, Congress excluded (1820), failed to exclude (1850), and then un-excluded (1854) slaves from various territories in the Trans-Mississippi West, as well as outlawed the domestic slave trade in the nation's capital (1850). Until the Civil War, the focus of congressional efforts to control the movement of people into and within the United States was black slaves.[10]

The second track of this policy area had the more significant effects on the development of the federal government, though mostly after 1842. The major effects were not felt until the United States Navy established a separate African squadron in 1843 under the terms of the Webster-Ashburton Treaty. In fact, they were not actually felt until the Buchanan administration doubled the size of the squadron in 1859 to transform it into an effective enforcement tool for interdicting American participation in the international slave trade.[11]

Congress first passed a law against American participation in the international slave trade in 1794, more than a decade before it could constitutionally ban slave imports. It subsequently enacted new, stronger slave-trade legislation in 1800 and 1818. Congress, however, did not allocate any funds to enforce its early slave-trade laws until 1819, and even then the Monroe administration diverted the money to African colonization.[12] Nevertheless, United States Navy crews captured suspected slave ships; United States marshals arranged for the care of the captains, crews, and Africans seized from those ships; and United States attorneys libeled the ships and prosecuted the captains and crews with much greater frequency in slave-trading than slave-smuggling cases during the 1819–42 period. Navy vessels seized a total of 15 suspected slave ships during this period—one with 220 Africans aboard and another with 82 Africans aboard—while a Treasury revenue cutter captured a slave ship in intercoastal waters with 281 Africans aboard. These seizures affected diplomatic relations with the nations whose citizens claimed a financial interest in the seized ships or their human cargoes— particularly France, Portugal, and Spain. The greatest diplomatic effect of this second track, though, was its impact on relations with Great Britain. British officials continually lobbied American officials to increase their interdiction efforts, both before and after the Webster-Ashburton Treaty, until the Lincoln administration finally signed a mutual search and seizure treaty with Great Britain on April 7, 1862.[13]

A concerted American effort to interdict slave trading only occurred after 1842 and, especially, in the last two fiscal years before the Civil War. While the navy spent an estimated $20,000 per year on slave-trade suppression from 1819 to 1842, it spent an estimated $385,000 per year from FY1843 to FY1859, and $830,000 per year in FY1860 and FY1861. In terms of the percentage of total federal expenditures, navy expenditures on slave-trade suppression rose from 0.01 percent (1819–42), to 0.82 percent (FY1843– FY1859), to 1.28 percent (FY1860–FY1861). In terms of the percentage of total navy expenditures, they rose from 0.46 percent (1819–42), to 3.93 percent (FY1843–FY1859), to 6.95 percent (FY1860–FY1861). Similar progressions occurred in ship seizures, from an annual average of 0.63 ships (1819– 42), to 1.41 ships (FY1843–FY1859), to 6.0 ships (FY1860–FY1861); and in recaptured Africans, from an annual average of 12.58 captured (1819–42), to 71.65 captured (FY1843–FY1859), to 2.67 captured (FY1860–FY1861).[14] The creation and, then, enlargement of the African Squadron greatly increased the effect of this policy area on the development of the navy, as well as prepared it for its Civil War blockade duties.

Yet even before the Webster-Ashburton Treaty, this policy area had affected the development of the United States Navy, as when it helped the American Colonization Society found Liberia in 1821, and instituted more regular slave-trade patrols along the west coast of Africa in 1839.[15] The navy had also taken effective steps to interdict slave smuggling during the earlier part of this period.

FUGITIVE SLAVES

The fugitive-slave policy area was similar to the slave-trade policy area in that it had two tracks with different timelines and effects on the development of the federal government. It was also similar in that its major effects on the development of the federal government did not occur until after 1842. Still, the 1787–1842 period witnessed significant developments on both tracks.

The two tracks of this policy area were fugitive-slave returns under federal law, and federal assistance in fugitive-slave recoveries and in securing compensation for slave losses by other, extralegal means. During the 1787–1842 period, state actors established important legal precedents on the first track that had some effects on the development of the federal government, but most of those effects were postponed until the passage of the Fugitive Slave Law of 1850, which, for the first time, created federal enforcement mechanisms for fugitive-slave returns. On the second track, federal officials assisted in fugitive-slave recoveries and in securing compensation for slave losses by diplomatic, military, and fiscal means throughout the period, with some important effects on the development of the federal government.

The Constitutional Convention delegates added a fugitive-slave clause to their plan of government almost as an afterthought, at the insistence of Pierce Butler (South Carolina), who wanted "fugitive slaves and servants to be delivered up like criminals." The delegates seemed to have no clear idea of how the clause would be enforced, though they seemed to believe that it would be a matter of interstate comity. The lack of comity between Virginia Governor Beverley Randolph and Pennsylvania Governor Thomas Mifflin over the fate of alleged fugitive slave John Davis prompted Congress to enact a fugitive-slave law in 1793 that, nonetheless, largely left the recovery process in the hands of slaveholders and their agents. Southern congressmen attempted to amend the law in 1817 to make the federal government more responsible for interstate fugitive-slave returns, but the bill died in the House. The *Prigg v. Pennsylvania* (1842) decision changed the dynamics considerably. In his majority opinion, Associate Justice Joseph Story (Massachusetts) ruled that federal, not state, officials were responsible for interstate fugitive-slave returns. The decision, along with the Northern "personal liberty" laws enacted in its aftermath, made a new, stronger fugitive-slave law one of the central demands of Southern congressmen in the late 1840s. They gained such a law as part of the Compromise of 1850.[16]

This policy track did not greatly affect state development during the

1787–1842 period. As in the slave-trade policy area, the Constitution provided for a shift in governing authority from the state to the federal level but the effects of the shift were not felt until much later. In the meantime, federal courts had, however, become increasingly active in interstate fugitive-slave cases.[17]

Much more federal activity occurred on track two during the 1787–1842 period. In the negotiations preceding the Jay Treaty (1794), John Jay (New York) did not press the Revolutionary War claims for slave losses on his British counterpart, Lord Grenville. The failure of the treaty to address the matter was one of the issues that almost cost it Senate approval.[18] The Jay Treaty precedent was *not* followed in later treaty negotiations.

At the insistence of the American negotiators, including John Quincy Adams (Massachusetts), the Treaty of Ghent (1814) required Great Britain to reimburse Southern slaveholders whose slaves had been "carried away" by its forces during the War of 1812. Subsequently, the British government claimed its forces had not "carried away" any Southern slaves but rather that they had fled to freedom behind British lines. At this juncture, the Monroe administration did not drop the matter, and it eventually went to international arbitration. Tsar Nicholas I ruled that at least some of the American claims were legitimate claims under the treaty provision. In the end, Great Britain paid $1,204,960 for War of 1812 slave losses.[19]

During the War of 1812, "hostile" Creeks raided "friendly" Creek and American settlements in Alabama. The ensuing Red Stick War (1813–14) pitted Creeks against Creeks, with the intervention of Andrew Jackson's Tennessee Volunteers proving decisive. After the War of 1812, the Monroe administration paid $195,418 for the property losses of both American settlers and "friendly" Creeks from the "Red Stick" raids. Of that total, $38,106, or approximately 20 percent, paid for slave losses.[20]

United States treaties with Native American nations invariably contained fugitive-slave clauses that required them to return runaway or "stolen" slaves. In the case of the Treaty of Indian Springs (1821), the federal government established a $250,000 annuity to pay for Creek "depredations" on Georgia citizens, in return for the Creeks ceding a sizable portion of their lands to the State of Georgia, meaning that the state would gain both ways from the treaty. Of that total, Georgia citizens were ultimately awarded $108,944 for their property losses; approximately $22,000 would have been for slave losses if the proportion was the same as in the case of the "Red Stick" claims.[21]

Seminoles had actually committed many of the Georgia "depredations."

U.S. relations with both the Seminoles and the Spanish in Florida were intimately connected with the problem of slave runaways from Georgia and South Carolina to Seminole Maroon communities in the colony. This problem was one of the motives for the four American incursions into Florida between 1812 and 1818, culminating in the First Seminole War (1817–18), which General Jackson labeled "this savage and negro war." When the United States acquired Florida under the terms of the Adams-Onís Treaty (1819), it agreed to reimburse territorial residents for their property losses from those incursions. The federal government eventually paid $1,199,669 for such losses; again, at a 20 percent ratio, approximately $240,000 would have been for slave losses. The claimants included many Americans who had settled in Florida prior to its acquisition and some who had even participated in one of the incursions.[22]

The acquisition of Florida did not end slave disputes between American settlers and Seminoles. It only exacerbated the problem. It also made the federal government directly responsible for solving the problem. Indian agents and army officers in Florida increasingly found themselves acting as slave catchers and slave arbitrators during the 1820s and into the 1830s. The perceived insecurity of American slaveholdings in Florida and the surrounding states built the pressure for Seminole removal. When the Seminoles resisted, a protracted Second Seminole War (1835–42) was the result. The war effectively nationalized a set of local disputes over slaves and slavery.[23]

Long before the federal government enforced interstate fugitive-slave returns, it assisted in fugitive-slave recoveries and in securing compensation for slave losses in United States territories as well as from Native American lands and European colonies. Southern slaveholders received almost $1.5 million for slave losses suffered during the Georgia "depredations," the War of 1812, the Red Stick War, and the Florida incursions.[24] After the Jay Treaty controversy, the federal government stood squarely behind Southern slaveholders in the nation's foreign relations.[25]

The effect of the second track of the fugitive-slave policy area on the development of the federal government was greater than the first track. This track affected relations with Great Britain and Spain, just as the second track of the slave-trade policy area did. It also affected relations with many Native American nations. The British government funded most of the $1.5 million total that was spent on the War of 1812 slave claims. Yet the federal government spent an estimated $300,000 in the other three cases. Even in the case of the War of 1812 claims, the United States spent $56,887 on the two commissions that were established to determine individual awards under the tsar's ruling.[26] The American total would represent less than 0.01 percent of total federal expenditures during the 1787–1842 period, but the symbolic effect was still significant in aligning the federal government with slave interests.

MILITARY DEPLOYMENTS

The two tracks of this policy area were military deployments in response to slave revolts—actual, rumored, or simply feared—and in order to facilitate the removal of Native Americans from the Southeast. The United States Army was very responsive to requests from state and local officials for more troops in cases of slave revolts, even when such revolts were simply feared.[27] The army also coordinated the removals of the Five Civilized Tribes— Cherokees, Chickasaws, Choctaws, Creeks, and Seminoles—from Southern states and territories.[28] In the case of the Seminoles, it did much more.

The Constitution made the federal government responsible for suppressing insurrections and domestic violence. At the Constitutional Convention, Rufus King (Massachusetts), Luther Martin (Maryland), and Gouverneur Morris (Pennsylvania) each supported banning slave imports on the grounds that the federal government would be responsible for suppressing slave revolts. In his typically acerbic fashion, Morris commented that the Northern states "are to bind themselves to march their militia for the defense of the Southern States . . . against those very slaves of whom they complain."[29] No one denied the possibility.

The first major slave revolt to occur in the United States during the 1787–1842 period occurred in January, 1811, on the German Coast of the Mississippi River, north of New Orleans. In response to the revolt, Territorial Governor William C. C. Claiborne requested troops from the army garrison in Baton Rouge. Though local plantation owners had suppressed the revolt by the time the troops arrived, an army regiment marched through the area to deter further unrest.[30]

In July 1822, Charleston officials uncovered the Denmark Vesey Slave Conspiracy. In addition to overseeing the executions of Vesey and thirty-six alleged co-conspirators, South Carolina Governor Thomas Bennett secretly wrote the state's "own" Secretary of War, John C. Calhoun, asking him to reinforce the army garrison in Charleston. Not surprisingly, Calhoun complied, redeploying an army company from Saint Augustine to Charleston.[31]

In 1830, a rumored Christmas Day slave revolt in Wilmington, North

Carolina, prompted local officials to ask Secretary of War John Eaton (Tennessee) to garrison more troops in the city. Eaton also complied, redeploying two army companies from Fort Monroe, Virginia, to Wilmington.[32]

Finally, in August 1831, the Nat Turner Slave Revolt occurred in Southampton, Virginia. Governor John Floyd decided to rely on the state militia to repress the revolt, to prove that the state could control its own slave population. The Department of War was, however, flooded with requests from other Southern locations for more troops. Secretary of War Lewis Cass (Michigan) contemplated a general redeployment of troops from Northern to Southern army posts, but he ultimately decided against the plan as it became clear that the Southampton revolt was an isolated event. Still, the army redeployed two companies from Fort Johnston, North Carolina, to Wilmington and New Bern, near the Virginia border, as well as stationed another two companies in New Orleans.[33]

The effect of these troop deployments on the development of the federal government was minimal. The effect on slaveholders in reassuring them of the security of their slaveholdings was *not* minimal. The two primary responsibilities of the army in Southern states and territories were Native American pacification and slave control.[34] Those two responsibilities often coincided.

The Native American removals from the Southeastern states had multiple motives. As in the case of the Northwestern removals, Euro-American settlers wanted Native American lands. They also wanted greater security from Native American hostilities against their persons and properties. Nevertheless, the presence of slavery in both Euro-American and Native American communities made the Southeastern removals distinctive.[35] Euro-American slaveholders especially wanted Native American lands. They also especially wanted to secure their slaveholdings against Native American raids on their plantations and to prevent their slaves from running away to Native American lands. The Indian Removal Act of 1830 targeted the Five Civilized Tribes for removal. In the House vote, the greater the percentage of slaveholders in a congressional district the more likely the member of Congress from that district was to vote for the act, even after controlling for party and section.[36] Seminole removal, however, stood out as a uniquely slavery-related removal, in terms of its motives, the Native American response, and the United States' counterresponse.

Ostensibly, the Second Seminole War was the violent means by which the federal government removed the Seminoles from Florida. Much more than in the case of the other Southeastern removals, slavery was at the core of Seminole removal and its violent nature. Slave runaways posed a special problem for Euro-American slaveholders in Florida, as well as Georgia and South Carolina, because of the relative proximity of the Seminole Maroon communities. The desire for Native American lands was a less significant motive in the case of Seminole removal, because Florida was sparsely settled and the Seminoles had already been pushed onto less desirable lands, farther away from Euro-American settlements, during the earlier incursions. Local Euro-American slaveholders who were most insistent on Seminole removal were also insistent that the Seminoles surrender any disputed property to them prior to removal. The Black Seminoles correctly suspected that they were the targets of such demands. Of all the Seminoles, they most violently resisted removal, because they believed that they would lose their freedom in the process. This combination of factors was the powder keg that exploded into war when the army deployed troops to Florida in 1835 to begin the removal process. Otherwise, Seminole removal would probably have assumed a much less violent character and been more similar to the other Southeastern removals.[37]

Even before Quartermaster General Thomas S. Jesup (Kentucky) replaced Territorial Governor Richard K. Call as the commanding officer in Florida, he told his superiors at the Department of War that the Second Seminole War was a "negro war," not an "Indian War." He warned them that if the Seminole insurgency was "not speedily put down, the South will feel the effect of it on their slave population before the end of the next season."[38] He also decided that the best strategy to end the war was to offer the Black Seminoles safe passage to Arkansas, notwithstanding any Euro-American claims to them. Local officials protested Jesup's decision and he was compelled to withdraw his offer. Yet he unofficially pursued the strategy. By the end of 1838, most of the Black Seminoles had been removed from Florida. Thereafter, the Second Seminole War wound down to a rather indecisive conclusion. Colonel William J. Worth (New York) simply declared the war over on August 14, 1842.[39]

The Second Seminole War cost the federal government an estimated $30 million and the lives of 1,565 military personnel. By the end of the war, the army had removed approximately 3,000 Seminoles from Florida. By comparison, Cherokee removal, which was the second most expensive Native American removal, cost the federal government an estimated $1.3 million to remove approximately 12,200 Cherokees. The per capita ratio between the two removals was more than 100 to 1. One of the tragic long-term effects of the war was that the Seminole nation suffered an estimated 53 percent decline in its population from 1835 to 1860.[40]

The United States Army opened new lands to slavery much quicker than would have been the case if the state and territorial governments or the settlers themselves had been solely responsible for expelling Native Americans. This acceleration effect was certainly evident in Florida, but also in Georgia, Alabama, and Mississippi. Southwest expansion was slavery expansion. At least from the Euro-American perspective, the expulsion of Native Americans, by whatever means possible, was essential to the process.[41]

The Second Seminole War had major effects on the development of the federal government. As the war progressed, the Department of War decided to shift the fighting force in Florida from auxiliary troops to regular soldiers. In 1836, army regulars constituted only 48 percent of the fighting force. By 1841, they constituted 100 percent. The professionalization of the fighting force in Florida essentially distinguished the Second Seminole War from the earlier incursions, which were largely irregular military operations. Local officials protested this shift in the fighting force, just as they had protested Jesup's decision to offer the Black Seminoles safe passage to Arkansas, because it deprived their constituents of a source of income. The army proceeded with the shift over their protests. It also decided to reduce its reliance on territorial residents and their slaves to perform non-essential services. Yet again, local officials protested, and yet again, the army proceeded over their protests. These decisions required more regular soldiers. Accordingly, Congress increased the authorized size of the army from 7,130 to 11,800 men in November 1837. This increase was the only such increase between the War of 1812 and Mexican-American War. It also had lasting effects. Actual troop levels fell after the Second Seminole War, but remained higher than they had been before the war.[42]

The Second Seminole War decisions were important steps in the development of the army. They increased its autonomy from the demands of local constituents, its authority relative to militia and volunteer units, and its state capacities. In 1837, the peak war year, 4,322 soldiers were stationed in Florida, which was 35 percent of the total army force and 11 percent of the total federal workforce. During the first five years of the war, army expenditures on the war were $18.9 million, which was 35 percent of total army expenditures and 13 percent of total federal expenditures. Over the first two years of the war, both total army and total federal expenditures more than doubled, from $5.8 million to $13.7 million, and from $17.6 million to

$27.2 million respectively.[43] The generalization is that wars drive state development. The Second Seminole War was such a case. It was also a case where slavery drove war.[44]

CONCLUSION

The aggregate effects of these three policy areas on the development of the federal government were significant. One way to think of those effects is to think of them counterfactually, as if the Constitution had not contained slave-trade, fugitive-slave, and domestic-violence and insurrection clauses, as if the federal government had never acted to enforce those clauses, as if it had not removed powerful Native American nations from Southern states and territories, and as if it had never assisted slaveholders in recovering fugitives slaves or securing compensation for slaves losses. Under this scenario, navy ships would have been less active in suppressing the slave trade, army forces would have been deployed less frequently to deter slave insurrections and remove Native Americans, and both military and civilian personnel would have been less involved in recovering fugitive slaves and seeking compensation for slave losses.[45]

Most of these activities occurred during the antebellum period. Earlier activities, however, prepared the ground for later ones. The navy seized suspected slave ships before the Webster-Ashburton Treaty. Indian agents, military officers, and foreign ministers resolved extraterritorial slave disputes before the Fugitive Slave Law of 1850. The army suppressed slavery-related domestic violence before "Bleeding Kansas" and Harpers Ferry.[46]

The Constitutional Convention delegates committed the federal government to protecting slavery as long as the institution existed in the United States. The passage of time affected that commitment, as did the sectional and partisan affiliations of key federal decision makers. Each of these three factors contributed, for example, to the different approaches a Northern-dominated Federalist administration took to the Revolutionary War claims for slave losses, and a Southern-dominated Democratic-Republican administration to the War of 1812 claims.[47] Nonetheless, the federal commitment to protecting slavery withstood the effects of time, party, and geography until the Civil War. A Northern Democratic-Republican official who later became a Whig antislavery congressman is, in fact, prime evidence for this commitment. First as treaty negotiator, then as Secretary of State, and finally as president, John Quincy Adams orchestrated a highly determined diplomatic effort to secure compensation for the War of 1812 slave losses.[48]

Recently, a number of excellent studies—several by authors in this volume—have pressed beyond congressional rule-making in the territories to explore what happened on the ground during the 1787–1842 period. We should explore other policy areas in the same way, especially those where the connections between the federal government and slavery were least visible, such as in its "unofficial" use of slave labor.[49] This injunction, of course, applies equally to the antebellum period. After all, it was not Douglas's failure to support a certain rule about slavery in the territories that most upset Southern Democrats in 1860. It was the prospect of a Republican administration that was not committed to protecting the institution.

NOTES

I would like to thank the James Madison Program in American Ideals and Institutions at Princeton University for the financial and intellectual support to pursue this project. I would also like to thank Karen Orren and Stephen Skowronek, as well as the editors of this volume, for their helpful comments on earlier versions of this essay.

1. See Don E. Fehrenbacher, *The Slaveholding Republic: An Account of the United States Government's Relations to Slavery* (New York: Oxford University Press, 2001), 291.

2. See Richard Franklin Bensel, *Yankee Leviathan: The Origins of Central State Authority in America, 1859–1877* (Cambridge: Cambridge University Press, 1990), 13; David Brion Davis, *Inhuman Bondage: The Rise and Fall of Slavery in the New World* (New York: Oxford University Press, 2006), 273; Ronald P. Formisano, "State Development in the Early Republic: Substance and Structure," in *Contesting Democracy: Substance and Structure in American Political History, 1775–2000*, ed. Bryon E. Shafer and Anthony J. Badger (Lawrence: University Press of Kansas, 2001), 7–35; James L. Huston, *Calculating the Value of the Union: Slavery, Property Rights, and the Economic Origins of the Civil War* (Chapel Hill: University of North Carolina Press, 2002), 47–48; Richard R. John, "'Affairs of Office': The Executive Departments, the Election of 1828, and the Making of the Democratic Party," in *The Democratic Experiment: New Directions in American Political History*, ed. Meg Jacobs, William J. Novak, and Julian E. Zelizer (Princeton, N.J.: Princeton University Press, 2003), 50–84; and Karen Orren and Stephen Skowronek, *The Search for American Political Development* (Cambridge: Cambridge University Press, 2004), 88. By the literature of politics and history, I mean the work of historians, political scientists, and sociologists who study American political development. The particular focus of this essay is state development, as opposed to other types of political development, and state development on the federal as opposed to the state and local levels.

3. Fehrenbacher would be the major exception. Many scholars who argue that the presence of slavery depressed state development present internal improvements as their sole case for that argument. Whatever the validity of the evidence, it is an extremely slender foundation upon which to build such an argument, even if one buttresses it with Robin Einhorn's excellent research on tax policy (see Robin L. Einhorn, *American Taxation, American Slavery* [Chicago: University of Chicago Press, 2006]). The argument appears all the weaker when one considers

the evidence on the other side, as I do in this essay and, more comprehensively, in *Slavery in the American Republic* (Lawrence: University Press of Kansas, 2011).

4. See Laurence J. Malone, *Opening the West: Federal Internal Improvements before 1860* (Westport, Conn.: Greenwood Press, 1998); David R. Mayhew, "Wars and American Politics," *Perspectives on Politics* 3 (September 2005): 473–93; and Charles Grier Sellers, *The Market Revolution: Jacksonian America, 1815–1846* (New York: Oxford University Press, 1991).

5. More specifically, in this essay I examine the period from the Constitutional Convention to the end of the Second Seminole War. Several excellent works have explored the relationship between the federal government and slavery during the earlier part of this period: see Paul Finkelman, *Slavery and the Founders: Race and Liberty in the Age of Jefferson* (Armonk, N.Y.: M. E. Sharpe, 1996); John Craig Hammond, *Slavery, Freedom, and Expansion in the Early American West* (Charlottesville: University of Virginia Press, 2007); Matthew Mason, *Slavery and Politics in the Early American Republic* (Chapel Hill: University of North Carolina Press, 2006); and Donald L. Robinson, *Slavery in the Structure of American Politics, 1765–1820* (New York: Harcourt Brace Jovanovich, 1971). Yet these works generally explore how the presence of slavery affected public policy, not state development. This generalization would also be true of Fehrenbacher's more comprehensive work.

6. Fehrenbacher criticized W. E. B. Du Bois's classic study of the American suppression of the slave trade for not distinguishing these two tracks in arguing that the federal government did little to enforce its own slave-trade laws. According to Fehrenbacher, it did, with respect to slave smuggling, at least after the War of 1812. Cf. W. E. B. Du Bois, *The Suppression of the African Slave-Trade to the United States of America, 1638–1870* (1896; repr. New York: Social Science Press, 1954), 109–10, 129–30, 182–83; and Fehrenbacher, *The Slaveholding Republic*, 149–50, 201–2, 385n67.

7. See *American State Papers, 1, Foreign Relations* 1:25 ("Message to Congress," 2 December 1806), 68–69; U.S. Constitutional Convention (1787), in *The Records of the Federal Convention of 1787*, ed. Max Farrand, rev. ed. (New Haven, Conn.: Yale University Press; London, H. Milford, Oxford University Press, 1937; originally published in 1911), 2:364–65, 369–74, 415–17; and Matthew E. Mason, "Slavery Overshadowed: Congress Debates Prohibiting the Atlantic Slave Trade to the United States, 1806–1807," *Journal of the Early Republic* 20 (Spring 2000): 59–81. On shifts in governing authority as a defining feature of state development, see Orren and Skowronek, *The Search for American Political Development*, 123–32.

8. See Eugene C. Barker, "The African Slave Trade in Texas," *Quarterly of the Texas State Historical Association* 6 (July 1902): 145–49; Fehrenbacher, *The Slaveholding Republic*, 201; Warren S. Howard, *American Slavers and the Federal Law, 1837–1862* (1963; repr. Westport, Conn.: Greenwood Press, 1976), 154; "Thomas J. Lawler-Smith M. Miles," 24th Cong., 1st sess., 1836, H. Rep. 574; "Message from the President of the United States, Transmitting (in compliance with a resolution of the Senate of 19th February last) a Report from the Secretary of the Navy, Showing the Expenses Annually Incurred in Carrying into Effect the Act of March 2, 1819, for Prohibiting the Slave Trade," 20th Cong., 1st sess., 1827, S. Doc. 3, 28–29; and Frances J. Stafford, "Illegal Importations: Enforcement of the Slave Trade Laws Along the Florida Coast, 1810–1828," *Florida Historical Quarterly* 46 (October 1967): 126–27. There were undoubtedly unauthenticated cases during this period, but based on the available evidence it seems unlikely that slave smuggling was prevalent. The only cases of slave ships landing their human cargoes on American soil occurred much later, in 1858 and (possibly) 1860 (see Sylviane

A. Diouf, *Dreams of Africa in Alabama: The Slave Ship "Clotilda" and the Story of the Last Africans Brought to America* [Oxford: Oxford University Press, 2007]; and Tom Henderson Wells, *The Slave Ship "Wanderer"* [Athens: University of Georgia Press, 1967]).

9. See Aaron S. Fogleman, "From Slaves, Convicts, and Servants to Free Passengers: The Transformation of Immigration in the Era of the American Revolution," *Journal of American History* 85 (June 1998): 50; and Daniel J. Tichenor, *Dividing Lines: The Politics of Immigration Control in America* (Princeton, N.J.: Princeton University Press, 2002), 1, 99, 106–7. The Alien Act of 1798 sought to restrict "seditious" immigrants, but it was only in force for two years, and no immigrant was denied entry into the country or deported under the Act (see Alan Taylor, "The Alien and Sedition Acts," in *The American Congress: The Building of Democracy,* ed. Julian E. Zelizer [Boston: Houghton Mifflin, 2004], 70). On the racial overtones of the slave-import ban, see Rogers M. Smith, *Civic Ideals: Conflicting Visions of Citizenship in U.S. History* (New Haven, Conn.: Yale University Press, 1997), 169.

10. See Fehrenbacher, *The Slaveholding Republic,* 263–66, 271–76; Hammond, *Slavery, Freedom, and Expansion in the Early American West,* chaps. 2–7; and Governor Arthur St. Clair to President George Washington, 1 May 1790, in *The Territorial Papers of the United States,* ed. Clarence E. Carter, 28 vols. (Washington: Government Printing Office, 1934–75), 2:248. This generalization would also be true of the state governments, and, in their case, would include free blacks (see Ira Berlin, *Slaves without Masters: The Free Negro in the Antebellum South* [New York: New Press, 1992], 138–39; and Leon F. Litwack, *North of Slavery: The Negro in the Free States, 1790–1860* [Chicago: University of Chicago Press, 1961], 66–74).

11. See Robert Ralph Davis Jr., "James Buchanan and the Suppression of the Slave Trade, 1858–1861," *Pennsylvania History* 33 (October 1966): 446–59; "Message from the President of the United States to the Two Houses of Congress, at the Commencement of the Third Session of the Twenty-Seventh Congress," 27th Cong., 3rd sess., 1842, S. Exec. Doc. 1, 31.

12. See "Message from the President of the United States, Stating the Interpretation which Has Been Given to the Act Entitled, 'An Act in Addition to the Acts Prohibiting the Slave Trade,'" 16th Cong., 1st sess., 1819, H. Doc. 11. In 1820, Congress also enacted a law making participation in the slave trade piracy, a capital offense. For these early slave-trade laws, see "Report of John Pendleton Kennedy from Committee of Commerce on the Memorial of the Friends of African Colonization," 27th Cong., 3rd sess., 1843, H. Rep. 283, 288–90.

13. See Judd Scott Harmon, "Suppress and Protest: The United States Navy, the African Slave Trade, and Maritime Commerce, 1794–1862," Ph.D. diss., College of William and Mary, 1977, 128–29, 238–39 (appendix E); "On the Capture by a United States Vessel of the Spanish Ship Fenix, with African Slaves on Board, and under Suspicion of Piratical Intent, with a Recommendation for the Maintenance, &c., of the Slaves," 21st Cong., 2nd sess., 1831, H. Doc. 54; "Report of John Pendleton Kennedy from Committee of Commerce on the Memorial of the Friends of African Colonization," 27th Cong., 3rd sess., 1843, H. Rep. 283; "Message from the President of the United States, Transmitting, in compliance with a resolution of the House, a Report from the Secretary of State in Reference to the African Slave Trade in 1859," 36th Cong., 2nd sess., 1860, H. Exec. Doc. 7; Matthew Mason, "The Battle of the Slaveholding Liberators: Great Britain, the United States, and Slavery in the Early Nineteenth Century," *William and Mary Quarterly,* 3rd ser., 59 (July 2002): 665–96; Matthew Mason, "Keeping Up Appearances: The International Politics of Slave Trade Abolition in the Nineteenth-Century Atlantic World," *William and Mary Quarterly,* 3rd ser., 66 (October 2009): 809–32; John T. Noonan Jr., *The*

"*Antelope*": *The Ordeal of the Recaptured Africans in the Administrations of James Monroe and John Quincy Adams* (Berkeley: University of California Press, 1977); and "Message of the President of the United States, Transmitting a Copy of the Treaty between the United States and her Britannic Majesty for the Suppression of the African Slave Trade," 37th Cong., 2nd sess., 1862, S. Exec. Doc. 57.

14. See Harmon, "Suppress and Protest," 238–44 (appendix E); *Historical Statistics of the United States Millennial Edition Online, http://hsus.cambridge.org,* tables Ea636–43; Howard, *American Slavers,* 214–23 (appendix A); Letters Received, September 17, 1860 to June 22, 1861 [inclusive], box 1, Letters Received from the Navy Department, 1823–1909, Correspondence of the Office of the Secretary of the Treasury, General Records of the Department of the Treasury, Record Group 56, National Archives, College Park, Md.; "Message from the President of the United States, Transmitting (in compliance with a resolution of the Senate of 19th February last) a Report from the Secretary of the Navy, Showing the Expenses Annually Incurred in Carrying into Effect the Act of March 2, 1819, for Prohibiting the Slave Trade," 20th Cong., 1st sess., 1827, S. Doc. 3, 10–29; "Message from the President of the United States to the Two Houses of Congress, at the Commencement of the Second Session of the Twentieth Congress," 20th Cong., 2nd sess., 1828, S. Doc. 1, 139–40; and "Report of the Secretary of the Navy, Showing the Annual Number of Deaths in the United States Squadron on the Coast of Africa, and the Annual Cost of that Squadron," 31st Cong., 1st sess., 1850, S. Exec. Doc. 40, 3. Until 1843, the fiscal year mirrored the calendar year; in 1843, the fiscal year was changed to July 1–June 30. The expenditure estimates are personal estimates; available upon request.

15. See Harmon, "Suppress and Protest," 92–93, 107–8.

16. See U.S. Constitutional Convention (1787), in *The Records of the Federal Convention of 1787,* 2:443; Finkelman, *Slavery and the Founders,* chap. 4; Thomas D. Morris, *Free Men All: The Personal Liberty Laws of the North, 1780–1861* (Baltimore: Johns Hopkins University Press, 1974), chaps. 2, 6–8; and *Prigg v. Pennsylvania,* 16 Peters 539 (1842), at 615–16.

17. See Fehrenbacher, *The Slaveholding Republic,* 214, 217–18.

18. See Jerald A. Combs, *The Jay Treaty: Political Battleground of the Founding Fathers* (Berkeley: University of California Press, 1970), 153–55, 160–61. The key vote was the 20–10 vote not to approve Aaron Burr's substitute motion (see *Annals of Congress,* 4th Cong., 4th sess., 861). Twenty votes was the bare two-thirds majority necessary for treaty approval.

19. See *American State Papers,* 1, *Foreign Relations* 3:271 ("Great Britain," 15, 16, and 20 February 1815), 746; and John Bassett Moore, *History and Digest of the International Arbitrations to Which the United States Has Been a Party* (Washington, D.C.: Government Printing Office, 1898), 1:390. All expenditures have been rounded to the nearest dollar unless otherwise indicated.

20. See Richard S. Lackey, *Frontier Claims in the Lower Mississippi* (New Orleans: Polyanthos, 1977). Jackson made both "hostile" and "friendly" Creeks cede land after the war, despite the fact that the latter had fought with him at the decisive Battle of Horseshoe Bend.

21. See Tim Allen Garrison, "United States Indian Policy in Sectional Crisis: Georgia's Exploitation of the Compact of 1802," in *Congress and the Emergence of Sectionalism: From the Missouri Compromise to the Age of Jackson,* ed. Paul Finkelman and Donald R. Kennon (Akron: Ohio University Press, 2008), 97–124; and "Claim of Creek Nation of Indians for Payment for Lands in Georgia," 30th Cong., 1st sess., 1848, H. Rep. 826.

22. See *American State Papers,* 1, *Foreign Relations* 5:347 ("Treaty with Spain of Febru-

ary 22, 1819, as Finally Ratified," 23 February 1821), 130–31; James G. Cusick, *The Other War of 1812: The Patriot War and the American Invasion of Spanish East Florida* (Gainesville: University Press of Florida, 2003), 305–7; "Message from the President of the United States, Transmitting Copies of Documents Referred to in His Communication of the Seventh Ultimo, in Relation to the Seminole War, &c.," 15th Cong., 2nd sess., 1818, H. Doc. 14, 58; John Missall and Mary Lou Missall, *The Seminole Wars: America's Longest Indian Conflict* (Gainesville: University Press of Florida, 2004), chaps. 2–3; "Report of the Secretary of the Treasury and the Attorney General, in compliance with a resolution of the Senate of the 3d of August 1846, on the Petition of Kingsley B. Gibbs, executor of Zephaniah Kingsley, Deceased, Praying Payment of Interest on His Claim Arising under the Treaty with Spain of 1819," 33rd Cong., 1st sess., 1854, S. Exec. Doc. 82; and "Message from the President of the United States, Transmitting, in answer to Senate resolution of December 5, 1883, a Report of the Secretary of State respecting the Execution of the Treaty of 1819 with Spain," 48th Cong., 1st sess., 1884, S. Exec. Doc. 158. The federal government did not pay the claims from one of the incursions because Congress decided that it was a legitimate wartime operation against the British forces that were occupying northwestern Florida at the time (see Moore, *History and Digest of the International Arbitrations to Which the United States Has Been a Party,* 5:4528).

23. I discuss this war further in the next section.

24. Spanish American and Native American slaveholders received a portion of this money, but most went to Southern slaveholders.

25. See Fehrenbacher, *The Slaveholding Republic,* chap. 4.

26. See Moore, *History and Digest of the International Arbitrations to Which the United States Has Been a Party,* 1:367n1.

27. See Tommy Richard Young II, "The United States Army in the South, 1789–1835," Ph.D. diss., Louisiana State University, 1973, 447–48.

28. See Grant Foreman, *Indian Removal: The Emigration of the Five Civilized Tribes of Indians* (1932; repr., Norman: University of Oklahoma Press, 1972).

29. See U.S. Constitutional Convention (1787), in *The Records of the Federal Convention of 1787,* 2:220, 222, 364 (quotation at 222).

30. See Young, "The United States Army in the South," 469–74. An earlier, 1795 slave revolt in Louisiana occurred while it was still Spanish territory. In the case of Gabriel's Rebellion in Virginia in 1800, state officials uncovered the conspiracy in its final planning stages (see Herbert Aptheker, *American Negro Slave Revolts* [1943; repr., New York: International Publishers, 1968], 215–16, 219–22).

31. See *The Papers of John C. Calhoun,* ed. W. Edwin Hemphill (Columbia: University of South Carolina Press, 1993), 7:210 (Bennett to Calhoun, 15 July 1822), 220 (Calhoun to Bennett, 22 July 1822).

32. See Young, "The United States Army in the South," 501.

33. Ibid., 507–11. Adam Rothman estimates that a third of the United States army was stationed in and around New Orleans during the early part of the nineteenth century (see Adam Rothman, *Slave Country: American Expansion and the Origins of the Deep South* [Cambridge, Mass.: Harvard University Press, 2005], 116).

34. See Young, "The United States Army in the South," 4–6, 520–21.

35. On slavery among the Five Civilized Tribes, see Donna L. Akers, *Living in the Land of Death: The Choctaw Nation, 1830–1860* (East Lansing: Michigan State University Press, 2004),

118, 127, 130, 140–42; James R. Atkinson, *Splendid Land, Splendid People: The Chickasaw Indians to Removal* (Tuscaloosa: University of Alabama Press, 2004), 23–24; Kevin Mulroy, *Freedom on the Border: The Seminole Maroons in Florida, the Indian Territory, Coahuila, and Texas* (Lubbock: Texas Tech University Press, 1993), 4–5, 7–8, 17–18, 20–23, 25; Theda Perdue, *Slavery and the Evolution of Cherokee Society, 1540–1866* (Knoxville: University of Tennessee Press, 1979), 50, 56–60, 68–72; and Claudio Saunt, *A New Order of Things: Property, Power, and the Transformation of the Creek Indians, 1733–1816* (Cambridge: Cambridge University Press, 1999), 120–21, 124, 134.

36. See Leonard A. Carlson and Mark A. Roberts, "Indian Lands, 'Squatterism,' and Slavery: Economic Interests and the Passage of the Indian Removal Act of 1830," *Explorations in Economic History* 43 (July 2006): 486–504.

37. A group of Creeks also resisted removal, leading to the short-lived Creek War of 1836–37, but it is unlikely that they would have resisted if the Seminoles had not first (see Kenneth L. Valliere, "The Creek War of 1836: A Military History," *The Chronicles of Oklahoma* 57 [Winter 1979–80]: 463–85). Otherwise, Native Americans resisted on an individual or legal level, as the Cherokees did.

38. See *American State Papers, 5, Military Affairs* 7:760 (Thomas J. Jesup to B. F. Butler, Acting Secretary of War, 9 December 1836), 821. Scholars have increasingly accepted Jesup's assessment (see Canter Brown Jr., "Race Relations in Territorial Florida, 1821–1845," *Florida Historical Quarterly* 73 [January 1995]: 303–4; George Klos, "Blacks and the Seminole Removal Debates, 1821–1835," *Florida Historical Quarterly* 68 [July 1989]: 77–78; Jane F. Lancaster, *Removal Aftershock: The Seminoles' Struggles to Survive in the West, 1836–1866* [Knoxville: University of Tennessee Pres, 1994], 67; John K. Mahon, *History of the Second Seminole War, 1835–1842* [Gainesville: University Press of Florida, 1967], 201, 326; Missall and Missall, *The Seminole Wars*, 126; Mulroy, *Freedom on the Border*, 29; Larry Eugene Rivers, *Slavery in Florida: Territorial Days to Emancipation* [Gainesville: University Press of Florida, 2000], 204; and Bruce Edward Twyman, *The Black Seminole Legacy and North American Politics, 1693–1845* [Washington, D.C.: Howard University Press, 1999], 130).

39. See Missall and Missall, *The Seminole Wars*, 128–30, 132–33, 179–80, 201–2.

40. See Michael F. Doran, "Population Statistics of Nineteenth Century Indian Territory," *The Chronicles of Oklahoma* 53 (Winter 1975–76): 498 (table 2); "Removal of the Cherokees, &c.," 27th Cong., 3rd sess., 1843, H. Rep. 288, 2; Missall and Missall, *The Seminole Wars*, xv, 224; and John T. Sprague, *The Origin, Progress, and Conclusion of the Florida War* (1848; repr., Gainesville: University Press of Florida, 1964), 548–50 (appendix). No reliable estimates exist of the number of Seminoles who died during the Second Seminole War. The fact that the first census in Indian Territory did not occur until 1860 dictated the time frame of Doran's estimate, but he argued that the post-removal population losses of the Seminoles and other Native American nations in Indian Territory were the result of the way that the removal process had physically and psychologically weakened their populations. On the Euro-American side, the casualty figures do not include the casualties in the militia and volunteer units.

41. See Rothman, *Slave Country*, 11–13, 40–42, 166–68, 219. On Native American removals in the states and territories of the Old Southwest, see H. Jason Combs, "The Platte Purchase and Native American Removal," *Plains Anthropologist* 47 (August 2002): 265–74; Kathleen DuVal, "Debating Identity, Sovereignty, and Civilization: The Arkansas Valley after the Louisiana Purchase," *Journal of the Early Republic* 26 (Spring 2006): 25–59; and Daniel H. Usner Jr.,

American Indians in the Lower Mississippi Valley: Social and Economic Histories (Lincoln: University of Nebraska Press, 1998), chaps. 5–7.

42. See *Historical Statistics of the United States Millennial Edition Online, http://hsus .cambridge.org,* tables Ed26–47; Mahon, *History of the Second Seminole War,* 226; and Sprague, *The Origin, Progress, and Conclusion of the Florida War,* 103–6, 268–69, 425–26. During the Second Seminole War, the army's auxiliary forces included Native Americans, mostly Creeks, as well as militia and volunteer units.

43. See *Historical Statistics of the United States Millennial Edition Online, http://hsus .cambridge.org,* tables Ea636–43, Ea894–903, Ed26–47; "Expenditures in Suppressing Indian Hostilities in Florida," 26th Cong., 2nd sess., 1840, H. Doc. 8, 7, 10, 12–13, 15; and Sprague, *The Origin, Progress, and Conclusion of the Florida War,* 104. Because tables Ea894–903 only provide figures for the number of federal civilian employees at ten-year intervals from 1821 to 1881, I calculated the Florida army force as a percentage of the total federal workforce on the basis of the 1837 figures for the army and navy and the 1841 figure for the number of federal civilian employees.

44. At least until the Civil War, the United States has usually been considered an exception to the generalization that wars drive state development. As noted above, Mayhew revised this view, but he only considered the War of 1812 and the Mexican-American War, not Native American conflicts. Specifically on the Second Seminole War and state development, see Mahon, *History of the Second Seminole War,* 326–27; and Samuel J. Watson, "The Uncertain Road to Manifest Destiny: Army Officers and the Course of American Territorial Expansionism, 1815–1846," in *Manifest Destiny and Empire: American Antebellum Expansionism,* ed. Sam W. Haynes and Christopher Morris (College Station: Texas A & M University Press, 1997), 72. More generally, see Ira Katznelson, "Flexible Capacity: The Military and Early American Statebuilding," in *Shaped by War and Trade: International Influences on American Political Development,* ed. Ira Katznelson and Martin Shefter (Princeton, N.J.: Princeton University Press, 2002), 82–110; Sheldon D. Pollack, *War, Revenue, and State Building: Financing the Development of the American State* (Ithaca, N.Y.: Cornell University Press, 2009), chaps. 4–8; Bruce D. Porter, *War and the Rise of the State: The Military Foundations of Modern Politics* (New York: Free Press, 1984), chap. 7; and Mark R. Wilson, "The Politics of Procurement: Military Origins of Bureaucratic Autonomy," in *Ruling Passions: Political Economy in Nineteenth-Century America,* ed. Richard R. John (University Park: Penn State University Press, 2006), 44–73.

45. On counterfactual history, see Martin Bunzl, "Counterfactual History: A User's Guide," *American Historical Review* 109 (June 2004): 845–58; and James D. Fearon, "Counterfactuals and Hypothesis Testing in Political Science," *World Politics* 43 (January 1992): 169–95.

46. See Robert W. Coakley, *The Role of Federal Military Forces in Domestic Disorders, 1789–1878* (Washington, D.C.: Government Printing Office, 1988), chaps. 8–9.

47. The Senate vote on the Jay Treaty was highly partisan and sectional. Ten of the twelve Democratic-Republican senators and seven of the twelve Southern senators voted for the Burr motion (see *Annals of Congress,* 4th Cong., 4th sess., 861). Time was a factor, because Southern opposition to the Jay Treaty cautioned federal officials, regardless of their partisan or sectional affiliation, against neglecting slave claims in future treaty negotiations. On time as a political variable, see Orren and Skowronek, *The Search for American Political Development,* 12–13,

195–96; and Paul Pierson, *Politics in Time: History, Institutions, and Social Analysis* (Princeton, N.J.: Princeton University Press, 2004).

48. See Mason, *Slavery and Politics in the Early American Republic,* 93. Adams's career also demonstrated the importance of one's political role as a variable, but even as a Whig antislavery congressman, he attacked slavery collaterally, not directly, as through his efforts to overturn the gag rule.

49. See Ernest F. Dibble, "Slave Rentals to the Military: Pensacola and the Gulf Coast," *Civil War History* 23 (June 1977): 101–13.

PART III

Slavery, Sectionalism, and Partisan Politics

"Hurtful to the State"

The Political Morality of Federalist Antislavery

Rachel Hope Cleves

On January 1, 1795, Massachusetts Federalist Congressman Samuel Dexter introduced an amendment to the Naturalization Act of 1790 requiring that if a new immigrant to the United States "shall hold any person in slavery he shall renounce it, and declare that he holds all men free and equal." Dexter's amendment hit the House like a bunker buster, penetrating deep and igniting a furious explosion. Virginia Republican William Giles declared that while he "lamented and detested" slavery, "it was impossible at present to help it." James Madison rebuked Dexter, for such remarks had "a very bad effect on that species of property." Virginia Republican John Nicholas complained that Dexter had "more than on one occasion hinted his opinion that possessors of slaves were unfit to hold any legislative trust in Republican Government," and Nicholas's response was that slavery and egalitarianism were fully compatible. Virginia Republican John Heath "read a clause of the constitution prohibitory of proposing an abolition for many years to come," and asked how Dexter dared to propose such an unconstitutional amendment. Finally, it was Massachusetts Federalist Theodore Sedgwick who rose to silence the incendiary debate before it consumed the Capitol. The session came to an acrimonious adjournment.[1]

At first glance, Dexter's antislavery amendment and the debate it engendered appear to illustrate the historical argument that in the First Party System predominately Northeastern Federalists "were more inclined to oppose slavery than [were] Republicans," a party dominated by "pro-slavery and anti-black" Southerners.[2] Dexter, a key Federalist who was later appointed secretary of war by John Adams, implied that slavery de-moralized masters and made them unfit to be republican citizens. Virginia Republicans responded that slavery did not conflict with republicanism, and that the danger of servile rebellion made discussion of abolition objectionable. A second glance, however, complicates this narrative and buttresses the historical counterargument that the Federalists had made "only a limited contribution to antislavery," because their critiques of slavery "were not meant to end slavery; they were meant to discredit southern Jeffersonians and their allies."[3] Dexter affixed his amendment not to the Naturalization Act itself, but to an earlier Republican amendment requiring French aristocratic refugees to renounce their titles in order to gain U.S. citizenship. The Federalists viewed Giles's amendment as an attempt to "fix a stigma" on critics of the French Revolution as "friends to a nobility." Dexter's proposed sub-amendment could be viewed as a retaliation against the Southern-dominated Republican Party—as having been motivated by partisan interests rather than by humanitarian concern for human rights.[4]

While the historiographical debate over the Federalist antislavery position has been compelling, taking a third glance at the Dexter-Giles debate usefully blurs this apparent interpretive binary. On January 2, 1795, the Congress reconvened to continue discussion of the Giles and Dexter amendments. North Carolina Republican Joseph McDowell stated that at first he had not believed Dexter was "sincere," but that "much to his surprise, Mr. Dexter [has] persisted in supporting the propriety of his motion." The evident sentiment behind Dexter's amendment made McDowell fear for national unity, and he accused Dexter of holding "monarchical or despotical principles" against the right to own slaves (which raises questions about how Southern Republicans defined "monarchical" during the 1790s). McDowell then challenged Dexter to tell the House "that men who possessed slaves were unfit for holding an office under a republican government." Pushed to the sectionalist precipice, Dexter backpedaled. He "excused his motion," based, in his own words, on the logic that his opponents wanted to "hold us up to the public as aristocrats," and countered that he, "as a retaliation, will hold you up to the same public, as dealers in slaves." Dexter placated his opponents by adding that he "did not want to irritate," and then withdrew the motion, asking only that the Giles Amendment be voted on silently. In sum, a Southern Republican slaveholder had insisted upon the "sincerity" of a Federalist antislavery attack, while the Federalist had retreated and admitted to its partisanship.[5]

In fact, Dexter's amendment was both moral and partisan: designed to smear the opposing party, but also threatening, precisely because it drew on a moral argument, compelling to Northerners, that slaveholding was un-republican. Southern Republicans believed that Dexter meant what he said, and even after he had withdrawn the sub-amendment, Virginia Republican John Nicholas attacked him "most violently." The proffered olive branch now broken, Dexter demanded that his amendment be reinstated. Twenty-eight Federalists voted in favor of Dexter's amendment, eighteen from New England, eight from the Mid-Atlantic, and one each from Delaware and Maryland. Only two Republicans voted for the measure, both of them from Massachusetts. The vast majority of Northern Republicans, a small minority of Northern Federalists, and virtually the entire Southern delegation, voted together to soundly defeat it. The voting pattern, both sectional and partisan, suggests the inextricable connections between regional morality and political imperatives in Federalist antislavery initiatives.[6]

The moral dimensions of the Federalists' distinctive political critique of slavery are easy to overlook when compared with later antebellum abolitionist arguments that focused more consistently on the suffering of slaves. Early national political and religious conservatives condemned slavery because its domineering spirit undermined republican government and it exposed the entire nation to the risk of civil violence. The Federalist antislavery critique made a moral claim that the common good depended on a political order free from slavery. Yet it is also vital to recognize that the Federalist moral-political antislavery argument blended seamlessly into partisanship. Warnings of the danger that slaveholding posed to political order overlapped with critiques of slaveholding politicians, the latter criticism also benefiting Federalist sectionalist electioneering.

The Federalists used antislavery rhetoric to fight partisan battles on two fronts. Attacks on Southern slaveholding Republicans were a defensive measure against local challenges posed by Northern Republicans, and represented a spirited offense against Southern domination at the national level. These twin goals operated simultaneously from the party's beginnings, although Federalists initially stifled their antislavery rhetoric at the national level, after Southern politicians threatened secession. Conservatives like Theodore Sedgwick, terrified by the potential for violent civil disintegration, placed their highest priority on political order above all; to push the critique of slavery to the point of bloody disunion would have defeated Federalist logic. This moral calculus did not change until the War of 1812 seemingly subsumed the republic in violence and many Northeasterners began to see secession as less dangerous than an alliance with the French "anti-Christ."

Identifying the republican ideology that underlay the Federalists' overriding commitment to social stability further illuminates the overlaps between their partisan and moral antislavery arguments. The republican ideology fueling Federalist nightmares of factional bloodshed also led them to see partisanship as a conflict between virtue and corruption. They identified electoral successes as salvos in a moral war. Instrumentalizing Northeastern antislavery sentiment seemed not disingenuous but morally consistent. The ideology of republicanism concatenated partisanship with righteousness. As Northeastern Federalists criticized Southern Republican slaveholding and sought to defeat their opponents at the polls, they acted simultaneously from moral and party imperatives that cannot be separated.[7]

The depth of Federalist antislavery feeling only becomes fully apparent when the high political realm is integrated with the political culture of sermons, poetry, newspapers, and public meetings. Although recent historians have emphasized the broad participatory quality of the Democratic-Republican Party, Federalism is often reduced to its elected representatives. This perspective impoverishes our understanding of Federalism as an ideology.[8] If egalitarianism provided the ideological glue of Republicanism, Federalist political culture was united by fear of human nature and distrust in man's capacity for self-governance. Federalists believed that humanity's basic predilection toward sinfulness made the new nation vulnerable to civil violence. Faith in republican virtue sustained many negativists throughout the Revolution, but their faith collapsed during the mid-1780s as, in Federalist eyes, Americans violently pursued self-interest by turning the techniques of forceful resistance against their legitimately elected governments.[9]

Fearing political disintegration, Northeastern conservatives in the 1790s began to identify slavery as one of the gravest dangers impelling the United States toward anarchy. In his 1781 *Notes on the State of Virginia,* Thomas Jefferson had famously argued that slavery encouraged the "perpetual exercise of the most boisterous passions, the most unremitting despotism on the one part, and degrading submissions on the other." In the 1790s, Northern Federalists turned the opposition leader's own words against him, and against other Southern Republicans, arguing that slaveholders' tendency toward violent despotism made them dangerous citizens and threatened to undermine the republic.[10]

The Reverend Jonathan Edwards Jr. strongly articulated this moral-political argument against slavery in a 1791 oration to the Connecticut Society for the Promotion of Freedom, and for the Relief of Persons Unlawfully Holden in Bondage—an antislavery society largely comprised of conservative clerics and Federalist politicians. Edwards depicted slavery as an institution of violence defined by cruel practices such as torture, starvation, and whipping. Edwards argued that such practices were "exceedingly hurtful to the state which tolerates them," because "they deprave the morals of the people." He went on: "The incessant and inhuman cruelties practiced in the trade, and in the subsequent slavery, necessarily tend to harden the human heart against the tender feelings of humanity in the masters of vessels, in the sailors, in the factors, in the proprietors of these slaves, in their children, in the overseers, in the slaves themselves, and in all who habitually see those cruelties." For Edwards, slaveholder violence was incompatible with republican citizenship, and his position laid the groundwork for Samuel Dexter's moral-political claims in 1795.[11]

Edwards had inherited from his father, Jonathan Edwards, a Calvinist theological orientation that emphasized the utter sinfulness and brutality of mankind. Edwards Jr. combined his father's convictions about human violence with a new concern—that the institution of slavery manifested human wickedness in the new nation, and threatened it with a Providential retribution. Slavery posed a doubled threat to the integrity of the state, both provoking God's punishment at the hands of an external enemy, and fashioning violent citizens who threatened the internal political order. The younger Edwards's oration—delivered on the eve of the development of the First Party System—contained no overtly partisan elements, but it formulated a political logic frequently deployed in future party warfare.[12]

The orators who followed Edwards at the Connecticut Society adopted and politicized his argument that slavery constituted an "uncivilizing process," that it transformed masters into petty despots whose violence would destroy the United States. In 1793, the Federalist newspaper editor, pedagogue, and propagandist Noah Webster delivered the Society's annual oration, declaring that slavery impeded the "public happiness" because it converted "the civilized man into a savage." Recapitulating Thomas Jefferson, Webster argued that "men who from their infancy hold, and those who feel, the rod of tyranny become equally hardened by the exercise of cruelty." Slave owners, according to Webster, were "haughty, capricious, and cruel," as well as "rough, boisterous, [and] irritable." Those characteristics made slaveholders a threat to the state, because in a republic it was necessary for men to learn to "moderate their passions." By evoking Jefferson, Webster smugly hoisted the emerging opposition leader upon his own petard, and criticized the Republican Southern political base in the words of its leader. Webster argued, following Jefferson, that the deleterious effects of slaveholding could be seen in the Southern states, where dueling and blood sports enjoyed a legitimacy shocking to New England sensibilities. Such a taste for blood, according to Webster, made men utterly unfit for political engagement. Webster's condemnation of Southern society, and concurrent celebration of New England, would become the meat and potatoes of Federalist propaganda in the upcoming decades, as the Southern wing of the Federalist Party shrank to minimal proportions.[13]

In 1794, when the First Party System had reached full swing, Theodore

Dwight, Jonathan Edwards Jr.'s nephew and an emerging leader of the Federalist Party, delivered the Connecticut Society's annual oration. Dwight, in keeping with the increasingly vitriolic political rhetoric of the period, presented the moral-political argument against Southern slavery in damning terms. Slavery consisted of "tyranny," "torture," "evil," "death," and "barbarity and murder." Slavery gave children the "disposition to cruelty and injustice," and taught them indulge their worst passions. Southern men were rapists who sold their children; even Southern women would "indulge themselves in the paroxysms of rage and . . . seize the engines of torture." Slaveholders were unfit republicans, whose violence threatened to reduce the nation to bloody anarchy. Dwight's remarks, delivered in the context of Republican support for the increasingly bloody French Revolution, exhibited clear partisan implications by associating Southern slaveholding Republicans with Jacobins. Astoundingly, Dwight's condemnations of Southern Republican slaveholding would grow even more fierce later in the decade. While serving in the House of Representatives in 1806, Dwight would argued that the penalty for illegally importing slaves to the United States should be death. Less than a decade later, Dwight's ethical and partisan condemnation of the slave states would lead him to serve as secretary for the quasi-secessionist Hartford Convention. Ever the partisan, there is no reason to doubt that Dwight despised slavery on moral grounds.[14]

The argument that slavery's violence threatened republican governance circulated throughout Federalist political culture, operating, for example, in the debates over the Dexter Amendment in 1795. Joshua Coit, a Federalist representative who voted for the amendment, was a member of the Connecticut Society. While his vote supported the partisan aim of retaliation against Republican maneuvering, it also reflected the consonance between Dexter's argument and Coit's own antislavery sentiments. Theodore Sedgwick, the Federalist representative from Massachusetts who had initially attempted to suppress the fractious debate, explained his ultimate support for Dexter's sub-amendment in terms similar to the arguments that had been made before the Connecticut Society, declaring that "in his opinion the relation of master and slave, generated habits at least as uncongenial with the principles of our government, as would exist by not requiring the renunciation of a title." This argument was not new to Sedgwick; he had expressed antislavery sentiments since at least the 1780s, when he played an instrumental role in securing judicial emancipation in Massachusetts. Sedgwick, whose home was invaded by looters during Shays's Rebellion in 1787, had an earnest fear of political anarchy that impelled him to seek to stifle the Giles-

Dexter debate before it burned the House down. That same fear placed him squarely in Dexter's camp when the conflict, irrepressible, came to a vote.[15]

The Maine-district Federalist George Thatcher likewise both voted in favor of Dexter's amendment and showed consistent moral-political antagonism to slavery throughout his long political career. From the beginning of his service, in the First Congress of the United States, Thatcher had voiced his antislavery sentiments. When Georgia representative James Jackson advocated taxing New England rum in 1789, Thatcher had retorted, "If the pernicious effect of New England rum have been justly lamented, what can be urged for Negro slavery?" Thatcher's antislavery remarks presented the institution as harmful to the society that tolerated it. In 1800, when Pennsylvania Federalist Robert Waln introduced an abolitionist free-black petition, the entire House voted to disavow any congressional discussion of emancipation, with the sole exception of Thatcher, who declared slavery a "cancer" of the body politic. Antislavery sentiment bubbled dangerously close to the surface throughout Thatcher's political career. To preserve political amity, he tamped it down, but when given full voice, his views were acidic. In 1820, as Thatcher worked to achieve Maine statehood, he complained bitterly that his state was being made "a mere *pack-horse* to transport the odious anti-republican principle of slavery into the new State of Missouri, against reason and the fundamental grounds of the great fabric of American liberty." Rather than compromise with the proslavery Missouri forces, Thatcher insisted that Maine statehood could wait until its entry was freed from the stain of slavery.[16]

Not all Federalists subscribed to the moral-political argument that slaveholding threatened to undermine the republic. As long as the Federalist Party retained some power in Maryland and South Carolina during the 1790s, Southern Federalists typically supported the slaveholding interests of their region. (Even so, Southern Republicans often used the identification of the Federalist Party with antislavery to defeat their in-state rivals.[17]) Additionally, the Federalists' central commitment to the maintenance of order, which underlay its antislavery argument, paradoxically guaranteed that some Northern Federalists would regard antislavery with suspicion as too potentially destabilizing. Harrison Gray Otis, the sectionalist Federalist leader from Massachusetts, attacked antislavery as a grave danger to the Union throughout his career. Otis anathematized Waln's 1800 free-black petition, stating that he had "never seen a petition presented under a more dangerous and unpleasant aspect." Otis shared his state's disregard for slavery, which he labeled a "curse," but he despised antislavery's tendency toward disorder even more, and proved notoriously unsympathetic to abolitionists when he served as mayor of Boston during the early 1830s.[18]

Despite Otis's anathema, a portion of the Waln petition dealing with complaints against the slave trade was referred to a committee headed by James Hillhouse, a Connecticut Federalist and a Dexter supporter. Like Thatcher, Hillhouse repeatedly argued throughout his political career that slavery posed a terrible threat to the republic.[19] Federalist action on the Waln petition helps to correct the argument that slave revolts in the Caribbean and the revolution in France dampened Federalist antislavery zeal, by illustrating the dangers that social upheaval posed to the state.[20] Certainly, after rumors circulated in 1800 that French agents had offered aid and encouragement to the Virginia slave conspirators of Gabriel's Rebellion, Southerners of all party stripes connected the French Revolution and slave rebellion as twin evils.[21] However, Northern Federalists only rarely associated antislavery and Jacobinism, and their hatred for the French Revolution did not lead them to disavow antislavery. When the South Carolina Federalist congressman John Rutledge Jr. described antislavery as a Jacobin scheme during the 1800 Waln debate, Massachusetts Federalist Samuel Dana explicitly rejected the charge, denying that the antislavery petition was "a farrago of the French metaphysics of liberty and equality."[22]

The partisan sectionalism of American politics led Northeastern Federalists to identify slaveholders, not slave rebels, as the gravest "French" threat to the nation. The logic for the charge derived from American foreign policy during the 1790s. Southern Republicans' advocacy for supporting the French Republic's wars against Europe's allied monarchs led Christopher Gore, a Massachusetts Federalist lawyer and occasional politician, to charge slaveholders with Jacobinism in a 1794 essay. Attacking the Republicans as "desperadoes of faction and anarchy" and "lovers of war," Gore explained that since Southerners "are supported by the labor of slaves; their habits and manners, from this circumstance, are necessarily in favor of domination; and against equal liberty or equal rights." Slaveholding habituated masters to the use of domination, driving them to Jacobin passions, including the desire to join France in war. American conflict over Jay's Treaty in 1795 intensified Federalist critiques that slaveholders embraced Jacobin violence. Federalists argued that Southern Francophiles were violently protesting the Anglo-American treaty because Britain was not compensating Southerners for slaves carried away after the Revolution. In sum, Southern radicals trained in brutality by the practice of slaveholding were risking national stability in the violent pursuit of self-interest.[23]

The charge of slaveholding Jacobinism carried into non-political aboli-tionist texts. Amynto, the pseudonymous author of the 1796 pamphlet *Reflections on the Inconsistency of Man,* argued for immediate abolition and attacked Southern Republican slaveholders as violent Jacobins. Amynto as-serted that among "the representatives of Congress from . . . the southern [states], where slavery is yet raging in all its horrors, a furious democracy copied from the Jacobin principles of France appears to be the wish of most of the southern gentry." Likewise, an 1803 pamphlet bearing the similar title *Reflections on Slavery* deployed the specter of Jacobin bloodshed to drive home the danger of slavery by arguing that the United States would suffer providential punishment, perhaps at French hands, if the nation did not "loose the bands of wickedness" and pursue the immediate emancipation of the slaves.[24]

While antipathy to democratic violence led Federalists to disavow the French Revolution, they proved surprisingly sympathetic to slave revolts both in the Caribbean and at home. Many committed antislavery Federalists acknowledged the justice and rationality of slave resistance. They described Toussaint Louverture, leader of the Saint-Domingue rebels, in heroic terms as a "very able and influential character," and even as an African Burke—the standard-bearer of political order. The Adams administration forged diplo-matic ties with Louverture, a decision excoriated by Northern Republicans such as George Logan and Albert Gallatin, who argued that the slave rebels were guilty of "rapine, pillage, and massacre." While Thomas Jefferson ranted about the danger of liberated blacks pouring into the Southern states, Adams sat down to dinner with Louverture's mixed-race emissary Joseph Bunel.[25]

The racially progressive foreign policy of the Adams administration was soon undone by the Jefferson administration, which ended diplomatic ties with the island and supported Napoleon's effort to re-enslave the Haitians.[26] But Northern Federalists continued praising slave rebels. John Sylvester John Gardiner, an arch-Federalist minister, delivered an oration to the Afri-can Society in 1810, on the anniversary of the abolition of the trans-Atlantic slave trade, that condemned slaveholders and praised "the gallant Tous-saint."[27] Even more galling to Southern opponents, Northern Federalists offered sympathy for slave rebels at home. Timothy Dwight expressed com-passion in a eulogy for Gabriel, warning the South that "a host remain / Oppress'd with slavery's galling chain," who would follow in the rebel's foot-steps. An 1802 poem published in the Federalist *Gazette of the United States* condemned Thomas Jefferson and Southern inhumanity after more slaves were executed in suspicion of plotting another rebellion.[28]

Thomas Jefferson frequently served as the particular target of Federalist antislavery sentiment, again revealing the overlap of partisan and moral-political arguments. Federalists described Jefferson as the very personification of Jacobin slaveholding. Theodore Dwight used this line of attack first in 1798, characterizing the Virginian as a violent slave owner who would terrorize the United States with Jacobin bloodshed. The charge became more common in 1800 as the presidential election neared. A series of essays entitled "The Jeffersoniad," published in numerous Federalist newspapers, condemned the candidate as the leader of a party of "bastard children owners," "bastard children starvers," "Negro-stealers" and "man-slayers"—a party that "knashes its teeth for rage and feels a thirst that nothing will slake but the blood of proscriptions." If elected president, Jefferson would "Jacobinize, revolutionize, and of course demoralize the people of these United States." The author's use of the word "demoralize" revealed the critical logic that connected his attacks on slavery and on Jacobinism: both systems destroyed the morals of their practitioners and led inexorably to bloodshed. The survival of the nation and its citizens depended on exclusion of Jacobinism and slavery.[29]

While anti-Jeffersonian literature could be vitriolic, commitment to union tempered Federalist antislavery political action, until the War of 1812 persuaded many that union with the South proved a graver danger to political order than disunion. The future antislavery editor William Cullen Bryant, still a Federalist youth, wrote to his father in 1814 seeking permission to join the Massachusetts militia in order to prepare for a potential civil war against "an intestine foe [the South] in the defense of dearer rights than those which are endangered in a contest with Great Britain."[30] The War of 1812 released Northern Federalists from the paralyzing fear of disunion, and invigorated their antislavery attack on Southern Republicans. Federalists made a moral-political argument against the war that indicted the Republicans' Francophilia, slaveholding, expansionism, and general bloodthirstiness. Ultimately, Federalist opposition culminated in a December 1814 meeting in Hartford, Connecticut, to discuss political solutions to slaveholder dominance of the Union. Former members of the Connecticut Society, including Theodore Dwight, James Hillhouse, and Zephaniah Swift, all attended the meeting, as did antislavery Federalists Nathan Dane (author of the antislavery clause in the Northwest Ordinance) and Samuel Sumner Wilde (supporter of the legal rights of fugitive slaves). When the Hartford Convention demanded an amendment to the Constitution eliminating apportionment of representation by slave population (the infamous three-fifths clause), its members clearly combined moral and sectionalist-partisan interests.[31]

The Hartford Convention's attack on slave power represented the conclusion of more than three years of attacks on the war's slaveholding advocates. Typical antiwar sermons and orations built on the Federalist moral-political argument against slavery to condemn the Southern authors of the war policy. "Pause and reflect," the Reverend Thomas Andros preached, "of the boast, in southern papers, of the number of scalps we take in an Indian expedition—to say nothing of advertising for sale, buying and selling men, as we buy and sell horses and cattle." According to Andros, slave society had produced a brutal culture that did not value human life; Southern Republicans' advocacy for war was a natural consequence of their slaveholding and Indian wars. The brutality of Southern slaveholders posed a grave danger to the integrity of the United States, argued Northeastern Federalist ministers. Not only did the war expose the United States to temporal destruction, by pitting its woefully unprepared army against the might of Great Britain, it exposed the United States to the wrath of God, who would punish the republic for its sinfulness. The Reverend Noah Worcester, founder of the Massachusetts Peace Society, described the War of 1812 as God's punishment for the ongoing crime of slavery. The Connecticut Federalist minister Nathan Strong warned his church that the whole United States would be reduced to slavery if the nation did not immediately cease from the crimes of chattel slavery and warmongering.[32]

Many political opponents to the War of 1812 accused the war hawks of a violent desire to enslave Northerners. John Lowell, an incendiary political critic of the war who favored New England secession, argued that Southerners' masterly desire to dominate was the real, sinister, source for the war. He charged the aristocratic, slave-owning "warm-bloods of the south," with making war as an excuse to subdue the North by sword.[33] Josiah Dunham fulminated that the "Virginia Influence" wanted to compel Northerners "to be substituted, perhaps, in process of time, for African slaves, and *to serve the same masters.*" Others accused the South of attempting to destroy commerce in order to force all men of capital to become slaveholding landowners. They implicated President Madison personally as a slave owner. They compared British impressment to the far greater evil of Southern slavery. And they described human bondage as a national sin.[34]

The most violent attacks linking the War of 1812 to the crime of slavery came from the Reverend Elijah Parish, an arch-Federalist minister from

Newburyport, Massachusetts. The sharp-tongued Parish reviled Republicans in language that drove war hawks to distraction. Republican newspapers accused Parish of "diabolical slander," "atrocious villainy," "libel," "virulence, outrage, sedition," and "prostitution of the pulpit."[35] Be that as it may, Parish's antislavery sentiments appear to have been deep and long-standing. Parish had celebrated Britain's closure of the trans-Atlantic slave trade in 1807, associating antislavery with a future of global salvation, and positioning it against the "licentious anarchy" of Napoleonic France. Like fellow conservative ministers, Parish depicted the war as a consequence of Southern slaveholding violence. Parish's antislavery sentiments went further, embracing the righteousness of slave rebellion. In an 1812 protest, Parish chastised the Republican leadership: "Let the southern *Heroes* fight their own battles, and guard their slumbering pillows against the just vengeance of their lacerated slaves, whose sighs and groans have long since gone up to the court of the Eternal, crying for the full viols of his incensed wrath." The violence of slave masters gave both slaves and Northern states the right to throw off the yoke of Southern dominance.[36]

Parish shared his sympathy for slave rebellion with another remarkable antiwar minister, the Reverend Lemuel Haynes. Haynes, the son of an African father and a white mother, led a white congregation in Rutland, Vermont, from the late 1780s through the late 1820s. An orthodox Calvinist, Haynes strongly supported Federalist politics throughout his career, publishing virulent anti-Jacobin sermons in 1798 and 1801. In 1813, he published a protest sermon that called into question President Madison's justifications for the war. Madison had claimed to be defending the rights of American seamen impressed by Great Britain. If the seamen were justified in their resistance to British power, Haynes asked, was it "the duty of [Madison's] slaves to rise and massacre their masters?" If audiences answered no, they had to repudiate the war. If they answered yes, as perhaps Haynes hoped they would, slave rebellion had gained a powerful sanction. Haynes's long antislavery commitment, and personal investment in the question as a black man, suggests the moral consistency of the partisan antislavery critique during the War of 1812.[37]

Haynes's participation also provokes the question of whether Federalist antislavery extended to support for racial equality. Throughout his long career, Haynes received the patronage and support of several prominent white Federalist antislavery figures, including Timothy Dwight.[38] He ultimately lost his pulpit because of increasing racism in the Northeast. This racism manifested in an exclusionary ideology, which argued that not only slavery, but black people, signified a corruption of the body politic that had to be removed. The most well-known product of this ideology was the American Colonization Society, popular among Northern conservatives following its establishment in 1817. However, Northern Federalists prior to 1817 evinced a broad range of racial attitudes, extending from the hopefully integrationist to the baldly bigoted, with a median point of inclusion and subordination.[39]

Most antislavery Federalists embraced a racial "middle ground," advocating civil inclusion and political rights for African Americans while demanding their social subordination until that supposed future moment when the race would have been "uplifted." Northeastern Federalists viewed African Americans as ignorant and degraded, yet they acknowledged the oppressive forces faced by black people and promoted education and other ameliorative reforms.[40] The anti-Jacobin minister and Federalist propagandist Jedidiah Morse exemplified this compromise position in a speech he delivered to a black audience at an 1808 celebration of the closing of the trans-Atlantic slave trade to the United States. Quoting from the Paulite teaching that God made man "all of one blood," Morse attacked slavery as sinful and violent, expressing empathy for the suffering of its victims. However, his sermon gave equal credence to Paul's more familiar defense of subordination as an appropriate principle for ordering society, and preached deference to the black audience.[41]

Many Federalists accepted environmentalist arguments for black inferiority but expressed deep revulsion toward Thomas Jefferson's speculations that black people constituted an intermediary species between orangutans and human beings.[42] Federalists accused Republicans of inordinate racism. Massachusetts Federalist Samuel Taggart complained in 1806 that Republicans had ended trade with Haiti because they had "a peculiar aversion . . . to considering any people with a black skin as free and independent" (Taggart would later be a committed opponent to the War of 1812).[43] On the other hand, Federalist propagandist William Cobbett incorporated grotesque racial stereotypes into his writings, both to invoke antislavery sentiment against the Republicans and to attack black people. Massachusetts minister John Sylvester John Gardiner likewise uneasily integrated antislavery and anti-black imagery, criticizing the brutal domination exercised by slaveholders while reviling the social integration of black people, suggesting deep internal conflicts within Federalist racial attitudes.[44]

Despite the mixed record of Federalist racial attitudes, enfranchised African Americans in the Northeast generally believed that their best interests lay with the fortunes of the Federalist Party rather than the Republicans. Free blacks frequently voted for the Federalists, often justifying their choice in terms strongly evocative of the logic presented by white antislavery Federalists. At an 1809 political meeting in New York City, the African American leader Joseph Sidney encouraged his audience to vote Federalist in the upcoming elections because the party represented liberty and prosperity. Despite their cant about representing the rights of man, Southern Republicans ruled by the lash and would destroy the nation with their "mad democracy." For reasons both political and moral, Sidney trumpeted the Federalist message to his audience of black voters. "Will you flock to the slavery-hole of democracy?" he challenged. The Republicans, he argued, threatened the political rights of black people in the state—a logic that gained proof in 1821, when the Republican-dominated state government revised the state constitution to disenfranchise black voters.[45]

Joseph Sidney had good reason to suspect the consequences of Republican political leadership for his community, but was his faith in Federalism equally well supported? At the national level, the Federalists advanced little antislavery legislation, and their support for the limited number of antislavery initiatives to come before the Congress was erratic. There are many practical explanations for these failures: the Constitution's protection of slavery left few opportunities for Northeastern Federalists to act upon antislavery sentiments; after emancipation advanced in each of the Northern states by 1804, Federalists could not justify interfering in the institutions of Southern states; the Federalists were consistently in the minority after 1800 and had little power to press for antislavery legislation; the Federalists could not push an antislavery agenda for fear of risking their Southern support (a counterargument to the claim that Federalist antislavery was motivated by partisanship). But ideology may explain better than pragmatism the Federalists' failure to press a legislative antislavery agenda. The Federalist moral-political argument against slavery condemned the institution because its brutalization of masters infected the Union with a dangerous tendency toward civil violence. Men like Theodore Dwight, while sympathetic to the sufferings of black people, worried most of all about the health of the republic. Pursuing political antislavery at the national level, congressional Federalists soon discovered, swiftly prompted secessionist outbursts from Southern representatives. And so an ideological commitment to social order led to the subordination of antislavery to the preservation of union and amity among the states.

Within the larger sphere of political culture, however, the Federalist legacy produced significant ideological outcomes. Federalist antislavery strongly inflected reform discourse in the nineteenth century. While an ideological commitment to preserving social order prevented Federalists from waging a national political assault on slavery, their willingness to violently repudiate slavery as a brutalizing institution reshaped attitudes toward slavery and played a key role in the nineteenth-century abolitionism of their biological and cultural inheritors.

NOTES

1. *Columbian Centinel* (New York), 14 January 1795. Federalist newspapers covered anti-slavery arguments provoked by the Dexter Amendment more attentively than Republican newspapers did; see, for example, the *New-York Gazette,* 7 January 1795; *Greenleaf's New York Journal & Patriotic Register,* 10 January 1795; *American Minerva* (New York), 12 January 1795; the *Massachusetts Mercury* (Boston), 9–13 January 1795; the *Worcester Intelligencer,* 13 January 1795; the *Herald* (New York), 14 January 1795; the *Massachusetts Spy,* 14 January 1795; and the *Aurora General Advertiser* (Philadelphia), 15 January 1795.

2. Paul Finkelman, "The Problem of Slavery in the Age of Federalism," in *Federalists Reconsidered,* ed. Barbara B. Oberg and Doron S. Ben-Atar (Charlottesville: University Press of Virginia, 1998), 141, 153. See also Matthew Mason "Federalists, Abolitionists, and the Problem of Influence," *American Nineteenth Century History* 10 (March 2009): 1–27; Dinah Mayo-Bobee, " 'Something Energetic and Spirited': Massachusetts Federalists, Rational Politics, and Political Economy in the Age of Jefferson, 1805–1815," Ph.D. diss., University of Massachusetts Amherst, 2007; David N. Gellman, *Emancipating New York: The Politics of Slavery and Freedom, 1777–1782* (Baton Rouge: Louisiana State University Press, 2006), chap. 6; Adam Rothman, *Slave Country: American Expansion and the Origins of the Deep South* (Cambridge, Mass.: Harvard University Press, 2005), 24–34; John Saillant, *Black Puritan, Black Republican: The Life and Thought of Lemuel Haynes, 1753–1833* (New York: Oxford University Press, 2003); Gary Wills, *"Negro President": Jefferson and the Slave Power* (Boston: Houghton Mifflin, 2003); Marc Arkin, "The Federalist Trope: Power and Passion in Abolitionist Rhetoric," *Journal of American History* 88 (June 2001): 75–98; William C. Dowling, *Literary Federalism in the Age of Jefferson: Joseph Dennie and the Port Folio, 1801–1812* (Columbia: University of South Carolina Press, 1999), 16–19; Linda K. Kerber, *Federalists in Dissent: Imagery and Ideology in Jeffersonian America* (Ithaca, N.Y.: Cornell University Press, 1970); and James M. Banner, *To the Hartford Convention: The Federalists and the Origins of Party Politics in Massachusetts, 1789–1815* (New York: Knopf, 1970).

3. David Waldstreicher, *In the Midst of Perpetual Fetes: The Making of American Nationalism, 1776–1820* (Chapel Hill: University of North Carolina Press, 1997), 252. See also Padraig Riley, "Northern Republicans and Southern Slavery: Democracy in the Age of Jefferson, 1800–1819," Ph.D. diss., University of California Berkeley, 2007; John Craig Hammond, *Slavery, Freedom, and Expansion in the Early American West* (Charlottesville: University of Virginia Press, 2007); Matthew Mason, *Slavery and Politics in the Early American Republic* (Chapel Hill: University of North Carolina Press, 2006), 4, 59; Sean Wilentz, *The Rise of American*

Democracy: Jefferson to Lincoln (New York: W. W. Norton, 2005), 162; idem, "Jeffersonian Democracy and the Origins of Political Antislavery in the United States: The Missouri Crisis Revisited," *Journal of the Historical Society* 4 (Winter 2004): 375–401; Lance Banning, "Three-Fifths Historian," *Claremont Review of Books* 5 (Fall 2004), www.claremont.org/publications/crb/id.821/article_detail.asp; John Kyle Day, "The Federalist Press and Slavery in the Age of Jefferson," *Historian* 65 (Winter 2003): 1303–29; Arthur Scherr, "'Sambos' and 'Black Cut-Throats': Peter Porcupine on Slavery and Race in the 1790s," *American Periodicals* 13 (2003): 3–30; Leonard L. Richards, *The Slave Power: The Free North and Southern Domination, 1780–1860* (Baton Rouge: Louisiana State University Press, 2000), 28–36; and Sean Wilentz, "The Details of Greatness: American Historians versus American Founders," *The New Republic*, March 29, 2004. The Federalists' elitism makes many historians antagonistic; see the subtitle of even a positive recent account of the Federalists by Allen C. Guelzo: "Learning to Love the Federalists: The Federalists Are So Hard to Love" (*Claremont Review of Books* 4 [Winter 2003], http://www.claremont.org/publications/crb/id.1184/article_detail.asp).

4. *Columbian Centinel* (New York), 14 January 1795.

5. *Philadelphia Gazette & Universal Daily Advertiser*, 3 January 1795. Another allusion to antislavery measures as "monarchical" can be found in "For the Gazette of the United States," *Gazette of the United States* (Philadelphia), 23 February 1793.

6. *American Minerva* (New York), 13 January 1795; *New-York Gazette*, 7 January 1795.

7. James Roger Sharp, *American Politics in the Early Republic: The New Nation in Crisis* (New Haven, Conn.: Yale University Press, 1993); Richard Buel Jr., *Securing the Revolution: Ideology in American Politics, 1789–1815* (Ithaca, N.Y.: Cornell University Press, 1972); Richard Hofstadter, *The Idea of a Party System: The Rise of Legitimate Opposition in the United States, 1780–1840* (Berkeley: University of California Press, 1969); John R. Howe, "Republican Thought and the Political Violence of the 1790s," *American Quarterly* 19 (Summer 1967): 147–65.

8. *Beyond the Founders: New Approaches to the Political History of the Early American Republic*, ed. Jeffrey L. Pasley, Andrew W. Robertson, and David Waldstreicher (Chapel Hill: University of North Carolina Press, 2004). Pasley argues that newspaper editors led the Republican Party, but he dismisses the significance of Federalist editors (Jeffrey L. Pasley, *"The Tyranny of Printers": Newspaper Politics in the Early American Republic* [Charlottesville: University of Virginia Press, 2001], 231–40). Catherine O'Connell Kaplan disputes Pasley's characterization in *Men of Letters in the Early Republic: Cultivating Forms of Citizenship* (Chapel Hill: Published for the Omohundro Institute of Early American History and Culture, Williamsburg, Virginia, by the University of North Carolina Press, 2008). See also Dowling, *Literary Federalism in the Age of Jefferson*. Many historians disparage the prominence of ministers in the Federalist Party as having been motivated by status concerns (see Waldstreicher, *In the Midst of Perpetual Fetes*, 147–52; Gordon S. Wood, *The Radicalism of the American Revolution* [New York: Vintage Books, 1993], 229–31; Stephen E. Berk, *Calvinism versus Democracy: Timothy Dwight and the Origins of American Evangelical Orthodoxy* [Hamden, Conn.: Archon Books, 1974]; and Gary Nash, "The American Clergy and the French Revolution," *William and Mary Quarterly*, 3rd ser., 22 [July 1965]: 392–412).

9. Rachel Hope Cleves, *The Reign of Terror in America: Visions of Violence from Anti-Jacobinism to Antislavery* (New York: Cambridge University Press, 2009), chap. 1.

10. Thomas Jefferson, *Notes on the State of Virginia*, ed. William Harwood Peden (Chapel Hill: University of North Carolina Press, 1954), 162.

11. Jonathan Edwards Jr., *The Injustice and Impolicy of the Slave Trade, and of the Slavery of the Africans* (Providence, R.I., 1792), 10. See also James D. Essig, *The Bonds of Wickedness: American Evangelicals against Slavery, 1770–1808* (Philadelphia: Temple University Press, 1982), 107–13.

12. Jonathan Edwards, *Original Sin,* ed. Clyde A. Holbrook (New Haven, Conn.: Yale University Press, 1970); Peter Hinks, "Timothy Dwight, Congregationalism, and Early Anti-Slavery," in *The Problem of Evil: Slavery, Freedom, and the Ambiguities of American Reform,* ed. Steven Mintz and John Stauffer (Amherst: University of Massachusetts Press, 2007); Kenneth P. Minkema and Harry S. Stout, "The Edwardsean Tradition and the Antislavery Debate, 1740–1865," *Journal of American History* 92 (June 2005): 47–74; David Brion Davis, *The Problem of Slavery in the Age of Revolution, 1770–1823* (Ithaca, N.Y.: Cornell University Press, 1975), chap. 7.

13. Noah Webster, *Effects of Slavery, on Morals and Industry* (Hartford, 1793), 18–19.

14. Theodore Dwight, *An Oration, Spoken before "The Connecticut Society, for the Promotion of Freedom and the Relief of Persons Unlawfully Holden in Bondage: Convened in Hartford, on the 8th day of May, A.D. 1794"* (Hartford, 1794). See also the Pelham essays that Theodore Dwight published and probably wrote, in the *Connecticut Courant* for 12 December 1796 and 22 May 1797. And see Theodore Dwight, *An Oration, Spoken at Hartford, in the State of Connecticut, on the Anniversary of American Independence, July 4th, 1798* (Hartford, 1798); and *Annals of Congress,* 9th Cong., 2nd sess., 239–41.

15. Connecticut Society, *The Constitution of the Connecticut Society for the Promotion of Freedom and the Relief of Persons Unlawfully Holden in Bondage as Revised and Enlarged on the 13th Day of September 1792* (New Haven, 1792), 3; *Gazette of the United States* (Philadelphia), 6 January 1795; Arthur Zilversmit, "Quok Walker, Mumbet, and the Abolition of Slavery in Massachusetts," *William and Mary Quarterly,* 3rd ser., 25 (October 1968): 614–24.

16. *Annals of Congress,* 1st Cong., 1st sess., 224, 229–45; "Letter of the Hon. George Thacher," in *Proceedings of the Massachusetts Historical Society* (May 1878): 179–80.

17. Anthony Iaccarino, "Virginia and the National Contest over Slavery in the Early Republic, 1780–1833," Ph.D. diss., University of California, Los Angeles, 2000; Rachel N. Klein, *Unification of a Slave State: The Rise of the Planter Class in the South Carolina Backcountry, 1760–1808* (Chapel Hill: University of North Carolina Press, 1990), 258.

18. *Annals of Congress,* 6th Cong., 2nd sess., 231; *Liberator,* 5 and 19 September 1835; Samuel Eliot Morison, *Harrison Gray Otis, 1765–1848: The Urbane Federalist* (Boston: Houghton Mifflin, 1969).

19. In 1804, Hillhouse proposed antislavery amendments to the act bringing Louisiana into the nation (see Everett S. Brown, "The Senate Debate on the Breckinridge Bill for the Government of Louisiana, 1804," *American Historical Review* 22 [1917]: 360–64; and Rothman, *Slave Country,* 31). Hammond and Wilentz stress the Republican support for the Hillhouse Amendment (see Hammond, *Slavery, Freedom, and Expansion in the Early American West,* 36–38, 184n2; and Wilentz, "The Details of Greatness").

20. David Brion Davis, *Inhuman Bondage: The Rise and Fall of Slavery in the New World* (New York: Oxford University Press, 2006); Mason, *Slavery and Politics in the Early American Republic,* 36–40; Davis, *The Problem of Slavery,* 329; Jordan, *White Over Black,* 375.

21. Elizabeth Fox-Genovese and Eugene D. Genovese, *The Mind of the Master Class: History and Faith in the Southern Slaveholders' Worldview* (New York: Cambridge University

Press, 2005), chap. 1; Douglas R Egerton, *Gabriel's Rebellion: The Virginia Slave Conspiracies of 1800 and 1802* (Chapel Hill: University of North Carolina Press, 1993).

22. *Annals of Congress*, 6th Cong., 1st sess., 230, 234. George Thatcher one-upped Dana, arguing that although he opposed French democracy, "it was an admirable attempt in them, and well executed, to liberate their slaves" (ibid., 239).

23. Christopher Gore, *Manlius: With Notes and References* (Boston, 1794), 6, 49, 51; *Connecticut Courant* (Hartford), 3 August 1795; Henry Wilson, *History of the Rise and Fall of the Slave Power in America* (New York, 1969), chap 9.

24. Amynto, *Reflections on the Inconsistency of Man, Particularly Exemplified in the Practice of Slavery in the United States* (New York, 1796); Humanitas, *Reflections on Slavery, with Recent Evidence of its Inhumanity Occasioned by the Meleancholy Death of Romain, A French Negro* (Philadelphia, 1803), 14, 36.

25. See, for example, Dwight, *An Oration, Spoken before the Society of the Cincinnati, of the State of Connecticut, Met in Hartford, on the 4th of July, 1792*, 16–17; "Reflections on the Slavery of the Negroes," *Rural Magazine, or Vermont Repository*, June 1796; "Slavery," *Balance & Columbian Repository* (Hudson, N.Y.), 13 July 1802, 221; Thomas Branagan, *Political and Theological Disquisitions on the Signs of the Times, Relative to the Present Conquests of France Etc.* (Trenton, 1807), 67–70, 55–56; Lemuel Haynes, *Black Preacher to White America: The Collected Writings of Lemuel Haynes, 1774–1833*, ed. Richard Newman (Brooklyn: Carlson Publishing, 1990), 153, 57; and Elijah Parish, *A Protest against the War: A Discourse Delivered at Byfield, Fast Day, July 23, 1812*, 2nd ed. (Newburyport, 1812), 16. Historians debate the balance of humanitarianism and pragmatism in Federalist policy regarding Saint-Domingue (see Ronald A. Johnson, "Diplomacy in Black and White: A Distinctive U.S. Foreign Policy toward Revolutionary Saint-Domingue" (paper delivered at the SHEAR Annual Conference, Philadelphia, Penn., 2008).

26. Douglas Egerton, "The Empire of Liberty Reconsidered," in *The Revolution of 1800: Democracy, Race, and the New Republic*, ed. James P. Horn, Jan Ellen Lewis, and Peter S. Onuf (Charlottesville: University of Virginia Press, 2002), 309–30.

27. John Sylvester John Gardiner, *A Sermon Preached before the African Society on the 14th of July 1810: The Anniversary of the Abolition of the Slave Trade* (Boston, 1810), 17.

28. "Triumph of Democracy," *New England Palladium*, 6 January 1801, cited in Kerber, *Federalists in Dissent*, 46; "Ode," *Gazette of the United States* (Philadelphia), 28 June 1802.

29. Dwight, *An Oration, Spoken at Hartford, in the State of Connecticut, on the Anniversary of American Independence, July 4th, 1798*; "The Jeffersoniad," nos. 1–16, in *Columbian Centinel* (New York), June–August 1800 (this series was reprinted in the *Newburyport [Mass.] Herald*, the *Gazette of the United States* [Philadelphia], the *Philadelphia Gazette*, and other journals). Antislavery attacks on Jefferson continued after 1800 (see Thomas Green Fessenden, *Democracy Unveiled, or Tyranny Stripped of the Garb of Patriotism, by Christopher Caustic* [Boston, 1805], 99–125).

30. William Cullen Bryant to Peter Bryant, 10 October 1814; and William Cullen Bryant to Peter Bryant, 18 October 1814, both in Bryant-Godwin Papers, New York Public Library.

31. Connecticut Society, *The Constitution of the Connecticut Society*; Paul Finkelman, *Slavery and the Founders: Race and Liberty in the Age of Jefferson* (New York: M. E. Sharpe, 2001), 41, 109; Kathryn Grover, *The Fugitive's Gibraltar: Escaping Slaves and Abolitionism in New Bedford, Massachusetts* (Amherst: University of Massachusetts Press, 2001); Hartford Conven-

tion, *The Proceedings of a Convention of Delegates . . . Convened at Hartford in the State of Connecticut, December 15th, 1814* (Hartford, 1815); Mason, *Slavery and Politics in the Early American Republic,* chap. 2.

32. Thomas Andros, *The Grand Era of Ruin to Nations from Foreign Influence* (Boston, 1812), 14–15; Joseph Estabrook White, "Thomas Andros: Captive," *New England Quarterly* 10 (September 1937): 516–26; "The Slave Trade," *Christian Disciple,* October 1814, 309–11, and December 1814, 357–60; Nathan Strong, *A Fast Sermon, delivered in the North Presbyterian Meeting House, in Hartford, July 23, 1812* (Hartford, 1812), 15–16. See also Kiah Bayley, *War a Calamity Greatly to Be Dreaded* (Hallowell, 1812); and John Sylvester John Gardiner, *A Discourse, Delivered at Trinity Church, Boston, July 23, 1812* (Boston, 1812).

33. John Lowell, *Perpetual War: The Policy of Mr. Madison* (Boston, 1812), 77. See also John Lowell, *Mr. Madison's War: A Dispassionate Inquiry into the Reasons Alleged by Mr. Madison for Declaring an Offensive and Ruinous War against Great Britain* (New York, 1812), 3, 16; Friend to Freedom, *Southern Oppression: An Address to the People of the Eastern States, Developing the Causes of Their Oppression* (New York, 1813); and James Sloan, *An Address to the Citizens of the United States, but Particularly Those of the Middle and Eastern States* (Philadelphia, 1812).

34. Josiah Dunham, *An Oration, in Commemoration of the Birth of Our Illustrious Washington* (Windsor, 1814), 30; "Letters of Samuel Taggart," in *Proceedings of the American Antiquarian Society* 33 (1924): 368; Elijah Parish, *A Discourse, Delivered at Byfield, on the Annual Fast, April 8, 1813* (Portland, 1813), 13; Noah Worcester, *Abraham and Lot: A Sermon, on the Way of Peace, and the Evils of War* (Concord, 1812), 25; Jonathan French, *Sermons, Delivered on the 20th of August, 1812, the Day Recommended by the President of the United States for Public Humiliation and Prayer* (Exeter, 1812), 5–6; Lewis Mayer, *The Crisis: A Sermon, Preached at Shepherd's-Town, Virginia, on Thursday, August 20, 1812* (Martinsburgh, 1812); Nathan Perkins, *The National Sins and National Punishment in the Recently Declared War Considered in a Sermon, Delivered July 23, 1812* (Hartford, 1812), 16.

35. "Fellow Citizens," *Northern Centinel* (Burlington, Vt.), 30 May 1811; "To Elijah Parish, D.D.," *New-Hampshire Gazette* (Portsmouth), 11 June 1811; "Prostitution of the Pulpit," *American Watchman* (Wilmington, Del.), 27 July 1811. For two modern appreciations of Parish, see Jonathan D. Sassi, *A Republic of Righteousness: The Public Christianity of the Post-Revolutionary New England Clergy* (Oxford: Oxford University Press, 2001); and Mason, *Slavery and Politics in the Early American Republic.*

36. "Sermon XIV," in Elijah Parish, *Sermons, Practical and Doctrinal, with a Biographical Sketch of the Author* (Boston, 1826), 281–91; Parish, *A Protest against the War,* 16. Parish's antislavery sentiment likely dated to a period earlier than 1807 (see Parish's February 1795 sermon, "Psal. 92.1," in the Elijah Parish Papers, Governor's Academy, Byfield, Mass.).

37. Lemuel Haynes, *Black Preacher to White America,* 67–69, 83, 153, 157. For Haynes's earlier antislavery sentiment, see Ruth Bogin, "'Liberty Further Extended': A 1776 Antislavery Manuscript by Lemuel Haynes," *William and Mary Quarterly,* 3rd ser., 40 (January 1983): 85–101; and Rita Roberts, "Patriotism and Political Criticism: The Evolution of Political Consciousness in the Mind of a Black Revolutionary Soldier," *Eighteenth-Century Studies* 27 (Spring 1994): 569–88. Federalist antiwar minister Noah Worcester also connected the justice of the war and of slave rebellion (Worcester, *Abraham and Lot,* 25–28).

38. Saillant, *Black Puritan, Black Republican,* 84, 89.

39. Joanne Pope Melish, *Disowning Slavery: Gradual Emancipation and "Race" in New England, 1780–1860* (Ithaca, N.Y.: Cornell University Press, 1998), 192–93.

40. See Richard Newman's essay in this volume. Also, James Brewer Stewart, "The Emergence of Racial Modernity and the Rise of the White North, 1790–1840," *Journal of the Early Republic* 18 (Summer 1998): 181–217.

41. Jedidiah Morse, *A Discourse, Delivered at the African Meeting-House, in Boston, July 14, 1808, in Grateful Celebration of the Abolition of the African Slave-Trade, by the Governments of the United States, Great Britain, and Denmark* (Boston, 1808). Timothy Dwight made similar uplift arguments (see Hinks, "Timothy Dwight, Congregationalism, and Early Anti-Slavery," 155–59).

42. Jefferson, *Notes on the State of Virginia*, 143. For critiques of Jefferson, see William Linn, *Serious Considerations on the Election of a President: Addressed to the Citizens of the United States* (New York, 1800), 13; Clement Clarke Moore, *Observations Upon Certain Passages in Mr. Jefferson's Notes on Virginia, Which Appear to Have a Tendency to Subvert Religion, and Establish a False Philosophy* (New York, 1804); John M. Mason, *The Voice of Warning, to Christians, on the Ensuing Election of a President of the United States* (New-York, 1800); and Branagan, *Political and Theological Disquisitions on the Signs of the Times, Relative to the Present Conquests of France Etc.*, 117.

43. Mayo-Bobee, " 'Something Energetic and Spirited,' " 96.

44. See the complex imagery of "Debate on the Appointment of a Stenographer," in *Porcupine's Political Censor*, March 1796, 25; and John Sylvester John Gardiner *Remarks on the Jacobiniad* (Boston, 1795). Federalists also made political hay out of Massachusetts Governor John Hancock's hosting of an "equality ball" for Boston's "Negro" citizens in 1793 (see Richard Alsop, *The Echo, With Other Poems* [New York, 1807], 65–68).

45. Joseph Sidney, *An Oration Commemorative of the Abolition of the Slave Trade in the United States Delivered before the Wilberforce Philanthropic Association, in the City of New-York, on the Second of January, 1809* (New York, 1809); Finkelman, "The Problem of Slavery in the Age of Federalism"; Mayo-Bobee, " 'Something Energetic and Spirited,' ", 299–301; Jeffrey A. Mullins, "Race, Place, and African-American Disenfranchisement in the Early Nineteenth-Century American North," *Citizenship Studies* 10 (February 2006): 77–91.

Slavery and the Problem of Democracy in Jeffersonian America

PADRAIG RILEY

From the American Revolution to the Civil War, antislavery critics of the United States converged on a stock image of American hypocrisy: the slave-holding republican who yelped for freedom while he drove his Negroes, declaimed in the legislature by day and abused his human chattels by night. From Samuel Johnson to Frances Trollope and beyond, the slaveholding republican was a damning metaphor, capturing in one instant the contradictory reality of early American political culture. Yet it was also fundamentally inaccurate. For many enslaved African Americans, masters who spoke of liberty while they raised the lash were an all-too-frequent reality. The large majority of white Americans, however, confronted slavery far less directly: they were neither slaves nor masters, but members of a nation in which slavery was both extremely powerful and yet not always so ominously present. All white Americans remained connected to slavery, because it was such a powerful institution in the Southern and national economies and because slaveholders held considerable power in national politics. Yet for many non-slaveholders, slavery remained both geographically and ideologically distant. Even those who confronted slavery struggled to explain their complex ties to the power and oppression at the heart of the institution.

This was especially the case in the post-Revolutionary North after 1790, as the Democratic-Republican and Federalist Parties became consumed by an intense conflict over freedom and power in representative government. During the heyday of what came to be called "Jeffersonian democracy," Northern Republicans fought to obtain the basic institutional conditions of a democratic political order: they removed suffrage restrictions and qualifications for political office based on wealth; they elected lesser men to positions of power; they fought against nativism and religious establishments; and they built an impressive political coalition that brought Thomas Jefferson to the presidency in 1800.[1] Yet as Federalists observed in 1800, and as more and more historians have come to argue in recent years, Jefferson's election was marked not by the triumph of democracy but by the triumph of slavery. Jefferson's base was in the Southern states, and the Democratic-Republican Party would remain strongest there throughout its history. While post-Revolutionary Northerners acted to bring slavery to an end, gradually but decisively, Southern Republicans were the political face of an expanding and powerful slave society. They often restrained democratic practices for white men in their own states, while fighting to protect and expand slavery in the new American nation.[2]

These two conflicting visions of Jeffersonian politics—one based on democracy, one based on slavery—dominate current historiography, but historians have been hesitant to integrate them. Doing so requires moving beyond the metaphor of the republican slaveholder and looking more closely at how non-slaveholding Americans encountered the power of slavery in the early nation. We especially need to know more about how Northern Democratic-Republicans, the vanguard of democratization in the 1790s and 1800s, came to terms with their supposed antithesis—the powerful slaveholders who were their comrades and leaders in the Jeffersonian coalition.

Some historians see racism as the primary explanation for these Northern Jeffersonians: by emphasizing the grievances of white men, excluding free blacks from political and social life, and embracing slaveholders' fears of emancipation, Northern Republicans formed a powerful racial bond to the slaveholding South.[3] Others historians seem to believe that ignorance of slavery was possible, to some degree. In their view, Northern politics were primarily local, while Southern slavery was a distant problem that most Northerners overlooked in favor of political struggles closer to home.[4] More recently, historians have begun to dissent from both of these arguments, by claiming that Northern Republicans frequently opposed slavery at the national level. While Northern Federalists made the boldest attacks against slavery, Northern Republicans routinely fought against proslavery legislation in Congress and maligned slaveholders (much as they maligned Federalist elites) as an anti-democratic force.[5]

Together, these three conceptions of the Northern Jeffersonian relationship to slavery seem inconsistent, yet all can claim equal validity, depending on who one is looking at and when. The infamous Jeffersonian printer, William Duane, for example, opposed slavery in 1796; reconciled himself to the institution after 1800; attacked slavery again after the War of 1812; and then ended his political career by reaffirming the commitments that had suppressed his antislavery convictions in the first place. Such variation allows for endless conflict between those who see democratic promise in the Jeffersonian tradition and those who see the origins of a white man's republic. Neither position lacks evidence, but both lack perspective. Interpretation should begin by recognizing that the Jeffersonian Republicans, North and South, were tightly bound to both slavery and democracy.

William Duane's ideological itinerary reflects a wider pattern. In the 1790s, many leading Northern Republicans opposed slavery in public. But their hostility did not prevent an alliance to Southern Republicans, in large part because all Republicans, slaveholders and non-slaveholders alike, were focused on their domestic battle against Federalism and the international crisis that followed the French Revolution. Yet slavery could not be fully ignored, and many Northern Jeffersonians therefore began to either suppress or transform their antislavery convictions after 1800. Had slavery remained a static institution, this state of affairs might have persisted for some time. But Southern Republicans ensured that slavery would remain a central issue in national politics, by facilitating the expansion of slavery to the West and by advocating for slaveholders in the federal government. They effectively forced Northerners to either relinquish their antislavery principles altogether or engage in sectional conflict.

Southern hubris on the slavery question frequently provoked Northern dissidence, but such dissidence had limited outlets in the Jeffersonian period: no political coalition openly opposed to slavery (other than, at times, the expiring Federalists) ever took hold in the early republic. This was due to the power of slaveholders, the persistent cupidity and racism of many Northerners, and the weaknesses of organized abolitionism. But it was mostly due to the multiple ways in which democracy had become entangled with slavery since the 1790s.[6] After building an egalitarian political culture in alliance with slaveholders, Northern dissidents found it difficult to salvage a democratic antislavery argument. In the end, they were undone by the resiliency of the Jeffersonian coalition, which continued to bring slaveholders to power while making Northerners free.

FROM ANTI-SLAVERY TO PRO-JEFFERSON

Before 1800, many Northerners who would later become prominent Republicans directly attacked slavery in the United States. William Duane, soon to become an infamous Jeffersonian printer from Philadelphia, closed a 1796 assault on George Washington by decrying the fact that Washington held "FIVE HUNDRED of the HUMAN SPECIES IN SLAVERY." In 1791, Abraham Bishop, later an important Jeffersonian in Connecticut, defended the Haitian Revolution in terms which would have appalled most Southern slaveholders. Other Northern Jeffersonians were less radical, but no less opposed to slavery. Back in 1781, Levi Lincoln of Worcester, Massachusetts, who served as Jefferson's first Attorney General, argued on behalf of Quock Walker in a case that helped to end slavery in that state. The lesser-known John Leland, originally a Baptist from Massachusetts, spent many years as a missionary in Virginia, and left the state in 1790 as an open opponent of slavery. In the federal government, the Northern Jeffersonians Albert Gallatin and Matthew Lyon defended the right of antislavery petitioners to have a hearing in Congress.[7]

The antislavery words and actions of these men were tied to a wider post-Revolutionary political argument about the nature and character of the American government, an argument that would come to define the Democratic-Republican Party in the North. That argument had multiple sources, and it varied in emphasis from moderates like Lincoln to radicals like Duane and Lyon. But it had some obvious common themes: a powerful critique of aristocracy that Northern Republicans applied to local Federalist elites as well as European states; a generic belief in human equality and a specific argument for the political equality of all male citizens of the new American republic; a strong commitment to religious liberty; and an enthusiasm for self-government that led to the open advocacy of "democracy," a word that remained something of an epithet for many early American political leaders. In 1781, Levi Lincoln had claimed that "the air in America is too pure for a slave to breathe in" and that all men were equal before "the law of God"; Leland's 1790 attack on slavery followed a long fight to bring religious freedom to Virginia; Duane's critique of Washington was part of a vehement diatribe against Federalist Anglophilia and conservatism; Bishop praised the rebels of Saint-Domingue soon after his alienation from the Federalist leadership in Connecticut; and Matthew Lyon's defense of the right of petition came but a few months before he infamously spat in the face of Connecticut Federalist Roger Griswold, precipitating a brawl on the floor of Congress.

All of these men supported Jefferson in 1800, and all helped to build the Democratic-Republican Party in the Northern states. Given their antislavery convictions, such an alliance appeared contradictory, since Jefferson's party was clearly dominated by the slaveholding South. In 1800, Jefferson won only 27 percent of the Northern electoral vote, but 82 percent of the Southern vote. The House races in 1800 told a somewhat different story, since Democratic-Republicans ran well throughout the country. Still, Southerners had a clear edge in the new Republican majority that came to the House in 1801, and Virginia, the largest slaveholding state in the Union, held over one-quarter of all Republican seats, twice as many as any other state.[8] These Virginian congressmen tended to be slaveholders, and as a class they were the closest thing to a European aristocracy in American political life. But in the national politics of the 1790s, they had become outspoken critics of Federalism and John Adams, allying themselves with a broad coalition of Northerners to undermine what Jefferson termed "kingly" government—by which he meant the Federalist-sponsored Alien and Sedition Acts, Federalist partiality for Britain, and the Federalists' unconcealed disdain for political upstarts like William Duane and Matthew Lyon.

The alliance between Virginia and Northern Democratic-Republicans paid obvious dividends when it came to defeating Federalism, but it created an ideological problem for Northerners who had spoken so militantly against slavery. Some of those Northern Jeffersonians who had once expressed strong antislavery views simply forgot or neglected them over time. Levi Lincoln, for example, never spoke publicly on slavery in his Jeffersonian years. Others, however, clearly attempted to reassess their feelings on slavery, now that they were allied to the most prominent slaveholders in the nation. Duane, for example, tried to argue that slavery was on a path to extinction, led by Thomas Jefferson, whose "whole life has been marked by measures calculated to procure the emancipation of the blacks." His newspaper, the *Aurora General Advertiser,* also echoed Jeffersonian rhetoric about the expansion of slavery, explaining that the growth of cotton production would lead to "the happy diffusion" of slaves "over a greater extent of country, so as to be mixed with and checked by the white people."[9]

Such racial considerations were not part of Duane's criticism of Washington as a slaveholder, but they became commonplace in his commentaries on slavery in the Jeffersonian years. Unlike Bishop in the 1790s, Duane saw the Haitian Revolution less as an expression of universal liberty, than as a racial catastrophe with dire lessons for America. Like many other Northern Republicans, he supported Jefferson's embargo of the island in 1805. Both Duane and Thomas Branagan, a militant Northern critic of slavery, fantasized about the horrors of American slave revolt, in which a local Dessalines would slaughter the white population of Philadelphia, while Branagan added crude details about the dangers of interracial mixture as well. These Northern fears of black rebellion made little practical sense, given the demography of Philadelphia compared to Virginia, let alone Saint-Domingue, but they made profound ideological sense. Racist paranoia about liberated blacks provided Northern whites with a compelling psychological reason to support Southerners and to discard their earlier opposition to slavery. By 1814, Duane would tell Thomas Jefferson that slavery was the appropriate condition for African Americans.[10]

Abraham Bishop did not overhaul his own heroic story about the slave rebellion in Saint-Domingue, but he too began to develop a powerful investment in whiteness. Rather than adopt the racist fears of Southern masters, Bishop glorified the struggles of Republicans in Connecticut. Such men were, he claimed, also slaves, to Federalists and Congregational ministers, and it was "high time that societies for the emancipation of white slaves were established in New England." John Leland, back in western Massachusetts, followed suit on behalf of the slaves of his state—the dissenting Christians who were slaves of conscience to the established Congregational church. Matthew Lyon had actually been the closest thing to a white slave among all of these men—he had come to the United States as an indentured servant from Ireland, a fact which Federalists often cited to his discredit. But Lyon's experience of bondage made him no convinced enemy of slavery: by 1803, he had become a slaveholder in Kentucky, and explained to Congress that he found blacks more useful as slaves than as free men.[11]

The Jeffersonian tendency to aggrandize the oppression of Northern whites, in addition to a growing Northern racism, helped bind Northern Republicans to their Southern colleagues. But there were also good instrumental reasons for Northern Jeffersonians to suppress or at least modify their antislavery convictions. Joining the Democratic-Republican cause paid obvious dividends, and blunt attacks on slavery at the national level were not likely to perpetuate party unity. Many Northern Jeffersonians benefited, or hoped to benefit, from political patronage: Levi Lincoln became the Attorney General, and a paper he founded in Worcester, the *National Aegis*, received federal printing contracts. Duane never received the patronage he thought he was due (and which he requested in letter after self-righteous letter), but he did obtain some federal business. Abraham Bishop fared far better—his father was appointed the customs collector at New Haven, Connecticut, and Bishop took the post on his death, and became fairly well-off.[12]

But while the combination of race, patronage, and self-aggrandizement may account for a lot, one still struggles to fully explain the bizarre story of John Leland and the giant cheese, recently retold by Jeffrey Pasley. In 1801, Leland and his fellow Baptists in Cheshire, Massachusetts, decided to produce what came to be called "The Mammoth Cheese," to celebrate President Jefferson's victory over Federalism. In December, Leland trucked this massive, 1,235-pound cheese by sled, ship, and wagon from the Berkshires to

Washington, D.C., arriving in early January. What motivated such an endeavor? Leland was not obviously looking for patronage or racial pride, though he certainly hoped to make a public spectacle—to demonstrate, one might say, on behalf of the oppressed Baptists of New England. More generally, though, Leland was simply inspired by a powerful democratic enthusiasm. "We believe the supreme Ruler of the Universe," Leland said, as he presented the cheese to his president, "has raised up a Jefferson at this critical day, to defend *Republicanism* and to baffle the arts of *Aristocracy.*"[13]

Such language may appear bombastic, but it was heard everywhere in Jeffersonian orations. Jeffersonian rhetoric had a distinct nationalist tone, but Northerners usually had local referents in mind when they decried aristocrats. To most Northern Jeffersonians, the Federalist Party, which continued to hold regional power in New England after 1800, remained the chief impediment to expanding democracy in the United States. New England Republicans like Lincoln, Bishop, and Leland constantly assaulted the Federalists, who still dominated their states, while Duane spent the late 1790s in a bitter newspaper war with rival Federalist papers. Federalism died out fairly quickly in Pennsylvania after 1800, but Duane soon became involved in a factional fight against the more elite members of the Pennsylvania Democratic-Republican Party. Consumed by local struggles, Duane and the New Englanders had plenty of aristocrats to attack without paying much attention to slaveholders.

These Northern conflicts were overdramatized by their protagonists, but they were also unambiguous fights for democratization. Lincoln and John Leland hoped to undermine the power of the Congregational church in Massachusetts and expand religious liberty, while Duane helped elaborate one of the most radical theories of democracy in the early nation. Northerners contributed most of the actual "democracy" to Jeffersonian democracy, and helped elevate their president, the Declaration of Independence, and the Republican cause to an almost sacrosanct political status. Jefferson arguably deserved such affirmation—not because he was such a wonderful thinker and person, but because he proved, for most of his presidency, to be an excellent political leader for his Northern allies. While Federalists scoffed, Jefferson received Leland and his cheese with fanfare at the White House, and acknowledged Duane as a party leader. Most important, Jefferson's election paid huge political dividends to his Northern partisans. Before the congressional elections of 1800, Democratic-Republicans held only 34 percent of the Northern seats in the House. Afterwards, they held 54 percent, and that majority grew over time. Combined with their Southern colleagues, they had an unshakeable majority in the Congress, and they overturned hated Federalist legislation of the 1790s.

But if that congressional success helped bind Northerners to Jefferson, it also created new sources of discord. Once in Congress, Northern Republicans had to confront slavery, because it was such a powerful institution in the national economy and because slaveholders dominated the Southern contingent in Congress. While president, Jefferson never took a strong public stance against slavery, for fear of alienating his Southern base, but neither did he publicly defend the institution. This was not true, however, of most Southern Republicans, as Northerners who came to Washington learned fairly quickly. Even moderate antislavery arguments were subject to unremitting attack on the House floor, as Southerners unified around protecting the inviolable rights of masters. Southern defiance helped catalyze a new antislavery passion among Northern Republicans, who began to see the power of slavery not only as morally illegitimate, but as a malignant force within their own political coalition. As they confronted version after version of the republican slaveholder, most of whom were far less palatable than Thomas Jefferson, some Northern Republicans began to question the ideological convictions that had brought them to Congress and brought the Democratic-Republican party to power.

SOUTHERN POWER AND NORTHERN DISSIDENCE

In Republican rhetoric, the Federalist Party was the most aristocratic force in the United States, bent on subverting liberty and democracy. But such pronouncements were easier to make in Massachusetts and Philadelphia than in Washington, D.C., after 1800. After Jefferson's first election, the Federalists were palpably weak at the national level: they were a minority in both houses of Congress and they never again proposed a serious contender for the presidency. Except for brief and minor revivals during the embargo of 1807 and the War of 1812, their limited numbers only waned during the Virginia dynasty. Yet Federalists proved a troublesome minority. On the subject of slavery, they consistently challenged Southern Republicans: they opposed the expansion of slavery into the new territory of Louisiana; the Jeffersonian embargo of Haiti; and the linchpin of Southern political power, the three-fifths clause of the Constitution. On all of these questions, the majority of Northern Democratic-Republicans were either indifferent or publicly hostile to Federalist criticism of the South.

The most significant Jeffersonian debates over slavery, however, focused on the international slave trade, which South Carolina had reopened in 1803, per the twenty-year exception allowed by the Constitution. Here, the Northern Jeffersonians would play a very different role, attacking first South Carolina and then the Southern Republican contingent as a whole. In doing so, they came to blows with the most obviously powerful group in early Washington: the slaveholders who dominated Congress, the presidency, and their own party. Northern Jeffersonians in the House caused major sectional fights over a proposed tax on the international trade in 1804 and 1806, and by 1807, when the House debated legislation to close the international trade altogether, sectional lines were firmly drawn. Most Northerners supported abolition of the trade on antislavery terms, while Southerners unified around the protection of domestic slavery within the United States. In the end, almost every member of Congress voted to abolish the international slave trade, misleading some historians to see a consensual antislavery intent in the legislation. The full record of debate and the larger history of American slavery indicate an opposite conclusion: that the slave trade debates marked the genesis of a full-fledged and ambitious defense of Southern slavery.

Outside of Washington, planters and merchants were laying the major foundations for antebellum slavery: aggressive Western expansion; the production of cotton; and an internal slave trade that grew substantially after 1810, tying the Chesapeake to the Deep South. Almost in tandem, Southerners began to articulate the major points of the proslavery argument during the debates over closing the international trade. They claimed that slaves were better off in America than in Africa; that slavery was not inherently evil; that free blacks could never be tolerated in a slave society; that the property rights of slaveholders were inviolable before federal law; and that slaveholders should have the exclusive right to frame any and all legislation affecting slavery. In response, Northern Republicans and Federalists gave notice that they wanted federal law to reflect the values and constitutions of their own states, which were, many claimed, hostile to slavery as an institution. Some Northerners argued that ending the international slave trade would be the first step in the abolition of domestic slavery. But Southern representatives won the major legislative conflicts in 1807, imposing critical weaknesses on the American ban of the international slave trade. This proslavery victory set the tone for an uneven American record in curtailing slave trafficking for years to come.[14]

Southern political unity gave slaveholders considerable power in setting national policy toward slavery. The 1807 debates recalled previous fights where the South, by acting with greater unanimity when it came to slavery, was able to prevail against a divided North. Sectional alignment in the House also anticipated things to come: as long as a relatively solid South could carry a crucial minority of Northern votes, it could win majority-rule contests on questions relating to slavery. Later termed "doughfaces" by the raving John Randolph, those Northerners willing to back the South came predominantly from the Jeffersonian camp.[15] But exertion of Southern power was a double-edged sword, since defiance on slavery repeatedly incited Northern dissidence. The Jeffersonian alliance, like the Jacksonian alliance which succeeded it, effectively suppressed debate on slavery, so long as proslavery voices were as marginal as antislavery advocates. But when men like Randolph and Peter Early of Georgia assaulted the Congress with their defenses of mastership, Northerners found it hard to maintain their Jeffersonian idylls, and some turned to open criticism of the South.

James Sloan, member of Congress from New Jersey, was a case in point. Sloan was an almost prototypical Northern Jeffersonian: he came from a middling background (before serving in Congress, he had been, among other things, a butcher) and rose to prominence during the electoral contest of 1800. Jefferson did not win New Jersey in 1800, but his partisans did extremely well in congressional races, winning all five House seats. They likewise swept the House races in 1802, and sent James Sloan to Washington.[16] Though he was one of the more active members in Congress, Sloan has not gone down in history as a very auspicious character. Many historians know him only through Henry Adams, who described Sloan at one point as "a sort of butt in the party," and at another as simply "the butt of the house." Federalists frequently singled out Sloan as a sign of democratic degradation. He "is emphatically the small end of small things," wrote Massachusetts Federalist Samuel Taggart, indicative of the "scum" on the boiling pot of democracy. He was described as "the honourable James Sloan, member of Congress, *and butcher*"; a man who "has been so often seen with his apron, his steel, and his cleaver, in the Philadelphia shambles, grease and blood to the eyes." A butcher in the Congress—to Federalists, this was democracy run amok.[17]

Given the barrage of Federalist insults hurled in his direction, one might expect Sloan's Washington years to reinforce the central narrative of Northern Jeffersonian politics, where aristocratic Federalists suppressed the democratic aspirations of virtuous Republicans. But Sloan moved in the opposite direction. Writing retrospectively in 1812, he complained that members of the "middle and eastern states" had joined with the Southern Republicans "under the specious pretex[t] of unity to prevent the Federalists from obtaining their former power." And yet the Southerners, since at least Jefferson's embargo, had proven far more oppressive than John Adams's Federalists had ever been. This was only to be expected, Sloan claimed, because their "education and local situation hath had a tendency to bias the mind in favour of that anti-christian, tyrannical, and inhuman principle of slavery of the human species."[18]

Sloan confronted slaveholders in almost every congressional session. He supported the call to tax the international slave trade in 1804, he moved to gradually emancipate all of the slaves in Washington, D.C., in 1805, and he introduced the tax again in 1806. He played a major role in the debates over the abolition of the trade, and, in 1808, he moved that the national capital should be removed to Philadelphia, causing a bitter sectional division in the House. He joined the Republican caucus to nominate James Madison for the presidency in January of 1808, but by April he had broken with the party and declared his support for George Clinton of New York, who ran a stunted campaign to challenge Madison. Alienated from the Republican leadership, Sloan only became bolder. In a floor fight over the embargo, he assaulted the Republican heartland in Virginia, where *"three hundred forty-six thousand nine hundred and sixty eight HUMAN SOULS are kept in a state of perpetual bondage,* and used as an article of *traffic,"* and where even free whites were denied full political power. "I will never hold up as an example," said Sloan, "any government, where the choicest of all earthly blessings, '*liberty,*' is extended only to a chosen few, and withheld from the many."[19]

Sloan had clearly crossed the Potomac, but his antislavery speeches led only to relative obscurity. He never returned to Congress, having lost the support of Republicans in New Jersey and at the federal level. As a final testament to his inauspicious character, a number of newspapers reported his death in the fall of 1811, a date that continues to stand in official records. Yet Sloan does not seem to have died in 1811. A few papers ran a notice claiming that Sloan was still alive; he published a pamphlet in 1812; and he was reported as a bank director in Trenton the same year. His actual death, meanwhile, received far less official notice, and he survives more or less in minor infamy, as the butt of the House.[20]

While I may not be able to redeem him from that reputation, it is important to recognize that Sloan, like other Northern Jeffersonians in Congress, did not make his peace with slavery. The course of Jeffersonian politics catalyzed a new antislavery argument among Northerners that was quite different from the sentiments of Republicans before 1800. Men like Sloan now viewed slavery not simply as an abstract political evil, but as a powerful institution in the American political economy with equally powerful ambassadors in the federal government. Northern Federalists had made similar arguments since Jefferson's first election, but they did so while maligning impetuous Democrats like Sloan. This in turn only reinforced the North-South ideological alliance that brought Jefferson to power. But when Northern Republicans turned toward a politically driven, sectional critique of slavery, they threatened to undermine the Republican alliance altogether. This was most obvious in 1812, when DeWitt Clinton, George Clinton's nephew, renewed an internal Republican challenge to "Virginia Supremacy" by running against James Madison. In what proved to be the most competitive contest for the presidency since 1800, DeWitt Clinton came close to victory, taking every Northern state except Pennsylvania and Vermont.[21]

The Clinton campaign drew on sectional feelings that were more pro-Northern than anti-slavery in nature. Many Northern Republicans were simply tired of being ruled by Virginians, and many remained angry on account of Jefferson's embargo of foreign commerce in 1807. Such dissidents believed that they would never obtain beneficial economic policies until a Northern man occupied the presidency. Slavery was at best a marginal issue in these sectional complaints, but its absence did not render them benign. Sectionalism was dangerous in and of itself, insofar as it worked to undermine the ideological bonds that had sustained the Republican alliance since 1800. When Clintonian Republicans did attack slavery, moreover, it was far more difficult to simply malign them as jealous regional elites. Had Clinton succeeded, he would have given Northern sectionalism greater legitimacy in national politics, and he would have made Northerners far more powerful in Congress, especially once the new House, reapportioned based on the 1810 census, sat in 1813. At that date, the Northerners held a 105 to 81 majority over Southerners, one that would only rise over time.

But the Clintonian threat did not persist long after the election of 1812, in large part because of the war with Britain that began earlier that same year. Initially, the War of 1812 maintained the possibility for a sectional rift in the Republican Party, but the progress of the conflict helped reinforce a nationalist ideology that brought Republican adherents closer together and destroyed Federalist opposition at the national level. Even as Federalists in New England bitterly resisted Madisonian war aims and objectives, Republicans in that region grew more attached to the national administration. Joseph Story of Massachusetts, for example, who had shown signs of Republican dissidence over Jefferson's embargo, vilified Federalist critics of the war as traitors. The same spirit of nationalism spread throughout the North: young Pennsylvania Republicans Richard Rush and Charles J. Ingersoll viewed the war as a glorious national cause, while freshman congressman (and Clinton supporter) John W. Taylor, from upstate New York, received letter after letter demanding a more powerful federal commitment to the war. By 1815, Republican nationalism was at high tide: Andrew Jackson's victory at New Orleans became a cause for celebration throughout the country, while the Federalist representatives from the Hartford Convention, arriving in Washington with a list of regional grievances, were slandered throughout the Republican press.[22]

Northern Republicans like Story and Taylor left the war convinced that the United States was on the verge of realizing a new political destiny: Story dreamt of "great national interests which shall bind us in an indissoluble chain"; Taylor was a strong supporter of a new national bank, a high tariff, and a more powerful (and well-paid) federal legislature. Both men envisioned a national political future that would transcend partisanship and sectional feelings, but their dreams would be short-lived. During the Missouri Crisis of 1819–20, both became outspoken critics of the South. That legislative fight remains the traditional starting point for serious consideration of the sectional politics of slavery, but the sectional passions of 1819 would have been no surprise to a man like James Sloan, or to many of the Jeffersonians involved in the bitter slave trade debates of 1807.[23]

For Joseph Story, the conflict over Missouri "let out the great secrets of Virginia, and blabbed that policy by which she has hitherto bullied us, and led us, and wheedled us, and governed us." By sowing political divisions in the North, Virginia Republicans insured that they would consistently claim national power. Sloan had already learned that lesson, but after the War of 1812, his dissent was replicated on a wider scale. William Duane, for example, echoed Sloan's attacks on Virginia as early as 1816, providing Republican dissidence with a national venue in his newspaper. During the Missouri Crisis he defined a radical Northern position, and the Virginian James Garnett considered him "designedly cooperating with the Abolitionists."[24] In the House of Representatives, John W. Taylor was equally blunt, exposing the underlying structure of Southern politics. "When have we seen a Representative on this floor," he wondered, "from that section of our Union, who was not a slaveholder?" Should a "laboring man" arrive in Washington as a representative of the South, Taylor claimed, it would be "an extraordinary event."[25]

Like Sloan before them, Northern Republicans during the Missouri Crisis began to insist that slavery had no place in democratic political culture. But now their voices were both louder and more widespread. To think that "FREEDOM and SLAVERY can exist long in the same country" was certainly absurd, claimed "Hancock" in William Duane's *Aurora*. The Southern argument on Missouri, especially from Virginians in Congress, was no less defiant, and only served to spur Northerners along the path of sectional self-consciousness. Joseph Story was aghast at the antics of the crazed John Randolph: "He said, 'the land is *ours*, (meaning Virginia's,) and we will have it, and hold and use it as we (Virginians) please.' He abused all the Eastern States in the most bitter style; and intimated, in the most direct manner, that he would have nothing to do with them." But again, anyone who had seen Randolph during the debates on the international slave trade could hardly have been surprised at his support for slavery in Missouri. Back in 1807 he had promised to personally violate any law that threatened a master's property rights in slaves.[26]

The eventual Missouri Compromise only briefly stemmed the tide of sectional passion. It was arguably less a compromise than a stalemate: many Northerners saw the compromise as a victory for slavery, while a key Southern contingent, dominated by Virginia, saw the 36°30" restriction as an invasion of property rights. John W. Taylor at first greeted the compromise as the best possible outcome under the circumstances. In late 1820, he was elected Speaker of the House of Representatives, which many Northerners took as a sign that sectional disputes might be suppressed in favor of "national interests," and that Northerners, rather than Virginians, might lead a new nationalist coalition. Republicans like Taylor and Joseph Story pursued such a coalition throughout the 1820s, and the breakdown of the Democratic-Republican Party in 1824 offered a clear moment of possibility, bringing John Quincy Adams to the presidency. He was the first Northerner to hold that office since his father, back in the 1790s. After 1828, however, both Story and Taylor grew pessimistic. Andrew Jackson became president in a landslide, and the old alliance between Northern democracy and Southern slavery was revived in a new form.[27]

For Taylor and Story, the rise of Jackson was a travesty, but for Jeffersonians like Martin Van Buren and William Duane, who helped build the Jackson movement, 1828 represented the rebirth of democracy in America. For Van Buren, Jackson meant a chance for institutional power; for Duane, he meant the chance to relive the ideological passions of his youth. For both, Jackson meant the return of "nothing more nor less than OLD FASHIONED JEFFERSONIAN DEMOCRACY," as Duane put it. Back in 1819, the *Aurora* had considered the coexistence of freedom and slavery downright absurd, but that statement was more than naive, considering William Duane's previous and subsequent history. He had helped bring Northern democratic freedom and Southern slavery together in his early Jeffersonian years, and after flirting with antislavery dissidence, he became one of Jackson's strongest supporters. Late in his life, he once again demonstrated the power of Northern democracy not to oppose slavery, but to accept it—an object lesson that would be repeated throughout the Jacksonian era.[28]

So was there ever a Jeffersonian antislavery tradition? Clearly, there were many Northern Democratic-Republicans who opposed slavery. But for Duane, Bishop, Leland, and Lincoln, opposition to slavery diminished in proportion to one's commitment to the Jeffersonian cause. Sloan's story, on the other hand, suggests that persistent opposition to slavery led only to dissidence: one could not be both Jeffersonian and antislavery at the same time. By the time of the Missouri Crisis, Northern Republicans like Taylor and Story seemed prepared to break with the South altogether. They chose nationalism over sectionalism, only to learn the hard way, as Sloan had before them, how thoroughly the combined force of Northern democracy and the Southern slavery could control national politics.

Jeffersonian and Jacksonian democracy recast national politics in terms which frequently made "slavery" more relevant as an abstract metaphor for the political and economic oppression of white men (and especially Northern white men) than as an extremely powerful institution in the national political economy. Focusing Northern attention on local elites allowed Southern slaveholders to appear as democratic icons rather than anti-democratic masters; aggrandizing the oppression of whites helped to build a racist democracy on which slaves had no claim and in which free blacks had no place. Finally, Jeffersonian and Jacksonian ideology helped preserve the political ties that produced "doughface" votes during sectional crises. The democratic passions of Northern Jeffersonians became a crucial part of a political system that protected slavery for decades.

The Jeffersonian and Jacksonian coalitions also contained the seeds of their undoing: defiant slaveholders and an egalitarian faith that refused to tolerate the claims of mastership. Yet dissident Jeffersonians, trapped by their own history, struggled to find a political coalition and a political language in which to press their claims. American democracy had never inherently opposed slavery, no matter how many protestations to the contrary. The very experience of democratic freedom in the North had sanctioned slavery from the outset, and overcoming that legacy proved difficult, if not impossible. Even the most antislavery Northern Jeffersonians became subject to the growing power of racism and proved unable to maintain the radical humanism of the 1790s. The Jeffersonian and then the Jacksonian alliance became vehicles not only for the political power of slaveholders, but for a racist social and political order in the North. From the perspective of Northern African Americans, "the slavery-pole of democracy" had triumphed.[29]

The rising virulence of Northern racism provides reason enough for scholars to remain skeptical of the egalitarian promises of Jeffersonian democracy. Yet it seems important not to lose sight of the lesson that Sloan learned so well: that slavery in the United States persisted because of the anti-democratic power of slaveholders. How and why men like Sloan first sanctioned that power and then attempted, but failed, to restrain it remain fundamental problems for the early republic. They are problems not of the republican slaveholder but of the confused democrat, struggling to define who is included in an egalitarian polity, what types of power are excluded, why oppression can or cannot be tolerated. Many Northerners in the early nation took the path of least resistance and answered these questions with racism and the elevation of white men. But, at heart, these are questions not about race but about the conflict between democratic ethics and arbitrary power, between individual freedom and the distant suffering of others. They continue to be hard ones to answer.

NOTES

1. Paul Goodman, *The Democratic-Republicans of Massachusetts* (Cambridge, Mass.: Harvard University Press, 1964); Alfred Young, *The Democratic-Republicans of New York* (Chapel Hill: University of North Carolina Press, 1967); Noble E. Cunningham, *The Jeffersonian Republicans: The Formation of Party Operations* (Chapel Hill: University of North Carolina Press, 1957); idem, *The Jeffersonian Republicans in Power: Party Operations, 1801–1809* (Chapel Hill: University of North Carolina Press, 1963); Joyce Appleby, *Capitalism and a New Social Order: The Republican Vision of the 1790s* (New York: New York University Press, 1984); Gordon S. Wood, *The Radicalism of the American Revolution* (New York: Vintage, 1993); David Waldstreicher, *In the Midst of Perpetual Fetes: The Making of American Nationalism, 1776–1820* (Chapel Hill: University of North Carolina Press, 1997); Jeffrey Pasley, *"The Tyranny of Printers": Newspaper Politics in the Early American Republic* (Charlottesville: University Press of Virginia, 2001); Andrew Shankman, *The Crucible of Democracy: The Struggle to Fuse Egalitarianism and Capitalism in Jeffersonian Pennsylvania* (Lawrence: University Press of Kansas, 2004); Sean Wilentz, *The Rise of American Democracy: Jefferson to Lincoln* (New York: Norton, 2005); Gordon S. Wood, *Empire of Liberty: A History of the Early Republic, 1789–1815* (New York: Oxford University Press, 2009).

2. Leonard Richards, *The Slave Power: The Free North and Southern Domination, 1780–1860* (Baton Rouge: Louisiana State University Press, 2000); Peter Onuf and Leonard Sadosky, *Jeffersonian America* (Malden, Mass.: Blackwell, 2002); William Cooper, *Liberty and Slavery: Southern Politics to 1860* (New York: Knopf, 1983); Robin L. Einhorn, "Institutional Reality in the Age of Slavery: Taxation and Democracy in the States," *Journal of Policy History* 18, no. 1 (2006): 21–43; Einhorn, *American Taxation, American Slavery* (Chicago: University of Chicago Press, 2006).

3. For Northern racism in the Jeffersonian era, see Leon Litwack, *North of Slavery: The Negro in the Free States, 1790–1860* (Chicago: University of Chicago Press, 1961); Gary Nash, *Forging Freedom: The Formation of Philadelphia's Black Community, 1720–1840* (Cambridge, Mass.: Harvard University Press, 1988); *Race and Revolution* (Madison, Wis.: Madison House, 1990); idem, *The Forgotten Fifth: African-Americans in the Age of Revolution* (Cambridge, Mass.: Harvard University Press, 2006); Joanne Pope Melish, *Disowning Slavery: Gradual Emancipation and "Race" in New England, 1780–1860* (Ithaca, N.Y.: Cornell University Press, 1998); Paul Finkelman, "The Problem of Slavery in the Age of Federalism," *Federalists Reconsidered,* ed. Doron Ben-Atar and Barbara Oberg (Charlottesville: University Press of Virginia, 1998); and Rogers Smith, *Civic Ideals: Conflicting Visions of Citizenship in U.S. History* (New Haven, Conn.: Yale University Press, 1997).

4. See Appleby, *Capitalism and a New Social Order,* 102. This view is an implicit, if never fully acknowledged, assumption of much of the work in the democratization tradition, especially that of Wood.

5. For the strong version of this argument, see Sean Wilentz, "Jeffersonian Democracy and the Origins of Political Antislavery in the United States: The Missouri Crisis Revisited," *Journal of the Historical Society* 4 (September 2004): 375–401; and idem, *The Rise of American Democracy.* For more balanced accounts, see Matthew Mason, *Slavery and Politics in the Early American Republic* (Chapel Hill: University of North Carolina Press, 2006); and John Craig Hammond, *Slavery, Freedom, and Expansion in the Early American West* (Charlottesville: University of Virginia Press, 2007). For the extension of this argument to the Jacksonian period, see Wilentz, "Slavery, Antislavery, and Jacksonian Democracy," in *The Market Revolution in America: Social, Political, and Religious Expressions, 1800–1880,* ed. Melvyn Stokes and Stephen Conway (Charlottesville: University Press of Virginia, 1996), 202–23; and especially Jonathan Earle, *Jacksonian Antislavery and the Politics of Free Soil* (Chapel Hill: University of North Carolina Press, 2004).

6. In emphasizing political rather than racial ties to slavery, I follow François Furstenberg's suggestive analysis of how early national concepts of political freedom helped justify slavery. In contrast to his emphasis on "autonomy," however, my analysis here focuses on the idea and practice of democracy (see Furstenberg, "Beyond Freedom and Slavery: Autonomy, Virtue, and Resistance in Early American Political Discourse," *Journal of American History* 89 [March 2003]: 1295–1330; and idem, *In the Name of the Father: Washington's Legacy, Slavery, and the Making of a Nation* [New York: Penguin, 2007]).

7. Jasper Dwight [William Duane], "A Letter to George Washington, President of the United States . . ." (Philadelphia, 1796), 46–48; Tim Matthewson, "Abraham Bishop, 'The Rights of Black Men,' and the American Reaction to the Haitian Revolution," *Journal of Negro History* 67 (Summer 1982): 148–54; "Brief of Levi Lincoln in the Slave Case Tried 1781," *Massachusetts Historical Society Collections,* 5th ser., vol. 3 (1877), 438–42; John Leland, "The Virginia Chron-

icle," in *The Writings of John Leland,* ed. L. F. Greene (1845; repr., New York: Arno Press, 1969), 96–97, 105–7; *Annals of Congress,* 5th Cong., 2nd sess., 656–70.

8. The electoral vote in 1800 was not an exact index of the popular vote, since many states chose electors in the state legislature. Congressional numbers in this essay are based on Kenneth C. Martis, *The Historical Atlas of Political Parties in the United States Congress, 1789– 1989* (New York: Macmillan, 1989).

9. *Aurora General Advertiser* (Philadelphia), 24 September 1800, 18 February 1803.

10. William Duane to Joel Barlow and Fulwar Skipwith, 2 January 1801, William Duane Correspondence, Library of Congress; *Aurora General Advertiser* (Philadelphia), 23 January 1806; Duane to Jefferson, 11 August 1814, "Letters of William Duane," ed. Worthington C. Ford, in *Proceedings of the Massachusetts Historical Society,* vol. 20, *May 1906,* 373–75. For comment on Branagan, see Nash, *Forging Freedom;* and idem, *The Forgotten Fifth.* On the American reaction to the rebellion in Saint-Domingue, see, among many accounts, Robin Blackburn, "Haiti, Slavery, and the Age of Democratic Revolution," *William and Mary Quarterly,* 3rd ser., 63 (October 2006): 643–74; and Michael Zuckerman, "The Power of Blackness: Thomas Jefferson and the Revolution in St. Domingue," in *Almost Chosen People: Oblique Biographies in the American Grain* (Berkeley: University of California Press, 1993).

11. Abraham Bishop, *Oration Delivered in Wallingford, on the 11th of March 1801, . . .* (New Haven, 1801), iii–iv; John Leland, "An Oration Delivered at Cheshire . . . ," in *The Writings of John Leland,* 268–69; Aleine Austin, *Matthew Lyon, "New Man" of the Democratic Revolution* (University Park: Penn State University Press, 1981), 131–33; *Annals of Congress,* 8th Cong., 1st sess., 543–44.

12. Pasley, *"The Tyranny of Printers,"* 203–19. See also the Lincoln-Jefferson correspondence in the Jefferson Papers, Library of Congress. On Duane, see Pasley, *"The Tyranny of Printers";* and especially Kim Phillips, *William Duane: Radical Journalist in the Age of Jefferson* (New York: Garland, 1989). For Bishop, David Waldstreicher and Stephen R. Grossbart, "Abraham Bishop's Vocation; or, The Mediation of Jeffersonian Politics," *Journal of the Early Republic* 18 (Winter 1998): 617–57.

13. Jeffrey Pasley, "The Cheese and the Words: Popular Political Culture and Participatory Democracy in the Early American Republic," in *Beyond the Founders: New Approaches to the Political History of the Early American Republic,* ed. Jeffrey L. Pasley, Andrew Robertson, and David Waldstreicher (Chapel Hill: University of North Carolina Press, 2004); Lyman Butterfield, "Elder John Leland, Jeffersonian Itinerant," in *Proceedings of the American Antiquarian Society,* vol. 62, pt. 2, *1952,* 155–242 (Leland's address to Jefferson is reprinted at p. 224).

14. *Annals of Congress,* 9th Cong., 2nd sess., 167–90, 200–204, 220–44, 264–74, 373–74, 477–87, 527–28, 626–27, 636–38; Matthew Mason, "Slavery Overshadowed: Congress Debates Prohibiting the Atlantic Slavetrade to the United States, 1806–1807," *Journal of the Early Republic* 20 (Spring 2000): 59–81; Robin Einhorn, "The Early Impact of Slavery," in *The American Congress: The Building of Democracy,* ed. Julian E. Zelizer (New York: Houghton Mifflin, 2004), 77–92; Adam Rothman, *Slave Country: American Expansion and the Origins of the Deep South* (Cambridge, Mass.: Harvard University Press, 2005); W. E. B. Du Bois, *Suppression of the African Slave Trade to the United States of America* (New York: Longmans, Green, 1896); Fehrenbacher, *The Slaveholding Republic,* 149–204; Walter Johnson, "White Lies: Human Property and Domestic Slavery Aboard the Slave Ship *Creole,*" *Atlantic Studies* 5 (August 2008): 237–63.

15. See Richardo, *The Slave Power*.

16. James Sloan, *An Address, Delivered at a Meeting of the Democratic Association* (Trenton: Mann and Wilson, 1801); *An Oration, Delivered at a Meeting of the Democratic Association . . .* (Trenton: Wilson and Blackwell, 1802); Carl Prince, *New Jersey's Jeffersonian Republicans: The Genesis of an Early Party Machine, 1789–1817* (Chapel Hill: University of North Carolina Press, 1967).

17. Henry Adams, *History of the United States during the Administration of Thomas Jefferson,* 723, 855; Samuel Taggart to John Taylor, 17 November 1804, in "Letters of Samuel Taggart . . . Part One," in *Proceedings of the American Antiquarian Society* 33, pt. 1, *April 1923,* 133; *Newburyport (Mass.) Herald,* 18 April 1806.

18. James Sloan, *An Address to the Citizens of the United States, but More Particularly to Those of the Middle and Eastern States* (Philadelphia: James Maxwell, 1812), 12–14.

19. James Sloan, *Politics for Farmers* (Salem, N.J.: Cushing and Appleton, 1809), 13; *Annals of Congress,* 10th Cong., 2nd sess., 915–30.

20. For reports of Sloan's death, see, among other papers, the *Trenton Federalist,* 11 November 1811; the *New York Evening Post,* 12 November 1811; and the *National Aegis* (Worcestor, Mass.), 20 November 1811. For counterreports that he still lived, see the *New York Evening Post,* 15 November 1811; and the *New-York Spectator,* 20 November 1811. Sloan was noted as a bank director in the *New England Palladium,* 17 November 1812, and in the *Tickler* (Philadelphia), 8 December 1812, and a pamphlet under his name was published in that year as well. A recent study of Sloan establishes a birth date of 10 October 1748 and a death date of 7 September 1831. See Bruce Bendler, "James Sloan: Renegade or True Republican?" *New Jersey History* 125, no. 1 (2010): 1–19. For 1831 obituaries, see the *Daily National Intelligencer,* 19 September 1831, and the *Philadelphia Inquirer,* 19 September 1831.

21. For an overview, see Steven E. Siry, "The Sectional Politics of 'Practical Republicanism': De Witt Clinton's Presidential Bid, 1810–1812," *Journal of the Early Republic* 5 (Winter 1985): 441–62; and Steven E. Siry, *De Witt Clinton and the American Political Economy: Sectionalism, Politics, and Republican Ideology, 1787–1828* (New York: P. Lang, 1989).

22. Joseph Story to Nathaniel Williams, 24 August 1812, in *The Life and Letters of Joseph Story,* ed. William Wetmore Story (Boston: Little and Brown, 1851), 1:228–29. In the John Taylor Papers at the New-York Historical Society, see: Barry Fenton to John Taylor, 13 January 1814 and 15 January 1815; Isaac Pierson to John Taylor, 15 January 1814; George and Thomas Palmer to John Taylor, multiple letters; and John Taylor to James Hawkins et al., 7 February 1814. See also Richard Rush to Charles J. Ingersoll, multiple letters, in the Charles J. Ingersoll Papers, Historical Society of Pennsylvania, Philadelphia.

23. Joseph Story to Nathaniel Williams, 22 February 1815, in *The Life and Letters of Joseph Story,* 1:254; John Taylor to Jane P. Taylor, 26 March 1816, John Taylor Papers, New-York Historical Society; Edward K. Spann, "John W. Taylor, The Reluctant Partisan, 1784–1854," Ph.D. diss., New York University, 1957.

24. For Duane's later hostility, see Matthew Mason, *Slavery and Politics in the Early American Republic,* 78–80, 101, 136, 144, 189–90, 194; Phillips, *William Duane,* 537–38; and Garnett to John Randolph, 22 February 1820, Randolph-Garnett Letterbook, Library of Congress.

25. Joseph Story to Stephen White, 27 February 1820, in *The Life and Letters of Joseph Story,* 1:362–63; *Annals of Congress,* 15th Cong., 2nd sess., 1170–79.

26. Phillips, *William Duane,* 537; Randolph in *Annals of Congress,* 9th Cong. 2nd sess., 528.

27. Robert Forbes, *The Missouri Compromise and Its Aftermath: Slavery and the Meaning of America* (Chapel Hill: University of North Carolina Press, 2007); Glover Moore, *The Missouri Controversy, 1819–1821* (Lexington: University of Kentucky Press, 1953); John Taylor to Jane Taylor, 1 March 1820, Taylor Papers, New-York Historical Society; Harlow Sheidley, *Sectional Nationalism: Massachusetts Conservative Leaders and the Transformation of America, 1815–1836* (Boston: Northeastern University Press, 1998); Richards, *The Slave Power*; Daniel Walker Howe, *What God Hath Wrought: The Transformation of America, 1815–1848* (New York: Oxford, 2007); Richard Brown "The Missouri Crisis, Slavery, and the Politics of Jacksonianism," *South Atlantic Quarterly* 61 (Winter 1966): 55–72.

28. For Duane and Jackson, see Phillips, *William Duane*, 638

29. To borrow a phrase from Joseph Sidney (see "An Oration Commemorative of the Abolition of the Slave Trade in the United States . . . " [New York, 1809]), in which he argues that free blacks should back the Federalist Party. See also David Gellman, *Emancipating New York: The Politics of Slavery and Freedom, 1777–1827* (Baton Rouge: Louisiana State University Press, 2006); David Gellman and David Quigley, *Jim Crow New York: A Documentary History of Race and Citizenship* (New York: New York University Press, 2004); and Dixon Ryan Fox, "The Negro Vote in Old New York," *Political Science Quarterly* 32 (June 1917): 252–75.

Neither Infinite Wretchedness nor Positive Good

Mathew Carey and Henry Clay on Political Economy and Slavery during the Long 1820s

Andrew Shankman

Most Jeffersonians came to power in 1801 in broad agreement about the conditions necessary to produce their empire of liberty, an egalitarian society of independent households. First, the nation's political economy should remain fundamentally agrarian and geared toward the export of agricultural surpluses. Second, the nation-state should remain small and aloof from domestic life. For the sake of republican liberty, the states were the critical locus of governance. Third, slavery was harmful to whites (much less importantly, also to blacks) and inconsistent with the "genius" of republican citizenship. Slavery, the result of a "culture of infinite wretchedness," warped republican citizens and undermined their institutions. Fortunately, many Jeffersonians insisted, slavery was unprofitable, Revolutionary ideology rejected it, and it would naturally in future play an insignificant role in American life.[1]

During their years in power, many Jeffersonians rejected all three assumptions.[2] Examining two central figures among the rethinkers—the American System's foremost publicist and popularizer, Mathew Carey, and its leading political advocate, Henry Clay—reveals how they justified a new political economy, which made full use of a burgeoning American slavery, as the way to establish the empire of liberty. During the long 1820s—beginning with the Missouri Crisis and the Panic of 1819 and ending with the Nullification Crisis of 1832–33—Carey and Clay argued that Jeffersonian ideals required an active nation-state and a domestic economy of agriculture, commerce, and manufacturing. As a result, they relied on slavery's growing significance and planned for it to play a vital role in their new political economy. Seeking the empire of liberty required reimagining slavery as something other than infinitely wretched.

Placing slavery at the center of American politics and political economy seems to work better after the mid-1830s, the decades of the gag rule, the "positive good" thesis, immediate abolitionism, and free-soil politics. Discussions of Jeffersonian political economy and the American System, on the other hand, focus on the years between the War of 1812 and the presidency of John Quincy Adams, and primarily treat conflicts between the nascent middle and working classes, capitalist and producer mentalities, and the connections between the rise of democracy and conflicts about capitalism. Slavery intrudes during the Missouri Crisis as an important but anomalous portent.[3] These literatures are valuable, but distributing the issues as they do obscures a crucial point: throughout the long 1820s those conceiving the American System were thoroughly preoccupied with slavery.

The American System assumed slavery's growing significance for the domestic economy. Carey and Clay accepted expansive slavery precisely because they sought a diverse economy of agriculture, commerce, and manufactures. This new political economy, they believed, would preserve a society of independent republican households. Like all Jeffersonians, their vision stemmed from the eighteenth-century Age of Revolution that had rendered slavery an intellectual and ideological problem as never before; yet during the long 1820s, Carey and Clay could no longer treat slavery as poison in the republican atmosphere. Slavery was not a positive good, but neither could it remain infinitely wretched. The new political economy required that Carey and Clay remove slavery as a source of doubt about republican institutions. During the long 1820s both explained how to view slavery as approaching something that was, under the right circumstances, distinctly "positively goodish."

After the War of 1812, Mathew Carey and Henry Clay argued that altered world circumstances demanded a new political economy for a new age. Clay explained, "We have shaped our industry, our navigation, and our commerce, in reference to an extraordinary war in Europe and to foreign markets, which no longer exist." Now "a new epoch has arisen," and we must "proclaim . . . the incontestable truth [and admit] the altered state of the world." Carey agreed, adding that the "nations of Europe could not be expected to allow us to continue the commerce that naturally belonged to them." The nation's citizen-farmers now confronted "the reduction of the price of our wheat [with] the return of so many of the soldiery to the labors of the field."[4] Carey and Clay invoked the new epoch to explain all of the nation's ills. Only the transformation of American political economy could establish the republic of independent households.

Carey and Clay insisted that the Panic of 1819 had proved them right. The republic needed a domestic market that absorbed a meaningful portion of farmers' surplus, which came with the development of manufacturing. Manufacturers purchasing agricultural surpluses reduced dependence on foreign wares and lessened the nation's specie drain. More specie allowed a rising supply of dependable paper currency. Carey and Clay argued that in the new epoch farmers would be destroyed by revenue tariffs below protective levels. Those who cared for yeomen had to promote manufacturing, banks, internal improvements, an expanding paper currency, and an ever-growing domestic market.[5]

Support for manufacturing and a domestic market did not mean turning away from Jeffersonian ideals, for in the new epoch agrarian political economy produced the very conditions it was meant to prevent. Superfluous farmers produced unmarketable surpluses, prices fell, debts rose, taxes went unpaid, and farms were foreclosed on. Under these conditions, lamented Carey, "citizens possessed of great wealth . . . increase[d] it immoderately by purchasing the property of the distressed . . . thus destroying the equality of our citizens, and aggrandizing the rich at the expense of the middle class of society." In the new epoch, overreliance on agriculture produced superfluous population, and with altered worldwide conditions, unprecedented land availability only worsened the problem. Carey and Clay realized that many Jeffersonians believed manufacturing had "debasing and demoralizing effects," but they insisted that the new political economy actually prevented a European social order.[6]

Carey and Clay argued that European economic and social conditions had nothing to do with republican America. The United States was a "wide" country, said Carey. Clay agreed that "the extent and the fertility of our lands constitute an adequate security against an excess in manufactures, and also against oppression, on the part of capitalists, towards the laboring portion of the community." In addition, explained Carey, republican banks would not "pursue [profits] to the disregard of public accommodation." Instead, they would "extend trade and commerce—and enable men of moderate fortune and good credit to compete with wealthy capitalists." Banks run by and for equal citizens would lend to smaller property holders, and would understand that "policy, as well as humanity, dictates an extension of accommodation, and . . . forbids banks to press upon their debtors." This combination of republican institutions, political freedom, freedom of movement, and millions of acres of "unsettled lands," allowed for a republican version of economic development that strengthened the nation; preserved independence, autonomy, and liberty for its citizens; and prevented "the lamentable and pernicious consequence of making the rich richer and the poor poorer."[7]

In Carey's and Clay's solution to the dangers of the new epoch, protective tariffs would stimulate manufacturing, a rising population of non-agricultural producers, and a home market. The republic would become much more a world within itself, where a robust slave economy both sustained and was sustained by the burgeoning capacity to manufacture. Planters and republican smallholders would flourish because of extensive domestic manufacturing; and manufacturers would thrive because of planters and smallholders. Sectional needs would be harmonized with "the transportation of raw materials from the southern to the middle and eastern states, and of manufactured articles from the latter to the former."[8] Land could again become a vital source of republican liberty once manufactures created demand for agricultural commodities. The new political economy would sustain an empire of liberty and a nation of farmers precisely because it would also nurture merchants, bankers, manufacturers, craftsmen, mechanics, and the growth of slave country. Once the republic pursued the new political economy, exulted Carey, it would be writ large a "little commonwealth," on the grandest scale on earth, Harmony, Indiana.[9]

More boldly, Clay imagined the United States shaping the Americas as a zone of liberty and freedom. The new political economy would make the nation "the great steward of the human family" and the source of "the hopes of the friends of free and liberal institutions, from all quarters of the Universe." Clay celebrated republican revolution throughout the Americas, and "the glorious spectacle of eighteen millions of people struggling to burst their chains and to be free." It was simple, said Clay. "An oppressed people were authorized, whenever they could, to rise and break their fetters." Clay's republic depended on Mexican and South American revolutions. He imagined a "counterpoise to the Holy Alliance . . . in the two Americas in favor of national independence and liberty, to operate by the force of example and moral influence; that here a rallying point and an asylum should exist for freemen and for freedom." Clay's earliest uses of the term "American System" referred to a North and South American zone of allied republics. This system could largely replace markets controlled by monarchies. Indeed, if European monarchies stifled pan-American republicanism, it would threaten "the interest, the safety, and even the independence of this country."[10]

Carey's and Clay's republican ideals exposed profound contradictions within this American System. They imagined republican liberty on a grander scale than ever before as they embedded slavery in their new political economy. Reducing reliance on European textiles and West Indian markets controlled by monarchies required slaves to grow cotton, and to be fed and clothed by the nation's citizens. Spanish-speaking republics could best fulfill the needs of the United States by retaining robust slave economies that supplied raw materials and consumed whatever the nation's domestic market did not absorb. When delineating Spanish crimes against the fledgling republics, Clay drew no distinction between slaughtering prisoners, refusing surrenders, violating flags, butchering in cold blood, and encouraging "slaves to rise against their owners."[11]

Carey's and Clay's methods for dramatically expanding human freedom required viewing slavery as other than infinitely wretched. Over the course of the long 1820s, they tried to conceive of how slavery could be removed from the criteria used when evaluating whether the United States measured up to its claim of being the leading nation in the defense of liberty. Harmonizing his political economy with slavery was both a personal and public goal for Clay. At times Clay conjured a future where all slaves simply disappeared. His fantasizing was genuine, but it should not overshadow the concrete world of the long 1820s and Henry Clay, slave owner. Clay bought, sold, and exploited men and women. The nation expanding as a slaveholding republic was organic to his reconception of political economy. Clay commiserated when correspondents missed opportunities to purchase slaves. He reflexively counseled a friend that his son should seek Alabama, of all the newer territories, to carve a law career, because "without wealth there can be no litigation."[12] Responsible men could only proceed as if slavery was the foundation of fortune. When it came to the practical matter of living life as well as possible, it never entered Clay's mind to imagine the republic without slavery.

Secretary of State Clay prided himself on being free of debt, beholden to no particular course of policy, and trustworthy to oversee the new political economy. In Washington, he exulted that he "resid[ed] in the best house . . . with the most spacious apartments and extensive grounds." Yet this prominence depended on his talents as a slaveholder. Ashland "operate[d] as a sinking fund of my remaining debt," since his salary was ample for his needs. Owning slaves meant "be[ing] entirely out of debt." Clay's slaves' hemp production, and the cotton bagging manufacture it sustained, depended on the growth of slave country in Alabama and elsewhere just as much as did his friend's son's career. Clay lamented the evil of slavery in an 1818 speech calling for a stronger fugitive-slave law, due to the "peculiar interest which the state of which he [wa]s a representative ha[d] in the passage of [a] bill," making it easier for masters to recapture slaves escaping so close to the borders of freedom. Clay behaved like any other master when pursuing escaped slaves, as in the case of seventeen-year-old Isaac, "a bright mulatto boy . . . [who] when spoken to has a downcast look."[13]

Acceptance of slavery's growth was the context for Clay's commitment to the American Colonization Society. If the Society focused primarily on removing free blacks, who were, according to Clay, "aliens—political—moral—social aliens, strangers though natives," then colonization could actually strengthen slavery, by reinforcing the connection between color and condition. Clay explained that, like most Southerners and Westerners, he believed colonization was for free blacks only and that the Society would not "touch or agitate, in the slightest degree, a delicate question connected with another portion of the colored population of our country,"[14]

Clay regularly disassociated the American Colonization Society from schemes to reduce significantly the number of slaves. Instead, the Society would rid the nation of its true evil. For, "of all the classes of our population," Clay explained, "the most vicious is that of the free colored. It is the inevitable result of their moral, political, and civil degradation. Contaminated themselves, they extend their vices all around them, to the slaves and to the whites." The horror was pervasive, for "the existence of free people of color is not limited to the states only which tolerate slavery. The evil extends itself to all the states.... [The free states'] cities . . . experience the evil in an extent even greater than it exists in the slave states."[15] The Society would help to make a republic of only slaves and whites. With the evil removed, there would be no reminder that blacks could be other than slaves.

At the beginning of the long 1820s Carey also understood that the nation's needs in the new epoch made slavery desirable. Carey was also a committed colonizer, though more often than Clay he considered the possibility of reducing the number of slaves as well as removing all free blacks. Like Clay, Carey insisted that slavery was a lamentable evil, while simultaneously considering the tremendous utility of slavery to the new political economy.[16] Carey did not have Clay's personal stake in slavery, but he believed slavery was essential for the full realization of his new political economy. Without the new political economy there could be no empire of liberty. Carey's interest in slavery, then, was no less real than Clay's. His life's work was to eradicate the exploitation and degradation that he believed threatened "men of moderate fortune." Placing the inspiring ideals of equality, dignity, freedom, and liberty at the center of his vision for the nation demanded that Carey, like Clay, explain why slavery and racial inequality in no way undermined or sullied his dreams for the republic in the new epoch. Both got their chance to do so with Missouri.

Carey and Clay both opposed restriction during the Missouri Crisis. As they did, they began subtly to treat slavery as something other than infinitely wretched. Clay's role in spreading slavery in the West is well known. Certainly Clay worried about disunion and was not solely seeking to further the interests of slaveholders by achieving compromise. Yet his speeches opposing exclusion began to challenge the traditional notion that slavery was toxic for republican institutions and citizens. Clay argued that denying a state's right to define its local institutions—the source of its republican capacities—was inseparable from preventing Missouri's entrance as a slave state.[17]

In this equation, a greater injustice than slavery was preventing its expansion west. In Missouri, republican institutions would be weaker without slavery than with it, since the absence of slavery meant that an overweening national government had violated states' rights. Enslaving people was not as much a threat to republican institutions as was the misuse of power that, among other things, made it more difficult to enslave people. Indeed, it followed that slavery demonstrated the soundness of republican institutions if its presence meant the arrest of this concentration and abuse of power. Clay never stopped saying that slavery was evil, though in the midst of debate on Missouri he suggested that it was so only for the slave, not the master.[18] Clay never thought that slavery was a positive good. But we must balance his traditional, Jeffersonian anxiety about slavery with the fact that his private life and public policy only made sense if the United States continued to grow as a slaveholding republic.

Carey did even more to divorce slavery from an assessment of the health and respectability of republican institutions. As with Clay, Carey's republican tender conscience demanded that he be enlightened about the "pernicious evil" that was slavery. But that fate of Missouri involved the fate of a nation that needed union and the new political economy in order to establish the empire of liberty. Since the Missouri Crisis threatened disunion, citizens had to decide "whether this great and admirable republic is to remain united and prosperous, a monument of the beauty and efficacy of free institutions, or to be violently resolved into its original elements, and to become the theatre and prey of a fierce intestine conflict."[19]

Carey acknowledged that "the freedom and comfort of the African race are... objects worth a strenuous effort to obtain; but if they are to be bought at the expense of the peace and happiness of the country, the price is too great." Dividing over Missouri would destroy union and the new political economy, and so provide "the possible destruction of our happy republic, the source of prosperity and comfort to millions of a better race."[20] Here Carey provided new thinking for a new epoch. Whether slavery eventually disappeared or not, the nation would remain a monument to free institutions, as long as it created a strong nation-state that pursued a proper political economy. If it did so, it would ensure the happiness of the "better race," and that was the only measurement for judging free institutions worthy of serious consideration.

Furthermore, those free institutions were meant exclusively for the "better race." Since free blacks were "depraved in their morals, debased in intellect, and unqualified to perform the duties of citizens," free republican institutions deserved no bad marks for excluding them. The condition of free blacks suggested that blacks were fit only for slavery. Missouri had every right to ban free blacks, because "the only object contemplated by the Constitution, was the placing of white citizens of each state on the same footing." Since the Constitution applied to whites only, there were no rights any blacks had that citizens were obliged to respect. Blacks as slaves were useful to the republic; free blacks had no place in it.

Spreading slavery west, argued Carey, did not weaken or render illegitimate republican institutions. Instead, Americans should judge the effectiveness of those institutions by measuring the extent to which "the better race" enjoyed the freedom that was available only in a society of independent households. That society would be preserved by building the new political economy in the new epoch. If the nation did so, citizens would enjoy their republican birthright. The enslavement of millions, lamentable though it might be, assisted citizens in living as they deserved. With Missouri, citizens had to acknowledge "that the peace and prosperity of eight millions of freemen and Christians, may [not] rightfully be sacrificed to promote the welfare of a million and a half slaves."[21] Seeking republican liberty and prosperity for the "better race" justified using slave labor to meet the needs of citizens. Slavery might be a "pernicious evil," but in 1820 Carey decided that denying new slave territory for his new political economy was more pernicious and more evil.

Carey's and Clay's vision for a new political economy, then, encouraged them to view slavery as other than infinitely wretched and automatically harmful to republican society. But the actions of many slaveholders during the long 1820s also prompted Carey and Clay to explain how republican society was compatible with, even strengthened by, slavery. For, from the onset of the long 1820s, it was clear how much their vision worried slave owners.[22]

The new political economy required a more centralized and vigorous nation-state than Jeffersonians had previously sought, and it was most obviously constitutional if the Constitution's powers were broad, expansive, and, at times, implied. Yet a proper nation-state required an elusive precision: to balance power and the constraint of power in much the same way that broad-based and democratized economic development would perpetually prevent the inequality and dependence associated with rapid and diverse economic growth. Clay understood the fear concerning implied powers: "that the chain of cause and effect is without end, that if we argue from a power expressly granted to all others, which might be convenient or necessary to its execution, there are no bounds to the power of this government." But Clay insisted that statesmen could precisely determine which powers belonged to the nation-state and which to the states.[23]

It was not a simple calculus. Clay dismissed the idea that the division was merely geographical, that internal matters belonged to the states and external ones to the nation. "The great mass" of what Clay termed municipal powers belonged to the states. But the nation retained modest (in Clay's mind) yet crucial municipal powers, to tax, regulate interstate commerce, and build post roads. Just as there was a moderate position on the municipal powers of the nation-state, so there was a moderate position on the implied powers that came with the enumerated ones. It was clear (to Clay at least) that regulating commerce and building post roads implied the power to pursue internal improvement in certain cases. The nation could not promote internal improvements "of a limited and local character," for to do so would violate the sovereignty of localities. But when internal improvements were "emphatically national," they could "be effected by the application of the resources of the nation." Once reasonable statesmen concluded that projects "promote[d] the good of the whole, the power and the treasure of the whole must be applied to their execution."[24]

Nevertheless, what was clear to Clay was unlikely to convince the more-extreme advocates of states' rights, particularly Southerners who viewed states' rights as essential to protect slavery.[25] Who were the reasonable statesmen doing the calculating? What constituted "emphatically national"? What precisely was the public good, and how was it measured and judged? During the 1820s, many slave owners' fears about national power and their commitment to states' rights intensified.[26] By 1824, Carey and Clay had identified Southern congressmen and the wealthiest slaveholders as the principal opponents of their new political economy. Those most concerned about their slave property appeared convinced that creative readings of the Constitution would allow national intervention within a state's borders and even interference with state laws essential for the protection of slavery. In addition, as Carey and Clay observed regular denunciations of their cherished political economy by Southern legislators, they concluded that too many slaveholders associated slavery's needs with worldwide free trade, and tariffs for revenue only.

During his 1824 presidential bid, Clay heard that Louisiana, South Carolina, and Virginia feared his new political economy and associated Andrew Jackson with an anti-tariff position. After John Quincy Adams's election, Clay received letters from Southern allies stating that their states equated support for the president with the endorsement of emancipation. Adams's free-state origins discredited him even in parts of Clay's Kentucky. By 1826, Clay worried that "a majority of [Virginia's] General Assembly [was] . . . a permanent opposition to the

General Administration." From the Southern Atlantic states to the Kentucky interior, Clay heard protective tariffs denounced and associated with hostility to states' rights. Hovering over these accusations was the omnipresent warning: soft on states' rights, weak on slavery.[27]

By the mid-1820s, Clay believed the divisions were primarily sectional, and that at stake was what he termed "D.M.I.I." [domestic manufactures and internal improvements]. To support D.M.I.I., Clay proposed the series of conventions planned by Carey's Society for the Promotion of Manufactures and the Mechanical Arts, which culminated with the Harrisburg, Pennsylvania, convention of 1827. Clay pleaded with the antislavery Ohioan Charles Hammond that "there should be mutual forbearance, and perhaps more on the side of the non-slavery holding states, as they are the stronger, safer, and happier party." Nevertheless, over the course of the long 1820s Clay concluded that many slave owners viewed advocacy of D.M.I.I. as an assault.[28]

As many slaveholders' hostility to the new political economy grew, Carey struggled to convince them that it best served their interests. Glutted foreign markets drove down prices for Southern staples, and cotton was "a mere drug everywhere, and the most vital injury [has] been inflicted on a section of the union . . . which nothing but a destructive policy could prevent from the enjoyment of the highest prosperity." But the new political economy provided slave owners "a grand domestic market, independent of the caprice of foreign nations." Without this market, competition from "Hindostan," and possibly Brazil, would cause prices to plummet. Carey's claim that a new epoch, produced by the disappearance of European markets and exemplified by the Panic of 1819, would cripple the Southern cotton market, seemed plausible after cotton prices declined by two-thirds between 1817 and 1825. Slaveholders, fearful of the new political economy, concluded Carey, needed to enter "the age of sober reflection," and consider "their own interests [as well as] the welfare of the nation." Planters, Carey explained, enjoyed that happy situation where personal and national interest coincided.[29]

Carey and Clay insisted that the new political economy nurtured the entire nation. By the middle of the long 1820s, they increasingly addressed to hostile Southerners what they believed were anodyne defenses of tariffs and implied powers. Nevertheless, the nation needed the new political economy, and the nation-state did have to "execute the great purposes of its institution." If Southerners refused to accept reason, said Clay regretfully, the nation-state would have to do so "without the co-operation, and, if indispensably necessary, even against the will of any particular state." Preventing the new political economy because of the national governing powers that promoted it and because those powers were imagined a threat to slavery meant that "the interests of the greater part should be made to bend to the condition of the servile part of the population. That, in effect, would be to make us the slaves of slaves."[30]

Planter hostility frustrated Carey and Clay. During the long 1820s, it seemed impossible to convince anxious slaveholders that the new political economy was compatible with a slaveholding republic.[31] Instead, slaveholders demanded free trade as they spread the Cotton South from the Atlantic Coast to East Texas. Slaveholders paid no attention to Carey's warnings. During the 1820s, the fall in cotton prices did not stop the new cotton regions from acquiring about 75,000 slaves from east of the Appalachians (in addition to the 225,000 sent west between 1790 and 1820). As Carey warned about glutted markets, cotton production increased from about 1.4 million (500-pound) bales per year, to 2 million bales (and the production capacity of U.S. textile mills rose sixfold).[32]

During the long 1820s, Carey and Clay began to worry that many slaveholders were so fearful about slavery's future, and so zealous to protect their slave property, that they would spread slavery as widely as the could. Owning slaves appeared to blind them to their and the nation's interests. Carey's and Clay's frustration caused them to think further about how best to use slavery in the republic of the new epoch. Soothing slaveholders required removing sources of concern while also fitting the economy of slave country more seamlessly into the new political economy. Carey's and Clay's efforts revealed how difficult it was in the long 1820s to consider the nation's needs without seeking to accommodate and placate those most devoted to owning slaves.

Seeking to reassure slaveholders forced Secretary of State Clay to confront the incompatibility of slaveholding and his republican internationalism. When celebrating the Latin American revolutions, Clay could not help but use language that terrified slave owners. During the long 1820s, as dissolution of the Spanish empire led to abolition in the new South American republics, anxious U.S. slaveholders began to mistrust Clay even more. In part to reassure U.S. slaveholders and safeguard slave property, Clay became determined to at least stop abolition and even republican institutions from spreading to Cuba, the closest prospective abolitionist republic to the United States.

By 1826, as Spanish-speaking republics appeared ready to liberate Cuba, slaveholders began to dread a second Haiti 90 miles from slave country. Clay feared that if Mexico and Colombia attacked Cuba, free blacks, or even slaves, might acquire arms. The prospect of armed slaves and the upheaval that might wreak on the United States meant that Cuba had to remain a monarch's colony. To preserve slavery in Cuba and safeguard it in the United States, Clay favored war with the other American republics. If, by seeking to liberate Cuba, they "put arms in the hands of one race of the inhabitants, to destroy the lives of another; if, in short, they should countenance and encourage excesses and examples, the contagion of which, from our neighborhood, would be dangerous to our quiet and safety, the government of the United States might feel itself called upon to interpose its power."[33]

In directions to the U.S. envoys to the 1826 Panama Conference of American States, Clay explained that an independent Cuba capable of preventing "all assaults from without, or within" was impossible, and liberation by Colombia and Mexico was insupportable. The United States viewed liberation as "a war of *conquest.*" If European monarchies intervened "merely to the object of preventing any change in the existing state of things, in respect to the Island, the United States, far from being under any pledge, at present, to oppose them, might find themselves, contrary to their inclination, reluctantly drawn by current events, to their side." In particular, the United States opposed "inva-sion *from Colombia, on account of the character of a portion of the troops of that Republic*" (italics in the original).[34]

The United States would not countenance a second Haiti. Just as it would not recognize the first black republic, it would oppose this new attempt at independence, since slaveholders "would live in continual dread of those tragic scenes which were formerly exhibited in a neighboring Island, the population of which would . . . employ all the means which vicinity, simi-larity of origin, and sympathy could supply, to foment insurrection; in order to gain ultimate strength in their own cause."[35] The Panama Conference was stillborn. The U.S. envoys never arrived to state the U.S. position, which was that in the Americas republican institutions were not for blacks, and that preventing those institutions from spreading to them justified monarchy, the survival of European empires, and U.S. alliance with kings to prevent the movement from slavery to freedom.

When considering Carey's and Clay's stance on Missouri, their eagerness to treat slavery as a vital institution within the new political economy, and Clay's willingness to abandon the Monroe Doctrine to defend slavery, the two could not be faulted for feeling that they deserved slaveholders' trust. Yet during the long 1820s they rarely got it, and both began to consider how slavery might be altered to remove the anxieties the new political economy clearly provoked among many who owned slaves. Since too many slavehold-ers believed that the new political economy threatened their interests, in several essays, beginning in the mid-1820s, Carey discussed the rapid and, to him, alarming growth of the slave population. The vast increase in slaves, Carey concluded, meant that cotton production, like American agriculture in general, outstripped demand. While the new political economy would solve this problem, slaveholders' blindness meant that they tried to prevent its formation. Slavery served the republic's needs in the new epoch if it did not prevent the new political economy. If it did so, Carey decided, it needed to be reformed so that those who lived by owning slaves could see their and the nation's interests more clearly.

Carey suggested that colonization should move beyond free blacks and also keep the slave population relatively constant as the white population grew. Slave owners should also explore new uses for their slaves. Carey argued that slaves could easily convert to labor in Southern textile factories. Free labor, he argued, would be more productive than slave labor, if the economy of slave country remained unchanged. But, Carey happily concluded, factories with slave laborers were more profitable than those using free labor.[36] Keeping the slave population relatively constant would make each slave more valuable; diversifying the Southern economy would make each slave more productive. Manifestly, slaveholders' hostility to the new political economy was the gravest threat to their prosperity.

Clay also sought to convince Southerners that they should diversify slave production in their own version of the new political economy. In Kentucky, he explained in a speech defending the 1824 tariff, slaves worked in rope walks, textile production, and in the manufacture of cotton bagging. Cotton bagging was vital to the cotton economy, but without protection, Clay explained, American manufactures had atrophied. The manufacture of bags was dominated by Scotland, and so "the price was raised upon the cotton grower." Carey took note of the possibilities raised by Clay and devoted an essay to the excellent prospects of Kentucky.[37]

While making these suggestions, Carey and Clay relied on their credentials as the respectful friends of slaveholders. In addition, Carey denounced immediate emancipation, claiming it would be far worse than even leaving slavery as it was. Immediate abolition threatened the Union, which was vital for "the security of the peace, happiness, and prosperity of our citizens." Abolition meant choosing the one and a half million enslaved blacks over the eight million free whites. Beyond that, convincing slaves to hate their bondage led to revolt and much greater misery for slaves and masters. By proclaiming the injustice of the slaves' condition, immediate abolitionists merely "render[ed] the slaves sullen, discontented, unhappy, and refractory." While seeking to transform slavery, then, Carey suggested that slaves were unhappy primarily because outside agitators made them so. Slaves were better off enslaved than liberated by their supposed friends. Slaveholders,

Carey implied, should realize that; unlike the immediate abolitionists, men such as Clay and himself merely wanted the slavery that was best for the nation and the master.[38]

Yet Carey and Clay made their claims just as many Southerners invigorated a defense of plantation slavery. During the 1820s, as traditional Jeffersonian predictions about slavery's future proved bogus, Southern political economists argued that slave labor was essential for subtropical staple agriculture, and more productive than free labor in such regions. Carey also dissented from the traditional claim that free labor was intrinsically more productive than slave labor. But he allowed slave labor greater productivity only as long as slave states reformed their political economy in the ways that he demanded. Southern theorists countered that plantation slave labor was uniquely productive precisely where it existed and where it could best expand.[39]

Thus, despite all their efforts, it seemed to Carey and Clay that too many slaveholders were immune to reason. Clay could not escape the American System's Southern problem. After his efforts in Missouri, after his careful explanations for why his policies would never threaten slave property, after his attempts to respond to every Southern concern, little had changed since he had been told by a Virginia friend that to win the election in 1824, he must "pledge that he would take care of the great interests of the south and the west." His friend went on: "The people of the south and the west . . . feel the progress of their impoverishment . . . by the northern and eastern capitalists, under the operation of the protecting system." Clay could only ask plaintively, "My dear Sir, what interests have Virginia and the south separate from the Union?" According to many slaveholders, plenty. Over the course of the long 1820s, Clay's Southern problem grew worse. In an angry 1826 speech given in Lewisburg, Virginia, Clay reminded his audience that he had secured slavery in Missouri. How could he now be "converted into a foe of southern, and an infatuated friend of northern and western interests?"[40] Yet that was how many Southerners did view him during the long 1820s. Clay heard about his Southern problem in letter after letter; he faced it in Congress after Congress.

Clay's frustration was exceeded by Carey's. Carey could not (he had no doubt) have made a more convincing case for the universal benefits of the new political economy. In a republic devoted to liberty, dignity, freedom, and rationality, all men should listen to reason. Yet Southerners refused. As the end of the long 1820s drew nearer, Carey's mounting frustration produced a series of angrier pamphlets denouncing what he viewed as selfish, yet ironically suicidal, ignorance.[41]

From Carey's perspective (and really also from Clay's), the most irrational slaveholders never listened to reason. Instead, wrote Carey, the long 1820s were ending with the nation moving "beyond the Rubicon." Nullification was the most searing evidence yet for Carey and Clay of their failure. Clay's conduct during the crisis is well known. When forced to choose (in his view, contrary to all reason) between union and the new political economy, Clay chose union and a compromise that gradually reduced tariffs below protective levels.[42] But here was the power of the politics of slavery in the long 1820s. Slavery finally severed Carey from Clay. For Carey, Southerners had done the unforgivable; they had committed republican original sin: they had sacrificed the needs of the eight million for the sake of their interests in the one and a half million. Their actions would destroy the new political economy—the only hope for the Jeffersonian dream.

Slaveholders had finally pushed Carey too far. The tireless advocate of a vigorous nation-state and Union now rejected the compromise Clay would make. The new political economy was more important than an unreformed slavery. In 1833, said Carey, it was time the Union dissolved. Carey's "Rubicon" pamphlet exuded a deep sense of relief, as if a truth long denied could be told. In January, Carey admitted that two weeks before he would have done anything to preserve the Union. Yet now that South Carolina would dissolve it, he found himself calm and unafraid. Why preserve the Union, he wondered? Now he saw clearly "that the southern states have been from the commencement of the government a mill stone about the neck of the other states." Finally, a vibrant republican nation could be "rescued from the evils and disgrace of slavery." Southerners could sink into their backward and impoverished sloth. The union of Northern and Mid-Atlantic states (Carey did not mention the West), with the new political economy, would forge the empire of liberty. Yet even here Carey could not bring himself to ask his "better race" to live entirely without the benefits of slavery. The new nation he imagined would include Delaware and Maryland, and, by his calculation, 108,861 slaves.[43]

From the Missouri Crisis and the Panic of 1819 at its onset, to the Nullification crisis that concluded the long 1820s, slavery was central to the period as lived by Mathew Carey and Henry Clay. The two could barely think a thought, plan a program, or imagine the nation's happy republican future without running into slavery and all the issues with which it intersected. Carey and Clay began the long 1820s convinced that they could construct national harmony and secure the republican birthright of citizens. They also chose the delusion that they would not compromise the republic's self-proclaimed reputation as the international example of liberty if they took full advantage of the undeniable growth of slavery.

To accomplish their goals, Carey and Clay moved slavery away from being something about which the republic should be anxious and ashamed. Both constructed methods for measuring the impact of slavery on the nation that did not start with the assumption that it automatically weakened republican institutions or corrupted republican citizens. Instead, slavery should be treated as just another policy, like the promotion of banks or domestic manufactures, that could be structured well or badly, with the only meaningful measurement of a policy's utility for the republic being whether or not it bettered the condition of what Carey called "the better race." Properly melding the new political economy with a reorganized and diverse slave economy required divorcing the presence of slaves from judgments about the integrity and viability of republican society. Despite their efforts to convince slaveholders to embrace the new political economy, and their subsequent ideas for reforming slavery, Carey's and Clay's only real impact on the issue of slavery during the long 1820s was to assist in building an alternative slavery discourse to lament and necessary evil. Carey and Clay contributed to ideas that helped make it easier to view slavery as other than infinitely wretched in precisely those years when that position gained some intellectual credibility.[44]

Carey and Clay believed they would build an empire of liberty: a society of independent households enjoying peace and harmony. At the end of the long 1820s, the nation was divided over the new political economy, slave owners threatened disunion, and Carey and Clay, for the first time, found themselves on opposite sides during a grave constitutional crisis. To get there, Clay had chosen slavery over his international republican ideals and had given up his tariff. With Missouri he had done at least as much as any other single man to spread slavery west. It is hard to see how he could have done more for slaveholders during the long 1820s, but in 1833 he had nothing to show for it except the alienation of his most prolific advocate.

Slavery was so central to the politics and political economy of the long 1820s that two of the most vital thinkers about the American System, the nation-state, the nature of federalism, and the Jeffersonian legacy could never really imagine living without it. But, in the end, Mathew Carey was willing to live with only about 100,000 slaves, while Clay's compromise meant that citizens would continue to coexist with millions. Carey and Clay thought they could bring lasting harmony to the nation, but at the end of the long 1820s they did not even have harmony with each other. There are no simple reasons why Carey chose the new political economy over union, while Clay, the statesman who could never become president yet still had to govern, opted for union over his cherished American System. But how much did it matter in 1833 that Henry Clay owned upwards of fifty slaves while Mathew Carey owned none?[45]

During the long 1820s, slavery was able to divide even such like-minded men as Carey and Clay. The end of that period marked the beginning of the gag rule and reaction to it, and the advance of the moral critique of immediate abolitionism and the aggressive response of the positive-good thesis. At the same time, with westward expansion white Americans began to learn how to draw on those two positions as they associated their most profound anxieties and aspirations with the success of either slavery's spread or confinement. At the end of the long 1820s, slavery could thwart the new political economy and divide Carey from Clay. With the political culture that emerged in response to those years, slavery divided much more than that.

NOTES

I would like to thank Ignacio Gallup-Diaz, John Craig Hammond, Matthew Mason, Daniel Richter, David Waldstreicher, and Michael Zuckerman for reading and urging me to improve this essay.

1. Thomas Jefferson, *Notes on the State of Virginia* (New York: Harper and Row, 1964), 159; *Philadelphia Aurora*, 8 May 1801, 18 June 1801, 21 September 1801, 29 March 1802, 30 November 1802, 23 November 1803, 11 February 1804, 6 May 1805, 29 July 1805; Drew R. McCoy, *The Elusive Republic: Political Economy in Jeffersonian America* (Chapel Hill: University of North Carolina Press, 1980); Lance Banning, *The Jeffersonian Persuasion: Evolution of a Party Ideology* (Ithaca, N.Y.: Cornell University Press, 1978); David Brion Davis, *The Problem of Slavery in the Age of Revolution, 1770–1823* (New York: Oxford University Press, 1975); Peter S. Onuf, "'To Declare Them a Free And Independent People': Race, Slavery, and National Identity in Jefferson's Thought," *Journal of the Early Republic* 18 (Spring 1998): 1–46; Gary B. Nash, *Race and Revolution* (Madison, Wis.: Madison House, 1990); Adam Rothman, *Slave Country: American Expansion and the Origins of the Deep South* (Cambridge, Mass.: Harvard University Press, 2005) (Rothman skillfully explains how Jeffersonians generally opposed slavery rhetorically but not meaningfully). See also Eva Sheppard Wolf, *Race and Liberty in the New Nation: Emancipation in Virginia from the Revolution to Nat Turner's Rebellion* (Baton Rouge: Louisiana State University Press, 2006); and Trevor Burnard, "Freedom, Migration, and the American Revolution," in *Empire and Nation: The American Revolution in the Atlantic World*, ed. Eliga H. Gould and Peter S. Onuf (Baltimore: Johns Hopkins University Press, 2005), 295–314.

2. Drew R. McCoy, "An Unfinished Revolution: The Quest for Economic Independence in the Early Republic," in *The American Revolution: Its Character and Limits*, ed. Jack P. Greene (New York: New York University Press, 1987), 131–48; Roger G. Kennedy, *Mr. Jefferson's Lost Cause: Land, Farmers, Slavery, and the Louisiana Purchase* (New York: Oxford University

Press, 2003); Matthew Mason, *Slavery and Politics in the Early American Republic* (Chapel Hill: University of North Carolina Press, 2006); John Craig Hammond, *Slavery Freedom and Expansion in the Early American West* (Charlottesville: University of Virginia Press, 2007); Rothman, *Slave Country.*

3. A sampling of the voluminous literature includes: Drew Gilpin Faust, *The Ideology of Slavery: Proslavery Thought in the Antebellum South, 1830–1860* (Baton Rouge: Louisiana State University Press, 1981); William Lee Miller, *Arguing about Slavery: John Quincy Adams and the Great Battle in the United States Congress* (New York: Vintage Books, 1995); Ronald G. Walters, *The Antislavery Appeal: American Abolitionism after 1830* (New York: W. W. Norton, 1978); Bruce Laurie, *Beyond Garrison: Antislavery and Social Reform* (Cambridge: Cambridge University Press, 2005); John Stauffer, *The Black Hearts of Men: Radical Abolitionists and the Transformation of Race* (Cambridge, Mass.: Harvard University Press, 2002); Michael A. Morrison, *Slavery and the American West: The Eclipse of Manifest Destiny and the Coming of the Civil War* (Chapel Hill: University of North Carolina Press, 1997); Jonathan H. Earle, *Jacksonian Antislavery and the Politics of Free Soil, 1824–1854* (Chapel Hill: University of North Carolina Press, 2004); Sean Wilentz, *The Rise of American Democracy: Jefferson to Lincoln* (New York: Norton, 2005); Charles Sellers, *The Market Revolution: Jacksonian America, 1815–1846* (New York: Oxford University Press, 1991); Harry L. Watson, *Liberty and Power: The Politics of Jacksonian America* (New York: Hill and Wang, 1990); John Ashworth, *Slavery, Capitalism, and Politics in the Antebellum Republic: Commerce and Compromise, 1820–1850* (New York: Cambridge University Press, 1995).

4. *The Life and Speeches of Henry Clay,* ed. James B. Swain, 2 vols. (New York: Greeley and McElrath, 1843), 1:140, 149–50, 222; Mathew Carey, *Essays on Political Economy; or the Most Certain Means of Promoting the Wealth, Resource, and Happiness of Nations: Applied Particularly to the United States* (Philadelphia, 1822), 200.

5. Carey, *Essays on Political Economy,* 69, 96; *The Life and Speeches of Henry Clay,* 1:150, 222, 228–29, 257.

6. Carey, *Essays on Political Economy,* 198–99; *The Life and Speeches of Henry Clay,* 1:220–21, appendixes 1–2; Carey, *Essays on Political Economy,* 62–63, 179–80.

7. *The Life and Speeches of Henry Clay,* 1:142–43, 257; Carey, *Essays on Political Economy,* 62–63, 184; Mathew Carey, *Reflections on the Present System of Banking in the City of Philadelphia, With a Plan to Revive Confidence, Trade, and Commerce, and Facilitate the Resumption of Specie Payments* (Philadelphia, 1817), 7–11.

8. Carey, *Essays on Political Economy,* 67.

9. Ibid., 11.

10. *The Papers of Henry Clay,* ed. James F. Hopkins, 10 vols. (Lexington: University of Kentucky Press, 1959–91), 2:514–17, 856–58, 3:80–81, 764–65, 4:521–22; see also 2:443–45, 580–81, 584–85, 590–91, 593, 803–16, 867–70, 4:2.

11. *The Papers of Henry Clay,* 2:518.

12. *The Life and Speeches of Henry Clay,* 1:279; *The Papers of Henry Clay,* 2:891–93, 3:116–17, 127, 310, 488–89, 562–63, 773, 872, 4:549–50, 2:418 (quotation); Rothman, *Slave Country,* chap. 5.

13. *The Papers of Henry Clay,* 2:391–92, 398, 432–33, 4:838–40, 5:216–17, 6:361–62, 471.

14. *The Life and Speeches of Henry Clay,* 1:270; *The Papers of Henry Clay,* 2:263–64; Eric

Burin, *Slavery and the Peculiar Solution: A History of the American Colonization Society* (Gainesville: University Press of Florida, 2005).

15. *The Life and Speeches of Henry Clay*, 1:282; *The Papers of Henry Clay*, 2:383–85, 3:497, 5:17, 6:283.

16. Mathew Carey, "African Colonization" (Philadelphia, 1829); idem, "Letters on the Colonization Society, with a View of Its Probable Results" (Philadelphia, 1832).

17. *The Papers of Henry Clay*, 2:740–47, 766–67, 774–75, 780–81, 788–89, 3:20–21.

18. At least according to a speech given in response to Clay's remarks by Pennsylvania congressman John Sergeant (a close ally of Clay's during the 1820s on economic issues). Clay's speech went unrecorded (see *The Papers of Henry Clay*, 2:776).

19. A Pennsylvanian [Mathew Carey], "Considerations on the Impropriety and Inexpediency of Renewing the Missouri Question" (Philadelphia: Mathew Carey, 1820), 3–4.

20. Ibid., 5–7.

21. Ibid., 52–55.

22. Duncan MacLeod, "The Triple Crisis," in *The Growth of Federal Power in American History*, ed. Rhodri Jeffreys-Jones and Bruce Collins (De Kalb: Northern Illinois University Press, 1983), 13–24; Richard E. Ellis, *Aggressive Nationalism: McCulloch v. Maryland and the Foundation of Federal Authority in the Young Republic* (New York: Oxford University Press, 2007).

23. *The Life and Speeches of Henry Clay*, 1:57–58, 170.

24. Ibid., 164–65.

25. Defending slavery was by no means the only reason to endorse states' rights (see Ellis, *Aggressive Nationalism*).

26. William Freehling, *Prelude to the Civil War: The Nullification Controversy in South Carolina, 1816–1836* (New York: Oxford University Press, 1965); Manisha Sinha, *The Counterrevolution of Slavery: Politics and Ideology in Antebellum South Carolina* (Chapel Hill: University of North Carolina Press, 2000); John Lauritz Larson, *Internal Improvement: National Public Works and the Promise of Popular Government in the Early United States* (Chapel Hill: University of North Carolina Press, 2001), 149–93.

27. *The Papers of Henry Clay*, 3:828, 5:220–22, 223, 635, 1023, 6:200, 435–36, 497.

28. Ibid., 6:320.

29. Mathew Carey, "A Warning Voice to the Cotton and Tobacco Planters" (Philadelphia, 1824); Mathew Carey, "Founding Memorial of the Proposed Society of Political Economists (Philadelphia, n.d.); Rothman, *Slave Country*, 171, 187; Carey, *Essays on Political Economy*, 69; Pennsylvania Society for the Promotion of American Manufactures, "Address to Congress: Being a View of the Ruinous Consequences of a Dependence on Foreign Markets for the Sale of the Great Staples of this Nation, Flour, Cotton, and Tobacco" (Philadelphia, 1820).

30. Mathew Carey, "Examination of the Charleston Memorial" (Philadelphia, 1827); "Colbert II" (Philadelphia, 1827); *The Life and Speeches of Henry Clay*, 1:166, 240.

31. Brian Schoen, "Calculating the Price of Union: Economic Nationalism and the Origins of Southern Sectionalism, 1790–1828," *Journal of the Early Republic* 23 (Summer 2003): 173–206.

32. Rothman, *Slave Country*, chap. 5; Kennedy, *Mr. Jefferson's Lost Cause*, 79, 109; Gavin Wright, *The Political Economy of the Cotton South: Households, Markets, and Wealth in the*

Nineteenth Century (New York: W. W. Norton, 1978), 96; Morton J. Horwitz, *The Transformation of American Law, 1780–1860* (Cambridge, Mass.: Harvard University Press, 1977), 40.

33. *The Papers of Henry Clay*, 4:271–74, 359–60, 5:331–34.

34. Ibid., 5:331–34.

35. Ibid., 5:331–34, 337–38; Alfred N. Hunt, *Haiti's Influence on Antebellum America: Slumbering Volcano in the Caribbean* (Baton Rouge: Louisiana State University Press, 1988), 29–30.

36. Mathew Carey, "Slave Labor Employed in Manufactures" (Philadelphia, 1827); idem, "African Colonization" (Philadelphia, 1829).

37. *The Papers of Henry Clay*, 3:642–44; Mathew Carey, "Some Notices of Kentucky: Particularly of its Chief Town, (Lexington)" (Philadelphia, 1828).

38. Mathew Carey, "Universal Emancipation" (Philadelphia, 1827), 4.

39. James Oakes, "The Peculiar Fate of the Bourgeois Critique of Slavery," in *Slavery and the American South*, ed. Winthrop D. Jordan (Jackson: University Press of Mississippi, 2003), 29–48.

40. *The Papers of Henry Clay*, 3:468–69, 477–78, 5:655; John Majewski, *A House Dividing: Economic Development in Pennsylvania and Virginia before the Civil War* (Cambridge: Cambridge University Press, 2000).

41. Mathew Carey, "Common Sense Addresses to the Citizens of the Southern States" (Philadelphia, 1829); idem, "Should the Nullifiers Succeed" (Philadelphia, 1832).

42. Mathew Carey, "Prospects beyond the Rubicon" (Philadelphia, 1832–33); Richard E. Ellis, *The Union at Risk: Jacksonian Democracy, States' Rights, and the Nullification Crisis* (New York: Oxford University Press, 1987); Freehling, *Prelude to Civil War*.

43. Carey, "Prospects beyond the Rubicon," 17–19, 21–23.

44. Oakes, "The Peculiar Fate of the Bourgeois Critique of Slavery."

45. Richard L. Troutman, "The Emancipation of Slaves by Henry Clay," *Journal of Negro History* 40 (April 1955): 179–81.

The Decline of
Antislavery Politics,
1815–1840

Donald J. Ratcliffe

The 1830s have traditionally been regarded as the time when sectional tensions over slavery heightened suddenly, dramatically, decisively. Historians have assumed that after the constitutional debates of 1787 argument over slavery disappeared for four decades. Then, the appearance of William Lloyd Garrison's *The Liberator* in 1831, the organization of the American Antislavery Society in 1833, and the evangelizing abolitionist campaigns that followed across the North, revived awareness of the issue and provoked a gradually intensifying confrontation with the slave states. Thus, the evolution of antislavery agitation is viewed from the perspective of the Civil War, as a key part of the story that tells how after 1830 a peaceable republic was carved apart by an issue that no one had cared about previously.

Such a view, as some early historians have protested, underestimates the power of earlier antislavery movements.[1] Recent work has established that Northern antislavery sentiment had a significant impact on national politics before 1830, frequently provoking bitter arguments within Congress over whether the United States should be a slaveholders' republic. From that perspective, it becomes reasonable to see the 1830s as marked not by "the rebirth of antislavery," but by antislavery decline—as a period when the slavery issue was deliberately removed from the mainstream of national political argument.[2]

This process had begun before 1830, as Northern politicians responded to the rising sectional sensitivity of the South, so evident by the late 1820s. Thus, in the early 1830s Garrison and his coadjutors were not starting a new, unprecedented crusade, but rather trying to breathe life into one that was fizzling out. For them, political antislavery had already lost out in the world of the nascent Second Party System, and they appreciated that the only way to achieve abolition was by stressing reform rather than politics, by transforming public consciousness in the North, both morally and racially. The apparent extremism of their standpoint had the effect, however, of accelerating the process of pushing the slavery issue still further to the political margins. Between 1815 and 1825, politicians had debated slavery openly in the North and had raised issues surrounding it in Congress. By 1835, public discussion of slavery in the North had become the preserve of perceived extremists, and Northern representatives sought to avoid the issue in national forums. As the slavery issue became more fraught, so it ceased to be the stuff of mainstream politics.

From this perspective, my object here is, first, to underline the political significance of antislavery sentiment before the late 1820s; second, to demonstrate how far things had changed by the late 1830s; and third, to suggest when and why this change came over American politics after 1825.

Basic to this argument is a distinction between "antislavery" and "abolitionism," a distinction not commonly made by historians, but one that illuminates the historical process. In this essay, "antislavery" refers to the growing belief that developed in the Revolutionary era that slavery was morally wrong, socially harmful, and inconsistent with the highest American ideals of liberty and democracy. This hatred of the institution could be compatible with racism, with respect for property, and with an unwillingness to threaten the sectional understandings upon which the Union had been erected. Some racial liberals embraced the antislavery point of view, but it was also compatible with those who favored the colonization of free blacks and who refused to interfere with slavery where it already existed.

The term "abolitionism," as used here, refers to the approach to slavery associated with William Lloyd Garrison, the Tappan brothers, and Theodore Dwight Weld in the 1830s. Their morally absolutist stand insisted on the immediate, uncompensated abolition of the institution, rejecting colonization as a solution, and they were willing to agitate for this point of view even in states where slavery already existed. True, earlier writers had preached immediate abolition—notably George Bourne in 1816 and John Rankin in 1824—but those men did not rouse the response that Garrison did in the evangelized Greater New England of the 1830s, when cultural conditions and techniques of organizational agitation were clearly different.[3]

But even after 1831, the older stream of antislavery persisted, with its proponents condemning the counterproductive extremism of what they called "modern abolitionism." Arguably, this older antislavery stream later provided much of the impulse supporting the free-soil movements that ultimately triumphed in the new Republican Party of the 1850s. Antislavery finally won the day, yet historians have tended to ignore its expression before 1830, when it indubitably shaped elections, legislation, and policy.

ANTISLAVERY POLITICS

Between 1789 and 1815, Northern antislavery sentiment reared its head fitfully but passionately. Usually it was Northern Republicans who objected to some concession to the slave interest and prominent Northern Federalists who insisted on recognizing the vested rights and interests of the slave states. But after 1808, as the Federalists of New England increasingly blamed their lack of national success upon the three-fifths rule, they adopted a strident antislavery rhetoric that superficially foreshadowed the style and rhetoric of the later Garrisonians. At the same time, the political conditions from 1808 through 1814 persuaded most Northern Republicans to accept the priority of commitment to the national party and avoid embarrassing their Southern partners, and so—while never consciously becoming the lackeys of slavery—they proved reluctant to pursue policies that upset the intersectional harmony upon which party success depended.[4] But then, after 1815, as the Federalists gave up formal opposition to the national administration and the Republicans became politically predominant in the North, the two parties came together to counteract the interests of slavery. They revealed the power of antislavery sentiment in their commitment to the cause of emancipation, the gains they made, and the conflicts they sustained.

Their great success came in New York in 1817, when the Assembly passed overwhelmingly a law freeing, on July 4th, 1827, all the slaves in the state who had been untouched by the state's emancipation act of 1799. This was the first *total* emancipation act passed by any state, guaranteeing the ultimate freedom (but not immediately) of all 11,000 slaves in New York. In Pennsylvania in 1815 and Ohio in 1817, state courts freed individual slaves who had been brought inside their borders by Southern slave owners. In the Old Northwest, antislavery activists beat back attempts to introduce slavery into Indiana and Illinois, and they prevented a suspected attempt to remove the prohibition on slavery from Ohio's constitution. The founding of the American Colonization Society (ACS) in 1817 was commonly approved of in the North as a means of encouraging Southerners to end slavery.[5]

Not everything gave cause for hope. Congress's prohibition of slave importations in 1807 had not ended the business. As international trading conditions improved after 1815, illegal importations increased; by 1818–19 Congress was toughening up naval enforcement of the prohibition, and in 1820 it declared international slave trading to be piracy. The demand for more slaves produced a spate of kidnappings of free blacks in the Northern states, which were sometimes disguised as fugitive-slave claims or legitimate domestic slave-trading. Free states along the Mason-Dixon Line passed anti-kidnapping laws, resulting in all sorts of incidents along the borders of North and South.[6]

Disputes over the return of fugitive slaves inevitably prompted a Southern attempt to secure a new fugitive-slave law in 1818. The object of the proposed law, according to a leading Washington editor, was "to make that law efficacious, which is at present little better than nominal." It would increase penalties for resistance, and transfer the formal judgment as to whether a detainee was indeed a runaway slave to judges in the putative slaveholder's state. To deter kidnappings, Northern congressmen inserted a clause that required the recording in the vendor's county court of the personal details of every slave sold across state lines, and in this guise the bill passed the House. When the Senate excised the registration clause, the House rejected the amendment and the bill lapsed.[7]

In many respects, this debate predicted the impending Missouri Crisis. Early one morning, someone placed on the seat of every senator a copy of John Kenrick's 1817 pamphlet *Horrors of Slavery,* which included "extracts, chiefly American, . . . demonstrating that slavery is impolitic, antirepublican, unchristian, and highly criminal; and proposing measures for its complete abolition through the United States." This and other antislavery protests provoked a long speech from William Smith of South Carolina defending the superiority of the Southern labor system, which was a forerunner of his famous promulgation of the positive-good argument two years later. Henry Clay made an even longer (and now lost) speech illustrating "the nature of slave property, its evils, and the rights of its possessors with great force." The vote on final passage of the original bill revealed a sharp sectional alignment, broken only because eighteen Northerners—harbingers of the "doughfaces" of 1820—were willing to "sacrifice some of their old prejudices to the spirit of harmony and mutual benefit," though their number dwindled decisively after the Senate excised the registration clause.[8]

The Missouri Crisis was also anticipated in the renewed arguments over the problem of illegal slave imports. In 1807, after a bitter debate in which some Southerners threatened secession and civil war, Congress had finally agreed that slaves intercepted as illegal imports should be handed over to the state where the interception was made or reported, and dealt with according to local law. After 1815, the illegal trade and the number of interceptions increased, and Northern newspapers soon reported that those intercepted were being sold as slaves by state governments, with the proceeds finishing up in the national treasury. By the 1818–19 session, national leaders feared that this sectionally divisive issue would reignite the controversy of 1807.[9]

The Slave Trade Act of March 1819 finessed the entire problem by handing rescued slaves over to the federal government and giving the president an appropriation to send them back to Africa. The ACS managers saw this issue as their entering wedge for federal financial assistance, and used the intercepted slaves as the main argument to employ the appropriation in founding an African homeland for the returnees. Desiring to avoid a potentially damaging argument over "recaptured Africans," the federal government in 1819 underwrote the unprecedented (if unofficial) colonial venture in Africa, marked by the founding of Liberia in 1821.[10]

Thus, the Missouri Crisis arose in the context of intensifying arguments, as local, state, and regional conflicts generated a national contest over slavery. James Tallmadge's antislavery amendment to the Missouri Enabling Bill in February 1819 was entirely predictable, given that only a year before he had tried to block Illinois' admission because its constitution did not adequately outlaw slavery. For many Federalists, the object in 1819–20 may have been to weaken the power of the Republican South, but for most Northern Republicans—the heart of the restrictionist cause—the central issue was always the expansion of an unacceptable institution. Many Northern congressmen searched for a compromise that might hold the Union together, but remained conscious that opinion back home adamantly opposed the admission of new slave states west of the Mississippi. On the decisive question of admitting Missouri as a slave state, they almost all voted against, whatever their private misgivings; and Missouri was admitted only because eighteen Northern congressmen either voted with the South or abstained. Only five of these "doughfaces" survived the scrutiny of the 1820–21 elections.[11]

The Missouri Crisis did not disappear from American politics quickly. This hostile popular response to the compromise persuaded most Northern congressmen to obstruct Missouri's admission in the lame-duck session of 1821 by defending the right of free black citizens to enter any state. They also refused to make any concession to continuing Southern demands for a new fugitive-slave law. At their final attempt in 1822, a New York congressman who avowed that he was not "one of those visionary philanthropists who would contend for immediate and universal emancipation," insisted that the proposed bill would be "a direct and efficient agency to promote the traffic which had been carried on to a great extent of seizing free blacks and selling them for slaves." Whereas the South had come close to securing the measure in 1818, in subsequent years they fell far short of the votes needed.[12]

This reflected the overall rousing of antislavery feeling that, according to Don Fehrenbacher, "crystallized into a reform movement of considerable force in the 1820s." Regularly, from 1821 onward, Congress received petitions for the abolition of slavery in the District of Columbia. Most significantly, the Ohio Resolutions of February 1824 called on the federal government to pass a law, with the consent of the slaveholding states, freeing at the age of 21 and then colonizing all slaves born after the passage of the act. The Resolves declared, moreover, that "the evil of slavery is a national one," and therefore the people of all the states should share the costs. Seven other Northern states, plus Delaware, endorsed the proposal.[13]

If the weakening of national party ties had made the Missouri Crisis possible, the passions aroused during the controversy finally ensured the end for the old Federalist and Republican Parties. As a consequence, the presidential election of 1824 marked the beginnings of a new system of party politics. Many Northern groups resented slavery's victory in Missouri and wished to shake off what Rufus King called the "black strap" in the national affairs. In particular, New Englanders throughout "Greater New England" demanded a non-slaveholding president. Since John Quincy Adams was the only Northerner with a chance of national success, even New England Federalists were willing to accept him, despite his well-remembered betrayal of their party in 1808. In New York, the famous People's Party of 1823–24 began as a movement among Republicans to prevent Van Buren Republicans from delivering the state to the "Virginia" candidate, William Harris Crawford of Georgia. In the critical local elections of 1823, the People's Party openly labeled the contest as between "Crawford and Slavery" and "Adams and Liberty." Significantly, the most successful statewide candidate in the People's election triumph of 1824 was James Tallmadge, of antislavery fame, who garnered 16,000 votes more for lieutenant governor than his gubernatorial running mate, DeWitt Clinton.[14]

The Panic of 1819 and the economic depression introduced other tensions into the national election—over banking, debts, internal improvements, tariff protection—that divided some states internally and created a sectional alignment that separated East from West as much as North from South. But the final result, which placed the Northern candidate Adams in the White House, with the aid of Henry Clay's Western supporters, could easily be perceived as a potential threat to slavery, and guaranteed that slavery issues would continue during Adams's presidency. The new president's enthusiasm for internal improvements revealed a willingness to interpret the Constitution broadly for the "general welfare," while higher tariffs would enhance the resources of an administration that was thoroughly identified with the colonization cause. Rufus King's Senate proposal of 1825 that the sale of federal lands be used to finance colonization gave substance to the fear that this federal administration might try to interfere with the South's control of its slaves. Throughout Adams's presidency, congressional debates touched on slavery in ways that left no doubt of the persistence of antislavery attitudes.[15]

Many Southerners were sufficiently alarmed by the evidence of continuing antislavery pressure from the North to propose strong measures of resistance. Nine Southern state legislatures condemned the Ohio Resolutions of 1824. Proposals to give federal aid to the ACS led Georgia legislators, in December 1827, to declare that they would "not permit their country to be made waste and desolate, 'by those who come among us under the cloak of a time-serving and hypocritical benevolence.'" Southerners eager to limit federal power and financial means proposed measures that would reduce both. They also threatened to take extreme measures, even secession, if the South was not allowed to treat visiting black seamen and uncooperative native tribes as it wished. Such threats alarmed many Northerners, and persuaded the more radical of them that traditional antislavery methods were unlikely to persuade the Slave South to embrace emancipation.[16]

A Union Safe for Slaveholders

By 1835, the world of antislavery concern had changed to a world of anti-abolitionist mobs and persecution in the North. One Northern editor later remarked that, whereas before the admission of Missouri "the sinfulness of the institution . . . had been thoroughly ventilated by pulpit, press and rostrum . . . without molestation," afterwards "a different state of things began to prevail." If twenty years later any editor had repeated the things openly written about slavery on the eve of the Missouri Crisis, his fellow citizens would have made a bonfire of his press and types. The appearance of immediate abolitionism, the efforts of the American Antislavery Society, and the abolitionist revivals conducted by Theodore Dwight Weld provoked severe racial fear in the South and a vicious reaction within the North that demonstrated how unacceptable the proposals of the modern abolitionists were. As a consequence, as the same editor said, Northern politicians were soon brought "into a state of non-resistance to the increasing demands of slavery."[17]

Symbolic reassurance and practical guarantees had first come with the election of a slaveholder to the presidency in 1828. President Jackson's attorney general reversed the official attitude toward South Carolina's (surely unconstitutional) practice of imprisoning visiting black sailors, and the administration blocked further federal appropriations for the ACS. The Indian Removal Act of 1830 removed a troublesome racial minority and opened vast acres for the cultivation of cotton with slave labor. In addition, Jackson's vetoes of in the years 1830–32 satisfied Southern fears over the principle of broad construction, while Congress in 1832 produced a compromise of the tariff acceptable to all but the ideologues in South Carolina. With their discontents appeased, most of the South refused to support South Carolina's challenge to federal authority in the Nullification Crisis.[18]

But then the swelling abolitionist campaign raised Southern anxieties to a new pitch of alarm, excitement, and apprehension. As a consequence, the congressional sessions of 1835–37 had to break away from the pressing problems of financial and economic policy that had occupied the preceding sessions, and devote most of their time to issues surrounding slavery. The immediate danger came in 1835–36 when the abolitionists flooded Southern post offices with pamphlets that Southerners feared might incite slave rebellion. Congress refused to allow Southern postmasters to police the mails, but in practice the sympathetic Jackson and Van Buren governments allowed them to take whatever action they thought necessary.[19]

Of greater political relevance was the massive petition campaign that began in 1835. As John C. Calhoun recognized, this marked a change in the character of petitioning, from the requests of a few well-meaning individuals and societies to a highly orchestrated mass campaign supported by thousands of signatures. By December 1836 the petitions' demands had extended from the District of Columbia to the interstate slave trade, slavery in the territories, and the possible annexation of Texas. To discuss such issues, Waddy Thompson of South Carolina warned, would "irritate, almost to madness, the whole delegation from the slave states." After much debate, the House resolved in May 1836 that petitions relating to slavery should be received and then automatically tabled without discussion. This gag rule reassured the South that Congress would not interfere with the interests of slavery, even in areas where arguably it had jurisdiction.[20]

In 1837, Congress made the most significant concession of all, a reform of the Supreme Court that has been largely underestimated by historians. Since 1802 each justice had been responsible for officiating on a specified federal circuit and had to reside in that circuit. From 1807, there were seven circuits, three Northern, three Southern, and one that covered Ohio, Kentucky, and Tennessee. Newer Western states were excluded from this system, and attempts to extend it had failed because of disagreements over circuit boundaries and fears of unacceptable appointments. The new "Judiciary Act" of February 1837 increased the court to nine justices, rearranged the one existing Western circuit, and added two more. One of the three Western circuits was in the Northwest, where there was already a resident justice, John McLean, appointed by Jackson in 1829. The other two were in the South, one for the Deep South and the other across the Upper South, although neither population size nor the weight of legal business justified giving the Southwest two circuits. Since new appointees had to be residents of the vacant circuit, the new arrangement gave the slave states five justices and the free states four. For the first time, the South had gained control of the Supreme Court.[21]

Ever since the Marshall Court's assertion of national judicial supremacy, Southerners had appreciated how the judiciary might undermine the constitutional defenses of the peculiar institution. That danger was now removed, especially with Roger B. Taney's appointment as chief justice in 1836. On the last day of his presidency—at the same time as announcing official United States recognition of Texas's independence—Jackson nominated two states' rights Southern Democrats to the new Supreme Court seats. Overall he had appointed seven of the nine justices, five of them in the last two years of his administration, when the slavery issue was rampant. Thus, Jackson's presidency ensured a built-in advantage for the South for the next quarter-century.[22]

This considerable Southern gain was soon followed by what Thomas Hart Benton described as "the most important proceeding on the subject of slavery which has ever taken place in Congress." In December 1837, Calhoun proposed six resolutions delineating the federal government's constitutional relationship with slavery. Although the resolutions expressed a state-sovereignty view of the Constitution, all (except one relating to Texas) passed the Senate in January 1838 by overwhelming votes. These resolutions affirmed the most advanced constitutional and political protection for slavery: supported by the gag rule, they established that Congress would not take measures that affected the institution's standing.[23]

There were, of course, protests against these concessions from some Northern representatives. In the House, John Quincy Adams gained everlasting fame as Old Man Eloquent in his nine-year defense of the constitutional right of petition against the gag rule.[24] In the Senate, Thomas Morris of Ohio followed a course that would retrospectively earn him the title of "the first Abolition Senator," repeatedly warning of the encroachments on constitutional liberties threatened by the "slave power," a term he coined.[25] Yet they protested alone. Morris found no support in the Senate for his counter-resolutions, and the Ohio Democrats replaced him as the end of his term approached. In January 1840 they read him out of the party, forcing Morris to turn his antislavery energies to the miniscule Liberty Party. Adams, too, stood virtually alone in his assaults on the gag rule. No other congressman came to his assistance on the main issue in the dramatic week-long controversy created by his provocative campaign against the gag rule in February 1837, although a handful of Northern antislavery Whigs, notably William Slade of Vermont and Joshua Giddings of Ohio, subsequently rallied to his support. Though their campaign would succeed in destroying the gag rule in December 1844, Adams himself was always careful publicly to distance himself from abolitionist criticisms of slavery, stressing instead the need to defend the citizen's constitutional right of petition.[26] Strikingly, there is no evidence of open Northern opposition to the 1837 "Judiciary Act," and it is surely significant that such opposition as there was could not even raise enough votes—20 percent—to have the "Yeas" and "Nays" recorded.[27] Other than Morris, no Northern politician used the opportunity provided by Calhoun's resolutions to launch philippics against slavery, as they undoubtedly would have done twenty years before. Far from seeing the rise of antislavery politics, the 1830s saw Northern politicians of both parties trying to bury the issue of slavery.

THE REVIVAL OF NATIONAL PARTIES

Clearly, a considerable change had occurred—from the open advocacy of the antislavery cause in national politics up to at least 1825, to the avoidance of such issues by almost all Northern politicians after 1835. The obvious explanation for this change in the political status of slavery agitation was the revival of party politics from the late 1820s onward, and especially the conscious revival of Mr. Jefferson's party in the form of the Jacksonian Democratic coalition. Martin Van Buren's role in this process has long been recognized. As he famously wrote to Thomas Ritchie in January 1827, "Party attachment in former times furnished a complete antidote for sectional prejudices by producing counteracting feelings." Only when that defense had been broken down could "the clamour ag[ains]t Southern Influence and African Slavery" be made effectual in the North, replacing the old party distinctions by "geographical divisions founded on . . . prejudices between free and slave holding states." Van Buren therefore advocated "the revival of old party feelings" to restore the "beneficial" political combination between "the planters of the South and the plain Republicans of the North."[28]

Such a resurrection of Mr. Jefferson's party had been the objective of many Old Republicans during the Missouri Crisis, as they tried to rally the party with the cry of "Federalist plot." In the 1824 election, some Northern politicians trusted that the traditional party nominating process—the congressional caucus—would still attract the support of loyalist voters and, like Van Buren, stuck to the nominated "Virginia" candidate in the face of local opposition. After 1825, Van Buren insisted that Jackson provided the only point the South could rally around, and reassured his allies that the slaveholding Jackson, for all his nationalism, was an Old Republican at heart. He insisted that the best way of winning sufficient support in the North in 1828 was by "combining Genl. Jackson's personal popularity with the portion of old party feeling yet remaining." In New York, Van Buren managed to carry most of the regular Republicans, especially his fellow Dutch Yorkers, into the Jackson camp. In the Middle and Northwestern states, the General's personal appeal to discontents of many kinds won much popular support, despite his association with Southern grievances.[29]

After Adams's election, his opponents had seized every opportunity to brand his administration dangerous to the slave South. In the Panama debate of 1825–26, they combined attacks on the new president's supposed disregard for constitutional limits on his power with warnings about the dangers of aligning the United States too closely with black republics. Some Northern observers thought it "manifest" that this Southern opposition was inspired by "the cloven foot of negro slavery and southern dominancy." Then, when the Jacksonians won control of Congress in December 1827, they appealed to the slave states over several minor knotty issues. For example, they defended the slave interest in a controversy arising from the *Antelope* case, which had dragged through the courts for years. The debate "produced much incidental discussion in the house of representatives, of slavery, and the slave trade," and in the end Congress agreed to allow thirty-nine illegally imported slaves to be retained in the United States. This de facto importation depended entirely on the support of Jacksonian "*doe* faces" from New York, Pennsylvania, and Ohio. Such assistance helped to unite the South behind Jackson in 1828, which then gained its reward in the package of measures and vetoes delivered during his first administration.[30] This appeasement was possible only because most Northern Jacksonians in Congress held to the presidential line, in spite of opinion back home. In practice, the force of party ties, reinforced by the concerns and grievances that had brought them into the Jacksonian coalition, was strong enough to overcome sectional considerations, and most Northern Democrats supported Indian Removal and Jackson's vetoes regardless of pressure from their constituents.

By 1835–36, the Jacksonians faced a different challenge, as party rebels in the South charged Jackson's nominated successor with being too close to New York abolitionists. In this presidential year, Van Buren deliberately countered his proslavery opponents by helping the South gain the defenses it demanded. Then, as president, he pursued policies that Daniel Walker Howe has reasonably characterized as underlining the proslavery, white-supremacist stance of the national Democratic Party. But by this point the Bank Wars of 1832–34 and the Panic of 1837 had introduced other issues of significant principle and practical effect, sharpening the ideological stance of the Democratic Party. Its supporters now had even stronger reasons for avoiding problems that threatened the political cohesion of the party. Accordingly, as the decade progressed, most Northern Democrats became firm supporters of the anti-abolitionist measures designed to reassure the South that slavery was safe within the Union. Some Northern Democrats in Congress spoke openly in defense of the South's interest in slavery, and in December 1838 the resolution to adopt the gag rule for the session was introduced by a Northern Democrat. As a group, Northern Democrats provided the votes that helped Southerners of both parties protect the peculiar institution.[31]

But does that mean that Northern Democrats were pro-slavery? They appeased the slave South, but they did so as part of their battle against an overly centralizing, apparently neo-Federalist Party. They did not adopt the arguments and ideology of the proslavery protagonists of slavery—who denied that Congress had any competence where slavery was concerned—but rather looked toward maintaining the principles upon which the Union might be preserved. As defined by the events of the Jackson administration, the Democracy was primarily concerned with establishing a strict-construction, laissez-faire, anti-aristocratic basis for government. As John Ashworth has argued, these concerns happened also to fit closely with the interests of slavery. According to the *Democratic Review,* even the gag rule could command "the free support of all the democracy of the north," once placed on "its true ground of the states-rights principle." Thus, many Northerners who combined antislavery with Democratic principle could find a place within the party, and keep it through the 1830s, conscious of the larger purposes the party served.[32]

Accordingly, the Ohio Democrats could safely replace the dangerous Thomas Morris in the U.S. Senate in December 1838 with Benjamin Tappan, eldest brother of the famous abolitionists and a man long vocal in his criticisms of slavery and colonization. Benjamin regarded himself as an "abolitionist in principle," but as senator would only act within the limits of the Constitution and according to the will of his state; when he got to Washington, he promptly refused to present abolitionist petitions to the Senate, even though he approved their objective. For this eldest Tappan, slavery was a distraction from the serious struggle over financial issues and American System policies—with all their ideological and symbolic overtones for the future character of the republic—that were involved in the battle between the major parties.[33]

Historians have long emphasized how this partisan logic, resulting from the structural pressure to build a national coalition capable of winning control of the federal government, operated on the Jacksonian Democrats. We need also to appreciate how it affected their opponents. The political coalition that fought for Adams's reelection in 1828 and Clay's election in 1832, by that time operating under the name National Republican, was essentially a union of New Englandism with the American System. Inevitably, that political grouping found most of its support in the North and united most of the South against it. Such a party might be expected to take up anti-Southern causes as a means of beating the Jacksonian Democrats in the North, and apparently did so with its opposition to Indian Removal in 1830–32 and its defense of the American System.

But on the slavery issue the National Republicans were very cautious. For one thing, they did not wish to jeopardize the Union by provoking the South; for another, they knew that Adams was unlikely to sweep the North in 1828 and so needed Southern electoral votes, which they had realistic hopes of getting in the Border states and Louisiana. Immediately on taking power in 1825, members of Adams's cabinet gave careful reassurances on slavery to the South. Then, when difficult issues connected with slavery came up in the Congress of 1827–28, the administration refrained from using them to unite the North. When a Louisiana slaveholder, Marigny d' Auterive, was refused compensation for a slave wounded at New Orleans in 1815 on the grounds that the United States government only ever paid compensation for the loss of property, not persons, Jacksonians pointed up the threat to slavery implicit in that doctrine. The Adams men were furious at the Jacksonians' irresponsibility but felt unable to answer the agitators in the spirit they deserved. Over the *Antelope* case, one Ohio congressman pointed out that the administration's organs in Washington were "so *delicate* on the subject of negroes that the debate is not even given." Even in the 1828 presidential election Adams men avoided the slavery issue, despite the attractions of running a sectionalist campaign. This restraint led James Tallmadge, twenty years later, to accuse President Adams of having "*betrayed* his friends in expectation to have gained the South for his re-election."[34]

Even when Southern support did not materialize in 1828, thanks partly to the Jacksonians' exploitation of fears for slavery, the defeated National Republicans avoided agitating the issue. They still retained some faith in colonization as a program upon which moderates in the North and the South might yet agree, though the decline of antislavery societies in the South was undermining that hope. They argued (fruitlessly) that the American System, far from threatening slavery, would benefit Southern planters. They presented their opposition to Indian Removal as a question of protecting legal rights and the benevolent work of Christian civilization, and made little of the slavery overtones. In his Second Reply to Hayne, in January 1830, Daniel Webster promised that the North would remain faithful to the Union as it was, implicitly a Union that respected the historic protections for slavery.[35]

With the rebellion against Jackson in the South in 1835 and the Hugh Lawson White campaign of 1836, Northern Whig leaders had a real incentive to lean over backwards to attract the Southern rebels. With the heightening of economic concerns after the Panic of 1837, they succeeded in doing so. This did not mean that the Whigs were united in protection of slavery—the Northern wing was always most reluctant to vote for proslavery measures—but Northern Whig politicians were cautious about what they said, and were always careful to distinguish themselves from the abolitionists. Henry Clay may have leaned too far toward propitiating the South in the congressional sessions of 1837–39, and thereby ruined his chances for the Whig nomination, but the successful nominee, the much underestimated William Henry Harrison, carefully maintained his ambiguity on such questions. He may have appealed to Northern evangelical reformers in 1840, but his protagonists could also point to his Virginia origins and his proslavery record as governor of the Indiana Territory and in the Missouri Crisis.

Significantly, in his inaugural in March 1841, Harrison would repeat Van Buren's commitment not to countenance any bill that interfered with slavery in the District of Columbia.[36]

Similarly, when the Whigs won control of Congress in 1839, it was Southern *Whigs* who introduced a permanent gag that ensured that petitions relating to slavery were not received at all. Northern Whigs of course voted against, and the rule passed in January 1840 only with the help of their Democratic rivals, but most Northern Whigs did not immediately campaign or agitate against it. Instead, they cooperated with their Southern brethren in organizing the two houses, placing some slaveholders in key positions. As Calhoun said in 1840, the Whig party wished not to be "blended" with the abolitionists "on the main question," but was "unwilling to lose their weight . . . in elections." Aware of the need to preserve partisan unity, Southern Whigs recognized the antislavery pressures on their Northern partners and did not press for the annexation of Texas, which would have revived the issues of the Missouri Crisis. Reciprocally, Northern Whigs appreciated that the gag rule would protect their party allies in the South in the forthcoming election. All Whigs, regardless of section, recognized that the "first duty of patriotism" was to rid the nation of Van Buren's "reckless, ignorant, unprincipled pack." Even some abolitionists—like the early immediatist John Rankin—decided that partisan issues mattered more than slavery and in 1840 chose to vote for Harrison. For most Northern politicians and voters, the sharpening of party contest in the mid-1830s had become so intense that men such as Slade, Giddings, and Tappan thought that slavery was neither the only nor the greatest issue at stake in current American politics.[37]

Existence of a national party inevitably required compromise between sections, and that meant compromise with slavery. What was new after 1825 were the growing demands of the South for tangible concessions and public protections, which meant that the ambiguities of the Jeffersonian era would no longer satisfy. Those demands persuaded many of the most radical antislavery evangelicals that something more revolutionary needed to be done.[38] Similarly, the most ideologically committed moral reformers—whether supporters of prohibiting Sunday Mails, or opposers of Indian Removal, or political Antimasons—saw that the new main parties would not sustain morally absolute stands that might adversely affect their chances of electoral success. Accordingly, as other causes declined after 1833, they tended to join not one of the major parties but the political margins of modern abolitionism.[39]

ANTI-ABOLITIONISM AND RACE

The ability of Northern politicians to appease the slaveholding South derived, of course, from more than just the centrality that major party politics acquired in the course of the 1830s. They were able to make concessions to the South because of the conspicuous change in public attitudes made clear by the response to the modern abolitionists after 1833. The outburst of mob violence in the North—the hounding of George Thompson and Garrison and the New York Tappans, the myriad riots in small towns whenever abolitionist evangelists appeared—reflected a shift in outlook among both populace and political elite, as attitudes concerning slavery and race were challenged by the demands and behavior of the abolitionists. What the abolitionists revealed were cultural and religious changes that had been underway for at least a decade, and they exposed to daylight the racist tendencies of traditional antislavery sentiment.[40]

Undoubtedly, much resistance to the abolitionists came from the established professional and mercantile classes, especially in urban areas. These "men of property and standing" objected to irresponsible agitation of issues that threatened the prosperity and viability of the Union without any hope of achieving their ostensible objective. In Philadelphia even abolitionists among the elite were most reluctant to press the slavery issue in the immediate wake of both the Missouri and the Nullification crises. Others disliked the techniques of agitation used by abolitionists within Northern communities, including the encouragement of women's activism and the employment of outside agents. Governor Edward Everett objected to abolitionist agitation in Massachusetts in 1834–36 in particular because it unnecessarily disturbed the peace of rural communities.[41] Yet agitation that undermined the authority of local elites was scarcely new, for Northern communities had already been stirred by protagonists of the burgeoning national parties, as well as by the extraordinary Anti-Masonic campaigns of 1827–33.

Far more significant in explaining the willingness to play down slavery issues, certainly among the populace at large, were public attitudes toward free African Americans. The outbreak of race riots directed against free blacks in Northern cities between 1824 and 1829 set the example for the attacks on black communities during anti-abolition riots of the mid-1830s. Racial prejudice against African Americans had, of course, existed in the United States from its founding, and for most Northerners traditional antislavery had been blended with racist presumptions. But since emancipation, free blacks had coexisted alongside whites—however uneasy and contested the relationship—and Northerners had generally recognized black claims to freedom even if they denied and opposed black claims to equality. After 1825, however, they increasingly denied that blacks had any right to freedom, or even residence in the United States. This hardening of racial attitudes made it much easier for each party, in its own way, to adjust to slavery as an inescapable fact of political life.[42]

A suggestive example of the shift in racial attitudes came from the state with the third largest white population. Ohio was never racially blind; it was in fact the first Northern state to write the word "white" into its voting qualifications at its founding constitutional convention in 1802, and yet did so only on the casting vote of the convention's president. It introduced black laws in 1804 and 1807, and yet administered them with some sensitivity: bonds were rarely actually required, and the registration process was partly intended to help protect genuinely free blacks against the Fugitive Slave Act. The pioneering "Negro" historian Carter Woodson decided that in early Cincinnati treatment of free blacks was marked overall by "toleration"—at least until 1826, when he detected a change to "persecution." By 1829, one of the nastiest antebellum race riots saw half the city's free blacks chased out of the city.[43]

This shift in attitude was articulated, and therefore made more conscious and deliberate, by the American Colonization Society. Though from the start it had been dedicated to removing free blacks, the national body was originally and for a long time perceived as essentially antislavery, providing a solution to the South's problem of what to do with slaves it may have wanted to free. In 1827 a state ACS was founded in Ohio, but now it pitched its appeal on the need to get rid of a dangerous population that threatened a *"servile war"* in a state where the Negroes "enjoy enough freedom to feel their chains . . . and are not under the watchful restraints of a master." As Clay said in Washington the same year, the "evil" lay in the existence of the "free African race among us," who were inevitably "aliens—political—moral—social aliens, strangers though natives." In effect, the ACS spokesmen extended the idea that blacks had no claim to a free existence in America, that they were a menace to society that must be removed. As a consequence of this changing attitude, the Ohio legislature passed stiffer black laws in 1829 to deter the immigration of free blacks. Thus, the ACS helped to exacerbate what Thomas Morris called in 1838 "the putrid mass of prejudice" that he believed had been deliberately created "to keep the colored race in bondage."[44]

This hardening attitude resulted largely from the growing visibility of free blacks. In Ohio their numbers virtually doubled in the 1820s, and many whites believed that the slave states were throwing their old and decrepit slaves into the state. As across the North as a whole, the growth was not disproportionate to the growth of the total population, but it was more obvious in the cities: the number of free blacks in Cincinnati tripled between 1826 and 1829. By the 1820s distinctions were made in many places between the established black population and newcomers, with incidents of violence directed essentially at the latter. At the same time, the increasing civic activism of Northern free blacks made their presence more obvious. Since 1815, black leaders had forged a black political community through print and public action, adopting group confrontation to force white politicians to recognize their wishes and needs. In Philadelphia, black activists established four times more reform associations in the 1820s than in the previous forty years, as well as founding outspoken newspapers. Black organizations led the campaign against colonization, which led some white citizens to perceive that America's basic problem was not slavery but the presence of blacks, free as well as slave.[45]

Apparently, the materials for the racist reaction that met the abolitionists in the 1830s were already being put into place by the late 1820s. For most Northerners, the rejection of abolitionism would not contradict their antislavery, which they had always reconciled with racist feelings of distaste and superiority. But those feelings had acquired a new edge: the anti-abolitionist mobs of the mid-1830s were an expression of the harsher racist consensus that most Northerners had come to share in the previous decade. And one consequence of that consensus was a latent feeling among many Northerners that slavery, however deplorable, could be tolerated, because at least it kept those savage Africans locked up within the South.

Given such changes in popular attitudes, the abolitionists of the 1830s sought to re-energize a reform movement that had proved incapable of achieving its avowed aims. Garrison's novelty lay not in trying to persuade people that slavery was a moral evil, but in recognizing the need for a transformative recognition of black rights and for immediate action. Nor was he politically naive, as some historians have suggested; antislavery had already been sidelined in the world of the nascent Second Party System, and the only way to transform its fortunes was by changing public consciousness. Hence, Garrison and his coadjutors adopted shock tactics, used extremist language, rejected standard moral authorities, and sought confrontation.[46] Of course they were right, though it was not their efforts that were to change the Northern perceptions of enslaved blacks, but four years of civil war. On this view, William Lloyd Garrison is important not just for initiating a more vigorous antislavery campaign after 1831, but for responding to the fact that popular antislavery was no longer the mainstream political force it was once.

The modern abolitionists of course had a huge impact on the development of political relations between slave and free states. They provoked crises upon which politicians had to take a stand and drove the South to demand ever greater reassurances that slavery was safe within the Union. Yet these abolitionists remained a deeply divided minority within the nation, and it is arguable that the non-Garrisonian abolitionists who did not eschew politics had the greater impact in building a free-soil coalition within the North.[47] Alternatively, some recent historians have pointed to the role of non-evangelical activists who came out of the Democratic Party, men usually of radical view on financial and economic as well as slavery issues—such as Thomas Morris and Marcus Morton of Massachusetts. Yet this view does not explain why only some Northern radical Democrats turned to abolition causes, while most remained loyal to their party and supported the ultra dough-faced regimes of the 1850s.[48]

The most realistic answer is that most of these abolitionists of Democratic antecedents were convinced antislavery men before 1825. The antislavery of Morris, Ben Tappan, and Morton was established through parental teaching, the writings of Jefferson, and early political controversy well before being subdued by political ambition, party loyalty, and economic radicalism. The near-silence of the main parties of the late 1820s and 1830s on slavery issues made it possible for Northerners of antislavery tendency who thought other political issues more salient to find a home in those parties. In time they began to be ejected from office, as early as 1840 in Morris's case, but after 1844 for most antislavery Democrats, including Morton. President Polk drove from minor office many long-serving Democrats of radical antislavery sympathy, and his conspicuously pro-Southern policies alienated many antislavery Northern voters.[49]

One consequence was a sharp decline in turnout in many Northern states, first detectable in the off-year elections of 1846. That pool of abstaining and alienated antislavery adults, from both main parties, was available to antislavery parties, such as the Free Soilers, and became an important source of voter support for the Republican Party in 1856.[50] For these voters, the old antislavery campaign had come to seem insignificant during the party battles of the 1830s, but gradually the aggressions of the slave South roused their old principles. What finally overthrew Southern political power in 1860 was not the "modern abolitionist" minority, but the long-established conservative and racist antislavery sentiment of the Northern majority that for a quarter of a century had been out of the headlines.

NOTES

1. William Birney, *James G. Birney and His Times* (New York: D. Appleton, 1890); Alice Dana Adams, *The Neglected Period of Anti-Slavery in America, 1808–1831* (Boston: Radcliffe College, 1908).

2. For recent use of the conventional term "rebirth," see John Ashworth, *Slavery, Capitalism, and Politics in the Antebellum Republic*, vol. 2, *The Coming of the Civil War, 1850–1861* (Cambridge: Cambridge University Press, 2007), 97. Recent revisionist work includes Don E. Fehrenbacher, *The Slaveholding Republic: An Account of the United States Government's Relations to Slavery* (New York: Oxford University Press, 2001); Richard S. Newman, *The Transformation of American Abolitionism: Fighting Slavery in the Early Republic* (Chapel Hill: University of North Carolina Press, 2002); Mathew Mason, *Slavery and Politics in the Early American Republic* (Chapel Hill: University of North Carolina Press, 2006); John Craig Hammond, *Slavery, Freedom, and Expansion in the Early American West* (Charlottesville: University of Virginia Press, 2007); Robert Pierce Forbes, *The Missouri Compromise and Its Aftermath: Slavery and the Meaning of America* (Chapel Hill: University of North Carolina Press, 2007); and the essays in this volume.

3. George Bourne, *The Book and Slavery Irreconcilable* (Philadelphia: Printed by J. M. Sanderson, 1816); John Rankin, *Letters on American Slavery* (Ripley, Ohio: D. Ammen, 1826; Boston: Garrison and Knapp, 1833).

4. Usually, Federalists are seen as anti-slavery and Republicans as pro-slavery. Recent views to the contrary include Leonard L. Richards, *The Slave Power: The Free North and Southern Domination, 1780–1860* (Baton Rouge: Louisiana State University Press, 2000); Sean Wilentz, "Jeffersonian Democracy and the Origins of Political Antislavery in the United States: The Missouri Crisis Revisited," *Journal of the Historical Society* 4 (Fall 2004): 375–401; and John Craig Hammond, "Race, Slavery, and Party during the First Party System in the North," paper delivered at the SHEAR Annual Conference, Providence, R.I., 2004.

5. Arthur Zilversmit, *The First Emancipation: The Abolition of Slavery in the North* (Chicago: University of Chicago Press, 1967), 213–14; David N. Gellman, *Emancipating New York: The Politics of Slavery and Freedom, 1777–1827* (Baton Rouge: Louisiana State University Press, 2006), 206; Eric Burin, *Slavery and the Peculiar Solution: A History of the American Colonization Society* (Gainesville: University Press of Florida, 2005).

6. Fehrenbacher, *The Slaveholding Republic*, 149–52; Thomas D. Morris, *Free Men All: The Personal Liberty Laws of the North, 1780–1861* (Baltimore: Johns Hopkins University Press, 1974), 30–41.

7. *Daily National Intelligencer* (Washington, D.C.), 27, 29, 30 January 1818, 2 February 1818; *Annals of Congress*, 15th Cong., 1st sess., 225–26, 231–38, 241–54, 257–58, 825–40.

8. John Kenrick, *Horrors of Slavery* (Cambridge, Mass.: Printed by Hilliard and Metcalf, 1817); *Daily National Intelligencer,* 2 February 1818, 15 June 1818; *The Papers of Henry Clay,* ed. James F. Hopkins and Mary W. M. Hargreaves (Lexington: University of Kentucky Press, 1961), 2:432–33.

9. Hazel Akehurst, "Sectional Crises and the Fate of Africans Illegally Imported into the United States, 1806–1860," *American Nineteenth Century History* 9 (June 2008): 97–122, especially 103; Donald Robinson, *Slavery in the Structure of American Politics, 1765–1820* (New York: Harcourt Brace Jovanovich, 1971), 324–46.

10. Philip J. Staudenraus, *The African Colonization Movement, 1816–1865* (New York: Columbia University Press, 1961), 48–58.

11. Robinson, *Slavery in the Structure of American Politics,* 408; Donald J. Ratcliffe, *The Politics of Long Division: The Birth of the Second Party System in Ohio, 1818–1828* (Columbus: Ohio State University Press, 2000), 54–55; Major L. Wilson, *Space, Time, and Freedom: the Quest for Nationality and the Irrepressible Conflict, 1815–1861* (Westport, Conn.: Greenwood Press, 1974), 22–48; Wilentz, "Jeffersonian Democracy and the Origins of Political Antislavery in the United States," 375–401; and John Craig Hammond's essay in this volume.

12. Morris, *Free Men All,* 41.

13. Fehrenbacher, *The Slaveholding Republic,* 68–69, 88 (quotation); Newman, *The Transformation of American Abolitionism,* 49–55; Herman V. Ames, *State Documents on Federal Relations: The States and the United States* (1900–1906; repr., New York: Da Capo Press, 1970), 203–5.

14. John C. Fitzpatrick, ed., "The Autobiography of Martin Van Buren," in *Annual Report of the American Historical Association for the Year 1918* (1920; repr., 2 vols., New York: Da Capo Press, 1973), 1:139 (for King quotation). For the elections of 1823, see the *Dutchess Observer,* reprinted in the *National Advocate, for the County* (New York), 25 November 1823.

15. Forbes, *The Missouri Compromise and Its Aftermath,* 179–291, especially 216–22; Fehrenbacher, *The Slaveholding Republic,* 1–11, 68–71.

16. Ames, *State Documents on Federal Relations,* 204–13 (quotation at 212); Donald J. Ratcliffe, "The Nullification Crisis, Southern Discontents, and the American Political Process," *American Nineteenth Century History* 1, pt. 2 (Summer 2000): 1–30, especially 2–8.

17. Eber D. Howe, *Autobiography and Recollections of a Pioneer Printer* (Painesville, Ohio: Telegraph Steam Printing House, 1878), 24, 48.

18. Ratcliffe, "The Nullification Crisis, Southern Discontents, and the American Political Process," 8–15; Daniel Walker Howe, *What Hath God Wrought: The Transformation of America, 1815–1848* (New York: Oxford University Press, 2007), 342–57, 414–23.

19. Richard R. John, *Spreading the News: The American Postal System from Franklin to Morse* (Cambridge, Mass.: Harvard University Press, 1995), 256–80.

20. William Lee Miller, *Arguing with Slavery: John Quincy Adams and the Great Battle in the United States Congress* (New York: A. A. Knopf, 1996), 30, 238 (quotation), 124–39; William W. Freehling, *The Road to Disunion,* vol. 1, *Secessionists at Bay, 1776–1854* (New York: Oxford University Press, 1990), 308–52.

21. *The Globe* (Washington, D.C.), 9 March 1837; *Daily National Intelligencer* (Washington, D.C.), 15 March 1837; Charles Warren, *The Supreme Court in United States History,* 3 vols. (Boston: Little, Brown, 1922), 1:676–84, 800–802.

22. *The Globe* (Washington, D.C.), 13 March 1837, reprinted from the *Richmond Enquirer*; Harold M. Hyman and William M. Wiecek, *Equal Justice Under the Law: Constitutional Development, 1835–1875* (New York: Harper and Row, 1982), 59–63.

23. [Thomas H. Benton], *Abridgement of the Debates in Congress, from 1816 to 1856* (New York: D. Appleton, 1858), 13:568n; Charles M. Wiltse, *John C. Calhoun: Nullifier, 1829–1839* (Indianapolis: Bobbs-Merrill, 1949), 370–73.

24. Leonard L. Richards, *The Life and Times of Congressman John Quincy Adams* (New York: Oxford University Press, 1986), 89–145.

25. B[enjamin] F. Morris, *The Life of Thomas Morris* (Cincinnati: Moore, Wilstach, Keep, and Overend, 1856), 106 (quotation), 119–20, 165, 174; Jonathan H. Earle, *Jacksonian Antislavery and the Politics of Free Soil, 1824–1854* (Chapel Hill: University of North Carolina Press, 2004), 37–48.

26. B. F. Morris, *The Life of Thomas Morris*, 85, 192–94; Miller, *Arguing with Slavery*, 351–57; Freehling, *The Road to Disunion*, 1:343–45, 349–52.

27. *The Globe* (Washington, D.C.), 9 March 1837.

28. Martin Van Buren to Thomas Ritchie, 13 January 1827, in *The Age of Jackson*, ed. Robert V. Remini (New York: Harper and Row, 1972), 3–7.

29. Martin Van Buren to Thomas Ritchie, 13 January 1827, ibid., 5; Norman K. Risjord, *The Old Republicans: Southern Conservatism in the Age of Jefferson* (New York: Columbia University Press, 1965); Ratcliffe, *The Politics of Long Division*, 131–310.

30. Quotations are from Ratcliffe, *The Politics of Long Division*, 139, 141–42. See also John T. Noonan Jr., *The "Antelope": The Ordeal of the Recaptured Africans in the Administrations of James Monroe and John Quincy Adams* (Berkeley: University of California Press, 1977).

31. William G. Shade, "'The Most Delicate and Exciting Topics': Martin Van Buren, Slavery, and the Election of 1836," *Journal of the Early Republic* 18 (Fall 1998): 459–84; Howe, *What Hath God Wrought*, 508–24, 544–46, 584–85; Richards, *The Slave Power*, 125–33.

32. John Ashworth, *Slavery, Capitalism, and Politics in the Antebellum Republic*, vol. 1, *Commerce and Compromise, 1820–1850* (Cambridge: Cambridge University Press, 1996), 323–50; *Democratic Review* (New York), April 1839, quoted in Miller, *Arguing with Slavery*, 344–45. See also John McFaul, "Expedience vs. Morality: Jacksonian Politics and Slavery," *Journal of American History* 62 (June 1975): 25–26; Joel Silbey, "'There are Other Questions Beside That of Slavery Merely': The Democratic Party and Antislavery Politics," in *Crusaders and Compromisers: Essays on the Relationship of the Antislavery Struggles to the Antebellum Party System*, ed. Alan M. Kraut (Westport, Conn.: Greenwood Press, 1983), 143–75; and Sean Wilentz, "Slavery, Antislavery, and Jacksonian Democracy," in *The "Market Revolution" in America: Politics, Religion, and Society, 1800–1880*, ed. Melvyn Stokes and Stephen Conway (Charlottesville: University Press of Virginia, 1996), 202–23, especially 202–7.

33. Benjamin Tappan to Lewis Tappan, 21 November 1839, Benjamin Tappan Papers, Ohio Historical Society, Columbus; Daniel Feller, "A Brother in Arms: Benjamin Tappan and the Antislavery Democracy," *Journal of American History* 88 (June 2001): 48–74, especially 52–64. For the issues at stake in the party battle, see John Ashworth, *"Agrarians" and "Aristocrats": Party Political Ideology in the United States, 1837–1846* (Atlantic Highlands, N.J.: Humanities Press, 1983); and Howe, *What Hath God Wrought*, 576–84.

34. Ratcliffe, *The Politics of Long Division*, 142 (quotation of Ohio congressman John C.

Wright); Tallmadge to Webster, 16 June 1848, in *The Papers of Daniel Webster: Correspondence*, ed. Charles M. Wiltse (Hanover, N.H.: University Press of New England, 1984), 6:298.

35. Ronald N. Satz, *Indian Policy in the Jacksonian Era* (Lincoln: University of Nebraska Press, 1975), 39–63; Mary Hershberger, "Mobilizing Women, Anticipating Abolition: The Struggle against Indian Removal in the 1830s," *Journal of American History* 86 (June 1999): 15–40.

36. Richard Carwardine, "Evangelicals, Whigs, and the Election of William Henry Harrison," *Journal of American Studies* 17 (April 1983): 47–75; Michael F. Holt, *The Rise and Fall of the American Whig Party: Jacksonian Politics and the American Civil War* (New York: Oxford University Press, 1999), 95, 109–10, 111, 113–21, 168–89.

37. Calhoun is quoted in David J. Russo, "The Major Political Issues of the Jacksonian Period and the Development of Party Loyalty in Congress, 1830–1840," in *Transactions of the American Philosophical Society* 62 (1972), pt. 5, 23; and also Freehling, *The Road to Disunion*, 1:345–50 (quotation at 346). For Rankin, see Theodore Dwight Weld, *Letters of Theodore Dwight Weld, Angelina Grimké, and Sarah Grimké*, ed. Gilbert H. Barnes and Dwight L. Dumond (1934; repr., Gloucester, Mass.: Peter Smith, 1965), 850. See also Miller, *Arguing with Slavery*, 357–73, 387; and James Brewer Stewart, "Abolitionists, Insurgents, and Third Parties: Sectionalism and Partisan Politics in Northern Whiggery, 1836–1844," in Kraut, *Crusaders and Compromisers*, 25–43.

38. David Brion Davis, "The Emergence of Immediatism in British and American Antislavery Thought," *Mississippi Valley Historical Review* 49 (September 1962): 209–30; David W. Blight, "Perceptions of Southern Intransigence and the Rise of Radical Antislavery Thought, 1816–1830," *Journal of the Early Republic* 3 (Summer 1983): 139–63.

39. Bertram Wyatt Brown, "Prelude to Abolitionism: Sabbatarian Politics and the Rise of the Second Party System," *Journal of American History* 58 (September 1971): 316–41; Hershberger, "Mobilizing Women, Anticipating Abolition," 35–40; Donald J. Ratcliffe, "Antimasonry and Partisanship in Greater New England, 1826–36," *Journal of the Early Republic* 15 (Summer 1995): 230.

40. David Grimsted, *American Mobbing, 1828–1861: Toward Civil War* (New York: Oxford University Press, 1998), 3–82, especially 18–32.

41. Newman, *The Transformation of American Abolitionism*, 40, 55, 152–68; Leonard L. Richards, *Gentlemen of Property and Standing: Anti-abolition Mobs in Jacksonian America* (New York: Oxford University Press, 1970).

42. James Brewer Stewart, "The Emergence of Racial Modernity and the Rise of the White North, 1790–1840," *Journal of the Early Republic* 18 (Summer 1998): 181–217, especially 188–202; and idem, *Abolitionist Politics and the Coming of the Civil War* (Amherst: University of Massachusetts Press, 2008), especially 35–57.

43. Ellen Eslinger, "The Evolution of Racial Politics in Early Ohio," in *The Center of a Great Empire: The Ohio Country in the Early Republic*, ed. Andrew R. L. Cayton and Stuart D. Hobbs (Athens: Ohio University Press, 2005), 81–104, especially 86–91, 94; Carter G. Woodson, "The Negroes of Cincinnati Prior to the Civil War," *Journal of Negro History* 1 (January 1916): 1–22, especially 2–4.

44. *A Brief Exposition of the Views of the Society for the Colonization of Free Persons of Colour, in Africa* (Columbus, 1827), reprinted in *Quarterly Publications of the Historical and*

Philosophical Society of Ohio 7 (1912): 79–89 (see especially 85); Henry Clay, "On African Colonization" (January 1827), in *The Life and Speeches of Henry Clay,* ed. James B. Swain (New York: Greeley and McElrath, 1843), 270, 283; Benjamin Morris, *The Life of Thomas Morris,* 85. See also Joanne Pope Melish, *Disowning Slavery: Gradual Emancipation and "Race" in New England, 1780–1860* (Ithaca, N.Y.: Cornell University Press, 1998), 190–208.

45. Paul Goodman, *Of One Blood: Abolitionism and the Origins of Racial Equality* (Berkeley: University of California Press, 1998), 5–53; Newman, *The Transformation of American Abolitionism,* 11, 13–14, 95–108, 112, 116–20; Paul A. Gilje, *The Road to Mobocracy: Popular Disorder in New York City, 1763–1834* (Chapel Hill: University of North Carolina Press, 1987), 143–70.

46. Aileen S. Kraditor, *Means and Ends in American Abolitionism: Garrison and His Critics on Strategy and Tactics, 1834–1850* (New York: Random House, 1967).

47. Richard H. Sewell, *Ballots for Freedom: Antislavery Politics in the United States, 1837–1860* (New York: Oxford University Press, 1976).

48. Earle, *Jacksonian Antislavery and the Politics of Free Soil;* Wilentz, "Slavery, Antislavery, and Jacksonian Democracy," 207–18; idem, *The Rise of American Democracy: Jefferson to Lincoln* (New York: Norton, 2005), especially 521–632.

49. Ratcliffe, *The Politics of Long Division,* 113, 144; Earle, *Jacksonian Antislavery and the Politics of Free Soil,* 37–40, 103–7; Eric Foner, "Origins of the Wilmot Proviso," *Journal of American History* 56 (September 1969): 262–79.

50. William E. Gienapp (*The Origins of the Republican Party, 1852–1856* [New York: Oxford University Press, 1987]) emphasizes the importance of new voters for the success of the new Republican Party in 1856, but these are defined as voters who had not voted in 1852. Arguably, many of them were regular voters before 1846 who had deliberately abstained in 1852.

Conflict vs. Racial Consensus in the History of Antislavery Politics

JAMES OAKES

H ere's one way to write the history of race and slavery in American politics between the Revolution and the Civil War:

The American Revolution unleashed a powerful antislavery movement that resulted in the abolition of slavery in every Northern state, thousands of manumissions in the Upper South, a ban on the expansion of slavery into the Northwestern territories, and eventually the closing of the Atlantic slave trade. But as quickly as this antislavery movement took hold, it just as suddenly collapsed; as impressive as its achievements were, they were also limited. Slaves in the North, for example, were freed only gradually, and even then, blacks were subjected to an increasingly restrictive series of racial discriminations. Technically, slavery was not abolished in the Northwest territories. Manumissions in the South stopped as quickly as they started. The new Constitution, far from completing the emancipation process, all but strangled it with a series of protections for slavery. Rather than ban the Atlantic slave trade outright, for example, the pro-slavery Constitution actually prohibited the new national government from interfering with slave imports for a generation—with the result that a huge wave of African slaves flooded into the newly United States. Thus did the antislavery impulse of the Revolution wither and die after 1790. For forty years, blacks organized and struggled to keep the antislavery movement alive, but not until after 1830 did radical abolitionism bring the movement back to life, and not for another generation did it begin to bear fruit. The villain of this piece—the worm in the apple of Revolutionary antislavery—was white racism. Whites may have subscribed to the abstract proposition that "all men are created equal," but when faced with the actual prospect of living with freed blacks as their equals, white Americans shrank back in horror. What flowered in the wake of the American Revolution was not its libertarian radicalism but a racist backlash against it.

This is a story familiar to all historians of the early republic, but the essays in this volume and the recent body of scholarship they represent suggest a different version of the history of race and slavery in American politics between the Revolution and the Civil War. This new version of early American history is still being constructed, but the outlines are becoming clear and they look something like this:

The American Revolution set in motion a long and bitterly divisive struggle over slavery and race in the new nation. A multifaceted Revolutionary ideology provided opponents of slavery with a powerful argument for universal freedom, but at the same time it inspired a popular defense of the inviolable rights of property that became the bulwark of proslavery politics. Out of this conflict came a series of struggles, the outcomes of which reflected the shifting balance of power in national and Northern politics. Where slaveholders were most power-ful, slavery could scarcely be touched. Where they were weakest, slavery was quickly abolished. Where the balance was more even—in states like New York and New Jersey—more protracted struggles took place, with the opponents of slavery eventually winning the day. Slave imports were banned in the Northwest, but the slaveholders who were already there waged a campaign to lift the ban, only to be beaten back. Antislavery delegates to the Constitutional Convention struggled to keep slavery out of the new charter but were checked by aggressive slaveholders who forced a series of compromises. The result was a Constitution that was no less ambiguous than Revolutionary ideology, and that ambiguity led to sustained conflict over the precise status of slave property. From the begin-ning, the slaveholders insisted that human property was just like any other property, and as such was protected as a constitutional right. But the Constitu-tion speaks of slaves as "persons" rather than property, and in the very act of singling slavery out for special protection the Constitution treated slaves as *dif-ferent* from other property. For slavery's opponents, this distinction stripped slavery of the "natural" right to protection that the Constitution otherwise guaranteed to land and houses. Instead, antislavery advocates held that slav-ery was protected more by the principle of federalism than by the sacred right of property. This difference meant that the national government had the right to outlaw the importation of slaves after 1808 and prohibit the expansion of slavery in the Western territories—restrictions that the Consti-tution did not specifically allow for any other form of property. On the other hand, federalism also decreed that the national government could not inter-fere with slavery in the states where it already existed. The result, as everyone knows, was an unending series of struggles over the power of the federal government to prevent slaves from being carried into the federal territories.

Far from withering after 1790, antislavery politics persisted, and eventually claimed many victories. Antislavery forces in New York and New Jersey grew stronger, overcame the slaveholders, and succeeded in passing gradual emancipation laws. But those laws were a beginning as much as a culmination. Many New York masters immediately began to renegotiate the terms of their relationship with their slaves, entering into indenture contracts that promised freedom after several years. Slavery itself was legally transformed. A few years after securing passage of the gradual emancipation statute, antislavery New Yorkers passed laws recognizing the marriages of slaves and allowing slaves to own property. It had long been illegal for New York masters to sell their slaves out of state, but after 1799 local governments shut down slave auction houses completely. In effect, New York had created a status somewhere in between slavery and freedom—in which "slaves" could not be sold, their marriages were legal, they owned property, and their children would be freed upon reaching adulthood. Finally, in 1817 New York revised its gradual emancipation laws to free all remaining "slaves" within ten years.[1]

In the Northwest, opponents of slavery abolished the institution in state after state, over the ferocious opposition of slaveholders. Long before the ban on the Atlantic trade, Congress had prohibited the importation of slaves into the Southwestern territories. All slave imports were banned at the earliest possible date, 1808, but Congress didn't stop there. After the War of 1812, antislavery politicians stepped up their attacks. International slave trading was criminalized—indeed, it was deemed a capital offense. By the time of the Missouri Crisis antislavery politicians had developed a critique of slavery so sweeping that it shocked the slaveholders and their allies.[2]

Over the next several years, proslavery forces struggled to build a coalition that could turn back the threat to national unity posed by antislavery politics, and by 1828 they succeeded. Just as the victory of Jefferson in 1800 had temporarily silenced antislavery republicans, the success of the Jackson Democrats in 1828 dampened antislavery politics for more than a decade. The Democrats employed a virulent racism to cement their coalition, but the point was not to defend slavery but to suppress it as a political issue. Instead, Democratic politics focused on democratic reform and economic policy. But the final suppression of antislavery politics was not complete until the Whigs emerged as the anti-Jackson party after 1832. They, too, were concerned chiefly with economic issues—virtually coming into existence in defense of the Bank of the United States, along with support for protective tariffs and federally funded internal improvements. Like the Democrats, the Whigs were concerned not with defending or attacking slavery, but with suppressing the issue entirely. Both were national parties with slaveholding and antislavery constituencies; rather than alienate those constituencies and undermine their national coalitions, both parties struggled to keep slavery out of national politics lest their coalitions collapse. Thus, the fortunes of antislavery politics rose and fell with the fortunes of nationwide party coalitions.

Yet the suppression of antislavery politics was real, and often ruthless. The silencing of Northern antislavery republicans after Jefferson came to power in 1800 was repeated with a vengeance in the 1830s. The Jackson Democrats summarily expelled men like Thomas Morris of Ohio and John Hale of New Hampshire—among the party's most determined antislavery colleagues. Whigs were less efficient at cracking the party whip, but it's worth remembering that when Whig congressman Joshua Giddings was censured for his vehement attacks on the notorious "gag rule," his fellow Ohio Whigs in Congress sat on their hands, and back home the Whig Party would not even endorse his reelection.

It was at this particular moment, in the 1830s—when party politics froze out antislavery politics—that a radical abolitionist movement emerged to fill the void created by the recent disappearance of antislavery activism within the political mainstream. And, not surprisingly, one of abolitionism's major goals—and its most enduring achievement—was to force antislavery back onto the national political agenda. First came the campaign to overwhelm the mails with antislavery propaganda. Next they tried "visitations" of candidates, aimed at securing support for antislavery policies. When that tactic failed, activists hit on a more successful tactic—flooding Congress with antislavery petitions. At first the proslavery forces succeeded in squashing the campaign by instituting the "gag rule" that sidelined all antislavery petitions. But the struggle persisted for nearly a decade, and by the time the gag rule was overthrown, antislavery politics was coming back to life.

Crucial to the ultimate success of a revitalized antislavery politics was an economic agenda that was incompatible with slavery. The Revolutionary generation, influenced by the critiques of Adam Smith and others, assumed that slavery was intrinsically inefficient and doomed to die out. The rise of the cotton economy undermined that assumption, and Jacksonian Democrats instead defended an unrestrained market in slaves, while their opponents, the Whigs, promoted an "American System" that assumed slavery's natural place in an integrated national economy. "Free Soil," by contrast, was more openly hostile to slavery than any of its predecessors, and it eventually became the ideological cry around which a broad coalition of antislavery politicians and voters could rally.

As disagreements over slavery were suppressed, disagreements over the place of blacks in Northern society generated a new source of conflict. Once emancipation in the North had been accomplished—a much more rapid process than most historians realize—the antislavery movement born of the Revolution was weakened in the North. As they would do again during the Civil War, the terms of debate shifted from slavery to the place of blacks in American society, in this case Northern society. On one side, committed opponents of slavery often led the resistance to various proposals for racial discrimination. They led the uproar in the North over racist restrictions in the Missouri constitution and South Carolina's Negro Seamen's Act. On the other side, growing numbers of whites clamored for various forms of racial discrimination, in particular depriving black men of the vote. The drive for black disfranchisement was often the product of partisan considerations. Jeffersonians, who watched in dismay as freed men emerged as a Federalist voting bloc, led the charge to disfranchise blacks.

In the two or three decades after 1820, supporters of racial discrimination won more often than the opponents, but they did not always win. In many Northern states, particularly west of the mountains, black voting was banned outright. But in 1820 Maine and Massachusetts granted blacks the right to vote. Rhode Island banned black voting in 1822, but restored it twenty years later. In New York, neither side won a complete victory. The disfranchisers were thwarted and had to settle instead for a property qualification that applied only to blacks.

In 1851, Indiana banned blacks from moving into the state, but two years earlier, Ohio lifted its ban. Who introduced the bill to lift the Ohio ban? Who voted for it? Why? Where was the constituency for opening Ohio's borders to free blacks? Surely the Western Reserve was not powerful enough to pass it by itself. At various times, racists attempted—and failed—to enact other discriminatory laws against blacks. Why did they fail? How did the opponents of discriminatory legislation explain and justify their position? We need to ask such questions if we are to understand the explosive conflict over racial equality that erupted in the 1850s between Republicans and Democrats.

The debate is obscured in part because Republicans insisted on separating the issue of slavery from the issue of racial equality. Though they took a principled and increasingly radical position against slavery, Republicans were formally agnostic about racial equality—often denying that they supported the civil and political equality of blacks and whites, but avoiding the issue entirely at the national level. As it turned out, however, Republican "non-racism" turned out to be a politically significant alternative to Democratic racism. In states where the Republicans took power, there was a tendency to repeal racially discriminatory legislation. Under Republican rule, schools were integrated, streetcars were desegregated, and voting rights were restored. In New York in 1860, the Republican legislature passed an amendment repealing the property qualification for black voters, but the proposal was defeated at the polls, even though a majority of Republicans voted for it. When Republicans vowed to revise the Fugitive Slave Act of 1850 so as to restore the "privileges and immunities of citizenship," it was not runaway slaves from the South they would be protecting, but free blacks in the North.

More importantly, the Republican critique of slavery had to be, at some level, an anti-racist argument. Northern Democrats, for example, freely invoked the Declaration of Independence, but they insisted that Jefferson's principle of fundamental human equality applied only to whites. Republicans invoked the same principle in opposition to slavery, but they insisted that the rights of life, liberty, and the pursuit of happiness had no racial qualifiers, that whites and blacks were equally entitled to them. So too with free labor. No Northern Democrats rejected the ideal of free labor, but once again they made a racial exception to it, and once again Republicans rejected the racial exception. Hence Lincoln's oft-repeated assertion that black and white workers were equally entitled to the fruits of their labor. Nor was it a mere accident that within a few years Lincoln's Republican attorney general would reverse *Dred Scott* and rule that blacks were citizens under the Constitution, or that that a Republican Congress would pass the landmark Civil Rights Act of 1866 and the Fourteenth and Fifteenth Amendments. There's a reason that Democrats denounced their opponents as "Black Republicans." Notwithstanding their claim that slavery and race were two distinct issues, Republicans found that a fight over slavery could not help being a fight over racial equality.

Here, then, is the second version of the history of race and slavery in American politics between the Revolution and the Civil War. Rather than a swift demise of antislavery politics, recent historians have recorded its persistence in the earliest decades of the new nation's history. Rather than a forty-year hiatus between the demise of Revolutionary antislavery and the rise of radical abolitionism, there was a relatively brief but crucial period between the late 1820s and the mid-1840s when antislavery politics was effectively frozen out of national politics. And rather than binding the fortunes of antislavery politics to the inexorable spread of white racism, recent scholarship emphasizes the shifting patterns of partisan politics and the changing balance of power between the supporters and opponents of slavery and racial discrimination.

There are other ways to tell the story of race and slavery in American politics—as the gradual, even inexorable efflorescence of Revolutionary ideology, as the triumph of abolitionist idealism over political expediency, as the triumph of capitalism over slavery. But the two versions of early American history recounted above—the rapid demise of Revolutionary antislavery beneath the heels of a hardening racial consensus versus the persistence of conflict over race and slavery—are the most influential, and their implications extend well beyond the mere revision of the historical narrative. Different stories raise different sets of questions that historians ask themselves, and very different ways of answering the questions.

The first story, of the quick demise of Revolutionary antislavery at the hands of rising white racism, has led scholars to ask these kinds of questions: Why did the antislavery zeal of the Revolution die so quickly? Why were its results so meager? Why did the struggle over slavery all but disappear after 1790? These are the trickiest kinds of questions historians ask, for they require us to explain not what happened but what failed to happen, not the conflict but the absence of conflict.

Traditionally, such questions lead historians to emphasize some form of consensus. In the aftermath of World War II, for example, many historians wondered why the United States had managed to avoid the extremes of fascism and communism that had recently torn Europe apart, and they answered the question by pointing to the consensual "American" commitment to pragmatism and an ingrained resistance to abstract political theories. Consensus history was one answer to what seemed at the time a pertinent question: Why was there no socialism in America?

In recent decades, a similar question has haunted historians of the early republic: Why was there no general and immediate emancipation in Revolutionary America? And their answers rely on what might be called "racial consensus history." Where the earlier generation spoke in broad terms of "American" values, recent scholars speak in slightly less general terms of "white attitudes" and of stereotypes that inhabit the "white mind."

Racial consensus history shifts the terrain of analysis away from political struggle, toward psychological turmoil. Consider this passage from Rich Newman's illuminating reconsideration of the dialogue between Thomas Jefferson and Benjamin Banneker. Newman wonders why it took so long for New Yorkers to pass a gradual abolition statute. He wants to explain a failure, to figure out why something that should have happened sooner instead happened later. Newman's answer centers on racial attitudes among whites. "New Yorkers would not adopt a gradual emancipation statute until 1799," Newman explains, because their growing "concerns about racial difference" tempered their commitment to emancipation. New Yorkers epitomized Jefferson's mental contradiction. They supported emancipation in principle, but in practice were held back by their racial prejudices. This explanation is largely psychological. "Jefferson expressed the American mind on race and emancipation—or, one might say, the divided American mind." A single, albeit divided "American mind" thus replaces a stark political division over slavery and race.

Donald Ratcliffe makes precisely this point in his outstanding account of the decline of antislavery politics in the 1830s. He identifies a "racist consensus that most Northerners had come to share" during the 1820s, and he describes it in psychological terms. "One consequence of that consensus," he writes, "was a latent feeling among many Northerners that slavery, however deplorable, could be tolerated, because at least it kept those savage Africans locked up within the South." Like Newman, Ratcliffe turns to racial consensus history to explain the absence of an antislavery struggle that should have been there or previously had been.

The emphasis on a white racial consensus is, in many ways, incompatible with an emphasis on conflict. But it has always seemed to me that to posit "conflict" as the stark alternative to "consensus" is overly simplistic. For Richard Hofstadter, the liberal consensus did not explain the absence of conflict so much as the ideological boundaries within which political conflict took place. His own books, for example, are bursting with conflicts—over slavery, immigration, monetary policy, or the role of intellectuals in public life. The fact that there was no socialism in America did not mean, for Hofstadter, that there was no conflict in America. His student, Eric Foner, has carried the implications of Hofstadter's work still further. In the predictable middle-class commitment to free labor Foner located the ideological reflection of an irrepressible conflict over slavery, and in the nearly universal commitment to "freedom" he discerned a breeding ground for a host of conflicts throughout American history.

But "racial consensus history" has no place for conflict. It is a totalizing thesis, in which an impregnable commitment to white supremacy flourishes in the near complete absence of conflict. Only blacks and a tiny handful of visionary radicals ever seem to question the consensus. In mainstream politics, the racial consensus leaves virtually no room for debate among whites over issues of racial equality. Among the many problems this approach to American history raises, surely one of the largest is its inability to explain what happened to the United States in the 1860s.

Toward the end of his life, Hofstadter examined the limits of the consensus approach by imagining a cartoon featuring a Yankee and a Confederate soldier who strike up a conversation in 1865, amidst the devastation of the war. "Well," one soldier says to the other, "at least we escaped the ultimate folly of producing political theorists."[3] Racial consensus history suffers from the same fundamental weakness. Imagine a similar cartoon, the two soldiers once again contemplating the ruins of the Confederacy, this time consoling themselves with the reflection that "at least we can agree that blacks are inferior to whites." No doubt many of them could agree on that, just as they could all affirm that George Washington was a great man and that Jesus Christ was their savior. But none of that would explain the Civil War, much less the abolition of slavery, the admission of blacks into the Union army, the Civil Rights Act of 1866, or the Fourteenth and Fifteenth Amendments to the Constitution.

The second story—of sustained conflict over race and slavery—avoids many of the pitfalls of racial consensus history. It begins from different assumptions, raises a different set of questions, and leads to a very different kind of answer.

Assume that the ideology of the American Revolution, instead of being unambiguously libertarian, had contradictory implications for slavery. Fundamental human equality led in an antislavery direction, but the inalienable rights of property led in the opposite direction. This was the point made by Virginia slaveholders in those familiar proslavery petitions from the 1780s. "We were put in Possession of our Rights of Liberty and Property" by the recent rebellion against Great Britain, the Virginians declared. "But notwithstanding this, we understand a very subtle and daring Attempt is made to dispossess us of a very important Part of our Property."[4] This ambiguity, and the conflict it sustained, was built into the Constitution. The rights of ordinary property were protected, but didn't the Constitution *single out* slavery and thus distinguish it from ordinary property? What the Revolution bequeathed, then, was a profound, intractable conflict over the moral and legal legitimacy of holding humans as property. Which aspect of "Revolutionary ideology" prevailed—universal liberty or the inalienable rights of property— was a question that was destined to be fought over, in politics.

A contradictory Revolutionary legacy transforms the questions historians are apt to ask and the answers they are likely to find. For example, instead of wondering why it took so long for New York to pass a gradual emancipation law, a historian might ask why they ever decided to abolish it and what might explain the timing of their decision?[5] The answer might begin with fact that the slaveholding interest was economically greater and therefore more polit- ically powerful in New York than in most Northern states. Because the balance of power was tilted in their favor, New York masters successfully turned back the first major attacks on slavery in the 1780s. But defeat led slavery's opponents to redouble their efforts, shore up their organization, and promote the antislavery cause more effectively. Meanwhile, extensive immigration in the 1790s transformed the demography of the state, weaken- ing the slaveholders' interest and strengthening popular support for aboli- tion. A decade after their initial failure, antislavery advocates renewed their campaign for a gradual emancipation law. By then they were better prepared to control the terms of the debate. The slaveholders tried again to use racial demagoguery to thwart abolition, but abolitionists succeeded in keeping public discussion focused on the principle of universal liberty. They also commanded wider support among the people. In this account, the history of antislavery politics in New York owes less to the "divided mind" of North- ern whites than to the shifting balance of political forces. Political conflict, rather than racial consensus, drives the explanation for the timing of eman- cipation in New York.

Throughout this volume there is abundant evidence of serious conflict over slavery in the young republic. We learn that Federalist opposition to slavery was partisan, for example, but that it was not *merely* partisan. As Rachel Cleves persuasively demonstrates, Jefferson's enemies articulated a serious moral critique of slavery alongside their polemical assaults on the third president. But there was also more antislavery agitation among North- ern Republicans than earlier scholars have acknowledged.[6] Black agitation against slavery never diminished, and, as Newman's examination of Ban- neker demonstrates, it was courageous and uncompromising in confronting even the most revered heroes of the Revolution.

Fights over slavery erupted at every turn—over the criminalization of slave trading, over banning slave imports into the Old Southwest, over at- tempts to undo the restrictions on slavery in the Old Northwest, over the proper response to Caribbean slave revolts, over congressional reception of antislavery petitions. Racial consensus is scarcely adequate to explain so much conflict. Rather, the inconsistencies in the Northern record were the predictably irregular outcome of a series of political struggles in which the advocates of racial discrimination fought against the opponents of racial discrimination, struggles in which neither side could ever claim total victory. Nor does racial consensus alone explain the waxing and waning of antislavery politics. Historians have long discerned a proslavery bias in Jeffersonian and Jacksonian economic policy, but Andrew Shankman's highly original analysis highlights the Whig Party's tacit acceptance of slavery in the "American System" of Matthew Carey and Henry Clay. Thus, the decline of antislavery during the 1820s and 1830s may have had less to do with a resurgent racist consensus than with the way Whigs and Democrats formulated their economic positions.

Political partisanship also seems to have influenced the relative strength of antislavery politics. Paddy Reilly points to the number of antislavery Republicans who muted their abolitionism after Jefferson's party triumphed in 1801. With the collapse of Federalism after 1815 came a corresponding collapse in Republican Party discipline—and with it a revival of antislavery agitation among Northern republicans. Donald Ratcliffe finds a similar pattern with the triumph of the Jackson Democrats in 1828. The Democrats who later became Free Soilers and Republicans had often been anti-slavery prior to 1828. The Jacksonians were adept at cracking the party whip, however, and they not only silenced antislavery voices but ultimately expelled many antislavery agitators from the party ranks.

These essay take us a long step toward a better understanding of the nature, persistence, suppression, and revival of antislavery politics in the early republic. It turns out there was far more conflict over slavery than earlier generations had imagined. The next step is to extend the analysis to the politics of race, to be more specific about the timing and sources of racially discriminatory legislation, to explain not merely the discriminations that were enacted but the ones that were repealed and the ones that were repudiated. As with slavery, there was more conflict over race than historians have heretofore imagined.

In the months leading up to the November 2008 presidential election, a story—perhaps apocryphal—circulated on the Internet about a pollster who knocked at the door of an older white couple in rural western Pennsylvania, where resistance to a black candidate was thought to be entrenched. When the pollster asked the woman whom she planned to vote for, she consulted her husband, who supposedly shouted from the living room, "We're voting for the nigger." Apocryphal or not, the story illustrates the limitations of the racial consensus as an explanation for complicated historical events.

This is not to deny the existence of a white racism, but merely to urge caution in the way it is invoked. Too often race becomes the default explanation, and the racial default is too often used to explain what failed to happen rather than what actually did happen. When invoked casually and indiscriminately, racial consensus risks becoming an all-explanatory principle that ultimately explains nothing. Matt Mason and Christopher Brown have made the point that, by themselves, antislavery ideals were rarely enough to sustain antislavery politics.[7] Only when they were attached to an issue that struck home—for British petitioners or Northern voters—did antislavery principles make headway.

The same can be said of white racism. It was there, it was pervasive, but it rarely operated as an independent cause. Racism usually worked in conjunction with something else. It may be, for example, that when voters became concerned about the economy or the role the state played in promoting capitalist development, they threw their support to parties that were, by the way, intensely racist and indifferent to slavery. If this was the case, a white racial consensus helped solidify popular support for Jeffersonian Republicans and Jacksonian Democrats but does not fully explain either of those movements. And yet the consequences—for blacks and for antislavery politics—were dreadful. On the other hand, when Northern voters, whether racist or not, elected a Republican congressional majority and a Republican president in 1860, they may have voted out of disgust for Southern belligerence, of out of patriotic commitment to the Union, but they were handing the reins of power over to politicians who believed that blacks and whites were equally entitled to the fundamental rights of life, liberty, and the pursuit of happiness.

Thanks to the authors of these essays, along with the scholars who have recently been reconstructing and rewriting the history of antislavery politics in early America, we now have a record of conflict over slavery that requires us to recalibrate the relative significance of conflict and consensus in the history of the early republic. Donald Ratcliffe's essay is a model of how this might be done. He identifies a series of intense conflicts over race and slavery in the early republic, specifies the points at which the conflicts reached the peak of their intensity, as well as the points at which conflict over slavery declined. In the process, Ratcliffe discerns a particular moment when the racial consensus hardened—the mid-1820s—and specifies the conditions under which it gained political salience—the election of Andrew Jackson and the subsequent threat posed by the emergence of radical abolitionism. In Ratcliffe's telling, the "racist consensus" is not a general explanatory principle, but the particular product of a specific moment with clearly defined but limited consequences for the fate of antislavery politics during the 1830s.

It is no easy thing for historians to explain the long political struggle over slavery that gripped the western world beginning in the late eighteenth century and continuing through the nineteenth. Nor has it ever been easy for historians to explain why, halfway through the Age of Emancipation, a civil war over slavery tore the United States apart. But surely an ideological consensus—over race or anything else—will never be an adequate explanation for that century of conflict.

NOTES

1. David N. Gellman, *Emancipating New York: The Politics of Slavery and Freedom, 1777– 1827* (Baton Rouge: Louisiana State University Press, 2006).

2. Matthew Mason, *Slavery and Politics in the Early Republic* (Chapel Hill: University of North Carolina Press, 2006); John Craig Hammond, *Slavery, Freedom, and Expansion in the Early American West* (Charlottesville: University of Virginia Press, 2007).

3. Richard Hofstadter, *The Progressive Historians: Turner, Beard, Parrington* (New York: Alfred A. Knopf, 1968), 462.

4. Fredrika Teute Schmidt and Barbara Ripel Wilhelm, eds., "Early Proslavery Petitions in Virginia," *William and Mary Quarterly*, 3d ser., 30 (January 1973): 139. See also Eva Sheppard Wolf, *Race and Liberty in the New Nation: Emancipation in Virginia from the Revolution to Nat Turner's Rebellion* (Baton Rouge: Louisiana State University Press, 2006).

5. For a similar approach to the timing of the British abolition movement, see Christopher Leslie Brown, *Moral Capital: Foundations of British Abolitionism* (Chapel Hill: University of North Carolina Press, 2006). Brown's concluding words offer a useful antidote to the cynicism that now pervades the scholarship on "the first emancipation" in the new nation. He writes: "In the end, what is remarkable about abolitionism in Britain [in the 1780s] is not that it took so long to emerge, that it was politically ineffective for many years, or that it was limited in its ambition and selective in its scope. Such movements often are. What is truly surprising about British abolitionism is that such a campaign ever should have developed at all" (461–62).

6. See, in particular, Jonathan H. Earle, *Jacksonian Antislavery and the Politics of Free Soil, 1824–1854* (Chapel Hill: University of North Carolina Press, 2004); and Sean Wilentz, *The Rise of American Democracy: From Jefferson to Lincoln* (New York: W. W. Norton, 2006).

7. Some years ago, Richard Sewell made a similar point about the salience of anti-Southernism in Northern antislavery politics (see Richard H. Sewell, *Ballots for Freedom: Antislavery Politics in the United States, 1837–1860* [New York: Oxford University Press, 1976]).

Contributors

RACHEL HOPE CLEVES is Assistant Professor of History at the University of Victoria and the author of *The Reign of Terror in America: Visions of Violence from Anti-Jacobinism to Antislavery* (2009), and of "On Writing the History of Violence," *Journal of the Early Republic* (2004).

DAVID F. ERICSON is Term Associate Professor in the Department of Public and International Affairs at George Mason University, and the author of numerous books and articles on slavery and the development of the American state, and on political theory. Among his many works are *The Shaping of American Liberalism: The Debates over Ratification, Nullification, and Slavery* (1993); *The Debate over Slavery: Antislavery and Proslavery Liberalism in Antebellum America* (2001); and numerous articles in the *Journal of Southern History* and in *Studies in American Political Development*. He is currently completing a book manuscript, "The Ghost behind the Machine: Slavery and the American State, 1791–1861," which is under contract.

JOHN CRAIG HAMMOND is Assistant Professor of History at Penn State University, New Kensington, and the author of *Slavery, Freedom, and Expansion in the Early American West* (2007), and of articles in the *Journal of the Early Republic*.

MATTHEW MASON is Associate Professor of History at Brigham Young University and the author of *Slavery and Politics in the Early American Republic* (2006), as well as articles in such journals as the *William and Mary Quarterly*, the *Journal of the Early Republic*, the *New England Quarterly*, and *American Nineteenth Century History*.

RICHARD NEWMAN is Professor of History at the Rochester Institute of Technology and the author of *Freedom's Prophet: Bishop Richard Allen, the AME Church, and the Black Founding Fathers* (2008), and *The Transformation of American Abolition: Fighting Slavery in the Early Republic* (2002), as well as articles in journals such as the *William and Mary Quarterly* and the *Journal of the Early Republic.*

JAMES OAKES is Graduate Professor of History at the CUNY Graduate Center and the author of numerous books and essays on the politics of slavery. He most recently authored *The Radical and the Republican: Frederick Douglas, Abraham Lincoln, and the Triumph of Antislavery Politics* (2007).

PETER S. ONUF is the Thomas Jefferson Memorial Foundation Professor of History at the University of Virginia and has edited and authored numerous books and articles on Thomas Jefferson and the early American republic. His most recent authored work is *The Mind of Thomas Jefferson* (2007).

ROBERT G. PARKINSON is Assistant Professor of History at Shepherd University. He is currently completing his book manuscript "The Common Cause: Race, Nation, and the Consequences of Unity in the American Revolution." He is the author of articles in the *William and Mary Quarterly* and the *Virginia Magazine of History and Biography.*

DONALD J. RATCLIFFE is Senior Associate Fellow at the Rothmere American Institute at the University of Oxford and the author of numerous books and articles on politics in the early republic. Among his works is an essay "The Crisis of Commercialization: National Political Alignments and the Market Revolution, 1819–1844," published in *The Market Revolution in America: Social, Political, and Religious Expressions, 1800–1880,* edited by Melvin Stokes and Stephen Conway (1996), and articles in *American Nineteenth Century History* and the *Journal of the Early Republic.*

PADRAIG RILEY is Assistant Professor of History at Dalhousie University and is currently completing his book manuscript tentatively titled "Northern Democracy and Southern Slavery: Politics in the Age of Jefferson, 1800–1828." He is the author of "Clark Kerr: From the Industrial to the Knowledge Economy," in *American Capitalism: Social Theory and Capitalist Reality in the American Century,* edited by Nelson Lichtenstein (2006).

EDWARD B. RUGEMER, Assistant Professor of History at Yale University, is the author of *The Problem of Emancipation: The Caribbean Roots of the American Civil War* (2008), and "The Southern Response to British Abolitionism: The Maturation of Proslavery Apologetics," *Journal of Southern History*, (2004).

BRIAN SCHOEN is Assistant Professor of History at Ohio University and the author of *The Fragile Fabric of Union: Cotton, Federal Politics, and the Global Origins of the United States Civil War* (2009). His essay "Alternatives to Dependence: The Lower South's Antebellum Pursuit of Sectional Development through Global Interdependence" appeared in *Global Perspectives on Industrial Transformation in the American South*, edited by Susanna Delfino and Michele Gillespie (2005), and he has also published in the *Journal of the Early Republic.*

ANDREW SHANKMAN is Associate Professor of History at Rutgers University, Camden. He is the author of *Crucible of American Democracy: The Struggle to Fuse Egalitarianism and Capitalism in Jeffersonian Pennsylvania* (2004), and of articles in the *Journal of the Early Republic.*

GEORGE WILLIAM VAN CLEVE is Scholar in Residence in the Corcoran Department of History at the University of Virginia and the author of "Somerset's Case and Its Antecedents in Imperial Perspective," *Law and History Review* (2006). His recently completed book is *A Slaveholders' Union: Slavery, Politics, and the Constitution in the Early American Republic* (2010).

EVA SHEPPARD WOLF is Associate Professor of History at San Francisco State University and the author of *Race and Liberty in the New Nation: Emancipation in Virginia from the Revolution to Nat Turner's Rebellion* (2006).

Index

New Jersey, 236

New Orleans, 146–47, 149

New York, 14–16, 41, 269, 300

Niles' Weekly Register, 101, 103, 148–49

North Carolina, 143, 191–93

Northern States. *See* states, free

Northerners, 21, 40, 41, 44, 149, 151, 152, 229, 231, 232, 242

Northwest, Old, 275, 293

Northwest Ordinance, 2, 16, 129–30, 142–43, 186

Notes on the State of Virginia, 71, 73, 210

Nullification Crisis, 162, 175, 176–77, 247, 261, 274

Ohio Resolutions (1824), 272, 273

Otis, Harrison Gray, 213–14

Panama Conference (1826), 258, 277

Panic of 1819, 247, 249, 256, 272

Parish, Elijah, 217–18

Pennsylvania, 76. *See also* Philadelphia

Pennsylvania Abolition Society, 50, 77, 105, 129, 132

petitions, 49–50, 53, 63, 72, 109, 214, 230, 272, 274

Philadelphia, 70, 76, 231, 282. *See also* Pennsylvania

plantation economy, 250, 257, 260

planters, 191, 235, 250, 257

Prosser, Gabriel. *See* Gabriel's Rebellion

Quakers, 19, 20, 34, 36, 50, 51, 53, 60, 64, 78

Quincy, Josiah, 23

race, 72–78; and equality, 80; and inequality, 81. *See also* racism

racism, 80, 172–78, 219, 228, 231, 242, 257, 268, 282–84, 295, 302

Randolph, Edmund, 78, 126

Randolph, John, 183, 236, 240

Red Sticks, 149, 168, 189

reform, 73, 77, 83, 268; moral, 73; and race, 75, 85; and slavery, 77

religion. *See* Christianity

Republican ideology, 34, 81–82, 126, 209–10, 247; and labor, 34; and slavery, 42, 208, 253

Republican Party. *See* Democratic-Republicans

Republican Party of the 1850s, 21, 26, 269, 285, 296

Revolution, French, 212, 214, 215

Revolution, Haitian. *See* Haiti

Rhode Island, 132

Roberts, Jonathan, 169

Rush, Benjamin, 37, 54

Rutledge, John, 26, 214

Saint-Domingue, 78, 95, 107, 144, 215, 229, 231. *See also* Caribbean; Haiti; insurrection, slave

sectional politics, 21–23, 25, 209, 214, 236, 238–39, 256, 267, 272, 277–78

Sedgwick, Theodore, 212

Seminoles, 189–90, 191

Seminole War, 189–90, 192–95

Senate. *See under* Congress

slaveholders, 25, 101, 127, 140, 149, 152, 190, 214, 228, 236, 255, 261

slave labor, 210–11, 250, 260; and free labor, 39

slave rebellion, 52, 55, 59, 64, 78, 94, 97, 107, 109, 130, 168, 191, 208, 215

slave representation: three-fifths clause and, 21, 22, 164, 217, 234, 269

slave resistance, 78, 130, 259

slavery: and capitalism, 234; defenses of, 122–23, 229, 245, 255; opposition to, 138, 140, 209–12, 213, 214–18, 230, 251, 268; and property rights, 127–30. *See also* abolition; abolitionists; Quakers; reform, moral

slaves, fugitive, 56, 129, 149, 168, 190

slave South. *See* states, slave

slave trade, 184, 187, 235, 237; and the Constitution, 184–85; domestic, 20–21, 147, 167, 274, 293; opposition to, 38, 185; transatlantic, 149, 269, 293

Sloan, James, 236–38, 241

Jeffersonian America

Jan Ellen Lewis and Peter S. Onuf, editors
Sally Hemings and Thomas Jefferson: History, Memory, and Civic Culture

Peter S. Onuf
Jefferson's Empire: The Language of American Nationhood

Catherine Allgor
*Parlor Politics: In Which the Ladies of Washington
Help Build a City and a Government*

Jeffrey L. Pasley
*"The Tyranny of Printers": Newspaper Politics
in the Early American Republic*

Herbert E. Sloan
Principle and Interest: Thomas Jefferson and the Problem of Debt (reprint)

James Horn, Jan Ellen Lewis, and Peter S. Onuf, editors
The Revolution of 1800: Democracy, Race, and the New Republic

Phillip Hamilton
*The Making and Unmaking of a Revolutionary Family:
The Tuckers of Virginia, 1752–1830*

Robert M. S. McDonald, editor
Thomas Jefferson's Military Academy: Founding West Point

Martha Tomhave Blauvelt
The Work of the Heart: Young Women and Emotion, 1780–1830

Francis D. Cogliano
Thomas Jefferson: Reputation and Legacy

Albrecht Koschnik
*"Let a Common Interest Bind Us Together": Associations,
Partisanship, and Culture in Philadelphia, 1775–1840*

John Craig Hammond
Slavery, Freedom, and Expansion in the Early American West, 1787–1820

David Andrew Nichols
Red Gentlemen and White Savages: Indians, Federalists,
and the Search for Order on the American Frontier

Douglas Bradburn
The Citizenship Revolution: Politics and the Creation of the American Union, 1774–1804

Clarence E. Walker
Mongrel Nation: The America Begotten by Thomas Jefferson and Sally Hemings

Timothy Mason Roberts
Distant Revolutions: 1848 and the Challenge to American Exceptionalism

Peter J. Kastor and François Weil, editors
Empires of the Imagination: Transatlantic Histories of the Louisiana Purchase

Eran Shalev
Rome Reborn on Western Shores: Historical Imagination and
the Creation of the American Republic

Leonard J. Sadosky
Revolutionary Negotiations: Indians, Empires, and Diplomats in the Founding of America

Philipp Ziesche
Cosmopolitan Patriots: Americans in Paris in the Age of Revolution

Leonard J. Sadosky, Peter Nicolaisen, Peter S. Onuf, and Andrew J. O'Shaughnessy, editors
Old World, New World: America and Europe in the Age of Jefferson

Sam W. Haynes
Unfinished Revolution: The American Republic in a British World, 1815–1850

Michal Jan Rozbicki
Culture and Liberty in the Age of the American Revolution

Ellen Holmes Pearson
Remaking Custom: Law and Identity in the Early American Republic

Seth Cotlar
Making Democracy Safe for America: The Rise and Fall
of Transatlantic Radicalism in the Age of Tom Paine

John Craig Hammond and Matthew Mason, editors
Contesting Slavery: The Politics of Bondage and Freedom in the New American Nation